An Unexciting Life

Reflections on Benedictine Spirituality

An Unexciting Life

Reflections on Benedictine Spirituality

Michael Casey
Monk of Tarrawarra

2005

ST. BEDE'S PUBLICATIONS
Petersham, Massachusetts

Copyright © 2005 by Michael Casey, OCSO
Published in the United States of America
All Rights Reserved

The majority of articles in this book have been published previously and permission to reprint is gratefully acknowledged. Complete bibliographic data is given in the Introductory paragraph of each article.

"Principles of Interpretation and Application of the Rule of Benedict," "The Hard Sayings of the Rule of Saint Benedict," "*Quod Experimento Didicimus*: The Heuristic Wisdom of Saint Benedict," "Ascetic and Ecclesial: Reflections on RB 73,5," "Strangers to Worldly Ways: RB 4,20," "The Benedictine Promises," "Taking Counsel: Reflections on RB 3," "Compassion, The Mainspring of Ministry," "Models of Monastic Formation," "Marketing Monastic Tradition Within Monasteries," "The Rule of Benedict and Inculturation: A Formative Perspective," and "The Monk in the Modern World," all previous published in *Tjurunga*. Used with permission.

"Orthopraxy and Interpretation: Reflections on Regula Benedicti 73,1," "'Community' in the Benedictine Rule," "Discernment and Pastoral Care," and "Intentio Cordis (RB 52,4)," all previously published in *Regulae Benedicti Studia*. Used with permission.

"The Dynamic Unfolding of the Benedictine Charism" previously published in *The American Benedictine Review*. Used with permission.

"The 'Humanitas' of the Benedictine Tradition," appeared in *St Benedict: A Man with an Idea*, University of Melbourne, 1981. Used with permission.

"Sacramentality and Monastic Consecration" appeared in *Word & Spirit*, St. Bede's Publications. Used with permission.

"The Journey from Fear to Love: John Cassian's Road Map," previously published in the proceedings of the *Prayer and Spirituality in the Early Church Symposium*, 1996. Used with permission.

Library of Congress Cataloging-in-Publication Data
Casey, Michael, 1942-
    An unexciting life: reflections on Benedictine spirituality / Michael Casey.
    p. cm.
    Includes bibliographical references.
    ISBN 1-879007-47-9
    1. Benedictines--spiritual life. 2. Monastic and religious life. 3. Christian life--Catholic authors. I. Title.

BX3003.C37 2004
248.8'942--dc22

2004058828

Published by: St Bede's Publications
    PO Box 545
    Petersham, MA 01366-0545

Contents

Foreword vii
Abbreviations x
An Unexciting Life:
    The Sober Spirituality of Saint Benedict 13

The Art of Interpreting the Rule

Principles of Interpretation and Application
    of the Rule of Benedict 29
The Hard Sayings of the Rule of Saint Benedict ... 41
Orthopraxy and Interpretation:
    Reflections on Regula Benedicti 73, 1 55

The Benedictine Tradition

Quod Experimento Didicimus:
    The Heuristic Wisdom of Saint Benedict 69
The "Humanitas" of the Benedictine Tradition . 101
Ascetic and Ecclesial: Reflections on RB 73,5 115
The Dynamic Unfolding of
    the Benedictine Charism 133

The Benedictine Community

Strangers to Worldly Ways: RB 4,20 161
"Community" in the Benedictine Rule 177
Discernment and Pastoral Care 189
The Benedictine Promises 209
The Value of Stability 239
Sacramentality and Monastic Consecration 263

The Journey from Fear to Love: John Cassian's
    Road Map 291
Taking Counsel: Reflections on RB 3 311
Compassion: The Mainspring of Ministry 325
Intentio Cordis (RB 52,4) 339

MONASTIC FORMATION

Models of Monastic Formation 365
Marketing Monastic Tradition
    Within Monasteries 411
The Rule of Benedict and Inculturation:
    A Formative Perspective 449

EPILOGUE

The Monk in the Modern World 497

Foreword

For the last 30 years I have been writing on different aspects of monastic spirituality. For the most part, my choice of topic has been dictated either by market demands (since I am often asked to address a particular topic) or by my own evolving interests. As the years pass, I have become aware that most of what I have written is part of an emerging synthesis. In my own mind, what I have done is like a large jigsaw puzzle in which, progressively, the separate pieces begin to cohere to form little islands which eventually connect. Unlike most practitioners I have not done the edges first. This omission means that the boundaries are always expanding—driven, as usual, both by requests from outside and by some inner urging of my own *daimon*.

This sense of everything fitting together became stronger when I reviewed various articles which have been brought together to form this volume. Although they were written in different inner and outer circumstances, I recognize that most of the issues that have engaged my attention are recurrent. This means that there is some inevitable overlap, on the one hand, and some equally inevitable changing or nuancing of positions on the other. I have made the decision to let what I have written stand as it is, even though nowadays I would have expressed myself differently. Partly this is because I am too lazy to rework everything. But it is also due to a respect for the authorial process; *Quod scripsi, scripsi*. I believe in rough edges.

At the heart of nearly all the articles in the collection is a specific approach to the interpretation of texts—particularly the text of Saint Benedict's Rule, but also including that part of the literature of monastic tradition with which I have been able to become familiar. In the titles of many of the articles occurs the word "reflections". This marks the literary genre in which I have chosen to communicate the fruit of my study. I have read whatever technical studies are available on the topic and, in dialogue with the Rule itself, I have tried to apply what I have learned to the contemporary situation as I know it. I am flattered that this method has been designated "existential hermeneutics" but, really, it is just common sense. Using my own experience of monastic life to understand what the monastic authors are getting at, trying to absorb their teaching and then to come back to my own situation and apply it in the real world. Inevitably there is a Cistercian flavor to the result, since that is the context in which I operate, and parallel to the studies included in this volume is an equal or greater number of other essays which deal more explicitly with aspects of Cistercian spirituality and history.

As I see it, three points stand out in this strategy. Firstly, in rereading old articles it seems to me that I have been long convinced of the importance of firsthand contact with the texts of tradition, believing that the message flows more freely from the text of the author than from any commentary or synthesis—including my own. Secondly, I find myself reaffirming the principle that any text of monastic tradition needs to be read in the context of both anterior and posterior tradition, watching history bring to the surface elements of the tradition that were partially concealed even from those who were its expositors. From here it is but a small step to the third point, seeing ourselves as continuators of this process, entering into dialogue with those who have gone before us and formulating new syntheses that communicate the ancient message to our times and places.

I see the Benedictine tradition as an ever-flowing stream, capable of being reinterpreted, reapplied and re-inculturated. Yet there are constant elements that do no more than change their outward garb. The conditions for the search for God vary only in accidentals. Perseverance, purity of heart and the negation of self-will are both necessary and difficult in any historical context. Monastic values such as prayer, separation from the world, poverty, chastity and community remain valid even though their embodiment in practices may change. And it seems that certain observances such as liturgy, prayer, reading and work continue to belong to the integrity of the Benedictine charism.

To those who live outside monasteries, monastic life can seem to be exotic, which it is, and interesting, which ideally it is not. Benedictine life is geared to opening up channels of communication with the spiritual world. This demands certain restrictions on sensate excitement and a willingness to lead a quiet life. A contemplative life doesn't just happen. It presupposes years of active asceticism as well as a certain largeness of heart that permits a monk or nun to persevere in giving priority to interiority, at the expense of more tangible benefits and gratifications. It is surprising how challenging is such a life-style, especially if one is thinking in terms of forty or fifty years of it. Like a duck on a dam, it may seem smooth sailing on the surface, but underneath there is a lot of paddling going on.

To highlight this unfashionable angle on monasticism, I have named this collection after one of its components, *An Unexciting Life*. Although most of the articles seem to offer a counterpoint to this theme, they all presuppose that the hard work has been done to create a fervent, disciplined and uncompromising collection, like the previous one published by St Bede's (*The Undivided Heart: The Western Monastic Approach to Contemplation*, 1994) aims to make available articles that many readers may find it inconvenient to locate. In offering this selection I am conscious of all those who have occasioned the various contributions that form its substance. I salute them gratefully. And I am grateful to those who have permitted the republishing of the various pieces.

Abbreviations in Notes

AAS	Acta Apostolicae Sedis
ABR	American Benedictine Review
ACW	Ancient Christian Writers
ANF	Ante-Nicene Fathers
CBQ	Catholic Biblical Quarterly
CC	Corpus Christianorum, Series Latina
CChrM	CorpusChristianrum, SeriesMedievalis
CCM	Corpus Consuetudinum Monasticarum
CIC	Codex Iuris Canonici
COCR	Collectanae Cisterciensia
CS	Cistercian Studies Series
CSEL	Corpus scriptorum ecclesiastoricorum latinorum
CSQ	Cistercian Studies Quarterly
CWS	Classics of Western Srirituality
DIP	Dizionario degle Istituti di Prefezione
DR	Downside Review
Dsp	Dictionnaire de Spiritalité
EO	Ecclesiastica Offica
FC	Fathers of the Church
GL	Geist und Leben
GS	Gaudium et Spes
ITQ	Irish Theological Quarterly
MS	Monastic Studies
MDS	Medieval Studies
NPNF	Nicene & Post-Nicene Fathers
NRTh	Nouvelle Revue Tneologiqué
PG	Patrologia Graeca (ed.) J.P. Migne
PL	Patrologia Latina (ed.) J.P. Migne
RAM	Revue d' Ascétique et de Mystique
RB	Rule of St Benedict
RBén	Revue Bénédictine
RBS	Regulae Benedicti Studia
RM	Rule of the Master
RTAM	Recherches de théologie ancienne et médiévale
SBO	Sancti Bernardi Opera

SC	*Sources Chrétiennes*, Cerf, Paris
SM	*Studia Monistica*
StA	Studia Anselmania
TDNT	*Theological Dictionary of the New Testament*
TJ	*Tjurunga*
Vox	*Vox Benedictina*
De Vogüé *La communauté*	Adalbert de Vogüé, *La communauté et l' abbé dans Régle de saint Benôit*
De Vogüé *The Rule*	Adalbert de Vogüé, *The Rule of Saint Benedict: A Doctrinal and Spiritual Commentary*
Bernard *Apo*	*Apologia*
Bernard *Div*	*Miscellaneous Sermons*
Bernard *In Cant*	*On the Song of Songs*
Bernard *Pasc*	*On Easter*
Bernard *Pre*	*On Precept and Dispensation*
Bernard *Quad*	*On Lent*
Bernard *VMal*	*Life of Malachy*
Cassian, *Conl*	*Conferences*
Cassian, *Inst*	*Institutes*

AN UNEXCITING LIFE
THE SOBER SPIRITUALITY
OF SAINT BENEDICT

This unpublished essay was the basis of a talk given for the launching of Sister Verna Holyhead's book, The Gift of Saint Benedict *on 26 June 2002. Its basic purpose was to counter the priority given to entertainment in many industrialized societies. Anything unseasoned by entertainment is considered insipid and boring. "Our goal is to educate and entertain" runs a policy statement of* Psychology Today *(February 2002, p.7). For very good reasons a life faithful to the spirit of St Benedict is not and cannot be entertaining. It seeks to activate deeper levels of the human psyche. For this a high level of sensory calm is necessary.*

Some years ago I read a quotation from a letter of Gustave Flaubert, the creator of *Madame Bovary*, which could easily serve as a summary of one aspect of the spirituality that stems from the Rule of Saint Benedict. As I remember it, the text ran: "Be regular and ordinary in your life, like a bourgeois, so that you may be violent and original in your work." What he seems to be saying is that the price paid for the release of the inner spark of creativity is low-impact living: the renunciation of superficial excitement, passive entertainment and mindless celebrity. In other words, exterior dullness is a condition for inner excitement. To describe this happy state I coined the phrase "creative monotony."[1]

For us who live in a sensate society dominated by an appetite for excitement, no matter how vacuous its source, the preferential option for a quiet life may seem a little peculiar. No doubt, in the midst of the helter-skelter of a busy life, the idea of an oasis of silence has a certain appeal, but relatively few of us seriously consider building into our lives the values by which Benedict lived.

This reluctance derives, in part, from a misunderstanding of the nature of an unexciting life. The serenity envisaged by the Benedictine motto **pax** is not the deathly stillness of a stagnant swamp where nothing ever happens, nor is it the lassitude resulting from the abandonment of all ideals and the dodging of every challenge. The outward calm that nurtures inward growth is the fruit of a disciplined life pursued through many years, and of battle-scarred victory in many struggles.[2]

It is precisely because Benedictinism is a commitment to facing the challenges of real life that it can serve as an inspiration and summons to many outside its immediate circle. On an existential level, the witness of Benedictine life fervently lived can be a reminder that humanity is enhanced and not diminished by renouncing self-indulgence, possessions and power. On a more interior plane, the beliefs and values incarnate in Benedict's Rule can be for us an antidote for some of the conditioning to which we are all subjected, who live in the twenty-first century. Attempting to assimilate the counter-cultural philosophy of Benedict's Rule is not an escape into an antique irrelevance, but a movement of reflection that is becoming increasingly necessary in a society that is fearful of any critical self-analysis.

I would like to address briefly five areas where Benedictine values are a challenge to the way most of us have learned to live. I have chosen to group these themes under the rubric of "sobriety."

1. A Settled Lifestyle

The very idea of living according to an externally generated rule seems absurd to many of our contemporaries who consider it a denial of individual choice and the consequent extinguishment of all creativity. In fact a consumerist culture constantly confronts us with such a multiplicity of meaningless options that we fritter away our power of choice through daylong involvement with making selections between trivialities. As a result, we are so entertained by the illusion of freedom that we never explore its deepest regions, nor are we conscious when its native breadth is constrained.

We are so much enamored of the notion of spontaneity that "regularity seems to trammel us," as Cardinal Newman observed.[3] We are afraid that any structuring of our personal life will depersonalize our activities. Of course, we do not want to examine how free our "spontaneous" choices are. Are they dictated by attitudes generated by mass media manipulation? Are they the expression of unconscious needs and drives? Are they truly the fruit of sober reflection and unhurried choice? We seem to think that instant availability is the law of the universe. What we want now always seems to be the right thing, so we want it immediately. We become impatient with the delays necessary for laying foundations and building infrastructure. How rarely do we reflect that those who become successful and worthy of admiration usually invest years of effort in refining the resources with which nature has endowed them. Athletes train and singers practice; years of study are concealed behind any expertise. Time in the spotlight rarely amounts to 1% of the years devoted to preparation—a lifetime of dedication condensed into 15 minutes of fame! And we overlook the fact of necessary sacrifice: doing one thing well often involves leaving aside alternative activities that are equally satisfying and potentially successful.

When it comes to the spiritual life, it is patently impossible to make any progress unless we take things seriously. This is one aspect of what Benedict means by the term "fear of the Lord."[4] We cannot even start on our spiritual journey until we are seriously committed to it. Ineffectual desire is no substitute for hard work. Our nature is such that every man, woman and child is visited by dreams of spirituality—whatever form these may take. Stranger still is the fact that the more disordered a person's life, the more persistent the fantasy. No credit is due for heroic virtue if it is exercised only at the level of daydreaming. It is only when these aspirations are translated into practice that progress begins; and it is only after years of persevering effort that solid gains become apparent.

So we are confronted by Benedict's insistence on **stability** which stands as an enduring challenge to a society where mobility is universal and the unspoken conviction that many of us have is that if we are faced with an unpleasant situation we ought to move on. The assumption is that the problem is always out there, and never in ourselves. Saint Anselm expresses well what Benedict had in mind as an antidote to this tendency.

> Just as any young tree, if frequently transplanted or often disturbed by being torn up after having recently been planted in a particular place, will never be able to take root, and will rapidly wither and bring no fruit to perfection, similarly an unhappy monk, if he often moves from place to place at his own whim, or remaining in one place is frequently agitated by his hatred of it, never achieves stability with roots of love, grows weary in the face of every useful exercise and does not grow rich in the fruitfulness of good works. And when he realizes if perchance he does reflect on it that he is making progress, not towards good, but towards evil, he unjustly assigns the whole blame for his misery not to his own behavior but to that of others, and hence unhappily works himself up to even greater hatred of those among whom he lives.[5]

Such stability is not just a stubborn refusal to change but, as Benedict notes, the willingness to keep working energetically on what has been begun under God's inspiration until that day when grace brings it to completion.

2. Avoidance of Extremes

Benedict is also boring because he does not make the mistake of identifying what is good with what is dramatic. Benedict was a man for whom any form of exhibitionism was abhorrent. In our times, now that news has become an exercise in entertainment, we tend to consider only that which is sensational as worthy of our attention.[6] It is becoming increasingly difficult to see as admirable a life that is ordinary, obscure and laborious. Steering a middle course is unremarkable, yet this is what nearly every wisdom tradition recommends. There are so many words in Benedict's rule that inculcate such an attitude: moderate, reasonable, temperate, sufficient, measured, suitable, appropriate. In such a context, there is not much scope for exaggeration, impetuosity or self-display. There is, rather, a consistent effort to keep working at improving the Gospel character of one's life, beginning first and foremost at the unseen level of the heart and only gradually moving outwards, "evangelizing" all that one does.

So we arrive at the point of saying that Benedict's monastery is ruled by a steady and unfrenetic **discipline**. The meaning of this term is twofold as far as the individual is concerned. Fundamentally it means continually submitting ourselves to a learning process, to be willing to continue as lifelong learners, ready to adapt to changing situations, both interior and exterior. There is a pre-existing pattern to which we are expected to conform. We are always in training. This conjures up the second aspect of discipline, which involves accepting an authority outside ourselves, together with the inevitable restraints and constraints on our freedom. We desire and agree to be governed by a prescriptive rule of life, by an abbot and by a community. Inevitably yielding control of our life is painful to those of us who treasure autonomy. There is much asceticism in submitting to a rule which distinguishes needs from wants, in giving obedience to a constituted superior whose priorities are the will of God, and the spiritual advancement of the community, and in trimming our activities to concord contentedly with the preferences of the people with whom we live.

Even so, the discipline demanded in a monastery following Benedict's Rule is not extreme. Not even Benedict practiced all that he preached.[7] In a community formed by Benedict's Rule, there is a constitutional balance between the different levels at which power is exercised based on accountability before the judgement-seat of God. There is a differential concern for the welfare of each. Benedict's emphasis on teaching has as its outcome, the inculcation of a broad philosophy of life common to all the members of the community, and despite or because of the profession of poverty, the standard of living is not low and financial anxiety is not high. As Saint Benedict envisaged it, lifestyle is not an issue in community. Ideally it is just there, leaving most of the community free to get on with the business of seeking God and living in objective conformity with the Gospel, in accordance with the promises they have made.

A challenging feature of Benedictine discipline, especially for compulsive communicators, is the emphasis on silence. It is difficult for many to appreciate how this regular suspension of conversation is the guardian of the quality of community life. Silence makes possible a more sincere searching of each one's inner dispositions, it facilitates prayer and is the seedbed in which wisdom grows. It is somewhat paradoxical that restraint of speech is an important factor in imbuing what we say with reflectiveness and insight for, as Benedict remarks, wise persons are known for the fewness of their words. Benedictine life is full of such ironies.

3. Embrace of Opposites

Our contemporaries sometimes confuse regulation with regimentation, obligation with coercion. The view unconsciously adopted by many who have had little personal contact with real monks is that it is a highly theatrical life that follows a tight script allowing little leeway for members of the community to express personal differences or manifest anything approaching flair, panache or eccentricity. We all know, of course, that this is far from the truth. Monasteries tend to provide habitat for astonishing array of personalities, all unique characters albeit unselfconsciously so. This leads us back to the statement of Flaubert with which we began. A life outwardly placid unleashes more creative torrents than an existence characterized by an unending succession of trivial excitements.

The equilibrium manifest in a well-ordered Benedictine community is not a happy accident, nor does it result from rigid control. It derives from a certain largeness of heart that is able to encompass differences and divergences without seeking to reduce them to an artificial consensus. Such an embrace of contrary values means that Benedictine life is remarkably flexible and adaptable, and so it is able to accommodate different personalities. Furthermore it is better equipped to survive social changes and thus to re-invent itself in different situations.[8]

To embrace difference in our own immediate ambience requires great inner security and a good sense of humor. It is a process that is like that, by which we rid ourselves of the fusty comfort of parochialism and become somewhat more cosmopolitan. There is an important advantage in such broadness. In giving others permission to be different from us, we are simultaneously giving ourselves permission to be different from them. We become free by allowing freedom to others. When life is not polarized between black and white, many subtle shades are found to exist between the extremes, and it is probable that each person's zone of comfort and challenge occurs at a different spot along the continuum. If all are encouraged to find their natural level, all will grow more easily, and a good community will result.

Such acceptance of differences is not confined to the present: it must also reach out and embrace both the past and the future. As far as the past goes we need tolerance of others' historical mistakes, especially those with a continuing effect, a generous measure of forgiveness, and the ability to let go of grievances. It means also being somewhat niggardly in the general absolution we accord to ourselves, openly admitting to errors of fact, misjudgement, inappropriate behavior and, alas, moments of malevolence.[9] We have to forgive ourselves also. For the future we need to view life as a marathon and not a sprint, and so not demand that progress be too rapid. By all means let our desire for perfection be fervent, but let it never become a channel of discontent. Only babies grow quickly. With adults decades can pass with little discernible change—but perhaps that is because we lack the eyes to see.

4. Invisibility

Notwithstanding the fact that we are fed up with arrogance and self-promotion, many of us do not feel fully at ease with Benedict's approach to humility.[10] Yet in reality it is a very safe spiritual path to identify with the little people. Here in Australia we are very lucky the Benedictine and Cistercian communities have such a low profile and are generally marginal to both Church and society.[11] How awful it must be to live in a community formed by inhabiting grand and pompous buildings, burdened with centuries-long privileges and expectations, and locked into a series of mutual obligations that benefit nobody. How refreshing is Saint Bernard's call to poverty.

> Those who are fully loaded cannot run well; those who are empty and unoccupied make progress more quickly and more safely. You must be naked to fight with a naked opponent, the devil, for he is not burdened with earthly possessions. See that you are wearing nothing by which he could get a grip on you.[12]

The mad thing about money is that the more you have the more you need. Once a certain standard of living is attained, it involves not only maintenance but constant improvement. Unprincipled amelioration can easily seep into monastic life as a reaction to the past, if monks and nuns carry a resentment about former conditions that they experienced as excessive deprivation. Today it is probable the average monk or nun costs more to support than ever before. Doubtless, some of the expenditure is necessary, because of education costs and the fact that they are expected to fill more roles and work at many more tasks. We should not close our eyes, however, to the possibility that some of the extra outlay may represent a dereliction of values dear to Saint Benedict.

Humility and poverty are not unrelated. The choice of a monastery that guarantees a lower standard of living amounts to a renunciation of an automatic hike in status. Enter a famous community and you become thereby a little famous, no matter who you are. Choose a small unendowed monastery and you will probably live and die in obscurity. Celebrity everywhere depends on money: but there is still a charm in a hidden life that defines itself apart from material possessions, status and social esteem. A community that is materially poor can be very rich if it is characterized by dedication, mutuality, communion, listening, hospitality. The lifestyle that is typically Benedictine is unexciting because it is poor and relatively unknown. It may not be famous but that does not prevent it from being true to the Gospel and, therefore, ultimately promotive of human growth and happiness. It serves as an evangelical leaven and a signpost in a society that is in danger of losing its way.

5. Vision of Community

If we agree that one of the most dehumanizing influences in Western society is the tendency to individualism, then what we need to offset that distortion is a strong theory and practice of community. The community Benedict desired to create was not just a gathering of like-minded individuals who enjoy one another's company, but a structured and purposeful group of people who are united by shared beliefs and values, and by common goals and objectives. Benedict's vision of community reflects his view of the human person: called to a corporate relationship with God in prayer, called to practical self-sustenance in common work, called to be open to "outsiders" through hospitality, called to ongoing reconciliation in the effort to become makers of peace, called not to self-righteousness and judgement but to mental and practical compassion. Benedict's community is not arcane or esoteric: it is simply a group of people who freely choose to walk the way of the Gospel.

We need never be ashamed of our investment in building community, nor in the fact that it involves struggle. It is, along with faith in God, one of the most strongly counter-cultural projects in which we are involved, even though it corresponds to the aspirations of many. Nearly half a century ago, Erich Fromm wrote about the madness of an individualist society—and the situation has certainly deteriorated since then. The solution he proposed, however, remains valid. "The transformation of an atomistic into a communitarian society depends on creating again the opportunity for people to sing together, to walk together, to dance together, admire together—together and not...as a member of a 'lonely crowd'."[13]

As monks and nuns we are called to witness to the holiness of God through a dedication to worship, but we are also summoned in a particular way at this period of history to be witnesses to the value of human community as the basis of our service of God. Our contemporaries need to be reminded that humanity desires above all things an environment from which violence, exploitation, manipulation and dominance have been excluded, and in which acceptance, respect and love are made the first priority.

Monastic life is not reserved to an elite. Perhaps, as Saint Bernard suggests, it will prove more attractive to those who are so impaired that without such intensive care they would not flourish.[14] This means that persons whose spiritual constitution is more rugged can practice the same beliefs and values, in a less structured way. And this explains the appeal of monastic spirituality to lay people. We who are more knowledgeable and experienced in this tradition need to recognize this need and to cater to it. No harm would be done also, if we were to extrapolate this vision of the local community or church, as the early Cistercians used to call their monasteries, into the sphere of the universal Church in its essential functions. We might discover a model of the Church more attractive than some which are being currently marketed.

It is perhaps not generally recognized that one of the strongest influences on the Second Vatican Council was the Benedictine Blessed Columba Marmion. It is a reasonable assumption that most of the conciliar Fathers had read Marmion's works, which had been standard fare for pious ecclesiastics for half a century before the Council happened. The vision of community and Church implicit in the Benedictine tradition came into its own as the Council decrees began to appear: Christocentric and liturgical, humane and hospitable, traditional and open. Surely the "Benedictine" values are precisely those expressed in the decrees of the Council and which correspond most fully to the aspirations of many in the Church today—most powerfully those who are alienated and disempowered.

In a homily preached at Monte Cassino, Pope Paul VI recognized that the Benedictine ideal of peace involves the renunciation of an exciting life. This leads, he said, to a sober way of life marked by "a spiritual style [expressed] in the elegant gravity of your actions."[15] The term *gravitas* that Pope Paul uses is one that is important for Benedict. It denotes that a monk ought to be a man of substance, a weighty man, someone who is solid and not easily upset. He is not saying that a monk should be overweight, or as solemn as a funeral director, or ponderous and self-important. He is suggesting that the monk's center of gravity is not susceptible to exterior pressures so that he is not easily bowled over. *Gravitas* suggests a certain removal from real or manufactured storms that move life in the direction of soap opera. There is a tendency to develop a spirit of calmness, a certain imperturbability and a sage sense of proportion that transcends temperament and has its source in a firm faith in God.

Perhaps we might conclude on the note with which we began. "Be regular and ordinary in your life, like a true follower of Saint Benedict, so that you may be violent and original in your work!"

NOTES

[1] The Spiritual Vision of Saint Benedict (Benedictine Studies Program, 1980) Unit 4, E.

[2] "Because the idea of peace is connected with that of calm, a cessation of disputes and their orderly solution, it often happens that we are easily led to think of peace as inertia, rest, sleep, death. And there is a whole psychology that accuses a peaceful life of inaction and laziness, of ineptitude and selfishness, and instead praises struggle, agitation, disorder, and even sin as sources of activity, of energy, and of progress." Paul VI, *Quale Saluto*, 24 October 1964 in *The Pope Speaks* 10 (1964) pp. 121-122.

[3] Quoted by Ian Ker, *John Henry Newman: A Biography* (Oxford: University Press, 1988) p. 93. On the next page the author quotes the pithy apothegm, "Go to bed in good time, and you are already perfect."

[4] On this see, M. Casey, *Truthful Living: Saint Benedict's Teaching on Humility* (Petersham: St Bede's Publications, 1999) pp. 95-119.

[5] Letter 37 to the novice Lanzo in *The Letters of Saint Anselm of Canterbury: Volume One* (CSS 96; Kalamazoo, Cistercian Publications, 1990) pp. 134-35.

[6] "What is the dominant mode of experience at the end of the twentieth century? How do people see things, and how do they expect to see things? The answer is simple. In every field, from business to politics to marketing to education, the dominant mode has become entertainment.... In other centuries human beings wanted to be saved, or improved, or freed, or educated. But in our century, they want to be entertained. The great fear is not of disease or death, but of boredom." Michael Crichton, *Timeline* (London: Arrow Books, 2000) 01.13.52; pp. 442-443.

[7] This is apparent if we draw up parallels between the Rule and the Benedict who appears in Saint Gregory's *Dialogues*. Despite quoting with apparent

approval the aphorism "Wine is no drink for monks" Benedict admits that it is hard to convince monks of the truth of this stance. It is to be noted that when the monks of Vicovaro decided to get rid of Benedict, they put the poison in his wine. In the *Rule* Benedict makes provision for the election of the abbot and the appointment of the prior by the one elected. In the *Dialogues* it seems that in making foundations he reserved to himself the nomination of both officials.

[8] See "Balance in Monastic Life," *TJ* 9 (1975) pp. 5-11; "The Benedictine Balances," in *Saint Benedict of Nursia: A Way of Wisdom for Today* (Paris: Editions du Signe, 1993) pp. 24-25; "The Dynamic Unfolding of the Benedictine Charism," *ABR* 51.2 (June 2000) pp. 149-168; "The Rule of Benedict and Inculturation: A Formation Perspective," *TJ* 62 (2002) pp. 15-46.

[9] "At one point in writing about the General Will, Jean-Jacques Rousseau said that for democracy to work, citizens must be willing to say, 'I was mistaken.' This is not something most of us are willing to do....."Andrew Hacker, "Twelve Angry Persons," in *New York Review of Books*, September 21, 1995, p. 46.

[10] Some of the reasons for this I attempted to analyze in *Truthful Living*, pp. 9-27.

[11] See M. Casey, "Australian Benedictine Spirituality," in *Benedictine Pathways: Benedictines in Australia and New Zealand* (The Benedictine Union of Australia and New Zealand, 2000) pp. 5-6.

[12] *Sent* 3.94; *SBO* 152.2-8.

[13] Erich Fromm, *The Sane Society* (London: Routledge & Kegan Paul, 1956) p. 349.

[14] Bernard of Clairvaux, *Apologia* 7: "I knew that my soul was so weak as to require a stronger remedy." *SBO* 3, 87, 26.

[15] *Quale saluto* 24 October 1964; translated in *The Pope Speaks* 10 (1964) p. 120.

The Art of Interpreting the Rule

PRINCIPLES OF INTERPRETATION AND APPLICATION

This article attempted to formulate some practical guidelines for interpreting St Benedict's Rule. It was more concrete and simpler than earlier articles in which I had reflected on monastic reading of the hermeneutical writings of Hans-Georg Gadamer. It began life in TJ 14 *(1977), was recycled to form part of the* Benedictine Studies Program *in 1979, and was reprinted in* Benedictines 36.2 *(1984) and translated in* Monastische Informationem 38 *(1984).*

Many communities that profess to follow the Rule of St Benedict (*RB*) experience a degree of difficulty in reconciling an honest fidelity to the Rule with responsiveness to the demands and opportunities of the present moment. It is easy to talk of "return to the sources" and the "signs of the times" as being dual animating principles of religious renewal, but achieving their harmonious interaction in practice is not quite so simple.

It is not that anyone seriously denies that *RB* is a substantial text. Its impact on the history of Western Europe is generally recognized, and even Australian history is marked, in its early stages, by the impress of Benedictinism. The problem lies with the Rule's archaic character. The scene it evokes is patently antique; it is the insular, pragmatic world of sixth-century Italy, rural, rugged, and prone to pessimism. The kind of life for which it legislates seems impossible in the modern world.

An observer might be forgiven for wondering whether *RB* has any effective impact on modern monastic communities. There is, undoubtedly, a certain cultural and linguistic continuity, which gives the impression of fidelity: the Rule is publicly proclaimed, its values are often held in high regard and many traditional observances survive. Yet often it seems that a conventional and standardized "Benedictinism" has more practical import than the Rule itself. Flowing garments, shaven heads, Gregorian chant, Gothic arches and other elements of the popular monastic image may be left aside without much regret, but other observances which have as little foundation in *RB* (such as daily Mass, education, general chapters) are followed with great zeal. On the other hand, departure from such crucial matters as the weekly Psalter, the prohibition of personal possessions, excommunication, and utter obedience is legitimated by reference to the famous Benedictine "discretion." The question arises whether *RB* is simply an historical element in the evolution of modern Benedictinism, which has been largely superseded. If it does have some role to play, a second question may be posed: how does fidelity to a sixth-century Rule interact with a concerned response to the real world of today?

It is good to allow our doubts about the value of studying *RB* to surface. Very often they can serve as indicators of the direction our studies should take. Just as the presence of pain can lead to the diagnosis of disease, so our antipathies to such a course of study can highlight the real questions that need to be asked at every stage of understanding. These doubts or difficulties are not irrelevancies or temptations to be brushed aside without examination. They are concrete indications of where effort is best expended. This introduction attempts to outline some principles by which *RB* is able to enrich contemporary community life without causing it to forget the real world or to overlook some areas of gain since the sixth century.

FIRST PRINCIPLE:

RB does not act directly upon community regimen, but on the minds and hearts of community members.

The Rule is no longer normative in deciding details of community life; this normativity is now exercised by the Constitutions and by other agencies delegated by them. *RB* is not normative but instrumental; it serves as a catalyst. It animates and gives form to a judgement about particular issues not by pre-determining the conclusion, but by stimulating a personal and communal sense of vocation. Understanding is not communicated materially and immediately, but formally and through a process of dialectic. What the Rule has to say is not spoken into a vacuum, but into a consciousness that is not without content. It influences a person or a community not by some form of automatic takeover, but by a gradual nuancing, a process of subtle broadening and enrichment. *RB* does not pre-empt the judgement on an issue by handing down a decision made fourteen hundred years ago; it enters into dialogue with other components of consciousness. Its total effect is not intended to produce a stale conformity with ancient models, but a lively debate in which neither the past nor the present is allowed a monopoly. *RB* (and other ancient texts) if properly used, has the capacity to ensure the freedom of our choices. They can ensure that the judgement of faith is brought into play in deciding a particular option, causing a personal sense of vocation and commitment to Christ to interact with urgent appeals of need and expediency. The result of such give-

and-take may not always be the same as spontaneous impressions and judgements made on the spur of the moment.

To be able to interact with more tangible forces, *RB* needs an assured place in our hearts and minds. We cannot hope to be influenced by *RB* unless we expose ourselves to it. If the *Exordium Magnum* is to be believed it was precisely the attentive listening to the daily reading of the Rule which triggered off in the hearts of the Fathers of Citeaux an awareness of God's call. Humbly and attentively to read RB, allowing it to speak to one's heart, is often a means by which we are confirmed and challenged in our monastic life. There is no question of interpreting it in fundamentalist fashion, but of using it as a means of making explicit our own conscience and sense of vocation.

Dialogue between a modern Benedictine and *RB* is possible only on the supposition that there is some common ground between them. The discovery of the area of overlap requires a realistic acceptance of the inherent difficulties of such communication and a deliberate attempt to overcome them.

SECOND PRINCIPLE:

Understanding RB is facilitated by appreciation of its historical, cultural and linguistic characteristics.

The fact that there are areas in *RB* which we regard as obscure at best, and at worst wrong (corporal punishment, the prohibition of laughter, the downgrading of individual initiative) alert us to the fact that *RB*'s particular approach to monastic life is something that is fundamentally foreign to our way of thinking. The easy assumption that we know what he is referring to without much effort is unfounded. There are many parts of *RB* which can be understood only within their proper context; this means that anyone who aims to let the Rule speak for itself must take some care that he appreciates the framework in which its ideas are set.

It is not correct to say that it is possible to abstract the "spiritual teaching" of the Rule from its organizational arrangements. Beliefs, values and actions form a unity. It is possible for several different actions to serve as alternative expressions of a single value, but it is not possible to understand the values inherent in the Rule without appreciating the concrete externalizations visualized by *RB* in their historical context. It is not here being suggested that the letter must be kept in order to comprehend the spirit but that the letter (the practical administrative details of daily life in *RB*) must be weighed and assayed as part of the process of appropriating the spirit. St Benedict was not purporting to write "ageless" spirituality; he simply adapted an earlier rule to serve as a kind of handbook for groups of monks known to him. What spiritual teaching he included was governed by the understanding that if monks knew why certain practices were advocated, their acceptance would be more complete. *RB* envisages monastic life in its totality as it existed in the sixth century; the complex of beliefs, values and practices that it describes cannot be arbitrarily broken up; first they must be appreciated as a whole.

There is a need for scholarly work to precede our attempts at interpreting *RB* and applying it to contemporary situations. This is not to say that only professional scholars may interpret the Rule; it means simply that those whose duty it is to administer the Rule cannot afford to overlook what scholars are saying about the climate of thought which pervades *RB*. It is not possible to appreciate the significance of *RB* without understanding the sense of the words; it is only through what it says that we can penetrate to what it means. To understand what the Rule is saying we have to be very patient. We must be steadfast in our refusal to project anachronistic modern notions back into the Rule; we have to allow our own horizons to broaden somewhat to take in something of the perspective characteristic of *RB* and try to see things from that standpoint. Above all we have to acquire the tight-rope walking knack of taking notice of what the experts say without completely evacuating our own judgement.

Just as our reading of *RB* is enriched by an appreciation of the setting out of which it speaks, any effort to interpret *RB* without this preliminary work will lead inevitably to bizarre inexactitudes, gross oversimplifications and eventually to a trivialization of its message. The whole point of reading the Rule is to broaden our minds: no such broadening takes place if we approach *RB* as a series of pre-ordained solutions to be applied automatically if the occasion warrants it. Getting to the heart of the matter and looking at it from another viewpoint is certainly a more arduous and less automatic procedure, but it does effect a certain stretching of consciousness; it is within the context of such an enlarged awareness that genuine solutions begin to be perceived.

THIRD PRINCIPLE:

RB is part of a living tradition. Understanding the Rule involves an appreciation of the values and beliefs of both previous and subsequent tradition.

The Rule of St Benedict was never intended as the final and definitive expression of his thought on monastic life. It is, rather, a workmanlike compilation of directives, which it seemed necessary for him to spell out in the situation in which he lived. Some elements are necessarily local and for his own time; some permanent elements may have been given little prominence in the Rule because they were well understood and needed no emphasis.

To understand the Rule, therefore, it is necessary to see it as part of an ongoing tradition. Benedict wrote in order that the tradition might become a living reality in the situation in which he and his contemporaries lived. He was trying to do in his milieu what Antony, Augustine, Basil, Cassian and Pachomius were doing in theirs. Therefore, it is important that the written work of Benedict be viewed within the context of the whole monastic program of formulating principles for evangelical living.

Furthermore, this tradition did not stop or become rigid with the writing of the Rule. Very often subsequent tradition allows what was implicit in Benedict's expression of the monastic ideals to become visible; it also offers correctives and elucidations to what were, perhaps, merely temporary measures. Sometimes, alas, subsequent tradition also distorted the original.

This holds especially with regard to the meaning of words. Monastic vocabulary is specific. It is not enough to look up in a Latin dictionary to find an English equivalent. There were many turns of phrase, which have a particularly evocative meaning within the monastic sub-culture. The precise meaning of what Benedict is saying is often accessible only to those experienced in the traditional language of this sub-culture.

It is especially in the level of values and beliefs that the meaning of the Rule is to be found. The directives given by Benedict for the practical organization of life in the monastery are almost useless unless we happen to be able to reproduce that life-style. In history this has often been changed. What remains permanent is concentrated far more on the inner elements than on external observances.

FOURTH PRINCIPLE:

Not all aspects of the thought of RB are worthwhile; having attended closely to the meaning of some sections, one may judge them to be inapplicable.

No matter how much reverence we have for the *auctoritas* of *RB*, nothing can alter the fact that it remains a sixth-century Italian rule. Nothing is gained by abandoning the present and taking up domicile in the past; the attempt to live a sixth-century life in the twenty-first century cannot succeed because it is contrived. In our efforts to understand where the teaching of the Gospels, our Benedictine vocation and our own conscience are leading us, the Rule can be of considerable help. But it is not normative; often we shall have to diverge from its practices and priorities and sometimes we shall have to take a step diametrically opposed to what it enjoins. This is to be expected. The important thing is not that we do what the Rule says, but that we listen to it.

The very fact that St Benedict himself consciously altered the tradition he received and made provision for the adaptation of *RB* cannot be overlooked. A positivist approach to *RB* is intrinsically erroneous. Not only is there no need for us to deny the skerries of wisdom we have laboriously acquired in our own life, it is precisely this understanding which will help us to appreciate what the Rule is saying. *RB* serves as one element in a dialogical progress; it interacts with other sources of guidance. This means that at times *RB* serves a very subsidiary purpose; in a discussion of television or the Third World or balancing the accounts, *RB* is likely to be the silent partner. Furthermore, many of the issues which seemed important to St Benedict are dead. The Rule does not contain all the answers; but it can sometimes help us to find what we are looking for.

FIFTH PRINCIPLE

Understanding RB is facilitated by a commitment to the program of which the Rule is part; participation in a living tradition gives "family access" to the texts, which give expression to the tradition.

Beyond the written word of *RB* there is another mode of access to St Benedict's thought: the tradition which emanates from him and which has, through many reversals of fortune, survived until today. Just as a spoken word is often nuanced by a person's demeanor, private jokes, personal history and so forth, so *RB* and other texts are often given supplementary meaning by the social institutions which stem from them. A text may enunciate a principle in black and white terms that brook no hesitation about their meaning, yet this harshness may be tempered in practice by a very lax enforcement of the principle. Thus there is no certain evidence that the practice of excommunication, as spelled out at some length in *RB*, has ever been effectively put into practice. Beneath the surface of community life there runs an underground stream of understanding, which assures that the letter of the Rule is not interpreted without reference to what is between the lines. It is precisely this absence of contact with a living tradition, which was, in part, responsible for the severity and literal-mindedness of the Trappist reform.

The person who seems most likely to be enriched by *RB* is the one who shares St Benedict's zeal in seeking the will of God, and responding to a sense of vocation on the one hand; and in trying to formulate practical measures which would allow people of today to flower within monastic tradition on the other. Without such common purpose, no real dialogue is possible.

SIXTH PRINCIPLE:

The capacity of RB to enhance the consciousness of a modern reader is grounded in the fact that it proposes an alternative perspective to that normally adopted by him or her.

The whole impact of an ancient text such as *RB* derives from the fact that it preserves a "memory" of a way of seeing and doing things, which is not governed by contemporary ideology. The ancient approach is not normative; there is no question here of advocating neo-primitivism. It does have the effect of reminding us of the sheer relativity of many aspects of thought and conduct, which we have come to think of as absolute. Too often we tend to accept uncritically, beliefs and values which contribute little to the unfolding of a vocation; it does us no harm sometimes to be reminded of an alternative system. If it is true that we are not easily able to assess the impact of values which we have absorbed in the process of growing up—we take them for granted; they are self-evident—then it is also true that we have internalized beliefs and attitudes that work contrary to our vocations, but without our knowing it. By allowing such presuppositions and prejudices to enter into dialogue some of their potential for harm can be voided. Out in the open we are able to assess them critically and either accept, modify or reject them. Such dialogue *works* best when it is transcultural, when we allow the views of one not reared in our culture to percolate through our awareness; then there is possibility of change. The very strangeness inherent in *RB*, which at first seemed to be such an obstacle to its understanding, now appears as an asset. It is good to read something about monastic life that comes from another setting and from a different world. It may challenge us to re-examine aspects of our thought and practice; it may also confirm us in what we hold and do. In either case it will have impact only to the extent that it acts as an autonomous agent, piercing the habitual shell of our customary positions and causing us to wake up.

CONCLUSION

In this introduction it has been possible only to outline elements of an approach to *RB* which would set it up in tandem with an enlightened contemporary awareness. The approach here summarized is not unlike the traditional practice of *lectio divina*; we read not for information or for detailed regulation of our lives. We read in order that our consciences may be stung by what we read and the will of God manifested thereby. The same applies to our reading of the Rule: what we aim for is the keeping alive of our sense of vocation. Once this instinct develops, practical issues can easily be solved.

THE "HARD SAYINGS"
OF THE RULE OF SAINT BENEDICT

In the years following the aggiornamento *of Vatican II, many communities were embarrassed by the hardline positions proclaimed in Benedict's Rule. In many cases the public reading of the Rule was curtailed or bowdlerized. Those who propagated the Rule preferred to dwell on its "positive" aspects. In this article, which first appeared in Tjurunga 3 (1972), I attempted to give some elements of background to Benedict's "hard sayings" and to suggest that in some cases Benedict's severity was no more than a reflection of the exigency of the Gospel.*

Notwithstanding the many instances of genuine humanity and even tenderness to be found in RB, there are many passages in the Rule, which seem, by our standards, excessively severe. The persistent emphasis on obligations and punishments, the prohibition of merrymaking and the cool detachment toward newcomers are examples of such "hard sayings." These passages pose a certain amount of difficulty for the modern reader who, if he does not reject RB altogether, is inclined to temper his acceptance of it by drawing a veil over its jagged edges and concentrating instead on its more positive aspects.

In this chapter I should like to suggest some guidelines to help in the interpretation of such passages and in their application to our own situations. In particular, I shall try to clarify what seems to me to be the key question. In a specific instance, is the severity of *RB* to be traced to a historico-cultural residue passively absorbed by Benedict or is it due to an active acceptance of some positive monastic value that even now cries out for implementation?

It seems to me that in examining any of the "hard sayings" of *RB* there are five aspects of the Rule that need to be kept in mind. These are its fidelity to its sources, its genre as legislative writing, the lofty goals it presupposes, the sort of people for whom it was originally written and the limitations and prejudices of its author. Let us now briefly examine each of these.

1. *Faithful to its Sources*

It is probably true to say that Benedict was to a large extent psychologically incapable of conceiving monastic life outside the theoretical and practical framework imposed by its own history. Just as we may find it difficult to think of the Papacy without reference to its more recent historical manifestations, so Benedict found himself unable to dissociate monasticism from its rugged beginnings. It is clear that Benedict has tempered the spirit of mainline monasticism with the milder traditions of Basil and Augustine, but the Rule remains in substantial continuity with Cassian and Pachomius and Anthony. The life-style described in *RB* is not Benedict's brainchild. He is simply describing the sort of life led in the monasteries of his acquaintance, a sort of life owing more to an accumulation of administrative decisions and common sense than to anybody's bright idea.

Because many of these practices were informed with traditional monastic theory and supported by the authority of the great men of the past, Benedict accepted them. In some cases he accepted such practices simply because they were traditional.[1] In other cases he deliberately modified the tradition.[2] And in many passages dealing with punishments, *RB* seems to have extended the treatment of its immediate source.[3] But despite the many changes in detail, the overall picture of monastic life remains the same as that delineated in the sources.

Our first task in trying to arrive at an interpretation of the "hard sayings" is to view them against the background of their own origins. In some cases it will be clear that the situation, giving rise to the particular tradition no longer occurs, in which case the tradition may be left to lapse. In other cases a closer examination of the issues will be called for. In almost every case, however, our understanding of what Benedict is driving at in the "hard sayings" will be nuanced and clarified by taking into consideration the sort of situation in which they arose and the problems they were meant to solve.

In some cases understanding can come from a consideration of the subsequent development of a tradition. By studying the history of the interpretation of *RB* we can sometimes bring to light aspects of the Rule not always apparent on a cursory reading. Thus, for example, the fact that to a large extent the history of the Benedictine Order is characterized by a certain dialectic between relaxation and reform, indicates that the tension between austerity and common sense is something internal to the Rule itself, and probably constitutes one of its most significant formative elements. Unless we appreciate this fact, our approach to *RB* will be considerably off target.

A first rule in interpreting the "hard sayings" is this: avoid isolating them from their context, from the rest of the Rule and from the ongoing tradition of which they are a part.

2. *A Legislative Document*

The great amount of valuable spiritual doctrine to be found in *RB* should not blind us to the fact that *RB* was written as a legislative document, not as a compendium of spirituality. The Rule is less concerned with giving a theoretical vision of monastic life than with providing a detailed description of its organizational framework. Principles are formulated to support policies and practices, not for their own sake. The basic thrust of *RB* is concerned with the visible aspect of life in a monastery, not with its secret dynamics. This is why so much space is devoted to admission of candidates, the appointment and duties of the various officials, the rubrics for the Work of God, the penal code and so forth. The theory behind much of the practice is presupposed. It is only formulated explicitly when there is a need to add emphasis or background to a stipulation, or to motivate a choice of one option among several.

The fact that *RB* is a rule influences its style and presentation as well as its content. It is due to the fact that parts of *RB* are written in "regulationese" that it sometimes sounds about as warm and inspiring as the railway by-laws. It is in many respects a typical Roman document,[4] showing a preference for clarity and reasonableness over personableness and flair.

Most important of all to remember is the fact that Benedict proposes his Rule, not as the unique source of obligation on matters touching monastic life, but as a code to be administered by the abbot in accordance with the teachings of the Gospel. The exceptions to the prescriptions of *RB*, demanded by common sense, are left to the abbot's discretion. There is no need to itemize them in the Rule itself. Furthermore, the abbot is several times reminded that the Rule is to be administered with an eye to the incapacity of the monks, so that in cases where the strictness of life described by *RB* is counter-productive, the injunctions of the Rule may be suspended.

A second rule in understanding the "hard sayings" is not to allow ourselves to be put off by their tone and general presentation, but to remember that they are set forth in *RB* as subject to the compassionate administration of the abbot.

3. A Ruder Readership

Both internal and external indications seem to suggest that among those for whom *RB* was written were included a certain number of rough diamonds, simple men who truly wanted a monastic life, but who expected (and maybe needed) a stern military-type discipline, with clearly delineated authority structures and swift retribution for offenders. In addition, we can be reasonably sure that even among the more sophisticated monks of the sixth century, a rugged life style would have posed relatively few problems. Their society was position orientated, not based on achievement. They had no access to the vast world of facts and interpretations that is diffused universally in our times. There was no trace of a class-consciousness of religious subjects vis-à-vis their superiors, such as seems to be emerging today. The overall picture was that they were apparently more reconciled to rough handling at the hands of their superiors than religious are nowadays.

When Benedict wrote his Rule, he presupposed this attitude in his monks. Whilst warning the abbot to be careful in his administration he still exhorts the monks to submit with patience.[5] *RB* is a plain man's guide to monastic life. There are few frills about it. It tends to state the issues clearly without becoming involved in the subtleties that real life often brings. It takes for granted that it is possible to categorize life into zones of black and white, and pays little attention to the vast grey zone in between.[6] This can lead us to conclude to a degree of insensitivity in Benedict that is offensive to our modern tastes, apart from being disastrous if put into effect in everyday life.

A third rule for understanding the "hard sayings" advises us not to impute excessive harshness to Benedict, but at the same time to be prepared to face issues and problems according to our heightened sensitivity and not to flee decisions by adhering rigidly to the black and white perspectives of the Rule.

4. *A Static World-View*

The modern world is very much aware of the phenomenon of development and its far-reaching implications. And here we have an edge over Benedict.[7] Benedict does not sufficiently appreciate the role of development in the life of a monk. The regimen he institutes for his monks is meant to apply to everyone, more or less, from the novice to the mature monk and to the abbot himself. There is no formation program; the novitiate is designed mainly to weed out unsuitable candidates and to ensure that those who are accepted, enter with the maximum deliberateness and awareness of what will be expected of them. Finally, throughout the Rule there is too much emphasis on words like "weakness" with their evaluative overtones, whereas often there is merely question of the monks being on the way to perfection, rather than established in the state of perfection from the beginning. Here, let it be said, Benedict's handling of the situations is usually very wise: it is his description of them that is unfortunate.

Now to answer some objections. It can be argued from the chapter *On Humility*, from the statement about the effects of growth of charity in the monk at the end of the Prologue, from the possibility of "graduating" into an eremitic form of life and from the view of monastic life as a journey to the Father that Benedict did recognize the fact of development. In addition, if development is such a basic factor of human life, how could one of such considerable experience and wisdom be unaware of its existence?

Yes, it is correct to say that some elements of the reality of development were apparent to the writers of monastic tradition. For example, almost all of them recognized that the program of monastic life is a long-term one. There are, to my knowledge, no texts that suggest that the sanctity proposed to us by the Gospels is attainable by any other means than a life of hard labor. The Master represents monastic life as an art or a craft at which the monk works all his years, finally producing what he set out to do. The same idea appears also in *RB*, especially in chapter 4. But this is not development. The end product is something resulting from steady application of skill and care, not something that grows as the result of an inner dynamism. And the price paid for the work of art, the reward given at the day of judgement is external and out of all proportion to the labor of its manufacture.

Likewise, the ladder described in chapter 7 is not the chronicle of the soul's ascent to God with the rungs being climbed serially. It is a description of the manifestations of humility in a person's life. The ascent may be considered complete when all the degrees are accomplished, but ascent begins not with an attack on the first degree but with a simultaneous attack on all twelve. [8] It is not correct to say that Benedict envisages a progression from interior virtues to exterior virtues, that humility of the heart comes before humility of the eyes or head, to use the Master's expressions. The sides of the ladder, be it remembered, which support all the manifestations of this virtue, are the body and the soul. "Taken literally," as de Vogüé notes, "this image rather signifies that *each* degree is *simultaneously* fixed in both sides, which are the body and the soul."[9]

Benedict's image of monastic life as a return to the Father from whom we have become distanced through sin is in some way parallel to our notion of development, but Benedict does not examine the idea in any depth. It is simply an image, suggested by the Bible and much used in the writings of early Christian tradition, and not a theory or an observation about monastic life in operation.

But Benedict does give evidence of some awareness of development. This is embodied in two important passages of *RB*. In a personal addition to the end of the Prologue, he advises the newcomer against being disheartened by the strictness of the life, which gets easier, he says, as time goes on.

> But as we **progress** in monastic life and in faith, we speed over the path of God's commandments with a heart enlarged by the indescribable pleasure of love...[10]

The second passage occurs at the end of the chapter *On Humility*. It too shows significant variations from *RM*.

> Having climbed all these rungs [of the ladder] of humility the monk arrives at the love of God that casts away fear and by which all that he did previously through fear he now begins to do effortlessly; it has become second nature to him.[11] He does this no longer from fear of hell but for the love of Christ and because of the pleasure he experiences in virtue...[12]

In both these texts Benedict shows himself aware of a progression taking place within the monk from laboriousness in the beginning to a degree of comfort later on. This is not the place for a full discussion of these texts. Suffice it to say that there is question of development only in a very narrow sense. On the level of brute fact the process described in *RB* is simply the socializing of the monk, the process in which he becomes accustomed to and familiar with the social life around him. He internalizes the values of the society in which he lives and forgets that he was ever any different. An inmate of a concentration camp goes through the same socializing experience. You can get used to anything, almost. This is almost certainly the phenomenon which *RM* is describing. Benedict goes deeper in ascribing the process not only to a "love of the custom itself" (*RM* 10:90), but to a growing relationship with Christ. The pity is that he nowhere develops the theme. As it stands in *RB*, we have to say that Benedict regards this as a development on a psychological level, not a development on a deep level of personal commitment. In his Rule he does not speak about or make provision for such a development, except maybe in the case of a cenobite becoming a hermit. Personal development toward a presently unspecified goal is not catered for by the Rule. This is why it can sometimes be experienced by people as rigid and stifling.

To conclude this long section let us formulate a fourth rule to help in the understanding of the "hard sayings." Wherever Benedict enjoins something without due respect for the role of development in human life, it must be understood to have only limited value, and the matter needs to be examined afresh *ab initio*.

5. A Specialized Life Style

RB was never meant for mass consumption. The attraction held by Benedictine life will always have a very limited following. The life-style envisaged by *RB* is not simply a cultural residue of a bygone age. It is also a remarkably apt description of a way of life still worth living. The "hard sayings" in *RB*, just like those of the Gospels, owe some of their severity to the very nature of monastic life as a long-term program of channeling one's efforts toward God as a discipline, self-forgetfulness and generosity. And none of us find these easy.

RB is acceptable only on the basis of a certain complex of motivations and goals. Only within the context of such an attitude is *RB* reasonable and effective. Wherever the subjective dispositions of a person do not coincide with those presupposed in *RB*, the setup described in the Rule is at once both unreasonable and counter-productive. We should not be too hasty in trying to explain away the "hard sayings" of *RB*, we need to cast a critical eye over our own life and commitment first. It would be a shame to throw the baby out with the bath water.¹³

Our final rule for understanding the "hard sayings" of *RB* is this: to the extent that the "hard sayings" represent a call to greater fidelity to the teachings of the Gospels and to our own sense of vocation, they stand.

NOTES

¹ Compare *RB* 10,3 with Cassian *Inst* 2,4, 'How throughout the whole of Egypt and the Thebaid the number of Psalms is fixed at twelve'.

² Compare *RB* 18,25 with *Vitae Patrum* 3,6. Compare *RB* 40,6 with *Vitae Patrum* 5:4,31.

³ It may be that Benedict simply wanted matters expressed more clearly than in *RM*, but the chapters have a chilling tone to the modern reader, though see note 12 below. In fairness to Benedict it should be noted that he buttresses his stance with considerable solicitude for those incurring the punishment.

⁴ *RB* bears a remarkable similarity in tone and content to the instructions left by the older Cato concerning his steward. In the 700 years separating them, the Latin language appears to have completed a full circle.

⁵ Especially in the fourth degree of humility. In *RB* 7, 34 Benedict has made a characteristic addition to the text of *RM*, adding as a motive for patience, the love of God, *pro amore Dei*.

⁶ For example, at the end of Chapter 58 Benedict seems to suggest that every departure from the monastery is the result of the devil's prompting. Nowadays it is generally recognized that in some circumstances it is the best thing to do.

⁷ Both the Romance word "develop"and its cognates and the Germanic word *Entwicklung* and its cognates are less than 400 years old. The origins of both are unclear, though it seems fairly certain that in the beginning they meant simply "unfold"or "unroll" as one would, for example, open a scroll. Whether the technical and more abstract meaning of the words is directly due to the influence of Hegel is hard to say. It seems probably however, that the appreciation of the notion of development and the use of the word must both have received a fillip from the dissemination of his writings. Benedict lived before Hegel. And not only Benedict, but Thomas Aquinas, Augustine and a substantial quorum of influential Church thinkers lived and thought in a world that appeared more static (or stable) than ours. There is no Latin word that corresponds exactly to "development." *Processus, progressus, progressio* (the word used by Paul VI in his encyclical *(On the Development of Peoples) evolutio, provolutio* and so forth are all modern makeshifts. As used by the ancient writers these words did not mean what we mean by "development," simply because they did not view reality as we do. Of course they did not totally neglect this aspect of things, but they did not recognize the extent to which things develop. More often than not, development was recognized only as an isolated phenomenon (e.g. growth) and the concept was thus limited in its area of application. The problem of change was central to Aristotle's thinking, but his approach was too analytic to grasp the broader outlines of the idea of development. The platonic thinkers were counter-developmental in the sense that they stressed

the idea of **return**, advance in perfection was recovery of a pristine state of blessedness. (This is not the place for a full treatment of this theme, but it may at least be pointed out that one reason for the persistence of this idea was that it represented one of the oldest strands of traditional Greek thought, as witnessed by the myth of Chronos. In the same vein, Odysseus is not an adventurer seeking new discoveries, but a man obsessed with the desire to return home. Note also that the Greek word for "never," *oupó*, means literally "not yet," implying that what never was never will be.)

The so-called "linear" view of the Bible is likewise unrelated to development. The Semitic worldview was either cyclic or static. The thinkers of Israel nuanced their idea of history with a certainty that Yahweh would intervene to save. But this was not a case of steady development from within (according to the Books of *Kings* things can only get worse) but a powerful intervention from without, in its way the most radical opposite to our modern point of view.

[8] "Attack" is to be read with the appropriate qualifications. The idea of making Cassian's list into a ladder was the Master's who was interested in tracking the soul's itinerary toward its Maker. He does not seem to have succeeded, simply because his material defies much classification. Benedict took the idea holus-bolus from *RM*, making only three small but significant changes. The most significant of these was to return to Cassian's idea that the goal of humility was not only exaltation in the hereafter, but perfect charity (which usually means love of God) in the present life. Benedict generally tries to tone down the eschatology of *RM*.

[9] Adalbert de Vogüé, *La Règle de S. Benoit*, vols. IV, V, VI (Paris: SC 184, 185, 186; 1971), 286-287.

[10] Prol 46-49.

[11] The literal translation is "as it were naturally, by custom." I am paraphrasing here on the basis of Augustine's *De Musica* 6:6, "Well is custom said to be a second, and as it were a manufactured nature." Cassian has simply *velut naturaliter*; the *ex consuetudine* is from *RM*.

[12] *RB* 7,67-69 = *RM* 10,88-90 = Cassian *Inst* 4:39,3.

[13] Maybe we are too casual in regarding parts of the Rule as obsolete. The practice of excommunication has probably never been observed in all its rigors, certainly it has lain in desuetude for more centuries than not, at least as part of normal administrative procedures. Yet the Confessing Church which grew up in Germany in the 1930s and was much under the influence of Dietrich Bonhoeffer accepted a very similar set of regulations to those of *RB*.

ORTHOPRAXY AND INTERPRETATION

REFLECTIONS ON REGULA BENEDICTI 73,1

This reflection was prepared for the Fifth International Regula Benedicti Congress held at Fleury in 1984 and was published in Regulae Benedicti Studia 14/15 (1988). *It took as its central theme the phrase that appears in RB 73,1: honestas morum. Benedict's Rule was written with a view to orthopraxy, and this primary concern must shape the ultimate response of readers and become the governing principle of interpretation.*

Although the *Rule of Benedict* is a short document, it is credited with an importance which goes beyond the monastic world, just as its presumed author has been named the patron of a Europe which he never knew. Because of the historical and cultural importance of subsequent Latin monasticism for the history of civilization and for an understanding of the medieval Church, the *Rule of Benedict* is studied not only as a guide to good living and an initiation into monastic life, but also as a key to certain salient themes of Western thought and history. The *Rule of Benedict* has, as successive papal statements continue to affirm, a significance which transcends the narrow world of the cloister.

There is ground for rejoicing here: that the philosophy of the Benedictine Rule is more widely studied, that the demands of critical methodology have weakened the grip of the benign fundamentalism of past centuries, that modern monks are exposed to a more sharply-focused teaching, less dominated by congregational ideologies. But there remains cause for concern. Are we, in making the *Rule of Benedict* the object of our study, approaching it in too intellectual a manner? Does our concentration on concepts somehow alienate us from the enterprise of which writing and reading the *Rule* are part?

If one were to conceive of what might be called a "monastic hermeneutic" of the *Rule*, it would seem to me that the chief part of such a project would consist in living according to the *Rule*. In other words, "orthopraxis" cannot be dissociated from the task of interpreting the text. This is not an advocacy of obscurantism, but the recognition that the interpretation of a monastic rule demands a specific hermeneutic which is not accessible to non-participant observers.

Let us reflect upon a concrete example: the role of the *Opus Dei* in the life of a monk. It is possible to trace the origins of the Benedictine schema for the liturgy of the hours, it is possible to formulate a theology and spirituality of liturgical prayer, one can speculate on the effects on consciousness resulting from regular participation in the office. And all of this can be formulated in terms of a commentary on the *Rule of Benedict*. But it seems to me that without the experience of the communal celebration of the Work of God, many of one's conclusions risk superficiality on the human level, no matter how rigorous the scientific basis. Such experience cannot be garnered in an occasional foray into choir; it comes from years of patient participation. Moreover, the question is further complicated by the close bond which exists between the monastic office and the other elements of monastic *conversatio*. What I am suggesting is that an authentic interpretation of the texts of the *Rule* which deal with the *Opus Dei* belongs to one who puts into practice the very specific beliefs and values which lie behind St Benedict's presentation.

The Practical Purpose of the Rule

St Benedict's purpose in writing is clearly stated in the last chapter of the *Rule*. It is not primarily the communication of ideas with a view to the crystallization of compatible values. What the author intends is to set forth a code of behavior. His aim is to tell monks how to act. Observance of its precepts will lead to a degree of objective goodness, a certain *honestas morum* (73,1).

There is, accordingly, question of legislation governing the way monks are to behave, if they are to be worthy of the outward signs of their profession (cf. 1,7). The nature of a monastic rule is such that it necessarily involves a measure of external constraint. The prospective monk is exposed fully to this aspect of the life he wishes to embrace: *Ecce lex sub qua militare vis; si potes observare, ingredere; si vero non potes, liber discede* (58,10). From the very beginning all are to accept the rule as master (3,7), to be content with the *status quo* (61,2-3) and to submit themselves to regular discipline and to the authority of the various monastic administrators (62,3-8). Nothing is to be done except what is commended by the ordinary regulation of the monastery and the example of the seniors (7,55) as well as by the will of the abbot (49,10). A detailed penal code is provided to punish and cure not only malice but also negligences and human infirmities. Once he has freely accepted this way of life, the monk consents to live under its coercion.

When Benedict sets up his school of the service of the Lord (Prol 45), he is not envisaging a Socratic or heuristic model for the training he gives. He recognizes quite clearly that there is much alienation in the early stages of monastic life: the young monk is playing a role, acting out a life which flows naturally from virtues which he does not yet possess. In some sense he is expected to act as though he were an old man who has passed beyond the passion, hot-headedness, ambition and lack of moderation which are characteristic of early adulthood. He acts gravely and speaks quietly; he is never brash or opinionated but sober, sage and (one would imagine) rather dull. There seems to be little scope in the Benedictine monastery for boisterousness, enthusiasm or initiative. Peace, tranquillity, moderation and order are important components of the Benedictine self-image. Mission, innovation, improvisation are not.

The training in monastic values foreseen in the *Rule* begins with the narrow observance of its obligations (Prol 47)—a task which Benedict recognizes as unpleasant and which the young monk undertakes only because he is afraid of the consequences of acting otherwise (7,68). It is a laborious task (7,68; Prol 2), sustained only by a high degree of faith in the validity of the process and in its capacity to achieve results.

Virtue is, accordingly, learned by rote. The repetition of good actions is believed to produce the corresponding habits and the progressive elimination of the opposite tendencies. There is, moreover, a concomitant process of internalization by which the monk acquires the beliefs and values which his actions signify and so, at the end of a long progression, he is a free man, no longer acting out of fear but from conviction (cf. 7, 69).

To most of our contemporaries this is a bleak and unappealing program of life or formation, one which runs counter to our conventional wisdom. It may be some consolation to recall that Benedict's anthropology and pedagogy are far more optimistic than that evinced in the *Rule of the Master*, that Benedict seems uncommonly aware of the dynamics of monastic development and that he has supplemented the police-state provisions of his legislation with a strong emphasis on motivation and on achieving suitable subjective dispositions. Indeed Chapter 72 seems to indicate his realization at the end of his life that "the last temptation was the greatest treason: to do the right deed for the wrong reason." All this is true, but the fact remains that he wrote a rule and expected that its prescriptions would be observed. Those who do otherwise are to be rebuked, excommunicated, whipped and expelled.

This is not the place to discuss the merits of such an approach considered as social or educational theory. What is of interest in the present context is that the *Rule* must be viewed as a hard document; it yields its meaning not to readers but to keepers. At the beginning it is sufficient merely to understand *what* is to be done. For this reason the *Rule* is to be read rather frequently in community (66,8). Almost anyone can understand the material dispositions of the *Rule*. Appreciating *why* particular courses of action are to be followed comes with time and wisdom, although it must be noted that Benedict takes for granted that the level of such understanding varies from person to person, and is in no way automatic (2,32). Understanding the beliefs and values involved is seen by Benedict as an aid to the implementation of regulations, so that he himself often indicates why particular deeds are to be done or avoided. Furthermore, the abbot and the deans are chosen for their capacity to communicate to others the meaning of monastic life: they must be able to teach as well as give orders (21,4; 64,9). It is supposed that the aptitude to win souls (58,6) is a capacity to convince others that the imposed norms of behavior are reasonable and constitute an apt means of achieving a desired goal.

Therefore, it has to be said that not all the content of St Benedict's teaching is contained in the text itself. The text delineates a manner of behavior in which the philosophy to be propounded progressively becomes apparent. It is the *conversatio* which forms; what the *Rule* does is to set up the situation in which the formative way of acting becomes possible. It demands of the prospective monk that he engage himself to continue with this manner of life until he dies. The meaning and message of the *Rule* is to be found in the process which it initiates and not merely in the word which it uses.

The Communal Context of the Rule's Observance

The foregoing is not to be taken as an invitation for an individual monk to embark on a crusade of unremitting fidelity to the precepts of the *Rule*, following his own interpretation. In fact, for Benedict, the primary interpretation of his prescriptions is to be found in their observance by a community—the establishment of monastic *conversatio*. An understanding of the *Rule* is the fruit of the living of a communal way of life, not the result of the transmigration of certain abstract beliefs and values into an individual consciousness.

It is the vitality of the concrete community which gives the monk the courage to submit himself to the process of "monastication." The credibility of the requirements which he faces is founded in the luminous lives of those around him. His defective appreciation of the monastic philosophy is compensated for by the *auctoritas* and attraction exercised by monks more advanced than himself. "This doesn't make sense, but if it is able to produce somebody of the quality of Brother X, then I am on the right track."

The *Rule* anticipates its contextualisation in an observant community. For this reason what it communicates beyond the purely practical—its occasional forays into monastic philosophy—is written in a sort of shorthand. Brief, lapidary statements are given which make sense if one knows about the matters to which they refer. For the tyro, the possibilities of misinterpretation are legion. There is an unexpressed content in the *Rule*, which is embedded in monastic *conversatio*. To try and interpret the *Rule* without reference to the tradition of life which stems from it is extremely precarious.

Chapter 73 reveals another aspect of the question. The author of the *Rule* is aware of the minimal content of what he has written, how stark, procedural and dry much of it is. He is aware that the life he is describing is far more lyric than his literary expression of it signifies, and so he points to the whole preceding tradition as to something which puts flesh on the bare bones of his own work. Benedict wrote a rule, concerned with the running of a monastery and with measures taken to prevent vice and the rupturing of charity (Prol 47), but it is not enough merely to observe the *Rule*. The measure of full righteousness is greater than that. Doing the right things with a hazy appreciation of why they are done and why they are right is only an *initium conversationis*. Real monks will look further, to the Scriptures, to the Fathers, to the whole body of monastic writings, of which the *Rule of Benedict* claims to be no more than a poor summary. It is in this wider reading that the monk strengthens his resolve to work against the bane of monastic life, *desidia* (Prol 2; 73,7); nonchalance, relaxation, slackness, *laissez-faire*, idleness, sloth, doing nothing. Benedict foresees that it is by giving himself to a profound assimilation of this tradition that the monk allows a certain degree of enthusiasm or fervor to be generated within him. The process begins with the observance of the *Rule* and its injunctions, but beyond this wooden compliance is a whole world of spiritual freedom accessible only to those who genuinely grasp the beliefs and values upon which monastic life is based.

The *Rule* is, accordingly, a condensation not only of the living tradition of monastic life but also of its concomitant written expression. It needs to be interpreted within this wider context. The *Rule* is not an end in itself and Benedict did not see it as such, as can be seen by a comparison of the statement in *RB* 66,8 about the public reading of the *Rule* with the exclusive concentration evinced in *RM* 24. Benedict does not see his own work as having the monopoly on the monks' allegiance: rather, if they were real monks they were to go beyond his words to their sources. History has often shown that in those sad cases where monastic philosophy degenerated into ideology, and the *Rule* had been absolutized in a particular interpretation, the iron circle was broken through recourse to the sources—the memory of the Apostolic Church, the example of the Fathers of the Desert, the teachings of the Scriptures themselves.

The bare text of the *Rule* is supplemented by the experience of those who have been formed by it, who have accepted its discipline and attained the goal it pursues. They know the realities about which the *Rule* discourses and are thus in a position to offer an interpretation of the text in the light of existing conditions. This formative community is itself guided by the broader monastic tradition out of which Benedict wrote and which remains accessible to us today.

The Whole Text

Misinterpretation can result from concentrating too exclusively on one part of the text without enough attention paid to certain other parts or to the *Rule* in its entirety. The basic fault with most wrong interpretations is that they are unlivable—at least in the context which Benedict envisages; they do not produce the fruit which he sought. The *Rule* is a practical document, intended to provide guidance in the concrete living of the evangelical ideal in a monastic milieu. The test of a good interpretation is its compatibility with this purpose not only for the moment but in the long term. The whole *Rule* comprises not only the text but the intentions of its author.

It may be that critical students of the *Rule* are inclined to scoff at the easy generalizations often made about the character of the *Rule's* author: that he is kind and gentle and moderate. Yet a comparison of the text of *RB* with that of *RM* convinces me that Benedict is more reasonable, compassionate, realistic and optimistic in his philosophy than the man whose work he borrowed. It does not seem to me that it is necessarily bad method to expect that these qualities would pervade Benedict's understanding of monastic life as a whole—even in those matters where they do not find literary expression. The whipping of children and of aberrant adults was widely practiced into the twentieth century, but a change in theory has latterly taken place. I do not think that it can be maintained that Benedict would have doggedly defended the practice even after its salutary effects had been discounted. Perhaps we need with much labor to do what some of the older commentators accomplished with such facility. Now to begin our treatment of the *Rule* with a critically-based effort to understand the personality and the priorities of its author.

In particular it needs to be re-affirmed that St Benedict was not a fanatic or an idealist; the image he conveys is that of a pastor. He is well aware that his sketch of the details of monastic life is approximative. Somebody else could, perhaps, do better (18,22). He is aware that not all of his recommendations are going to be greeted by the monks with submission—the famous example being the matter of wine (40,6). Although his chapters on the disposition of the "Work of God" won adherence beyond the monasteries, his careful injunctions on the matter of excommunication seem never to have been scrupulously followed. His reservations about appointing a prior and his preference for deans have not been persuasive through the centuries. An interesting dissonance appears in the matter of *scurrilitates*. In the chapter on silence he condemns them with uncharacteristic immoderateness: *aeterna clausura in omnibus locis damnamus* (6,8), yet in the chapter on Lent he offers the suggestion that as part of a program of watering down their vices the monks might consider reducing the level of *scurrilitas* (49,7). Monks are not to have private property (33,1-8; 54,1-5; 58,24-25) and the abbot is to search the beds to make sure of this (55,16), yet there is no deprivation. A beautiful theology of distribution based on need is enunciated (34,1;7), the cellarer is instructed to be sensitive and gracious in his dealings with the brothers (31,6; 13-14) and as a means of avoiding private ownership, the abbot is instructed to give the brothers everything they need (33,5; 55,18-22) and is warned to consider spiritual principles and his own judgment rather than material profit (2,33-36; 55,22).

The examples could be continued. The picture which emerges is not of a man writing a rule that is anything else but a practical expression of the Gospel. If, because of existing conditions, the keeping of the *Rule* voids its fundamental purpose, then such literal fidelity is foolishness. Nor is there any ground to insist that the only authentic expression of the Benedictine charism is to be found in the sum totality of the *Rule's* precepts. The reality is far more subtle than that. The spirit is more dynamic than the letter.

One of the problems which can be seen in the literature on the *Rule* is that often the pastoral purposes of the *Rule* are more closely followed by non-technical treatments than they are by critical work. Immediately the scholars deny this, affirming the practical utility of erudite studies, if searchers are prepared to work a little. This is probably true, but often an essay full of facile generalizations, contemporary applications and devotional overtones will automatically command more attention than a well-researched monograph, scientifically presented. At least this is true for monks and nuns themselves. I am not minimizing the importance of either *genre*. I am simply suggesting that some fusion of horizons is necessary if the inanities of an outdated fundamentalism are to be avoided and the sterility of a treatment which does not aim at life can be minimized. Scientific studies need to be more acutely aware that the interpretation of a monastic rule, above all things, is a matter of *praxis*.

At the same time there is no need to diminish the challenge which the *Rule* offers, precisely because it stems from a different vantage point. We do not want to interpret the *Rule* in such a way that it conforms substantially with our twentieth century, bourgeois preoccupations. We wish for it to retain its antique flavor, to challenge our rapid conclusions about the nature of Christian and monastic response with the convictions of a bygone age, to shame our mediocrity by the clarity of its own vision (cf. 73,7). We need to think more profoundly about some elements of the *Rule* which we readily take for granted. An example is patience. It is arguable that Benedict makes this the normative monastic experience (Prol 50; 7,35-43; 72,5), perhaps deliberately modifying Cassian's more active conception of the immediate goal of monastic life with something more passive (and less semi-Pelagian!). What does the centrality of patience have to teach a generation that lives in the wake of the nineteenth century's myth of progress and in an age which cherishes achievement above all? We have to take the *Rule* seriously, even when its emphases seem to differ from ours and especially when it offers a counter-balance to values thoughtlessly assimilated and blindly believed.

Living the *Rule* does not mean following a particular monastic ideology with a complacency which permits one to believe that no one else has access to the *Rule's* meaning. Interpreting the *Rule* does not mean secluding oneself from the complexity and ambiguity of concrete situations. To live the *Rule* means that one is an active and even ardent seeker after the meaning of the *Rule*, using all available means to enrich one's understanding. Thus, in the trial and error of real situations and in the continuing expansion of one's appreciation of the monastic tradition, the capacity to interpret the *Rule* develops. The *Rule* itself becomes an agent, for those who thus observe it, in introducing them to goodness of life and to the beginnings of monasticity.

The Benedictine Tradition

QUOD EXPERIMENTO DIDICIMUS
THE HEURISTIC WISDOM
OF SAINT BENEDICT

This article, appearing first in Tjurunga *48 (1995), aimed to illustrate the idea that St Benedict was a flexible man, more concerned with adapting the lifestyle of the monastery to the reality of its internal and external situation than in proposing an unchanging code of laws to be set in concrete for ages to come. This means that in writing the Rule he was far more tentative than is often thought. This openness is what grounds the adaptability of subsequent Benedictine tradition.*

The phrase that serves as the title of this article occurs in Chapter 59: *On the Offering of the Sons of Nobles or Poor People.*

> If it happens that one of the nobility offers a son to God in the monastery and the boy is a minor, his parents are to make the petition of which we spoke above. Then, at the Offertory, they are to wrap the petition and the boy's hand in the altar cloth and so to offer him. Regarding their property: they are to promise under oath in this present document that they will never, either personally or through an agent, in any manner or at any time give him anything or offer him an opportunity of owning anything. If they are not willing to do this and wish for due reward to offer an alms to the monastery, let them make a donation to the monastery of the things they wish to give, reserving the

income for themselves, if they so desire. In this way, having blocked every possibility, the boy will not be deceived by any expectation and so come to grief. God forbid. We have learned this by experience (*RB* 59,1-6).

A chance remark in a curious context opens another window into the personality of Benedict of Nursia. He appears as a man who can learn from experience. Perhaps we might read more into the text and infer that he was that *rara avis*, one who can learn from mistakes. Benedict had burned his fingers once and was determined not to repeat the experience. A similar phrase is found in Smaragdus, *Quia multis hoc experimentis doctum est*.[1] Perhaps it may be a characteristic of monastic growth.

Far from being a blueprint issuing from the far-seeing mind of a genius the Rule is, perhaps, better understood as a working document, progressively nuanced on the basis of a lifetime's experience. We all know, nowadays, that Benedict based his text on a pre-existing rule that is attributed to an anonymous Master. In the beginning Benedict's reliance on this model is almost complete; as the Rule progresses, its author becomes more independent from his primary source, more confident in his judgments and more strikingly original in his outlook on life.

The Master's Rule is a work of great learning and organizational imagination. Although there is no evidence that this earlier monastic code was ever put into practice, its creator was clearly a man who knew monastic sources and had more than a smattering of understanding about the way monasteries run. The two qualities that are noticeably lacking in the Master are tolerance of human limitation and benignity. He is a suspicious and authoritarian man, so possessed by an ideal that he interprets every imperfection as positive vice. He sometimes seems like a young man who has never discovered for himself how toilsome and rough is the way that leads to God. He seems not to understand human nature. His writing does not bear the hallmark of long experience.

How different Benedict is. He took a harsh, almost inhuman, document and progressively toned down its crusading zeal and filtered out its crabby demands. Benedict's text concludes gently and on a note of warmth and humanity. Benedict himself had changed during the years in which he wrote the Rule. He remains uncompromising in his view of monastic life as a single-minded search for God, but he has become more aware of what has to be done to help monks persevere in this pursuit. Age has made him wiser and more mellow. In more ways than one, Benedict has learned from experience. This is probably why Gregory the Great describes the Rule as "noteworthy for its discretion."[2] To appreciate better this aspect of Benedict's approach, let us review some characteristics of his work that are sometimes overlooked.

1. Less than Perfect Legislation

Admirers of Saint Benedict sometimes claim that the *Rule* indicates that Benedict had a fine legal mind.[3] For them the key to the longevity of the Benedictine tradition is the fine legislative structure that Benedict left behind. Benedict of Nursia was certainly a great man, but this does not necessarily mean that every flattering statement made about him is true. To penetrate to the heart of his character perhaps it may be necessary to set aside the faint praise of his prowess as a man of jurisprudence.

Let us begin by looking at some of the liabilities of Benedict's work considered merely as legislation.

a) Confusion of Genre

Law concerns the ordering of external actions; it has no direct bearing on the dispositions in which these actions are done.[4] Good law clearly prescribes what is to be done and what is to be omitted. There is no ambiguity. Exceptions to the ordinary run of events are exhaustively catalogued and a solution is offered for each dilemma. The relative gravity of each obligation is defined and different levels of sanction are prescribed in case of infringement. In this way the written code facilitates and guides the work of administrators and enforcers. Within its own limits it imposes a particular way of action and excludes alternatives.

Superficially it may seem that Benedict is attempting to write the *Rule* as legislation. There is detailed prescription and, apparently, a code of punishments. Despite this, the result is very amateurish. I am much impressed by the opinion that Benedict enjoyed using solid-sounding legalese (such as "regular discipline" and "congruent satisfaction"), but did so without particular competence. In other words, he lacked the narrow band of skills required to draft good law.

Here is an example of imperfect draftsmanship. One of the significant ways in which Benedict habitually deviates from the text of the Master is by the addition of adverbs and adverbial phrases intended to indicate the appropriate subjective dispositions in which the prescribed actions are to be performed. Pastorally these are helpful, but such determinations are beyond the scope of law. Benedict's *Rule* is not pure law. It is interested in the personal content of prescribed actions.[5] At the end of his life he distinguished life-giving acts from those that lead to hell, according to the quality of zeal which animates them (72,1-2). Even in judging forbidden actions, the abbot is instructed to pay attention to attitude as well as the malfeasance itself. Obstinacy, arrogance and contrariety add to the gravity of the crime. These unmeasurable qualities are nowhere defined; their assessment belongs to the abbot's judgment (24,2; 44,10). Likewise the same consideration holds in sentencing: the maturity and intelligence of the sinner are to be taken into account (2,27-28; 23,5). And making a clean breast of the transgression is a means of avoiding humiliation and punishment altogether (46,5-6). Contrary to the tendency to objectivize sin that we see evidenced in the *Poenitentiales*, Benedict refuses to dissociate external negligence from personal disposition. In this he shows himself an excellent pastor and a shrewd knower of human nature, but it means that in terms of legal clarity, the *Rule* is often defective.

b) Tentativeness

Good law is imperial and self-confident. It does not welcome the advent of any consideration outside its own terms of reference. Issues of morality, justice and common sense cannot stave off a parking fine. Good law is comprehensive and detailed; no loopholes are left. No quarter is given to those who may, for whatever reason, seek to evade its injunctions.

Here again Benedict shows that he is not a lawyer. He begins by apologizing:

> Therefore a school of the Lord's service is to be established by us. In regulating it we hope to enjoin nothing harsh or heavy. If it is a little restrictive this is, as reason and equity dictate, to effect the amendment of vices and the preservation of charity (Prol 45-47).

This text, inserted into the Master's introduction, seems to recognize the austerity of the way of life mapped out by the *Rule*. Benedict protests that it is not his intention to be harsh. It is, as it were, a temporary necessity until the new monk becomes socialized, so that "what he used to observe in fear, he may begin to keep effortlessly, naturally and out of habit" (7,68). This fear of frightening the pusillanimous (64,19) leads to a level of moderation or discretion that sometimes seems like mediocrity (48,9). Benedict admits to a certain reluctance in making material prescriptions for others: "It is with some scrupulosity that we define the measure of others' virtue"(40,2). He is apologetic in the case of monks having to haul in their own harvests (48,7), reluctant to impose his own carefully wrought system of psalmody (18,22), and unable to convince monks of the value of traditional monastic abstinence (40,6). In his maturer years he ceases to call even for the elimination of vices. Coexistence is the name of the game. The very activities that poison the heart of monastic *conversatio* are merely to be moderated during Lent (49,5).[6] The peak of this tendency to relativize his own prescriptions comes with Benedict's final chapter: *The Whole Observance of Justice is not Established in this Rule*. The precepts of the *Rule* are to be interpreted in the light of a vast, unwieldy body of literature that few will read in its entirety and none could synthesize.

c) Inconsistency

Designedly, well-drafted legislation does not contradict itself. Actions are evaluated according to a stable system of values that admits of impartial administration. In particular a specific enactment must not seem to go against a general right or obligation, without a stated reason for derogation and clearly defined limits. Otherwise you end up with chaos...and wealthy lawyers.

Benedict does not score especially well in the area of consistency. He is far too aware of exceptions for that. One example of outright contradiction is his attitude to *scurrilitates*.[7] In his much-shortened chapter on silence Benedict states clearly:

> *Scurrilitates* and words that are idle or provoke laughter we condemn *in all places* to an eternal exclusion. We do not permit a disciple to open his mouth in such conversation (6,8).

Thus, in his younger days, Benedict follows the monastic precedent and condemns such buffoonery.[8] Of the 51 verses in the Master's chapter on silence, Benedict adopts only nine; this is one of them. He makes it even more restrictive by adding the phrase, *in omnibus locis*. This is probably another illustration of the toughness associated with people who come from Nursia, the *Nursina durities* that Lentini mentions.[9] By Chapter 43 Benedict is forced to admit that giddiness is not so easily banished from the cloister; it can be readily triggered by any lack of seriousness, even excessive haste in trying to arrive punctually at the liturgy (43,2). But Benedict's apparent acceptance of what he had so irrevocably rejected is most evident in the chapter on Lent. Here *scurrilitas* reappears as one of the everyday monastic vices that the fervent disciple might consider reducing during this time of special effort (49,7). It is not that such jesting has become less subversive or less distracting, it seems rather that Benedict is learning to appreciate the limits of human possibility and becoming reconciled with them.

Benedict's organizational structure is often praised, but if we read the *Rule* literally, we find chaos. Like the Master, Benedict believed that "the omnipotence of the abbot is a fundamental and constant principle of cenobitism."[10] He seems to have had bad experiences with ambitious deputies, and so he tends to favor a more collegial model of middle management. Thus he suggests deans, placing each in charge of a group of ten monks, following biblical and monastic precedents (20,1-7; 65,12). Once appointed, the deans seem almost to disappear. The difficulty with this institution is that deans have authority over persons with no mandate to intervene in the general administration of the community. That leaves a gap in authority, which Benedict was reluctant to concede, but in this case he has been overruled by history and common sense. In fact, the prior, supplemented by a subprior and even a third prior, assumed the major responsibility for domestic administration and is sometimes more visible in medieval customaries than the abbot or cellarer.[11] Even when the notion of deanery did not slip away, the deans never bypassed the subordinate superiors, as Smaragdus explains.

> The subordinates ought to obey the deans and the deans ought to obey the *praepositi* and all the community alike ought to fall in with the instructions of the abbot.[12]

There are those who have a general though subordinate authority in the community. Benedict is prepared to permit some devolution of power if his conditions are met (65,14-15),[13] but he remains suspicious. Whereas he is generous to the Cellarer, admonishing him to be like a father to the community (31,2), for the Prior he has only warnings and threats. No specific qualities are required of the Prior,[14] nor are there any particular functions attached his office. He is simply to do what he is told (65,16). Contrary to this, there are others who have functions but no office. These are the *priores* or *seniores*,[15] who play an important role in the maintenance of the community but who are, in some manner, outside the law. The *prior*[16] who presides at the community meal and has the right to add a few edifying words (38,9) is not the abbot, since the superior eats with the guests in a separate facility (66,1).[17] Nobody knows which of the *priores* he may have been (Is it one of the few seniors who take their meals in the common refectory (66,2)?) or perhaps he was the *praepositus*, as it was in twelfth-century Cîteaux.[18] Benedict seems aware that his arrangements are confusing, so he attempts to clarify matters in chapter 63. The principle is stated thus in the opening verse:

The monks keep their order in the monastery according to:
    a) the time of their monastic life
    b) the merit of their life, **and**
    c) the abbot's decision (63,1; see 2,19).

Benedict thus gives three distinct sources of seniority. Later he tries to ensure that option C coincides with Option B and so reduces the possibilities to two: "the order they have [by entry] and the order the abbot has established" (63,4), except that he forgets that the *Rule* has already made an exception for priests and clerics (57,5; 57,8, but see also 58,11-12). And if this is not enough he varies his vocabulary:

	iunior	63,8
priores	iuniores	63,10
priores	minores	63,10
priores	iuniores	63,12
nonnus	frater	63,12
maior	minor	63,15
senior	iunior	63,15

All this concern about rank is to be interpreted, of course, in terms of Benedict's fundamental theory about equality in the service of Christ (2,16-22).

Another area of legal confusion concerns Benedict's insistence on the differential distribution of material goods. In some places he adopts an objective measure, based on sufficiency: (39,1; 40,2; 55,4; 55,15), but then he has a whole chapter refuting the propositions that all should receive necessities in the same measure (34,1-6). In the previous chapter he states the principle that the monk should possess nothing as *proprium* (33,3), the reason being the monk's radical incapacity to own anything (58,25). Yet he has the right to hope for everything necessary from the abbot (33,5) who is instructed to give to all what they need (55,18-19) interpreting "needs" generously rather than strictly (55,21).

There are other inconsistencies which need not be discussed in detail here. What is the first degree of humility? *RB* 5,1 and 7,10 do not coincide.[19] Monks are discouraged from leaving the precincts of the monastery (66,7; 4,78) yet there is much more in the *Rule* on conduct during journeys than about enclosure.[20] To define the daily portion of wine as one hemina (40,3) seems clear enough. The trouble is that nobody seems to know how much that is. Even the ingenious translation of *RB 1980* "half a bottle" leaves us in the dark about Benedict's precise intentions. Likewise his note on hermits in 1,3-5 is far from unambigous; there is little consensus among researchers about Benedict's attitude to the solitary life. Is it something that is superior to cenobitism and thus a form of post-graduate monasticism? Some, especially the disciples of Dom Anselm Stolz, have thought so. Others do not accept this. The point at the present, however, is that this important text is seriously ambiguous. Furthermore, the interpretation of the whole *Rule* could hinge on what option is adopted at this moment.

d) Ineffectual

Good legislation concerns itself with what is possible. It is canny enough not to formulate decrees that will be ignored. Law maintains its credibility by prescribing only what is acceptable to a substantial majority of those who are bound by it. This means postponing cherished ideals and reforms. The law pretends to be absolute and enforceable, but this secretly presupposes its reception by most. Without this nod, "people power" takes over, and law and order come under threat. Laws that are ignored with impunity undermine the authority that issues them.

Many of Benedict's institutions have been remarkably enduring. His plan for the celebration of the Liturgy of the Hours is one example. The ritual for the profession was another, although this was enriched by the introduction of consecratory elements drawn from Eastern practice. Even minor rituals have been maintained, such as the blessing of weekly officers. This, however, is to be expected of a Rule. It is surprising to find that, although the *Rule* was universally accepted (or imposed) in its totality, there are elements in it that have been apparently discarded. As we have seen, Benedict's vision of a community governed by an omnipresent abbot aided by deans without a second level of administrators seems never to have been realized. Partly this was because he misread what was taking place in the monastic world. It can also be argued, however, that the strategy of governance that he established was not feasible.

Far more serious, however, is the fate of his penal system. There are seven full chapters dealing with excommunication, making up about 5% of the total text of the *Rule*. Like the chapters on psalmody, they are detailed and carefully constructed. Like the Master, Benedict has in mind to establish logical and evangelical structures intended to bring healing to brothers with behavior problems and to protect the rest of the community from the worst of their excesses. An admirable project, but one which seems never to have been implemented in the way Benedict envisaged. The idea of introducing a stage of sequestration between punishments inflicted in community on the one hand, and, on the other, total expulsion is also found in other monastic authors and commentators, often borrowing from one another.[21] There is not much evidence of the practice in the Customaries; the monastic prisons were not medicinal means but punishments for those whom civil law could not touch—in any case they were small and usually unoccupied! The chapters are worth reading for their spiritual principles, but as law they seem to have had little impact.

e) Revisionist

It seems to me that Benedict's perspective on monastic life changed as he wrote the *Rule*. Initially he was very dependent both on the text and the spirit of the *Rule of the Master* as this was interpreted by his own austere temperament. This is progressively modified in the later chapters due, I believe, to two principal causes. The first was his broad reading, especially beyond the confines of the monastic ethos, in the gentler fields of ecclesiastical tradition. The second source of change was his willingness to learn from experience.

Let us try to appreciate the extent to which Benedict mellowed. This is not to say that his basic ideal has changed, he has become more attuned to the subtleties of human behavior. The final six chapter give some evidence of areas in which Benedict had second thoughts and wanted to nuance what he had already written. In some senses these chapters constitute a kind of *retractatio* to the *Rule*. Perhaps they should be read first, certainly they need to be kept in mind when attempting to apply any of the earlier parts of the *Rule* to real situations. These chapters bespeak a man who has learned by experience.

68 If the Abbot Misjudges a Situation

The chapter is a derogation from the absolutism occasionally imputed to St Benedict. Abbots sometimes act unfairly because of defective information; if the victim cannot cope with this there should be some possibility of appeal. In this case the principles enunciated in Chapter 3 are applied: the abbot accepts the new data, reflects on it and makes a judgment about what is *salubrius*.[22]

69 The Dangers of Patronage

Although Benedict came to appreciate the horizontal values of community as contributing much to monastic progress, he was also aware of the possibility of a pseudo-affection that is only a respectable façade for an inappropriate (and possibly mutual) dependency. Such a relationship not only sets up political currents that disrupt the harmony of the community, it also inhibits those involved from experiencing the full range of dynamics inherent in normal community living. For as long as the patronage lasts, progress will be slowed. Monks must avoid this delusional closeness.

70 The Dangers of Vigilantism

Equally monks must avoid an excessive distance that is the opposite of fraternity. This expresses itself in a tendency to make judgments, to regard others with severity, to rebuke and even, as St Benedict describes, to inflict punishments on perceived malefactors. There is always something suspicious about those who are zealous crusaders for some values, while neglecting others. St Benedict will return to this idea in Chapter 72.

71 Qualifications about Obedience

This chapter is so startling that few institutions are really able to come to grips with it. Benedict begins by affirming that obedience is such a good thing that we ought to extend its scope as far as possible, with due regard for good order.[23] So brothers also obey one another. Indeed this informal horizontal obedience is spiritually more effective since it is freer—being outside the realm of reward and punishment. And so Benedict says, "it is by *this* way of obedience that we go to God." *Hanc* (as distinct from *illam*) indicates the latter in a list of two, i.e. fraternal obedience is the way to God. Yes, we obey the abbot and his officials because this contributes to a smoothly-running house. We may be rewarded subtly if we obey or subtly punished if we do not. If our motives are good then such obedience will be spiritually profitable. To obey our equals, however, is purer obedience. It is giving priority to the preferences of another (72,7) and leaving our passionate desires in abeyance. Mutual obedience is the sweetest way of negating willfulness, because it not only brings advantage to us, it also makes life easier for others.

72 Qualifications about Observance

This Chapter removes any possibility that we might conclude that observance of the *Rule* automatically leads to holiness. The happy outcome of the monastic endeavor depends not only on deeds done, but also looks to subjective dispositions. What determines the result is the quality of zeal that animates observance. Bitter zeal separates from God and leads to hell, irrespective of good works. It is only a life lived according to good zeal that produces the fruits sought in monastic life. Good zeal is simply self-forgetfulness, patience, benignity, love. It is such close attachment to Christ, the ideal of the monk, that Christlike characteristics begin to flower. This is the ultimate goal of Benedictine life: observances must remain merely the means.

73 Qualifications about the Authority of the Rule

In his final Chapter Benedict eschews every claim to the last word. He has written a practical manual for beginners in the hope that it will lead them to lusher pastures. Although history seems reluctant to accept the author's evaluation of his own work, the point Benedict makes is valid. Spiritual life cannot be codified because it involves the exercise of the liberty of God. Its tracks cannot be precisely predicted because there comes a point at which everyone is on their own. So Benedict renounces any attempt to contain human life within a framework. Instead he refers us to the divine chaos of Scripture and tradition, with its unwieldy and contradictory variety,[24] and tells us to trust in God and take our guidance from there. His *Rule* is only rudimentary instruction, it is not a comprehensive survey of monastic progress. It seems that in the course of a lifetime Benedict has made the transition from Master (Prol 1) to servant.

Part of the reason for the inconsistency of emphasis in the *Rule* is that Benedict has learned that monastic community and the persons who constitute it are infinitely complex and little amenable to simplistic prescription. Such a conclusion is a fair indication of progress in experience and wisdom, but it results in untidy legislation.

Just as charism precedes and eludes institution, so a monastic Rule cannot be categorized as mere canonical legislation.[25] To interpret the *Rule* as law undermines its potential as "a book of experience" to influence and inspire. Speaking of the reference to the *Rule* in the text of Gregory's *Dialogues*, De Vogüé notes that Benedict's biographer had a similar assessment of the quality of the *Rule*.

[Gregory's] design was not legislation but edification. For him the *Rule* was less important as a monastic code whose prescriptions were to be followed exactly, than as a spiritual text that reflected the soul of a saint.[26]

2. Interferences

Let us look at some of the factors that interfered with Benedict's capacity to envisage and implement a tight organized system of control in the monastery. In many ways the reason is simple. As the years progressed Benedict grew in that quality of humility that he esteemed so highly and described so fully. He came to accept that there were limits to his knowledge and experience, that he could not necessarily prescribe remedies for every ailment and that many things were beyond his competence or control. One can only do what is possible and leave the rest to God.

a) Realism

The truth is not always as we hope. Among those who dream of a better world, only those who know how to interact with imperfect reality ever make progress in implementing their vision. To persevere in the face of disappointment and setbacks is not merely moral virtue, it is the condition of success for every venture. Pursuing an ideal to its inherent conclusion means coping with unforeseen resistances and occasional opposition. "If you can't tolerate the heat, get out of the kitchen." There is a tendency for dreamers to stay with their dreams and leave practical affairs to pragmatists. Leaders are those who have the knack of translating a dimly-seen objective into practical plans in a way that others willingly fall in with them.

Benedict seems to have been aware that, although monastic life can seem very uncomplicated to outsiders, the reality is different. There is no guarantee that a monastery will not be, at some time or other, the playground of a wide range of human emotion and behavior. A monastic leader needs patiently to keep applying the primary principles of Benedictine *conversatio* to unprecedented circumstances without becoming surprised, dismayed or discouraged by the reactions generated. At the same time such complex situations must be allowed to nuance the expression and presentation of the principles themselves. Thus emerges that common sense wisdom that is unafraid of truth and unfazed by differences. A tradition in dialogue with reality. Such, it seems, was Benedict. His monastic ideal was not predicated on the basis of a perfect community and a *Rule* that covered all bases. Within his basic structure there is an openness to alternative possibilities.

b) Flexibility

Living reality demands a flexible response. If the rigid, mechanist viewpoint of classical physics is allowed to dominate human interaction, then everything is expected to be measurable and predictable and the whole world of spontaneity, imagination and discovery is excluded. In such a framework development is channeled and inevitably curtailed. Every course of action has its policy and the possibility of heuristic evolution dims. Part of the distinctly modern mentality is an appreciation that the same goals can be achieved by various means, that pluriformity is not necessarily an affront to unity.

Benedictine history with its emphasis on local autonomy attests that there is much flexibility inherent in the tradition. Lifestyle, like the monastic habit, is to be adapted according to local conditions and climate and measured to fit the person (65,1.8). There is no suggestion that one size suits everybody; distribution is made on the basis of subjective need (34,2), and according to the special grace of each (40,1-2; 49,5-7). Pastoral action is to be differential (2,23-32), assignments are to expand and contract according to work demands (53,19-20) and "every age and understanding is to have its own measure" (30,1)—a flexibility not only dictated by nature but sanctioned by law (57,1). All this makes for livable community. It may not be good law but it offers the possibility of human growth and keeps the legal structure as a means and not a master.

c) Acceptance of Limits

There is a boundlessness about the enthusiasm of youth that makes it difficult for the young to accept limitations. Even into middle age there are many who find it difficult to be reconciled with the reality of moral impossibility. On the other hand, one of the signs of emergent wisdom is the capacity to work within one's own limitations and not to be upset by the imperfection of others. There are, no doubt, many monastic leaders who would willingly spend their days leading others into close and conscious communion with God. In fact their work is different. It consists, more often in dealing with immature expectations, humdrum administrative details, petty squabbles and occasionally major crises. Perhaps they are tempted to dream of a mature community where the only concerns are the attainment of the proper goals of monastic life. Alas for the illusion! Their proper task is not that of a mystagogue, but more like that of a garbage collector, facilitating progress by patiently clearing away the detritus of past unhappy years. As far as Benedict is concerned it is not the abbot's function to be a prince over a group of spiritual giants, but a shepherd and carer for the weak and faltering (27,6).

There are many recommendations in the *Rule* that demonstrate Benedict's realization that human beings never quite escape from finitude, no matter how flourishing their spiritual life. Sometimes it even seems that it is only after some progress that the cracks in the façade begin to be noticeable. The monk who has been raised up through all the levels of humility/exaltation is aware only of his own sinfulness and his need for divine mercy. No matter how holy a monk becomes he never graduates from the concrete need for dependence on God. Benedict cautions the abbot against a crusading zeal that is too harsh. The recommendations in the second (27-28) and third (64,7-22) abbatial directories show a remarkable mellowing. Benedict cautions the abbot not to break the rusty pot by scrubbing too hard at the rust (64,12).

In all his actions he is to show love, be prudent, mindful of his own fragility, have regard for the consequences of his actions (*providus*), thoughtful, discerning, moderate so that "the strong may have something to desire and the weak are not frightened away" (cf. 64,11-17). This merely repeats in compact form what Benedict has been saying elsewhere, "not to terrify or overstrain the weak (48,24-25), to accept to work with the weak and imperfect (35,3.13) and perhaps have faith enough never to lose confidence in the mercy of God (4,74). There is, perhaps, a theological substrate to all this. The divine is manifested in human weakness according to the incarnational economy. It does not displace limitation but integrates it in a new dynamic. Meanwhile space, time, culture and human fragility remain, but charity cloaks all this and limitations lose their capacity to impede the return to God.

d) Acceptance of Persons

Benedict calls on the abbot to renounce all distinction of persons based on social class (2,16-20), reminding him in God, whom he represents, there is no favoritism (*personarum acceptatio*) (2,20; 34,2).[27] His appeals to equity (Prol 47: *aequitatis ratione*), justice (2,19; 3,6), reason (Prol 47; 8,1; 64,1; 70,5, along with the frequent use of *rationem reddere*) and measure (11,2; 24,1; 25,5; 30,1; 31,12;39; 40; 48,9; 49,6; 55,8; 68,2; 70,5) serve as a reminder that the abbot's power is not absolute. It must be tempered not only by the constitutional restraints of the *Rule* but also by the inherent rights of the monks. There is a certain egalitarianism in Benedictine monasteries (2,20; 2,22). They are called to live together as a flock (*congregatio*), they come together in prayer (*conventus:* 20,5) they are summoned to meet as a chapter (*convocet:* 3,1). Together (*pariter*) they worship (20,5), do penance (49,3) and make their way to eternal life (72,12).[28] They exist in a state of communion because of what they are by God's creative act; as individuals and as Christians they have an intrinsic dignity and holiness. Their fundamental unity is deeper than the external convergence produced by common observances. There is in Benedict's *Rule* a strong sense of reverence for the person.

e) Trust

One of the most patent qualities of the *Rule of the Master* is its profound distrust of the monks and its reliance on exhaustive legislation as a means of closing every loophole through which they might slip into willful negligence. This unsavory pessimism leads to a futile attempt to foresee every eventuality and to prescribe detailed directives to cover every situation. Benedict has more confidence in the capacity of monks to be formed positively by their exposure to the good word and the good example that the ordinary monastic community conveys. For the most part, he is content to operate at the level of principles and to leave the application and administration of these principles to the abbot and his helpers. Monks correctly formed in beliefs and values will normally try to live in accordance with them; when they fail it is not because the situation is unclear and needs authoritative definition. More often it is simply human weakness or malice that generates unmonastic behavior. For this different remedies are needed.

Benedict does not try to claim a monopoly on truth or to impose a rigid correctness on thinking. His provisions for wider readings in Chapter 73, as in the liturgy and in the refectory, together with the actual practice of Benedictine monasteries in accumulating libraries and encouraging reading, remind us that he was open-minded enough to leave scope for differential development. Perhaps he understood what is implied in Teilhard de Chardin's axiom, "What ascends must converge." There are many avenues to truth and each must take the path that leads there most directly.

There is much more subsidiarity in Benedict's *Rule*. The bald statement about sounding the signal for the Work of God provides us with a principle that seems true of Benedict's approach as a whole. "Let [the abbot] take this charge upon himself or give it to a brother careful enough to ensure that all will be done at the right times" (47,2). The abbot can discharge his obligation of administrative concern personally or through other capable monks. The one provision is that those appointed should be able to do their job well. This means that their service is helpful to others and not harmful to themselves (47,3-4; see also 38,12).

f) Respect for Freedom

In understanding how a monastic rule is able to instill a spirit of freedom into those it forms, it is useful to recall Jacques Maritain's important distinction between two kinds of freedom: from obligation or from coercion. From the former none can dispense. We are all bound by a network of duties that derive from our personal commitments and from the rights of others. Nothing can change this fact. When we speak of "freedom" we are not conjuring up a life without debts to be paid, but a life in which we are able to pay our debts as free adults and not as indentured slaves or as children kept under rigid control. We are allowed to be present to our action as its total agent instead of being the reluctant executive of another's decision.

At first glance the *Rule of Benedict* can seem reminiscent of a police state with its emphasis on authority and supervision. A lot depends here on interpreting Benedict in the context of history. This means seeing how Benedict's regulations compare with those of his sources and contemporaries. It also involves transcending fundamentalism by looking at the way in which such regulations have been interpreted in subsequent centuries.

First we have to insist that Benedict is more interested in obedience than in authority. It is less a question of having a well-administered monastery than of offering the prospective candidate the benefit of obedience (*oboedientiae bonum*: 71,1). This asset is not external order, but an initiation into likeness with the obedient Christ (5,13; 7,32;34) the goal of which is mystical identification with the Word. "This is right for those who hold nothing dearer than Christ" (5,2). Learning to displace self-will is why "they desire to live in monasteries with an abbot over them" (5,12). Obedience must be interpreted as a spiritual reality and not merely an element in the social organization of the monastery.

It is true that Benedict recognizes that *reason demands* some policing of monastic behavior in the interests of fostering love and eliminating vice (Prol 47).[29] Thus he provides for "circators" who patrol the monastery to ensure that the time reserved for *lectio divina* is not frittered away.[30] The dual motivation is explicit: to avoid the danger of a monk giving into *acedia* and not only wasting his own time but also distracting others by his conversation (48,17-21). Benedict is serious about the realizing of goals for which a monastery exists and he has enough common sense to know that this realization is threatened if obstacles to it are not faced and dealt with. Also we have to be careful that our interpretation of Benedict's provisions is not mere projection of our own ideas. Those who conjecture that the lamp left burning all night in the dormitory (22,4) was for the purpose of supervision should be reminded that Benedict's regulation may simply be an extension of the Master's concern (*RM* 29,5) to facilitate navigation for those needing access to the *locus necessarius*.[31]

Benedict prefers to operate at the level of reason; it is only in cases where words are ineffectual that browbeating and punishment are recommended (2,24-29). The monastery's lifestyle is a given. The potential candidate is exposed to it, is obliged to study the *Rule* and to ponder well before his application for vows will be accepted (58,10). Everything is revealed and he is left free to embrace or to go elsewhere. No pressure is applied. The decision is his. Once made, however, such a choice entails commitment and obligations, not only to the community but also to God.

g) Optimistic Anthropology

In all of this some adumbration of Benedict's theological picture of human reality begins to emerge. His appreciation of the role of grace and his opposition to semi-Pelagianism meant that he regarded the monastic enterprise as one in which God was operative. The monastery is not merely a place to do penance for personal sins, but the possibility of coming close to God. It follows from this that Benedict sees human beings as having a fundamental capacity for divinization. "To be transformed by this *deificum lumen*, this divinizing light, not only in our intentions but even in the profoundest recesses of our being—such is our goal."[32] The particular additions made by Benedict at the end of the Prologue and the chapter of humility make it clear that he considered the human being capable of transformation by grace. The eschatology he embraced differs from that of the Master. It is relocated in this life. Even on earth the monk becomes a luminous icon of the unseen God. What more can be said about the extent of human potential?

3. What Benedict Became

Benedict's project of writing a monastic rule was too much stamped with his own humanity to be technically perfect legislation. It is an untidy, inconsistent and tentative text, just as human reality is. Above all it is teaching that constantly checks itself against reality and makes whatever changes reality demands. In this we begin to perceive some delineation of the features of the author's personality. Most of these characteristics revolve around the trait manifested in the text quoted at the beginning of this article: Benedict's capacity to learn from experience. Let us list different facets of this quality.

a) Willing to Learn

It is a comparatively rare human being who does not wish to quit the stage of apprenticeship and assume the mantle of the master. There is a stage in life when we are receptive. It is possible that we appreciate so much what we have already learned that we underestimate the substantial level of ignorance that remains. Many mistakes in human history come simply from people being oversupplied with answers and unaware of the real questions. Benedict remains open to guidance, even as an abbot and founder of monasteries, even as a recognized master surrounded by disciples. Chapter Three shows that he appreciates the counsel of the community, including the inexperienced. Benedict seems to have been aware of the complacency and infallibilism that can follow local autonomy (which later centuries would seek to moderate by visitations and general chapters) and so he cautions the abbot to be very attentive to the observations of visiting monks (61,4).[33]

b) Tolerant

Not only does Benedict preach toleration to his monks (72,5) but he also practices it. Of differences he does not complain, but accepts them as part of the fabric of life. In any community there is variety in age (30,1; 37,1-3), status (2,18), education (8,3), personality (2,31-32), grace (40,1-2), inspiration (20,4; 49,6), health (36,1-10; 39,1-2), strength (48,24-25), subjective disposition (2,12.24-29; 31,6-7). Benedict takes this for granted and tries to frame his recommendations in terms that include such a range of personal possibilities.

c) Capable of Change

We have already noted the revisionism inherent in Benedict's developing outlook. By concentrating mainly on principles, Benedict leaves open the possibility for local adaptation "according to local and climatic conditions" (55,1), and for judicious modification by the abbot (2,19). With regard to the appointment of a prior, Benedict is prepared to have his own preferences overridden, if there is good reason (65,14). The same is true of his arrangement of Psalms for the Work of God (18,22). Whatever the details, everything should be tailored according to its purpose and function (*pro modo conversationis*: 22,2; 55,8).

d) Able to Read Deeply

Perhaps it is in a lifetime's habit of reading, as reflected in Chapter 73, that we can find the source of Benedict's willingness to keep learning and to be open to new things as well as old (64,9). He stamped his institution with a love of letters no less than with a desire for God. He insisted that the abbot appoint to positions of subordinate authority those who were imbued with *doctrina* (21,4), as he himself was obliged to be (64,2). This is not a positivistic authority, but a regimen based on fraternity in Christ (2,20) and our common service of the same Lord (61,10). Master of monks though he be, the Benedictine abbot remains with them, a lifelong disciple in the school of the Lord's service. The abbot represents Christ; he does not replace him.

If, as is generally supposed, Benedict's portrait of the abbot is autobiographical, then one of his most salient qualities is his love for holy reading (4,55).

e) Discerning of Priorities

There is much detail in Benedict's *Rule*. Much less than in the *Rule of the Master*, but still considerable attention is given to the finer points of monastic observance. What becomes clear with familiarity is that Benedict never gets lost in *minutiae*. He always maintains a clear idea of what monastic life is about. He never concentrates so much on the eddies that he loses sight of the tides. The ultimate goal of the monastic enterprise remains paramount: everything else is of merely relative importance. Benedict's particular concern is to ensure that the myriad of elusive details that constitute monastic *conversatio* are marshaled under one or two basic priorities. "Nothing is to be preferred to the work of God"(43,3), following St Cyprian, "nothing is to be preferred to the love of Christ"(4,21) and, as virtually his last word, "absolutely nothing is to be preferred to Christ"(72,11).

f) Accepting of Mellowness

All are entitled to be a little rabid in their youth. In the usual course of events, however, the experience of life has the effect of blurring the categorical distinction between black and white and permitting some sensitivity to the finer nuances of issues. Mellowness is a normal sign of a person who has learned from experience. In most respects it seems that the author of the Benedictine *Rule* is entitled to be regarded as a mellow man: we find in him a fundamental benignity, an acceptance of what is human and a certain hopefulness about the future. The Master often appears as an irritable bigot; Benedict presents himself as someone who has lived long and has learned wisdom.

Perhaps the conclusion to these reflections is the inference that Benedict was a man who was not afraid of saying "yes" to the softening of grace. For him the cumulative effect of years of monastic experience was to become simultaneously more human and more divine.

There is no doubt that Benedict's *Rule* is one of the masterpieces of Western monastic literature. It deserves all the attention and some of the adulation it receives. It seems to me, however, that one of its significant characteristics is that both text and author are demonstrably open. The provisions of the *Rule* are not frozen for eternity, but are open to being adapted and made relevant by the passage of events and by the work of the Holy Spirit. If Benedict was a man who could learn from experience, then it is appropriate that the Benedictine charism should be equally willing to draw new expressions from the different situations in which it is embraced. The interpretation of the *Rule* need not confine itself to understanding an ancient text; it can also animate the formation of future monastic consciousness and practice.

NOTES

[1] *Expositio*, 21.2; p.212.

[2] *Dialogues*, 2,26; SChr 260, p.242. *Nam scripsit monachorum regulam discretione praecipuam, sermone luculentam.* On this text see, Adalbert de Vogüé, "La mention de la `Regula Monachorum' à la fin de la `Vie de Benoît' (Grégoire, *Dial.* II, 36)," *RBS* 5 (1976), pp. 289-298.

[3] Thus, Anselmo Lentini, *San Benedetto: La Regola*, Montecassino, 1980, p. liv: *uno del più insigni monumenti di sapienza legislativa.*

[4] In some countries the ambit of law is limited to the public sphere. Since law and its enforcement are concerned with social order, they are considered to have no right to intrude on private or domestic matters. The opposite tendency is evident in George Orwell's "Thought Police" and in the various approximations to such total control.

[5] See Adalbert de Vogüé, *La communauté*, pp. 487-489. I note that the title given to this section, "Souci de la Subjectivité" is not adequately translated in the English version: "Care for the Inner Life". See *Community*

and *Abbot in the Rule of Saint Benedict: Volume Two* (CS 5/2), Cistercian Publications, Kalamazoo, 1988; p. 432.

⁶ The verb used is *temperare*, later (49,7) supplemented by *subtrahere de*. I am attracted by the argument that *diluere* in 49,5 can be translated not only by the usual "wash away" but by "dilute." Faults are eliminated not by being swept away by a dramatic onrush of water but subverted by being steadily diluted through the addition of the contrary virtue. In this sense Lenten observance would be a means of weakening sin's interior hold upon us rather than the elimination of the outward defilement resulting from committing sins.

⁷ For background to this term see Philip B. Corbett, "Unidentified Source Material Common to Regula Magistri, Regula Benedicti and Regula IV Patrum," in *RBS* 5(1976), pp. 27-31.

⁸ Thus Cassian *Conference* 9.3; *SChr* 54, p.42: *scurrilitates quoque similiter amputandae*. This with a view to having a clear mind, ready for prayer.

⁹ *Op. cit.*, p. lv.

¹⁰ De Vogüé, *La communauté*, p. 437.

¹¹ In some sources, the Prior became, as De Vogüé points out (*La communauté*, p. 425) a sort of managing director. Isidore, for example, nominates eight areas of responsibility: concern for the monks, action in legal matters, care for possessions, the sowing of the fields, the care of the vines, concern for the flocks, the construction of buildings, the work of carpenters and tradesmen. This was in addition to a supervisory responsibility for all the internal departments of the monastery, including the sacristy, the cellars and the guesthouse.

¹² *Expositio in Regulam S. Benedicti*, 21.2; *CCM* 8, p. 211.

[13] Though, if Gregory the Great is to believed, Benedict himself appointed both abbot and prior. On being requested to establish a monastery at Terracina, "[Benedict] granted the request and having designated the brothers named the Father and his Deputy (*secundus*)." *Dialogus*, 2.22; p. 202.

[14] Smaragdus is more eloquent on this subject, drawing from Waldbertus' *Rule for Virgins* 2 (*PL* 88, 1054-1055 = *PL* 103, 948-949). He lists over 20 qualities, most of them positive

[15] In 27,2, the seniors constitute an informal back-up to the abbot's authority in the process of reconciling an alienated brother. Their presence has the beneficent effect of damping down any tendency to indiscipline, in the dormitory (22,7) around the monastery (48,17—referring to the "circators") and in the refectory (56,3). It seems that they also had a role in spiritual guidance (4,50; 46,5).

[16] I have given some brief indications about Benedict's use of *prior* (as distinct from *praepositus*) in "Leadership in a Benedictine Context," *TJ* 22 (1982), p. 40. The usage in the *Rule* is clearly equivocal.

[17] Oral tradition recounts how, not so long ago, certain visiting abbots were sometimes invited to partake of the meager monastic collation "to edify the brethren." They were then secretly led forth into the guest area to be wined and dined as befitted their rank. I am presuming that Benedict does not expect such bilocation of the abbot.

[18] *EO* 76, *passim*. See Danièle Choisselet and Placide Vernet, *Les Ecclesiastic Officia cisterciens du xiième siècle*, La Documentation Cistercienne, Reiningue, 1989; pp. 225-229. The abbot always ate *in hospitio*, *EO* 110.11; p. 312.

[19] The same clash is found in *RM* 7,1 and 10,10.

[20] See chapters 50, 51, 67.

[21] In 65,20-21, a rebellious prior is not offered this intermediary penalty; if he does not settle down after admonition and deposition, he is to be expelled.

[22] The word used in 3,5 can be translated blandly by "more advantageous" or "more beneficial." It is difficult to accept as literal the "more prudent" of *RB 1980*. Because of its connection with *salus*, *salubrius* would better be rendered "healthier" or "more wholesome." If *salus* is interpreted in a more theological sense, then the sense of "what contributes more fully to salvation" would be indicated. In this last case the faith-dimension is emphasized and the groundwork is laid for a "supernatural" motivation that overrides human evaluation. Transcending reason means acting *altiori consilio* (63,7) as distinct from ordinary good judgment *saniore consilio* (64,1).

[23] It has to be remembered that Benedict is far more interested in obedience than in authority. His perspective is spiritual rather than organizational. He sees obedience primarily as a means of conformity with Christ, so the monk who ardently desires such communion will seek out as many possibilities of obedience as possible.

[24] See M. Casey, "Ascetic and Ecclesial: Reflections on *RB* 73.5," *TJ* 28 (1985).

[25] In contemporary religious life, the role of legislation is carried by constitutions and statutes. This leaves to the *Rule* a more spiritual but not less real function.

[26] De Vogüé, "La mention," p. 297.

[27] The phrase *acceptatio personarum* occurs in Rom 2:11; for the usage see also the Vulgate Is 42:2, *neque accipiet personam*. See also Terrence Kardong, "Respect

for Persons in the Holy Rule: Benedict's Contribution to Human Rights," *CSQ* 27.3 (1992), pp. 199-207.

[28] See Marian Larmann, "The Meaning of *Omnes Pariter* in RB 49:3," *ABR* 26.2 (1978), pp. 153-165.

[29] Benedict's nuanced phrase, *dictante aequitatis ratione* is poorly translated in *RB 1980* by "The good of all concerned ...may prompt us."

[30] On the evolution of Benedict's fluid provision into a particular office see, Hugh Feiss, "*Circatores*: From Benedict of Nursia to Humbert of Romans," *ABR* 40.4 (1989), pp. 346-379. Feiss understands the evolution of circators as a benign means of attending to disciplinary tasks. In some monasteries of women a "Mistress of Discipline" was appointed. Having officials responsible for correction reduces the possibility of interpersonal friction arising from necessary intervention. "They are now a dim (if not too distant) memory and unmourned. Yet, the purposes for which they arose are still valid: to enforce a certain level of observance, to free superiors from petty disciplining, to provide constructive channels of mutual correction, to eliminate backbiting, recrimination and tale-bearing" (p. 379).

[31] For background to this question, although it is not treated directly see, Nancy Bauer, "Monasticism after Dark: From Dormitory to Cell," *ABR* 38.1 (1987), pp. 95-114.

[32] John Eudes Bamberger, "Anthropology, Pedagogy, Humanism in RB," *TJ* 9 (1975), pp. 67-74; p. 73.

[33] One is reminded of the observation of Dorotheos of Gaza: "If a man really sets his heart upon the will of God, God will enlighten a little child to tell that man what is his will." This is from the peroration to the fifth discourse, "On the Need for Consultation", in

Dorotheos of Gaza, *Discourses and Sayings* (CS 33), Cistercian Publications, Kalamazoo, 1977; p. 129.

THE "HUMANITAS" OF THE BENEDICTINE TRADITION

This short piece was delivered at a 1980 Symposium to mark the fifteenth centenary of Benedict's birth. It was published in John Stanley Martin [ed.], St Benedict: A Man with an Idea (University of Melbourne, 1981). The main idea was to emphasize the human values inherent in the way in which Benedict envisaged a monastic community operating.

Traditional orthodoxy, in its teaching about the person of Jesus Christ, has insisted that within the unity of a single personality were englobed both integral humanity and the full weight of the divinity. In Jesus Christ, it is affirmed, humanity attains its most complete expression in the context of a dynamic unity with the divine. In the words of the Athanasian Creed he was *perfectus Deus, perfectus homo*.

Underlying many of the great Christological heresies was the unexpressed belief that ultimately humanity and divinity were incompatible. If Christ were perfect man, he could not be regarded as divine; if he were God, then, in some sense, his humanity must be either illusory or defective. What is at stake in this question is not only the nature of godhead. Also involved is an understanding of humanity. Discussion of the person of Christ raises the issue of the fundamental compatibility of the human and the divine.

In the centuries which may be characterized as "Benedictine," the Churches of East and West strongly affirmed the innate spirituality of human being—given in creation, weakened through sin but restored and elevated by grace. *Formed* in the image of God, *deformed* through loss of likeness, *reformed* by being *conformed* to Christ in grace, ultimately to be *transformed* in glory. It was the belief of the church as a whole that growth in godliness necessarily involved becoming more human and that sin was not only a denial of God; it was, by that fact, a denial of man's self. To be estranged from God coincided exactly with being alienated from oneself.

It is within the context of this climate of thought that St Benedict's emphasis on human values needs to be understood. When he compiled his *Rule for Monasteries*, Benedict had a single aim before him: to gather material which might serve his immediate followers as a compendium to guide them in the living of a life based on Gospel priorities according to the circumstances then obtaining. Benedict proposed to his disciples nothing more or less than the realistic living of Gospel values in a changing world. If there is *humanitas* in the Benedictine tradition, it must be viewed, not as an outcome sought in itself, but as the effect of a life lived in substantial conformity with Christian values.[1]

Accordingly, there is a paradox evident in speaking of the *humanitas* of the Benedictine tradition. What Benedict sought, above all, was to divinize human life, to render it responsive to divine grace. The human values which were so important to the great masters of the Benedictine tradition were viewed within the perspec-tive of conformity with the divine plan; they were never understood as elements of an autonomous "humanism."

Let us, therefore, look at some of the characteristic values propagated by St Benedict which substantiate the claim that as well as being a holy man of God, the first abbot of Monte Cassino was a genuine humanist.

1. Human Scale

One of the distinctive marks of Benedictine monasticism is its concentration on the local monastery. The *Rule* of Benedict is not a plan for the evangelization of the world or the re-direction of history; it is a series of simple directives drawn up to help a small group of people live according to Gospel values in an environment permeated with the same spirit. It begins and ends on the practical level of what an individual or a community can do to diminish those factors which disturb human growth and well-being and thereby inhibit the flowering of spiritual potential.

There is always something to be done to render the present situation more in harmony with fundamental Christian priorities. Opportunity is not postponed until favorable conditions obtain; some small step is always possible. The Benedictine tradition of spirituality tends to emphasize the quality and personal content of action rather than its importance or result. The creation of an island of Christianity in a sea of indifference was considered to be a matter of raising up stone after stone until a base was established and then, step by step extending the base and building upon it.

We do not have, in Benedictinism, a system or method pursuing a pre-determined goal by a sequence of finely-measured procedures. The goal of monasticism, as formulated by John Cassian—one of Benedict's sources—was twofold. Ultimately the monk sought to advance the Kingdom of God; what he did was done "so that in all things God might be glorified." More immediately the monk pursued "purity of heart"—freedom from instinctual domination and self-interest in order to be undivided in the service of God.[2] Such goals focused attention less on the work being done and its results, and more on the disposition of the doer. What mattered most was the personal content of action.

This concern with motivation was paramount in the mind of Benedict. He repeatedly qualifies his sources by adding adverbs and phrases which give precedence to the personal and qualitative aspects of what a monk does.[3] A recent commentator summarizes this concisely:

> It is not the routine of monastic life that sanctifies: no routine will ever sanctify. It is the act of the human will at each little crossroads, as it occurs in the individual life, saying yes to that choice which identifies the Saviour's good pleasure, that means progress.[4]

It was in monastic milieu that a morality of intention was nurtured at a time when the church in the West, as a whole, was swayed by the material and legalistic mentality of the *Poenitentiales*.[5]

Benedict's view of the importance of subjective dispositions is nowhere clearer than in his chapters dealing with the exercise of authority. The abbot's task is not one of ruling grandly over a robust elite, but one of constant care for those who are less than perfect.[6] He is not to force them to conform to his preferences, but is, on the contrary, to adapt himself so as to be at the service of their several dispositions: *multorum servire moribus*.[7] Benedict repeatedly reminds the abbot that he is not to treat all monks the same; they are not ciphers but distinct individuals. He is to recognize the uniqueness of each and to respond to it; this means that with some he will have to be severe, with others forbearing and tolerant and with a third group willing to sit down and explain the issues involved.[8] He is to recognize that not all have the same requirements when it comes to material needs,[9] and that some have a greater capacity for fasting and abstinence from wine than others.[10] Two pithy statements summarize what St Benedict expects of the ideal abbot. "Let him so order all things that the strong may desire more and the weak may not be discouraged."[11] "He should so moderate and arrange everything both to save souls and in such a way that the brothers do what they have to without justified grumbling."[12]

This respect of individual differences is a hallmark of monastic spirituality. It is evident in the *apothegmata* of the Desert Fathers and, in a more systematic way, in the writings of Evagrius of Pontus. It reaches a climax in the *Pastoral Rule* written by Gregory the Great, the first biographer of St Benedict. He distinguishes no less than 36 ways in which individuals differ and bids the pastor accommodate his ministry to the temperaments and dispositions of those he is caring for.[13] The Benedictine tradition does not view monks as stereotypes, totally shaped by the pious routines which make up their days and years. They all remain individuals; many of them become "characters."[14]

In an age which was more static than our own, Benedict's sensitivity to personal development is remarkable. In two famous texts he demonstrates his awareness that quality of personal experience changes over the years as values deepen and life become simpler.

> As a person grows into the monastic way of life and in faith, his heart is enlarged and he begins to run the path of God's commands with that indescribable sense of pleasure which is love.[15]

The second passage comes at the end of the longest chapter in the *Rule* which is dedicated to a detailed phenomenology of growth, described in terms of humility.

> Therefore, having gone up all these steps of the ladder of humility, the monk comes at once to that love of God which, when complete, entirely eliminates fear. It is by such love that the monk now begins to observe and do effortlessly and naturally, as if by habit, all those things which previously were done through fear. He is no longer animated by the fear of hell, but by love of Christ, by good habits and by the attraction of good living. The Lord, in his goodness, causes this to happen in his workman, who is now purified of vices and sins, through the Holy Spirit.[16]

In his formulation of values and goals, Benedict never lost sight of the fact that he was dealing with concrete individuals with varying bundles of assets and liabilities. By tying monasticism down to a local community, he ensured that it never became a disembodied series of abstractions nor an alienating system of religious repression. In preserving the human scale in his teaching he made it possible and real and, in some sense, timeless.

2. Wholesomeness

Although Benedict fully appreciated the fact of human variation, he did not conceive of his monks as essentially individualist. He understood that a man becomes a monk in order to learn to discriminate between the disordinate tendencies of instinct and the authentic expressions of personal identity, between following the self or living in accord with the call of God resounding in the heart. What the monastery provides is a way of life which counters the instincts and fosters purity of heart. The daily regimen of the monastery is not a mould, but a model which flexibly forms individuals in authentic living and in inner undivision. The monastic way of life is a mirror which enables the monk to find his heart.[17]

The means which Benedict proposes is a balance between different sorts of activity: *ora et labora*, between physical and spiritual tasks, between solitude and community, between conservation and progression, between human and divine. Benedict has the typically Roman abhorrence for extremes—even in good things. Everything is to be done in moderation, *propter pusillanimes*—on account of the faint-hearted.[18] Every value is balanced by its complement.[19] Even contemplation is not sought as an end in itself, but only as an aspect or dimension of a life progressively given over to God.[20]

The result of such an approach is a very wholesome life. Especially because the Benedictine tradition has been purified and filtered in the course of many centuries, there is a question of a life-style that is founded not on theory but on long experience of practical living. Its basis is wisdom and its outcome is radically humane. There is no question of unnatural specialization terminating in the atrophy of certain faculties declared irrelevant. There is less possibility of pressure to conform to institutional expectations, since a Benedictine community has no goals outside the personal growth of the monks. What is fostered by Benedictine life is the capacity both to listen to the music in the soul *and* to play in time with others.

The tranquillity and freedom from anxiety bespoken by the Benedictine motto, *Pax*, is not the drugged state of heedlessness typical of those for whom religion has become a substitute for life. It is, rather, the condition of stability and harmony produced by the acceptance of discipline which leads to fruitfulness and growth.

3. Creativity

Monastic history is peppered with incidents which demonstrate the flexibility and adaptability of the Benedictine ideal. Polding and Salvado are examples of this, adapting the settled routines of established monasticism to the wild ways of the infant Australian colonies. The creativity of Benedictines is not restricted to the fine arts.[21] Wherever a problem presented itself, solutions were found, in agriculture, in plumbing, in architecture, in astronomy, in medicine, in sanitation. Practical skills developed and, in the course of centuries, were passed on and refined, until with the emergence of talented individuals—many of whom remain nameless—crafts became arts.

The role of Benedictines in the preservation and enhancement of the ancient Greco-Roman civilization can be but mentioned here.[22] Benedict did not envisage his monks as pious scribes or as custodians of culture in the way that his contemporary, Cassiodorus Senator, did. He wanted them simply to be good Christians and good monks: their cultural contributions were simply providential by-products of a more basic commitment. To preserve what was good among human resources followed, naturally from the sort of life they led.

In particular, their creative skills were employed in the creation of a liturgy which was so endowed with the fruits of human genius that it was redolent of the divine. The quality of communal worship is always an accurate gauge of the stature of a Benedictine community. At its peak it represents the marriage of human and divine, both in prayer and in life. As it recedes from this ideal it betokens a community less transfigured by grace and further away from humanity itself.

4. Fraternity

A characteristic of the *Rule of Benedict* relative to its immediate source (the *Rule of the Master*) is the increased emphasis on fraternal interaction.[23] In the monastic tradition it was believed that the more a monk attained purity of heart, the more liable he was to love. The greatest obstacles to love were thought to be the instincts to possess, to manipulate and to be violent. As a monk grew toward *apatheia*, or freedom from the passions, love progressively asserted itself. Far from becoming cool and clinical, monks became warmer and more affectionate according to their spiritual progress. True monks are great lovers. This is why the monastic tradition gladly appropriated the classical theme of friendship and baptized it, seeing in spiritual friendship a primary source of encouragement, guidance and correction in personal and religious development. [24]

5. Transcendence

The whole thrust of Benedict's ascetical teaching is to allow the monk to grow—to pass beyond the limitations of background and temperament and to realize the full potential of his being. The community constantly encourages him to grow.[25] He is referred back to the Scriptures and forward in hope to the end of time. He is taught to be detached from all things, yet simultaneously he is expected to reverence the meanest objects "as the vessels of the altar."[26] Benedict proposes no mean goal to the monk—not a functional expectation achieved by appropriate techniques, but the ultimate goal which none but the complete humanist would dare envisage, one which "eye has not seen nor ear heard nor has it entered into the heart of man to conceive what God has prepared for those who love him."[27]

The mysticism of the Benedictine tradition is not one which consists in denying human values. Faithful to the tradition of evangelical living which he inherited, Benedict affirms that a life lived wholly for God is ultimately human and that the way toward the perfection of such a life is not by the denial of what is human but through the purification of the human, of whatever distorts its candor or inhibits its nobility.

The celebration of this centenary is a challenge to us: how divine do we consider humanity to be?[28]

NOTES

[1] Perhaps the term "humanism" is an anachronism when applied retrospectively to St Benedict and his followers. It does, however, have the advantage of initiating that "fusion of horizons" necessary for a modern reader if he is to come to an understanding of an ancient text. Cf. M. Casey, "Principles of Interpretation and Application of RB," in *TJ* 14 (1977), pp. 33-38.

[2] Cf. John Cassian, *Conl* 1.4.

[3] Cf. A. de Vogüé, *La communauté*, p. 488.

[4] David Parry, *Households of God: The Rule of St. Benedict with Explanations for Monks and Lay-People Today*, Darton, Longman and Todd, London, 1980, p. 32.

[5] Something of the evolution of the term *intentio* is indicated in M. Casey, "Intentio Cordis (RB 52,4)," *RBS* 6/7 (1980).

[6] *RB* 27,6.

[7] *RB* 2,31.

[8] Cf. *RB* 2,23-25.

[9] *RB* 34.

[10] *RB* 40,1-2.

[11] *RB* 64,15.

[12] *RB* 40,5. Cf. also, M. Casey, "Discerning the True Values of Monastic Life in a Time of Change," in *RBS* 3/4 (1974/1975), pp. 75-88; especially pp. 79-81.

[13] Gregory the Great, *Pastoral Care* III.2-35; trans. H. Davis, (ACW #11), pp. 92-226; Longmans, London, 1950.

[14] Cf. Dominic Milroy, "Benedictine Education," in *The Benedictines*, a supplement to *The Tablet* (London), 12 July 1980. "Benedictine monasteries for all their appearance of uniformity and calm tend to be full of enthusiastic eccentrics." (p. xi).

[15] *RB* Prol 49.
[16] *RB* 7,67-70.
[17] Cf. M. Casey, "Cardiomimesis," *TJ* (1980), pp. 118-122.
[18] *RB* 48,9.
[19] Cf. M. Casey, "Balance in Monastic Life," *TJ* 9 (1975), pp. 5-11. See also, C. Dumont, "St Aelred: The Balanced Life of the Monk," in *MS* #1, pp. 25-38.
[20] Cf. M. Casey, "Saint Benedict's Approach to Prayer," in CS 15 (1980:3), pp. 327-343. Also, *Id.*, "Thomas Merton within a Tradition of Prayer," CS 13 (1978), pp. 372-378, and CS 14 (1979), pp. 81-92
[21] Cf. T. Bedford Franklin, *A History of Scottish Farming*, Nelson, London, 1952; pp. 21-105. David Knowles, *The Monastic Order in England*, Cambridge University Press, (2nd edition) 1963; pp. 487-560, 643-649. F. G. Cowley, *The Monastic Order in South Wales, 1066-1349*, University of Wales Press, Cardiff, 1977; pp. 53-96, 139-164.
[22] Cf. M. Casey, "St Benedict and Civilisation," in *The Australasian Catholic Record*, 57 (1980), pp. 359-365. The most accessible treatment of the outflowering of monastic culture during the Middle Ages is Jean Leclercq, *The Love of Learning and the Desire for God*, Fordham University Press, New York, 1963.
[23] Cf. A. de Vogüé, *op. cit.*, pp. 485-486.
[24] Cf. Adele Fiske, *Friends and Friendship in the Monastic Tradition*, Cidoc, Cuernavaca, 1970. Cf. M. Casey, "'Community' in the Benedictine Rule," a paper read at the Third International Congress on the Rule of St Benedict, Kremsmünster, 15 October 1980.
[25] Cf. M. Casey, "The Formative Influence of the Benedictine Community," *TJ* (1977), pp. 7-26.
[26] *RB* 31,10; cf. 32,4-5.
[27] 1Cor 2:9, quoted in *RB* 4,77.

[28] An expansion of some of the ideas given here with particular reference to the opportuneness at this time of history is to be found in M. Casey, "The Monk in the Modern World," a double address given at the Benedictine Union Symposium, 9 July 1980 and published in *TJ* 21 (1981) with the other papers of that gathering.

ASCETIC AND ECCLESIAL REFLECTIONS ON *RB* 73,5

The many ways in which Benedict's Rule has been faithfully observed in the course of history may be traced to a tension inherent within the Rule itself. St Benedict has drawn on two sources of influence, John Cassian and the tradition of the desert on the one hand, and on the other the ecclesiastical authors such as Augustine and Basil. This makes it possible for a follower of the Rule to lean more heavily towards its ascetical emphases or, alternatively, to be more open to the more humane, communitarian and ecclesial values that Benedict drew from the "Catholic Fathers." At least some of the dialectic inherent in Benedictine tradition can be traced back to the Rule itself. This article appeared first in Tjurunga 28 (1985).

The significance of *RB* 73,5 is not always noted by commentators. It is a very important text for the understanding of the whole *Rule* as well as for the appreciation of some of the variations in observance for which Benedictine history is remarkable.

In the context of locating the material regulations of the *Rule* within the doctrine of the Scriptures and of the Church, Benedict gives some indication of the monastic provenance of his spiritual philosophy:

> There are also the *Conferences* of the Fathers, their *Institutes* and their *Lives*, as well as the *Rule* of our holy father Basil.

This short verse is often treated as though it were a bald statement of the pedigree of Western monasticism which is already too well known to require further comment. In fact, there are a number of remarkable things inherent in this statement which lift it above the level of the banal, and make reflection on it a worthy project.

Firstly, Benedict wrote a Rule; his first concern was to legislate for the way in which monks live. *RB* was not conceived primarily as a spiritual testament but as a code of law. If elements of a philosophy of life were included, it was only because Benedict understood that, in practical terms, disciples are more likely to render obedience when they understand why certain things are enjoined on them.[1] This being so, it is interesting that the sources nominated by Benedict, are, in large measure, unorganized and even contradictory. The Scriptures and the books of the Catholic Fathers are concerned with broader issues than monastic regulation, and neither Basil nor the desert tradition approached monastic life in such a regulatory and perhaps even repressive way as witnessed in *RM* and *RB*.[2]

Secondly, no mention is made of *RM*. St Benedict could have saved Dom de Vogüé and others a great deal of labor if he had included the *Rule of the Master* in his listing. Its omission could be due to two factors. The first is that Benedict intended his condensed version of *RM* to replace the original; he believed that he had extracted whatever was of value in it so that no purpose was to be served in returning to it. A second possibility is that in the course of writing the *Rule*, Benedict became progressively disenchanted with his basic text, relied on it less heavily, and finally refused to include it in his list of useful reading.

Thirdly, Cassian is not named, although there is clear reference to his *Conferences* and *Institutes*. Two points can be made also about this. In the first place, Benedict is concerned about orthodoxy. In a time when the well-established order of both state and Church seemed under threat, and even monasticism had its share of disturbers of the peace and contrary thinkers, Benedict probably considered it important to ensure that the regimen of monasteries be stable, and their doctrine safe. Cassian was not named in the Council of Orange's condemnation of semi-Pelagianism, but his name was tarnished by association with that stream of thought,[3] and by his lack of sympathy with St Augustine's theological view.[4] Benedict, writing in the midst of the controversy, demonstrates a degree of caution, not untypical of the whole tenor of the *Rule* itself. The second factor is associated with the first. Perhaps Benedict is more interested in demonstrating the continuity of Cassian's doctrine with the teaching of the original Egyptian monks. Cassian is only their interpreter—a role he himself frequently claims—the doctrine itself stems from the heart of the desert experience.

Fourthly, a minor distinction: Basil never wrote "a rule"[5] but compiled two series of "rules"—practical, scriptural responses to questions posed, a monastic catechism as it were. He was more concerned with the doctrinal basis of monastic life than with its detailed regimen.

Finally there is a very important point. Many readers pass over this verse without realizing what a paradox it contains. Benedict cites as the broader background for an understanding of his own thought two sources: the Desert Fathers and St Basil. The fact is that, to some extent, these worthy sponsors are not compatible. At least they seem to represent opposite polarities in the range of monastic values. On the one hand is the desert tradition represented by the *Vitae Patrum* and the sayings and anecdotes related to individuals who manifestly had made great progress in spiritual living. This experiential base, lived out in the wilderness, remote from ordinary secular life and from the life of the urban churches, was given great psychological depth by Evagrius Pontikus, whose work Cassian gladly made his own. On the other hand is Basil, in a Cappadocian context, with a great deal of theological acumen and a feeling for the Scriptures, trying to formulate a guide for monks living in urban communities as part of a local church.

Taking for granted that such schematic representations are of limited value, let us attempt to indicate graphically what this polarization of values meant:

Basil	Desert Tradition
More communitarian	More eremitical
More humane	More ascetic
More theological/scriptural	More psychological/experiential
More institutional	More spontaneous
More ecclesial	More withdrawn
More horizontal	More vertical

There are several considerations to be kept in mind if such a schematisation is to be useful. All the qualities listed are good things. It is not a matter of opposing something desirable in monastic life to something that has no right there. It is, rather, a question of establishing a balance between two monastic components, or better, of setting up a dialectic which produces growth by allowing them to interact.[6] Secondly, it is hard to envisage any monk, who had arrived at some degree of earthly holiness, completely eliminating any of the qualities listed. This means that all of them, in their own way, would have tried to live the whole gamut of Christian virtue, and would have recommended the same to their disciples. The issue is, however, that in their teaching, as this has been handed down to us, there is often an emphasis to one or other series of qualities. Thirdly, neither Pachomius nor the monasticism which stemmed from him is included in the category "Desert Tradition." Pachomiam monasticism constitutes a special case both in itself and in its influence on *RB*.

When Benedict coolly instructs his disciples to draw from both streams of tradition, he is making provision for the avoidance of extremism and ensuring that the full range of monastic doctrine is available to guide their behavior. It is the openness to different and even divergent aspects of the one truth that gives to *RB* its "catholicity"—its universal appeal.

> If the monastic tradition was catholic in this sense, by joining to Christ the best of the secular heritage, **it was so as well in virtue of its openness to different, sometimes opposing currents**, which witness as to its capacity for assimilation and to its vitality. In the same breath Benedict mentions the works of Cassian and Basil's *Rule*, whose opinions on eremitism are scarcely compatible, and his esteem for Cassian's *Conferences*, affirmed here and elsewhere, does not prevent him from following Augustine in his doctrine of grace as well as in his presentation of the common life.[7] [Emphasis added].

It seems arguable that the longevity of the Benedictine tradition derives from this solid base. Within itself it contains the elements which permit it to adapt to a wide range of situations, to nuance its philosophy in favor of new challenges. To some extent the history of Benedictine monachism can be seen as a continuing variation between an ascetic emphasis and an ecclesial emphasis. At times this has led to a conflict of observances in which Benedictines of one variety are impugning the validity of other embodiments of the one tradition. Recrimination, hostility and suspicion have been the result. The recurrent question was often formulated in terms of whether the *Rule of Benedict* propagates a *conversatio* primarily ordained to the contemplative life, or to participation in the mission and ministry of the Church. Are Benedictines "active" or "contemplative"? The answer is that often they are neither, but ideally they are both.

The problem has been compounded in several ways. One was the curialist attitude in the Middle Ages which tried to arrive at a common category which might include both monks and canons regular, and thus was engendered a dilemma which affected both parties; the monks were clericalized and the canons were monasticated.[8] Another factor which complicated the dilemma was the preponderance of the ascetic influence in monastic theology. The case for the ascetic values was argued far more strongly by monastic tradition than for their complements. As a result most reforms seem to have taken as a primary premise the need for tightening monastic discipline: stricter rules of silence and separation, more penance, less flexibility. Monks of every generation have been invited to feel guilty that their level of monastic observance is considerably lower than that of their forbears—the real monks. It is only comparatively rarely that one hears of monasteries being rebuked for their failure to live as part of the Church: for their lack of positive virtues rather than for the presence of visible aberrations.

There is room for variety within the monastic order, as Bernard of Clairvaux affirmed in his *Apologia*.[9] The expressions of the Benedictine charism are pluriform. It is not right to take two observances and assign them different locations on a single calibrated scale of "fidelity." Rather each local community has to achieve its own specific blend of the monastic elements taking into consideration its own particular traditions as well as the more universal monastic values; it needs to take account of the challenges and demands of its own time and place. Most importantly, people have to be considered. It is no good arriving at a formula for a theoretically perfect monastic observance if the monks won't buy it. Monastic life is, above all, doing the best in the real world without pining about the absence of ideal conditions.

Let us now reflect on some aspects of this interplay of values, as it can be seen in *RB* and verified in our own experience.

I. The Significance of the End of the Rule

Chapters 67-73 of the *Rule of Benedict* are often considered as a later supplement to the main body of the text, representing the author's afterthoughts on what he had written. This block does not follow *RM*, but is in large measure, independent of it and in fact, breathes a different spirit. There is a stern chapter on monks going out, and two dealing with unhealthy relationships within the community—perhaps both are the fruit of lessons which the author learned by sad experience (cf. 59,6). There is an extraordinary chapter dealing with difficulties in obedience, giving the monk sound practical advice on dealing with impossible situations, and another which extends the range of obedience from compliance with the orders of superiors to a willingness to defer to all. Thus obedience ceases to be an external military-type of subordination and a material fulfillment of commands, and more of a willingness to be humbly submissive to all out of love and respect for each. Although Benedict sees this attitude principally in terms of juniors with regard to their seniors, it is interesting that he sees it important that the *bonum obedientiae* be understood as more than cultivating the hierarchy. He even says that it is such mutual obedience that leads to God.[10] This is because it is an obedience that is unrewarded in this life; there are no advantages to be gained, such as follow automatically on co-operation with those who have discretionary power over the range of monastic perquisites.

Chapter 72 goes even further. To some extent Benedict cuts the ground away from the rest of the *Rule* by saying that even if one has accomplished all that is enjoined, it is as nothing if it is not done for the right motives, that is, from love. "The last temptation was the greatest treason, to do the right deed for the wrong reason." Monastic observance is a means to an end: the end of the *Rule* is love. Strict observance profits nothing if it hardens the heart and causes envy, intolerance and lovelessness. Love thus becomes the measure of all the virtues. It is not a matter of exuding a universal beneficence and abandoning self-denial, asceticism and the practice of the virtues. Rather, love becomes the incentive for discipline and goodness. One can volunteer one's services out of self-denial or duty, but it is far sweeter to do so out of affection for a brother. One can forego a pleasure out of abstemiousness or scrupulosity, but it is a far more buoyant experience when one does it so that another might be gratified. One can practice discipline and become hardened by it, or one can do the same, not for one's own perfection, but so that another's life might be easier, and such a practice will not lead to complacency. Love is thus the main motive force in the cenobite's virtue—not "perfection," nor the elimination of vice, but the good of the brother.

The final chapter of the *Rule*, which is our focus in this present paper, continues this work of relativization. The precepts of the *Rule* are not to be taken as a program which, of itself, leads to perfection. It is not a closed system but a series of open doors: not a series of prescribed actions but an invitation always to remain alert to the challenge of the Word of God conveyed through the Scriptures and the Church. If one does this then one will become more and more aware of what one is **not** doing and somewhat less complacent in one's ability to fulfill to perfection the minutiae of a material code.

There is a revisionist tone to these chapters. They constitute a sort of *retractio* to the *Rule*. What has been the subject of legislation is to be qualified not only by the compassionate administration of a God-fearing abbot, but also by the imperatives of love and the totality of revelation. When Benedict sends his readers to opposite sources in 73,5, he is taking a step to ensure that this human and divine complexity is not simplified into a rigid, single-minded (and probably oppressive) system.

II. The Balancing of Sources

It is not possible to reach a sympathetic understanding of the Benedictine charism if one regards it merely as an imperfect derivative of the Desert tradition. It is certain that Benedict made use of the insights of this monastic current of thought, but he has deliberately balanced what he drew from it with other material drawn from general Church sources. He has softened some of the potential extremism of the Egyptian monks by emphasizing values which were ecclesial, communitarian and humane. This is clear not only from the content of the *Rule* but also from his choice of source material.

In the opening sections a strong dependence on the *Rule of the Master* is evinced. As the *Rule* progresses, this is weakened. A good example is the question of the abbot. Benedict's Chapter 2 closely follows *RM*, although there are several significant modifications. What he writes in Chapters 27-28, although occurring in a harsh context, is considerably more pastoral. The directory for the abbot given in 64,7-22 is different again, considerably influenced by the writings of Augustine and noticeably mellow in tone. It is as though, throughout the course of a lifetime, Benedict is becoming more comfortable with a gentler view of life, through his experience, and—arguably—through his continuing contact with the Catholic Fathers.

Benedict is strongly influenced by some of the major figures in the Western Church, most of whom were bishops and pastors. This is evident to a significantly greater degree in *RB* than in *RM*. Thus Benedict owes much to Augustine, to Cyprian and also to Ambrose, Clement of Rome and Jerome. There is, likewise, independent recourse to Basil and to Pachomius. The effect of such wider reading was to add a certain complementarity to Benedict's sources which, in turn, was a good foundation for a sober, moderate and balanced form of monastic life, filtered free of eccentricities and with an inbuilt capacity for variation.[11]

III. Horizontalism

It seems that Cassian, although he wrote for cenobites, was never quite satisfied with the cenobitic ideal, and privately hankered after the eremitical life as the sovereign goal of a monk's development.[12] *RM* is certainly committed to a communitarian form of life, but it is so rigidly and minutely organized that there seems to be scarcely any opportunity for the development of **affective** community—much less any encouragement to do so! "Community" appears more as an objective, external unit of organization and control, rather than a factor in subjectivity, which might have some bearing on spiritual development.

Benedict's *Rule* is different. Community is more than just the place where the monastic process happens. He accords it a positive role, so that growing into the community coincides with, and witnesses to, the authenticity of growth in the inner life of prayer. The influence of Augustine is probably in evidence here. Augustine begins his Rule with love of God and neighbor, and insists on the importance of unity of heart. Elsewhere he writes even more emphatically:

> The love of God comes first in the order of commandment, but the love of neighbor comes first in the order of practice...By loving the neighbor you cleanse your eye so that you are able to see God.[13]

This horizontalism[14] can be seen in Benedict's cumulative understanding of the role of the abbot. He is not a purely vertical figure whom the monks encounter on their upward journey to God. He is a brother.[15] He is not an absolute tyrant but is repeatedly subjected to God and his law, to the demands of justice, to the *Rule* with all its devices for reducing the possibility of impetuous decisions and also, it seems, to the local bishop. On the other hand, provision is also made for the re-allocation of some of the abbot's powers through delegation within the community.[16]

One coming newly to the monastery finds there more than the abbot; he encounters a community of brothers. St Benedict recognizes that there will be situations in which an abbot is pastorally powerless to assist an individual; in that case he counts upon the *seniores spirituales* to supply for this defect, (27,2-3). In the structuring of his monastery, he envisages a host of officials—deans, the cellarer, the senior who looks after newcomers, the prior—as adjuncts to the abbot. There are other seniors too, who have no title, but who are expected to ensure that the quality of monastic living is not diminished: the seniors whose beds are near to those of the juniors (22,7), those who patrol the monastery to ensure that all are engaged in their reading (48,17), and those who maintain order in the refectory when the abbot is eating out (56,3). Benedict is always aware of the potential for influence among the brothers, which is why he hates grumbling. They are bound to remain brothers, not to elevate themselves into some sort of mini-superiors (70,1-3); they are to encourage one another (22,8), and pray for one another (28,4). In normal circumstances there is scope for *consortium* and *colloquium* (25,2). Despite his absolute interdiction of *scurrilitas* (6,8), Benedict seems to have realized that joking and small talk would be ordinary components in a monk's day and is content to make provision for their containment so that they do not invade time for spiritual duties (43,8; 48,18), and suggests that during Lent they be restricted even further (49,7). Gravity, taciturnity and withdrawal from others, have spiritual significance only when they stem from a heart fully occupied with God. If they derive from personal preference, or an inability to relax or communicate, they probably serve more to reinforce vice than to promote virtue. Beyond the basis necessary to maintain monastic discipline, and to ensure the tranquillity of the monastic environment, there is no reason to suggest that Benedict would have sought to inhibit fraternal relations; his provisions are intended rather to enhance them, and to give them the possibility of greater profundity.

IV. Challenge

There are other aspects which could be discussed here: the relationship between the *Rule* as ideal and the pragmatics of daily life, the emergence of an understanding of the role of the monastery in the Church's mission and ministry, the merely relative value of a legal document as a guide to what actually went on in monasteries. For the moment it is important simply to underline the fact that within the *Rule*, and within the history of Benedictine monachism, there is a duality of theory and practice which has not always been well understood.

There are two poles which mark the extremes of this monastic dialectic: the ascetic and the ecclesial. It is too simplistic to aver that white monks espouse the former and black the latter, but there is a grain of truth in it, at least as concerns the English-speaking world. The thing is, however, that all who claim to participate in the Benedictine charism need to exhibit **both** qualities.

In the chapter on Lent, Benedict insists that when a monk decides on a program of self-reformation, he check it out with his abbot to make sure that his efforts are well-directed (49,8). There is a danger that instead of strengthening areas where he is defective, the monk will simply go on reinforcing qualities that are already firmly established. Thus one who is naturally withdrawn may espouse a crusade of silence: perhaps he would do better to learn to communicate. One who is already loquacious, may decide to be more sociable: he should try working on solitude. The "ascetic" should learn to relax and the *bon viveur* to restrict his pursuit of pleasure. We grow by opposites, not by endless progression in a single line. This is something that Gregory the Great clearly recognizes in his *Pastoral Rule*, at great length specifying what virtues are most needed by different temperaments. There is always the danger of a blind spot; we can be easy on ourselves by working only on the virtues which come naturally, and failing to develop the complementary skills and resources, which would admirably complete our nature with the fruits of grace and struggle.

A Benedictine community needs to take steps to ensure that it is both ascetic **and** ecclesial; this may involve conflict and disagreement and hardship, but it is the only way to grow according to its basic charism. It seems also likely that this will be the best road to renewal: filling out the generally ascetic emphasis of monastic ideology with the more ecclesial note recommended in the documents of the Second Vatican Council and, perhaps, demanded by the tenor of the time.

The key to the longevity of Benedict's inspiration and institution is this self-correcting polarity; it is also the substance of monastic renewal and a valuable factor in personal fidelity.

NOTES

[1] Cf. M. Casey, "Orthopraxy and Interpretation: Reflections on *RB* 73.1," RBS 14/15 (1988).

[2] Cf. Simon Tugwell, *Ways of Imperfection: An Exploration of Christian Spirituality*, (London, 1984), pp. 71-82. Not all agree with the basic orientation of this chapter, but it has a point.

[3] *Conf* 13; SChr 54, pp. 146-181.

[4] *De Incarnatione* 7,27. Cassian refers to Augustine rather abruptly as *sacerdos*, without any of the honorifics he gave to other figures.

[5] Although the *Small Asceticon* of Basil bears the title *Regula* in Benedict of Aniane's *Concordia Regularum* in PL 103.487.

[6] Cf. M. Casey, "Balance in Monastic Life," *TJ* 9 (1975), pp. 5-11. Lonergan's definition and description of dialectic are useful for clarity's sake: "For the sake of greater precision, let us say that **a dialectic is a concrete unfolding of linked but opposed principles of change**. [Emphasis added.]" Bernard Lonergan, *Insight: A Study of Human Understanding*, (London, 1958), p. 217.

[7] A. de Vogüé, *The Rule of Saint Benedict: A Doctrinal and Spiritual Commentary*, (Cistercian Publications, Kalamazoo, 1983), p. 316.

[8] This problem was explored in an unpublished conference of E. Schillebeeckx on *"Monachism and the Priesthood,"* given to Cistercian monks at Tilburg in June 1959, a transcript of which I have seen.

[9] Bernard *Apo* 7-9; *SBO* 3.86-89.

[10] *RB* 71,2; the *hanc* refers to the closer element in a list of two, that is, to obedience to the brothers rather than to the abbot.

[11] Some of the ecclesial values of *RB* can be seen in his references to episcopal intervention (62,9; 64,4), the borrowing from the Roman (and Milanese) liturgies (13,10; 9,4; 12,4; 13,11; 17,8), the primacy accorded to Scripture and the Catholic Fathers, and the general usage of biblical imagery primarily intended for the Church. The use of the term "Household of God" is significant, as also is the sense of identification with the wider church evident in the use of the term from Gal 6:10, *domesticus fidei* (53,2). On humane values see M. Casey, "The Humanitas of the Benedictine Tradition" in John S. Martin (ed.), *St Benedict, a Man with an Idea*, (University of Melbourne, 1981), pp. 27-35.

[12] Cf. Julien Leroy, "Le cénobitisme chez Cassien," *RAM* 43 (1967), pp. 121-158: "It is clear that in the thought of Cassian the inner man is the anchorite, or, at a pinch, the cenobite to the extent that he goes beyond the asceticism proper to cenobitism and the active life to give himself also to the struggle against thoughts. Now we have seen that this conception is given scarcely any scope in cenobitic asceticism" [Translated from p. 155]. Cf. E. Pichery, "La pensée de Cassien touchant l'anchorète et le cénobite et le but de son oeuvre

monastique," in the Introduction to *SChr*, 42, pp. 51-58; and A. de Vogüé, *The Rule*, pp. 45-63.

[13] Augustine, *In Ioannem* 17.8; (*SChr* 36, p. 174).

[14] Cf. A. de Vogüé, *La communaúte*, (Paris, 1961), pp. 485-487. M. Casey, "'Community' in the Benedictine Rule," *RBS* 8/9 (1982), pp. 59-65; Anselm Grun, "Benediktinische Gemeinschaft: Ein Modell fur christliches Zusam-menleben," *GL* 56/4 (August 1983), pp. 243-252.

[15] Cf. M. Casey, "Leadership in a Benedictine Context: An Interrogation of Tradition," *TJ* 22 (1982), pp. 5-103, especially pp. 89-90.

[16] *RB* nominates as candidates for middle management those who have an understanding of monastic values and a capacity for communicating these to others. They need to be industrious and efficient within the parameters of their mandate. They are not rivals to the abbot, but yet are expected to exercise a degree of initiative in their own areas of responsibility. Neither yes-men nor creators of private empires, they accept their subordinate position and within the terms of that subordination act creatively.

THE DYNAMIC UNFOLDING OF THE BENEDICTINE CHARISM

Despite its image of medieval timelessness, the Benedictine way of life has been constantly adapted in the centuries that followed the death of Benedict. This adaptation has been the key to its survival. Rather than measuring the fidelity of a given interpretation against a fixed standard, we need to appreciate that creative adaptation according to the reality of concrete situations is the soul of the Benedictine tradition. This article appeared in The American Benedictine Review 51.2 (2000).

To be found in many monasteries in the years before the Second Vatican Council was a pious novel entitled *Brother Petroc's Return*. It was the story of a medieval monk who had slipped into a coma and was buried in that state. Several centuries later, in the mid-twentieth century, he regained consciousness. Rejoining a Benedictine community, Brother Petroc continued where he had left off — undeterred by the social and technological changes "outside." The novel was a celebration of the essential timelessness of Benedictine *conversatio* as a pure reflection of universal human nature, unaffected by the fluid patterns of civilization.

Brother Petroc was wise not to have delayed his resurrection any longer. Another ten or twenty years and the romantic fantasy of a "life unchanged for centuries" was completely destroyed. This was not, however, a sudden rupture. *Aggiornamento* more grievously wounded the illusion of continuity than the reality. If we ask those who remember the former times, we will soon discover that, even before the Council, monastic life was only superficially medieval. The same is true even of the nineteenth century—despite the pious efforts of the brothers Wolter at Beuron and of others—and of most periods since the end of the Middle Ages. Benedictinism has always been in a state of continual flux.

There is certainly a strong conservative strain in Benedictine history. Conservation does not, however, imply resistance to change. On the contrary it demands a continual response to the movements of the external environment. If Benedict's charism has survived intact for 1500 years, it is only because it contains within itself a predisposition to adapt and so to avoid extinction. A skyscraper able to withstand earthquakes is one that can sway with the rocking of the earth. Solid buildings resist the movement and so tend to split.

In this article I would like to concentrate on the texts and themes in the *Rule* that provide a foundation and justification for continuing change in the monastic lifestyle. My focus will be not on the fixed deposit of monastic wisdom but on the elements that call for an ongoing expansion of the frontiers of monastic philosophy.

I am aware of potential pitfalls in this approach. The conclusions at which we arrive in our reading of Benedict's *Rule* are usually determined by the sections of the *Rule* to which we attach most importance. If we concentrate on one block of text or ignore another, our assessment of Benedict's vision is likely to be no more than a subjective recycling of our own priorities. If, for instance, we read only the Prologue and not the chapters on excommunication something of the integrity of St Benedict disappears. The result may be more marketable, but is the product genuine? I have suggested elsewhere that the later chapters of the *Rule*, as they are now located, are such a substantial qualification of what Benedict had earlier taught as to appear almost as a *retractatio*.[1] We cannot base ourselves simply on the first seven chapters and leave aside Benedict's subsequent reflections on the life he had set out to describe. Moreover, we cannot hope to gauge the personality and wisdom of this man if we restrict ourselves to a bowdlerized text. There are important insights to be gained even when a section seems irrelevant to our concerns.[2] Though my presentation concentrates on one angle of Benedict's thought, I hope that the reader will bear in mind certain complementary ideas. Otherwise the result will be a distortion.

Faced with the irrefutable fact of development and change in historical Benedictinism, and aware of the reality of massive multiformity in the monastic world of today, we are confronted with alternative conclusions depending on whether we view change positively or negatively. It is possible to view the successive departures from a fixed ancient ideal as a history of deformation and thus something to be regretted. Or we can conclude that there is, in Benedict's projection of ideals, an intrinsic openness to development: in which case the ideal is not degraded by historical evolution but re-framed and even re-vivified.[3]

The first approach could be stated baldly thus: there is a single genuine expression of the Benedictine charism and the various "Benedictine" lifestyles can be assembled along a continuum of fidelity to this prototype. A strict, primitive observance is the norm: what we see around us are watered-down approximations—no doubt laudable but not truly as St Benedict intended. This seems to have been the line followed by Adalbert de Vogüé in discussions with abbots at the General Chapter of the Strict Observance Cistercians not long after the Council. He was heard to assert that the only way to be sure of maintaining the spirit of the *Rule* was to keep in its integrity the letter of the *Rule*.

The second approach sees the *Rule* in a different light. It does not regard the *Rule of Benedict* as a *kanon*— originally a reed used as a measure of length, thence a standard of comparison, a fixing of limits as in the "Canon" of Scripture. Instead, it takes seriously the dynamic aspect of *regula*. The *Rule* is meant to provide direction to movement beyond the initial starting point. A graphic illustration of this aspect of the word is its ancient military use to describe the channel in a catapult which gave the missile its initial direction. In modern terms we might speak of the *Rule* as a guidance system: a means of maintaining direction amid the variables of the real world.

It is in support of this latter approach to Benedict's *Rule* that I would like to reflect on certain themes and emphases in its text.

1. The Benedictine Meaning-System is Dialectical

When, in the last chapter of the *Rule*, Benedict identifies the specifying sources of his monastic meaning-system, he does so in a way that was intended to widen the monk's mental horizon rather than constrict it. His own work Benedict qualifies correctly as incomplete: it does not propose a complete observance of righteousness, but draws a practical picture of a good moral life and basic monasticity. Once the monk has mastered these rudiments he is encouraged to go further by the observance of the teachings of the Holy Fathers. Observance of doctrine presupposes knowledge, knowledge comes by reading and reflection. When each monk reads a different book (48,15), knowledge grows variably. Formation is not confined within the limits of Benedict's own wisdom; monks and communities are invited to appropriate for themselves the wide world of the monastic and Catholic traditions. Future policy decisions will, therefore, be contingent on the haphazard—or providential—results of this more ample *lectio*.

The world of meaning that Benedict owned was not a closed and orderly system but a ferment of not-always compatible ideas at different stages of evolution. When in 73,5 he refers to the desert tradition — represented by the (unnamed) John Cassian and the *Lives* of the desert monks—he supplements this reference by mentioning the "Rule" of St Basil.[4] The oddity of this double indication should not escape us. Cassian and Basil do not sing the same song. The network of values that animate the spirituality of the desert is not the same as that to be found in Benedict's ecclesiastical sources. The most obvious divergence is the choice made between the solitary life and cenobitism.[5] The spirituality of the *eremos* or desert was eremitical (sidelining Pachomius for the moment). On the other hand, the text of Basil's *Long Rules* 7 (in the Latin version Ch. 3)[6] is a sustained polemic against the life of the anchorite, which the Cappadocian bishop rejected as unevangelical.

By suggesting a non-exclusive reading list, Benedict is opening the way to a genuine growth in an understanding that is wider than ideology. It is indicative of the same principle of complementarity that Gregory the Great applies systematically in his *Pastoral Rule*. To every virtue there is a corresponding opposite that is itself also a virtue. Pastoral discernment is a matter of knowing which end of the polarity to recommend to a particular person at a particular time. The Middle Way enunciated by Benedict attempts to capture the benefits of opposite virtues while minimizing their liabilities. This is the much-praised Benedictine "balance"—remembering of course that balance always requires the creative interaction of two opposed forces; it is never the single-minded pursuit of an extreme.[7]

Benedict may be said to have established a dialectic in monastic life, in which opposed but connected values act together to maintain direction in the midst of external change. It is this interaction that has ensured the survival of the Benedictine way of life. Instead of self-destructing either through stagnation or by loss of identity through dispersal of energies, Benedictinism has constantly re-expressed and re-energized itself by internalizing "new" values without loosening its hold on what it has received.[8]

So we observe a basis in the *Rule* for different emphases, all of which are valid in the appropriate circumstances. A Benedictine community will locate itself somewhere on the continuum between such pairs of values as the following.

The Way of Negation		*The Way of Affirmation*
Wilderness-living	and	Urban-living
Rusticity	and	Urbanity
Simplicity	and	Sophistication
Solitude	and	Community
Silence	and	Dialogue
Repetitive work	and	Meaningful work
Introspection	and	Outreach
Enclosure	and	Openness
Monastic liturgy[9]	and	Roman liturgy
Apophasis	and	Kataphasis
Contemplation	and	Ministry
Uniformity	and	Pluriformity
Structure	and	Latitude
Abnegation	and	Fulfillment
Austerity	and	Sufficiency
Poverty	and	Provision
Fasting	and	Feasting (!)
Experience	and	Theology

At any particular moment in a community's history, its physiognomy may, thus, be determined relative to other Benedictine groups. Each community has a unique lifestyle that will set it apart from other communities and congregations. This inevitably entails particular blind-spots in the perception of priorities; knowing about them opens up creative avenues of challenge. In general, "the way of negation" is seen most strongly in recently-reformed groups and among those who profess to pursue a secluded, contemplative orientation. "The way of affirmation" follows naturally on the choice of an active, ministerial lifestyle, more fully interacting with contemporary society.[10] Groups that are neither "active" or "contemplative" or try to be both may be riven by factions, each accusing the others of deserting the Benedictine ideal; it is not unknown for those who enter such a community to be watched; everyone waits to see to which faction they attach themselves.

All the qualities listed may be regarded broadly as "Benedictine" and none is absolutely excluded.[11] The most creative communities are those which manifest a strong showing at both ends of the spectrum. Sometimes the specific blend of elements comes from tradition or community custom, sometimes it is a response to unique local conditions by means of "inculturation." In certain cases a particular orientation is the result of a policy consciously-adopted to "correct" or re-direct what was perceived as a deviation from the ideal.

A creative Benedictine community embraces some affirmative policies and some negative policies. As a result it has a range of strengths that may appear inconsistent, but yet support and extend one another. Alternatively, a group may achieve an excellent balance between seemingly opposite qualities: if a community embodies the values of both silence and dialogue it lives well. The combination of qualities seemingly pulling a community in different directions need not be divisive or chaotic. To the extent that various pairs of opposites produce a disciplined yet adaptable community there is no need to insist on conformity to a safer average. On the other hand, another monastery that finds itself immoderately average may be there simply because it embraces neither "extreme". It is not silent and does not engage in meaningful dialogue; it encourages neither self-denial nor self-affirmation, enclosure is poorly observed without any genuine openness. It is passionate about nothing. It instinctively chooses the path of least challenge. Such wishy-washiness is the bane of Benedictine history, producing a comfortable but unfulfilling life, one with no purpose beyond survival. To compound matters, local autonomy may cause this directionlessness to be perpetuated.[12]

Each Benedictine group forges a specific identity by its particular blending of the various elements possible in a lifestyle governed by the *Rule*. As a consequence a monk visiting another monastery has the experience of a curious ambivalence toward this similar yet dissimilar community. He may, as St Benedict notes (61,4), be able to offer constructive criticism of the local scene. Simultaneously, however, he may well be taking note of certain elements that he would wish to be introduced into his own monastery. Less creatively, divergences in the blend of elements often lead communities to engage in a "war of observances"—"slanging off" at each other with little regard for truth, charity or moderation. The twelfth-century controversy between Cistercians and Cluniacs is but one example among many of the disedifying consequences of failing to appreciate how broad is the scope of the Benedictine vision.

The relative strength with which the values at each pole of the dialectic are held probably relates to the kind of reading that occurs in the community—on the supposition that monks are *ex professo* serious readers. The genius of Benedict was that he combined monastic sources such as Cassian and the Desert monks with Augustine, Basil, Clement, Cyprian and other "Catholic Fathers." The difference in tone between *RB* 2 and *RB* 64 is probably due to the fact that in one Benedict is following the Master, and in the other he is much influenced by Augustine. A monastery that restricts its intake to monastic sources will probably lack the richness and adaptability that St Benedict achieved; community, "horizontalism" and personalist values may be underdeveloped.[13] On the other hand, the practical exclusion of these archetypal monastic writings will eventually lead to a lack of contact with monastic roots: monks become generic religious distinguished only by wearing hoods. In a worse condition than either is a monk or community that does not read at all. All that remains in that case is the dim option between soulless custom and mindless innovation.

2. *Benedictine Constitutional Law Operates under Checks and Balances*

In an age where the power of secular rulers was untrammeled by constitutional restrictions Benedict has legislated for a system of government in which the power of the abbot was circumscribed. Likewise, the *Rule* was not an absolute. The most explicit statement of this duality occurs in 1,2, where cenobites are said to "live in monasteries and serve (*militans*) under a rule and an abbot." The ordinary monk is undeniably "under" the abbot, but both the monk and the abbot are equally "under the rule." "In all things let all follow the rule as master...The abbot himself is to do everything in the fear of God and observing the rule, knowing that he will certainly render an account of all his judgments to God who, above all, judges with equity" (3,7-11). "Especially, [the abbot] must keep this present rule in all things" (64,20). An abbot may attempt to reign as king, but St Benedict envisages no more than a constitutional monarchy. In fact there is no basis for autocracy at all, since the abbot has only borrowed or delegated authority; he is called to act as Christ's representative (2,2; 63,15). As such he is not permitted to teach, establish as policy or command anything that is not an expression of Christ's instructions: *extra praeceptum Domini* (2,4), St Benedict reiterates that the abbot is subject to God not in the sense that he is beyond human authority but because there will be a *discussio* about the effectiveness of his pastoral action on the Day of Judgment (2,6; 2,39). Sometimes this doom may be visited on an aberrant superior earlier than expected. If an abbot does not shape up, the Church, through the bishop or others, may intervene to remove him (64,3-6).

The concrete history of shared life in a monastery is another well-known but less-documented inhibitor of abbatial tyranny. A group of men living together for many years develops an implicit sense of corporate identity. An abbot may have the most dazzling plans for reform and be in total accord with the *Rule*, but his efforts will come to nothing if there is no continuity between the inertia/momentum of the community and the abbot's proposals. Benedict's experience at Vicovaro confirms this. We may be excused, therefore, for expanding the **abbot rule** dyad by the addition of a third element: the community. An abbot needs to apply the *Rule* in accordance with the concrete condition of the community: its history, aspirations, needs and graces. By instructing the abbot to ensure that his actions are a response to the real pastoral needs of the community, Benedict is effectively reducing the scope for originality and initiative. The abbot is restrained on the one hand by being called to act as the icon of the invisible Christ, and on the other to be a servant of the different *mores* found in the community. The abbot is to conform and adapt himself to the monks, not vice-versa (2,31-32).

It is possible that the **abbot community rule** triad will produce gridlock and victory for the status quo. In this case Benedict's dream of a solidly flexible community will not be realized. Granted, however that the abbot has been formed in the community and chosen by it, and that he shares with the body of monks the same basic monastic philosophy, there is no reason to be pessimistic about the possibility of eventual consensus. In addition to formation in a common *disciplina*, one has to consider the agglutinative effect of *doctrina* in the community, whereby the meaning-system that undergirds practical policy is constantly expressed and reinforced. The fusion of horizons achieved by the **abbot community rule** offers a prudent, creative and dynamic basis for adaptation.

3. Benedictine Conversatio is Tailored to Fit Persons

Benedict's prescriptions about the monks' clothing in Chapter 55 can easily be read as expressive of his monastic philosophy as a whole.

> Clothes are given to the brothers
> according to what sort of place they live in
> and the climate...
> The abbot is to give consideration to these things...
> The abbot is to make provision for measurement
> so that these clothes are not short
> but are measured for those who have the use of them.
> (55,1-8)

If clothing has the same characteristics as *conversatio* as a whole (22,2), then Benedict is saying firstly, that monastic life should be localized "according to the region in which they live"—a principle which can be extended as a warrant for attempts at inculturation. Secondly, instead of being a mute advocate of generic observance, the abbot should certainly be at pains to reflect on the modalities of necessary adaptation. This is more a matter of acting according to commonsense data than of satisfying prejudices and whims. To do otherwise is ridiculous, as is the case where monasteries turn on the heating on a fixed date, without regard for the vagaries of climate, or when details of daily living are decided on another continent. Thirdly, monastic life has to fit individual monks, that is, its standard form must be able to accommodate the variation consequent on different genetic make-ups, personal histories and graces. In a sense, each monk incarnates the charism uniquely. This we are prepared to acknowledge sometimes, when we are in a more mellow mood, but can easily forget when we experience frustration at the otherness of others. We jeopardize recruitment or formation by forgetting that the pattern according to which every potential monk is made is to be found more in the candidate than in the community. Monastic education consists in first *educing the person* and only then attempting to enrich him or her with the substantial wisdom inherent in the monastic community. It is quite the opposite to drowning the neophyte in the overwhelming but secure blanket of a monastic sub-culture.

There are several sections of the *Rule* where Benedict accepts a grass-roots determinant of observance. There is a recognition that the size of a community and the layout of the monastery[14] will modify the demands of a task such as kitchen service (35,4). The size of a community will also govern choices made about liturgy (17,6), administration (31,17) and the participation of officials in common chores (35,5). Local necessity or poverty (40,5; 48,7), heavy work and summer heat (39,6; 41,4) are all considered as sufficient to modify or mitigate normal practice.

Because situational factors are necessarily varied, achieving the ends Benedict proposed will sometimes demand that different means are employed. The abbot has to be some sort of alchemist. "Let him so temper and arrange everything that souls are saved and that the brothers do what they must do without justifiable murmuring." (41.5).

The Cistercian reformers of the twelfth century adopted *unanimitas* as an ideal, and saw its application in a hefty measure of uniformity. As the new Order quickly multiplied and expanded geographically, it became obvious that the *a priori* imposition of a rigid pattern would not work. These solidly-formed monks concluded that unanimity need not be weakened by the application of common sense. The Cistercian customary, which evolved between the 1130's and the 1170's, contains a text that expresses this principle.

> For this and for all other things appropriate to this time [of harvesting], each monastery is to act according to the placement of its lands (*secundum positionem locorum*) and the arrangements made by the abbot and prior, since it is not possible to observe these things equally in all places.[15]

4. Distribution is Made According to Need

The statement of need-based distribution at the beginning of Chapter 34 relies on Acts 4:32 and the various reprises of the theme indicate influence from the *Rule of St Augustine*. Benedict's preferred criterion is that of sufficiency, but this is a subjective standard: what is enough for one may be either excessive or inadequate for another. Benedict is squeamish about offering an objective norm. "It is with some scrupulosity that we are establishing the measure of food and drink for others" (40,2). In matters concerning the measure of food, drink, daily manual work and clothing Benedict qualifies his injunctions with the phrase *credimus*. He uses the auctorial plural of dignity, but insists that his judgment is not absolute (39,1; 40,3; 48,2; 55,4). It is as though he were adding "let him order it himself if he judges it better otherwise" (18,22). Such tentativeness is due not to indecision or lack of principle, but to a refined sensitivity to individual differences, especially those based on personal need.

Merciless to aberrations deriving from rebelliousness, indiscipline or vice, Benedict recognizes that the window of possibility for optimal observance exists mainly in the mature years of middle life; it takes time to develop and will eventually weaken. This is human nature and not the result of will. "Every age and level of understanding ought to have its distinctive measure" (30,1). It is for this reason that Benedict gives free rein to the natural instinct of mercy in the case of the old, the young and the weak. But just in case there might be someone who might feel impelled to insist on common norms, the "authority of the Rule" provides that "loving concern" should take precedence (37,1-3) over inflexible adherence to written law. Benedict is constantly aware that differential standards apply in the monastery. "[The abbot] must temper everything so that the strong may desire something more and the weak will not take flight" (64,19). "For brothers who are not strong or delicate some work or craft should be enjoined so that they will not be idle, but neither will they be oppressed by violent labor so that they run away. Their weakness must be taken into consideration by the abbot" (48,24-25). As a consequence, we notice that there is a radical departure from the Master's approach in Benedict's evangelical attitude to the sick and weak, care of whom is given absolute priority (36,1-2). Many relaxations of ordinary discipline are permitted to hasten their recovery, but it is attentiveness, care, love and solicitude that Benedict most desires to characterize his disciples' attitude.

Moral weakness attracts the same compassion as physical ill health. Chapters 27-28 point the abbot beyond police action in his dealing with delinquents. His zeal for the sinner's amendment is to be tempered by a skilled reading of the causes of the problem followed by persevering and imaginative intervention. Concern for the person is more evident in these chapters than zeal for a high level of monastic observance. Even the ultimate response of dismissal is not seen as a vindictive act, but as a means of preventing the problem from infecting the whole community (28,6-8).

It is an enlightening exercise to take note of all the exceptions and derogations to be found in the Rule.[16] Sometimes an abbot may have to abandon cherished principles because they cannot be marketed to the community. We can find a precedent for this in Benedict's attitude to temperance. Having cited the traditional saying that "wine is no drink for monks," he observes that "in our times monks cannot be persuaded of this"(40,6). Instead of surrendering completely, Benedict makes a strategic withdrawal and is content, since his monks cannot stomach total abstinence, that they stay within the limits of sobriety. The same discretion is earlier evident when Benedict restricts his demands for psalmody to what the monks will accept (18,22-25). In framing his words of guidance, Benedict seems to have before him the whole panorama of personalities that constitute a typical monastic community. His awareness of individual differences, special occasions and particular circumstances makes him reluctant to impose a regimen that in some or many cases might be counterproductive. Although he insists that a candidate understands the *Rule* and accepts the possibility of living by it (58,9-10), he also recognizes that circumstances change and genuine needs sometimes become apparent only after some time has elapsed. Inevitably special arrangements will have to be made because of the infirmities of different people, *propter diversorum infirmitatibus* (39,1). "It is not a matter of accursed favoritism (*personarum—quod absit— acceptio*) but of consideration of weakness" (34,2). The

Rule breathes the spirit that Benedict hopes will animate the abbot's practical administration. Monks should be secure in knowing that their needs will be accommodated: *omnia vero necessaria a patre sperare monasterii* (33,5). If an abbot sees that his ministry as taking care of weak souls rather than tyrannizing the strong (27,6), he will certainly respond to the revelation of such needs "not timidly, not reluctantly, not half-heartedly or grumbling and with an expression of unwillingness....For God loves a cheerful giver."[17]

The hardest thing about accepting the discerned needs of individual monks as a primary principle of governance is that it means that administrators have to be detached from their own need to be in full control. The arrival of data about subjective dispositions is always unpredictable, and reaching consensus through a thicket of outraged monastic sensibilities is beyond the imagining of those who think monasteries are zones of placid detachment and peace. This is not to say that running a monastery is an exercise in crisis-management. There is, however, a cloud of doubt above every master-plan. Though it is clear that Benedict envisaged a well-organized and provident administration, it is also evident that he hoped that the abbot would not attempt to achieve this by bulldozing his way through the legitimate needs and aspirations of his monks. "Let [the abbot] know what a difficult and arduous thing he undertakes in governing souls and being at the service of the manners of many" (2,31).

5. Different Gifts of Grace Exist

Need-based governance creates a climate of sympathy and compassion. But there is a danger—one recognized by Ayn Rand in her novel *Atlas Shrugged*. An administration that concentrates its energies on the weak and wobbly may inadvertently neglect the strong and the creative. If we believe the behaviorists, those who are constantly rewarded for being fragile may never develop an inclination to be strong. The result is a happily co-dependent community. Challenge is excluded. In such a community the imaginative and resourceful may be mindlessly exploited until they burn out, or there may be a partly-unconscious discrimination against them. In either case such one-sided concern is a parody of what Benedict intended

The ninety-nine are left in the mountains (27,8), but they also each will take a turn in being the wanderer. The abbot, meanwhile is to show "a single love to all equally," St Benedict says first but then qualifies the thought with his personal addition, "applying discipline in all matters according to their merits" (2,22). Differential love is the basis of the abbot's *auctoritas*; he does whatever he has to help individual monks to grow, according to the circumstances and the *kairos*, having respect for situations that can change from one moment to the next: *miscens temporibus tempora* (2,24).

This means that the abbot's ministry is not only propping up the feeble, but also energizing and directing those in whom, at a particular season, the grace of God is powerfully active. This may involve encouraging them to a level of temperance beyond the community norm and even beyond Benedict's own practice (40,4).[18] During Lent there is also the encouragement for individuals to follow the attraction of grace even beyond the accepted measure (49,5-10). The strong will chafe at the bit and desire more (64:19), they will not envy those from whom a lesser observance is required (34,3). There is a certain sense in which it is anticipated that fervent monks will refuse to remain at the gentle minimalism proposed for communal observance and will constantly stretch the limits towards a higher and purer embodiment of their vocation (7,67-70). If the abbot is called to obey God's will manifested through human limitation, he is equally obliged to submit to that will expressed in the gifts of grace, seemingly distributed so randomly.

Bernard of Clairvaux pulled no punches when it came to condemning individualistic behavior (*singularitas*), but he also knew that the harmony and progress of a community depend on a general capacity to tolerate differences, not only those based on special need but also those deriving from grace, giftedness and vocation.

Furthermore there will even be different gifts of grace and not all members will appear to follow the same course of action. Nevertheless interior unity and unanimity will gather and bind together this very multiplicity with the glue of charity and the bond of peace.[19]

To a large extent the well-being of the community demands not only that needs are met, but also that the creative energies present in the community find due expression, not only for the benefit of the gifted themselves, but as a providential means of life for the community and maybe for the Church.

6. Benedict's System is not Closed or Complete

It is easy to assume that intangible qualities like identity and morale are the result of a tight, all-pervasive, self-contained system that is somewhat insulated from contaminating "external" influences. In fact the opposite seems true. Social control often provokes an ambivalence in which exterior conformity cohabits with seething inward rebellion. Actions are enforceable and good habits follow with time, but the beliefs and values presupposed by norms and prescriptions are not automatic. Conflict is inevitable. The "feel-good" quality of a community is largely a function of compatibility between what is externally prescribed and the interior givenness of its members. Laws can disguise an unwilled *malaise* and limit its expression, but refusing to acknowledge the existence of dissatisfaction can never reduce the anxiety to which it gives birth.[20] It seems that a more open and flexible system is needed, notwithstanding the trouble it gives in the short term.

Benedict himself learned from experience (59,6) and from a lifetime's reading. It is to be presumed that he expected those who followed in his footsteps to be equally open to change. The abbot is expected to listen to the counsel of his community (3,2), not just in times of crisis but as an ordinary measure. Furthermore Benedict recognizes that often the Lord reveals a better way to those who have not been as fully monasticated (3,3). It is as though he was aware of the dangers of ideology and institutional blind spots. In a closed system what is done customarily is considered as necessarily the best; the organization protects itself from challenge by marginalizing every initiative for change. It is only the simple and non-socialized that can see that the emperor has no clothes. Thus the importance of giving double weight to every slight criticism that juniors make—especially considering the price they pay in official disapproval. The same outsider-insider quality is found in the visiting monk whose feedback the abbot is to consider prudently (61,4). In both cases, for St Benedict, the critic is not the originator of the message. He says it explicitly: it is the Lord who reveals and directs the human agent so that the need for change of direction is made manifest. If the trouble-maker is really a prophet then the abbot would do better to pay attention instead of trying to shut him up or put him down.

Resistance to data is one cause of stagnation; monastic politics is another. Specific projects are tendentiously labeled sometimes, with the result that instead of due discernment any vote divides along factional lines. In particular there is a strange duality in attitudes toward what is considered "old" and what "new." For many "the old is good" and the most dismissive epithet than can be applied is "novel." "Modern" is not generally a monastic compliment. Yet, for others "old" or "traditional" can mean outdated, worn-out and of no further use. Issues are not being looked at squarely as St Benedict wished. Instead of examining data and intercalating it with the wisdom born of experience and reading, prejudice and prejudgment rule the day, irrespective of how many authoritative *topoi* are alleged to add a semblance of weight to opinions discreditedly arrived at.

In the twelfth century the Cistercians attempted to leapfrog the detritus of centuries and return to a more primitive observance of the *Rule*. Yet they were viewed by traditional Black Monks as purveyors of novelties, presumptuously dissatisfied with the status quo, violators of the *Rule* they claimed to follow. As a result an insoluble and meaningless argument developed which had as its only effects, the politicization of monastic observance, and the introduction of a polarity between "return to the sources" and *aggiornamento*. Nowadays a cease-fire exists between Benedictines and Cistercians; I am not sure whether a peace treaty has been signed.

A similar situation is found today among the Strict Observance Cistercians (Trappists) and those Cistercian congregations that chose to follow what used to be called the "Common Observance." Which group can claim historical continuity with the reform of 1098? The Trappists own the real estate of the monastery of Cîteaux, and allege a closer approximation to the original lifestyle. The Order of Cîteaux regards the self-styled "reformed Cistercians" as a group that, in the nineteenth-century, broke away from the ongoing Cistercian reality to form a new Order. Which are the "old" Cistercians and which are the "new"? Who are the "real" Cistercians? Which is the more faithful embodiment of the Cistercian charism? How long is a piece of string?

"Creative fidelity" may seem to some like an oxymoron, but perhaps it is really tautology. Is it possible to have a fidelity that is not creative? It has been argued that the great Trinitarian and Christological heresies of the first millennium were all conservative heresies. Their adherents refused to go beyond the limits fixed by the penultimate Council. It was only the latest Council that was rejected. If the Church, theology and monastic life are essentially developing realities, then lagging behind becomes a clear danger and a temptation. Of course "progressives" can go too far also, but their appeal is mostly limited to the already-disenchanted. Those who resist change see themselves as defenders rather than attackers, armed for their task with the powerful weapons of nostalgia and sentiment and preying on the dread that is near-universal in confronting the unknown.

It has been my explicit intention in this article to argue that the *Rule of Benedict* is a text that creates a favorable environment for ongoing change and to imply that those periods of history were the most life-giving when Benedictinism responded positively and energetically to the special situation in which it was placed. No single expression of Benedictinism is universally normative. Like some good wines monasticism does not travel well—it is best in the place it is created.

Returning to the recently-resurrected Brother Petroc, we have to admit that almost every element of *conversatio* has changed while he slept: from the beds to the habits to the monks' philosophy of life. Yet perhaps we can qualify this statement with a distinction much in favor when the novel appeared. Benedictinism remains formally the same even though there have been many material changes. Just as it was commonly said that form is educed from the potentiality of matter, so from the raw materials of modern man the Spirit has produced many unique and unrepeatable species of monkhood—of which St Benedict probably would have been proud.

NOTES

[1] M. Casey, "Ascetic and Ecclesial: Reflections on RB 73.5," *TJ* 28 (1985), pp. 14-23.

[2] "A line-by-line, word-by-word analysis must be undertaken.... The hardest thing of all is the simplest to formulate: every word must be understood. It is hard because the eye tends to skip over just those things which are the most shocking or most call into question our way of looking at things.... The argument or example that seems irrelevant, trivial or boring is precisely the one most likely to be a sign of what is outside one's framework and which it calls into question. One passes over such things unless one takes pencil and paper, outlines, counts, stops at everything and tries to wonder." Allan Bloom, "The Study of Texts" in *Giants and Dwarfs: Essays 1960-1990*, (New York: Simon and Schuster, 1990), pp. 306-307.

[3] The two tendencies may be paralleled with what Giles Constable has termed "backward-looking" reform and "forward-looking" reform. "Both of these views of *reformatio* are strongly historical, but in different ways. One stresses a point in the past, where the Church should strive to remain or to return to; the other stresses changing circumstances in the present and the future, in accordance with which the Church must change." "Reformatio" in *Religious Life and Thought (11th- 12th centuries)* (London: Variorum Reprints, 1979), Article II; (p. 332 in the original pagination).

[4] The seriousness of Benedict's indebtedness to Basil is argued by Jean Gribomont in "The Commentaries of Adalbert de Vogüé and the Great Monastic Tradition," *ABR* 36.3 (1985), pp. 229-262. See also A. de Vogüé, "Entre Basile et Benoît: L'*Admonitio ad filium spiritualem* du Pseudo-Basile," *RBS* 10/11 (1981/82), pp. 19-34.

[5] I appreciate the point made by Columba Stewart that these terms can be descriptive of successive levels of spiritual progress rather than different external

lifestyles. "Another example of monastic allegory was Cassian's use of labels such as 'cenobitic' and 'anchoritic'. The words have obvious meanings based on common usage, but they also denote developmental stages within any form of monastic life." *Cassian the Monk* (New York, Oxford University Press, 1998), p. 28.

[6] Benedict would most likely have been familiar with the Latin version of Rufinus done about 396. Klaus Zelzer [ed.], *Basili Regula a Rufino Latine versa* (*CSEL* 86; Vienna: Hoelder-Pichler-Tempsky, 1986).

[7] See M. Casey, "'Balance' in Monastic Life," *TJ* 9 (1975), pp. 5-11. "The Benedictine Balances," in *Saint Benedict of Nursia: A Way of Wisdom for Today* (Paris: Éditions du Signe, 1994), pp. 24-25.

[8] "The goal of liberation is the creation of a new level of consciousness capable of synthesizing and of transforming the existing order. When conflict is conceived of in a dualistic system, the opposing systems are seen as irreconcilable—light against darkness, spirit against flesh. But the Hegelian concept of liberation does not involve the annihilation of one pole by the other. Instead a new identity emerges which is strong enough to appropriate the strengths of the dominant ethos, and then to synthesize them with the energies of the antithetical pole." Nancy Tenfelde Clasby, "Malcolm X and Liberation Theology," *Cross Currents* 38.2 (Summer 1988), pp. 173-184; p. 178.

[9] For a simple discussion on the distinction see Paul F. Bradshaw, *Two Ways of Praying* (Nashville: Abingdon Press, 1995) pp. 13-26. The divergence in liturgical style is best viewed in the extremes—with medieval Cluny at one end of the spectrum and Cistercian, Carthusian and Vallombrosan practices at the other. There is a contrast between rich ceremonial on the one hand and apophatic simplicity on the other. In a more contemporary analysis, the distinguishing elements of a

Western "monastic" liturgy include: a) priority given to a *nocturnal* office of Vigils, b) emphasis on the importance of all three Minor Hours as a means to continual prayer, c) use of the *whole* Psalter on a one-week or two-week cycle, d) tendency to *lectio continua* of Scripture and to leaving readings unedited and unexcerpted, e) ferial focus: its true nature is revealed in daily sobriety rather than in solemn celebration.

[10] To say that the line of distinction approximates that which divides White Monks from Black Monks is too facile to be of much utility.

[11] Even feasting. The youthful Benedict was rebuked by Romanus for fasting at Easter: Gregory the Great, *Dialogues* 2, 1, 7 (*SChr* 260, p. 134). In the course of the Cistercian-Cluniac controversy the author of the *Riposte* (ed. A. Wilmart in *RBén* 46 [1934], pp. 309-344) countered the criticism of feast day treats by saying "It is human—*humanum est*" (line 590, p. 324).

[12] The two traditional remedies for institutionalized inertia have been the regular visitation of the community by a monastic outsider, and supervision by a general chapter.

[13] It is probably true that a monastic philosophy developed in isolation from contemporary thought and vocabulary will, at first, attract by its exoticism, but later become alienating. A theology that is centered on real life is necessarily open to whatever influences life. That means that it continually draws popular beliefs and devotions into itself and monasticates, them. "La théologie monastique avait un caractère pastorale prononcé, parce que doctrine et vie y étaient dans une harmonie réciproque. De ce fait, elle était très ouverte aux idées qui vivaient dans le peuple." A. H. Bredero, "Le moyen âge et le purgatoire," *Revue d'histoire ecclésiastique* 78.2 (1983), p. 445.

[14] This phrase is a more adventurous rendering of *secundum...positionem loci* than the usual "according to...local conditions."

[15] Danièle Choisselet and Placide Vernet, *Les "Eccclesiastica Officia" cisterciens du XIIème siècle* (Reiningue: La Documentation Cistercienne, 1989); 84.32, p. 244.

[16] See M. Casey, "*'Quod experimento didicimus*': The Heuristic Wisdom of Saint Benedict," *TJ* 48 (1995), pp. 3-22. pp. The first section is entitled "Less than Perfect Legislation." The following paragraph is from pg. 20: "Not only does Benedict preach toleration to his monks (72,5) but he also practices it. Of differences he does not complain but accepts them as part of the fabric of life. In any community there is variety in age (30,1; 37,1-3), status (2,18), education (8,3), personality (2,31-32), grace (40,1-2), inspiration (20,4; 49,6), health (36,1-10; 39,1-2), strength (48,24-25), subjective disposition (2,12; 2,24-29; 31,6-7). Benedict takes this for granted and tries to frame his recommendations in terms that include such a range of personal possibilities."

[17] *RB* 4,14-16. May St Benedict forgive me for changing the context of this quotation! He uses it of the monk's obedience to God's will manifested through the abbot's orders. I use it of the abbot's obedience to God's will manifested through the reality of genuine human need.

[18] When monks of Vicovaro wished to poison St Benedict, they emptied their potion into the wine, presumably with the certainty that it would not go undrunk.

[19] Bernard of Clairvaux, "Second Sermon for Septuagesima, 3"; *SBO IV* (Rome: Editiones Cistercienses, 1966) pg. 352, lines 11-14.

[20] Diane Vaughan, in her study *Uncoupling: How and Why Relationships Come Apart* (London:Methuen, 1988), gives a descriptive analysis of marital and other relational breakdown. She locates the beginning of the process in a certain secretiveness that conceals the fact that

the person feels uncomfortable in the situation. If the secretiveness is broken and the difficulty exposed to view, dialogue and negotiation can often prevent it from reaching a point where it will destroy the relationship. There are probably lessons for monastic formation in this.

THE BENEDICTINE COMMUNITY

STRANGERS TO WORLDLY WAYS: *RB* 4,20

This article from Tjurunga *29 (1985) explores the monastic value of "separation from the world" from the standpoint of Benedict's Rule. It concludes that, although seclusion was an important observance for Benedict, the heart of this practice was a change in beliefs and values that is demonstrated in "unworldly" behavior. This evangelical distinctiveness will be expressed differently in particular circumstances, but it remains a constitutive element of the Benedictine community.*

I. The Question at Issue

One of the more difficult questions facing the Church and religious life is the determination of sound theological and pastoral principles to govern the relationship between the Christian community and that remnant of the human race which remains, as it were, "outside the fold." What relationship should exist between the Church and "the world"?

The instinctive answer is probably the most important element in a solution. The Church can have only one attitude toward the world and that is the attitude of evangelization. The Church exists for-the-world; its very definition includes that it is sent into the world, as

Christ himself was thus sent. If the world outside the Church did not exist, then the Church in its present form would disappear. The Church exists only in function of the task of evangelization.

This missionary stance has three irreducible components:

> a. The positive proclamation by word and example of the Gospel, and the preaching of the centrality of the person of Jesus Christ, to every human being irrespective of culture or social condition.
>
> b. The affirmation and acceptance of all that is good in "pre-Christian" culture and its incorporation in an ever-new Christian synthesis through the instrumentality of reverent, yet discerning, dialogue.
>
> c. The rejection and condemnation of all that cannot be harmonized with the Gospel. This includes not only those palpable evils such as superstition and violence in all their myriad forms, both subtle and blatant, but also those less distinguishable attitudes which prevent growth by cocooning people in complacency and dull their sensitivity to the need for change.

The first two items are reasonably well-established in the conventional church wisdom of the post-conciliar period. *Lumen Gentium* and *Gaudium et Spes* are in the process of re-orienting our thought and may well begin to produce fruit by the end of the century. The question of rejecting what is evil, of "calling lies "lies" and abominations "abominations" is rather more difficult. Partly this is because we have had a surfeit of facile condemnations in the past (which is where many church leaders continue to operate), and partly it comes from the intrinsic heroism required for such a task. If a denunciation really derives from the Gospel and not from personal psychological quirks, then it needs to be buttressed by large measures of prudence and moral courage—two virtues that rarely co-exist. It has to be stated, however, that the disciples of one who drove the traders from the Temple and pronounced a litany of woes against an unbelieving people, cannot afford to be less than uncompromising in their refusal of anything that distorts the Gospel, or in any way quenches the vitality of the human spirit. The fact that no one is saved without suffering does not excuse us from having, as a priority, the minimalization of pain in the lives of those whom God has created. This means not only the service of tending the wounded but also the task of defending them from attack by confronting the sources of error and oppression with the truth and justice of the Gospel.

To be "the salt of the earth" it is not enough to do good; we must also avoid evil. This means that we have to invest a certain amount of energy in resisting "that spirit of vanity and malice which transforms into an instrument of sin those human energies intended for the service of God and people."[1] We cannot attain to evangelical living by drifting; a certain amount of positive assertion is necessary. We have to take active steps against our acceptance of the goals and methods of the prevailing bourgeois philosophy of life as normal and desirable. True followers of Christ cannot be anything but distinctive.

This is what the New Testament means when it preaches a renunciation of "the world."[2] It is not demanding that we remove ourselves physically—by going to the moon, perhaps. It does not even insist on our becoming recluses to the extent that the possibility of our acting as salt or leaven would be voided. It is more a matter of *behavioral distance*—Christians refuse to act as unbelievers act when they sin. More fundamentally, what is involved is having a new way of looking at life. To act habitually as a Christian one needs a Christian philosophy of life, with beliefs and values shaped by the Gospel. It is a question of complete change of heart and mind, a *metanoia*. When Maximus the

Confessor wishes to distinguish between monks and worldlings, his criterion is not where they live or what they wear, but what fills their *minds*. "Worldlings are those who allow their minds to rest in material things.... A monk is one who separates his mind from material things and by self-mastery, psalmody and prayer, devotes himself to God."[3] The difference in identity and action is determined by the contents of the mind and heart. "Where your treasure is, there will your heart be also."

The question of separation from the world in the Benedictine Rule needs to be treated from this perspective. It is a fundamental and perhaps even constitutive monastic observance, but its importance derives from its universal applicability to all who accept the Gospel rather than from the peculiar forms which monasticism has developed in order to express this value.[4]

In fact there are a number of fairly basic problems associated with separation from the world which demand that those in monastic life re-assess their practice in the light of the Gospel and in submission to the Church's understanding of the monastic role in the world of evangelization.

> a. Firstly, it has to be admitted that the *Rule of Saint Benedict* is a bit weak when it comes to evangelization. Missionary attitudes are not a priority in the text itself. This defect can be corrected by reading the *Rule* in the context of its ecclesial sources[5] and with regard to the way in which monasteries following this rule have, throughout the centuries, often been animated by a genuine zeal for the Kingdom of God, which expressed itself in a monastic form of evangelization.[6] The charism itself is sound, but the text of the *Rule* needs to be supplemented.
>
> b. Perhaps monastic men and women need to identify themselves a little more closely with the Church, seeing themselves as organs of its work—not an élite doing

something different for their own advantage, but rather the Church at prayer.[7]

c. It is important that the concrete expressions of separation from the world are not identified with the fundamental value itself. Sometimes enclosure can be a cloak for an unwillingness to deal with the unpredictable and one might be excused for thinking that a "heroic" fidelity to enclosure may be an undiagnosed case of agoraphobia. The placid rhythms of the so-called contemplative life can suit those who prefer not to exert themselves very much and who, in other circumstances, might be called idle. Sometimes a closed community appeals to those who enjoy a situation in which authoritarianism and emotional dependence can thrive unchallenged—to say nothing of heresy and error. This is not to intimate that every enclosed community is a Port Royal, or an asylum or a country club, but it is to recognize that sometimes it is very difficult to maintain enthusiasm and to keep on the right track, without outside contacts of a substantial nature. Separation from the world is primarily a matter of the avoidance of worldly values and actions not their transposition into an enclosed situation. Observances are designed to aid evangelical living not to set up a life-style which substitutes for it.

There can be no doubt that there is scope for an institutionalized expression of separation from the world and that this can be of great utility to the members in following the Gospel. We have, however, to ask ourselves what form this institutional expression will take, having due regard to the changed reality of life today. A day spent reading newspapers, absorbed in radio and television and given to idle communication in the guest-house, or by telephone or letter, does not become less "worldly" by virtue of the fact that one does not leave the monastery precincts. It is not the keeping of enclosure that is significant, but what one does inside.

It is because there are so many questions that can be asked in the spheres of both theory and practice that it is good to leave them aside for a moment and to turn to the *Rule of Benedict* and to ask ourselves what his teaching was on this matter about which we are called to discern.

II. The Rule of Benedict

There can be no real doubt that the monastic situation envisaged by St Benedict entailed a solid amount of physical separation. This is reflected in his choice of a site for his monastery on top of a mountain but perhaps it is also a comment on the chaotic conditions experienced in sixth-century Italy. But there is a spiritual side to it. The monastery was seen as having the responsibility of providing for the monk that stability which would enable him, with the passage of the years, to become a man of *gravitas*, a person of depth. Worldliness is the opposite of this; it is giddiness, superficiality, frivolity, immaturity.

There is, accordingly, a negative campaign waged in the monastery against everything that would keep the monk mobile, on the understanding that wisdom is only possible when the monk settles down and lets his mind and emotions become calm.

> a. The monk closes off alternative futures by making a solemn promise to God to remain in this particular monastery until his death (58,15-16).
>
> b. The monk understands that his way of life does not permit him freedom of movement outside the monastery. It is inside the monastery precincts that the action will take place (1,11; 4,78; 66,7) and if he does go abroad it will only be at his abbot's bidding and according to his instructions (Chs. 50, 51, 67).
>
> c. Benedict takes steps to restrict the flow of worldly news in the community (67,5).

d. Monks are not permitted indiscriminately to mingle with visitors or guests, but only as they are appointed to do so by the abbot (53,24). The guesthouse is to be administered by one who is god-fearing and wise (53,21-22) and the one assigned to be porter is to be old, wise and possessed of *maturitas* (66,1).

e. There is no room in Benedict's monastery for jokes and fun (6,8; 7,59; 49,7).

f. Benedict likewise shows himself set against theological novelties; his insistence on solid orthodoxy is noteworthy (9,8; cf. 73,5). Furthermore he shows a marked preference for sobriety even in the expression of standard tenets of the faith, as instanced in his toning down of the Master's eschatological lyricism at the end of the chapter on humility.

g. There is no room for novelty or innovation in the day-to-day life of the monks; most things are done *per ordinem* (11,2; 13,12; 18,5; 47,2; 48,15; 63,4; etc.).

h. Worldly systems of rank and preferment end at the monastery gate: guests who are poor are to be given special attention (53,15), and no distinctions are to be made among monks on the basis of worldly condition or dignity (2,18-20; 63,8).

i. The avarice or cupidity which is the goal of worldly work is not to be found in the monastery: monks are to sell their produce at a price deliberately lower than that asked by seculars (57,7-9).

j. Monks are not permitted to receive letters and pious tokens from the outside (54,1-5).

k. Benedict carefully takes measures to ensure that party politics and divisions inside the community do not distract the monks from their real purpose, and thus divert their energies into siding with one faction or the other (65,9).

l. It is a little difficult to establish how closely Benedict believed the world to be allied with the devil. Certainly he prescribes prayer in the greeting of one coming from outside in case the devil is at work (53,5). Also the monk who leaves is thought to have done so at the devil's suggestion (58,28). However, the evidence is too sparse for a solid conclusion.

In the light of this, it is surprising to read in an article by Dom Victor Dammertz that "Benedict, the 'master of civilization' (Paul VI) has no place for *fuga mundi*, flight from the world."⁸ Admittedly the former Abbot Primate then goes on to interpret this term as "a contempt for human values"—a sense insufficiently nuanced. But the fact is that Benedict did not desire his monks to be anything else but "unworldly" and perhaps even "other-worldly." He wanted them to breathe the atmosphere of the Kingdom of God rather than be the playthings of human opinion and desire.

To make progress along this way, stability was of the utmost importance. This was, if we accept an Evagrian-Cassianic approach, primarily a *stabilitas mentis*, a solidity or steadiness of mind. It was the opposite of mobility of mind. *Stabilitas loci* or stability of place, staying in one community or monastery, was one means to this end; it was not itself the goal.

Separation from the world is thus seen to be more a matter of working toward an evenness of life in which prayer becomes possible. It is in the avoidance of meaningless mental stimulation rather than a question of bodily location. We see the same teaching in St Bernard of Clairvaux, who was certainly not a light-minded man, although he was a well-traveled one. Not only does he accept Benedict's list of things to be avoided, he makes it even more specific by his satire on monks who spend their time seeking novelties, the victims of curiosity, inquisitiveness and sheer busybodiness.⁹ Ambition too is an unwarranted diversion of energies.¹⁰ The practice of dialectic, and the effort of a philosophy not oriented toward living, he regards as pernicious for monks, a waste of time and a real abandonment of their vocation.¹¹ Thus his aesthetics of austerity, music "without frills," buildings without pretentiousness and cloisters without all the entertaining "cartoons" that were then coming into vogue.¹² To advance in prayer, inner quiet is needed, and this state is aided by the monastic environment and supported by monastic values.

In the light of Benedict's general approach, perhaps it may now be possible to understand what he means when he includes among the "instruments of good works" one which instructs the monk that he should be "a stranger to worldly ways," (4,20).

III. The Instruments of Good Works

Reflecting on the last verse of this chapter (4,78), it becomes apparent that what is intended when Benedict reproduces the Master's list of elements of monastic *conversatio* is to give concrete shape and form to what goes on behind monastery walls. In fact **all** the series could be seen as a potential description of what it means to be "a stranger to worldly ways."

We do, however, have some glimpse into the author's mind by looking more closely at the instruments which have been assembled in the immediate vicinity of 4,20. Whether it is an accident, or the result of some unconscious association of ideas or some latent structuring, we do have a rather precise notion of *fuga mundi* formulated in the group of aphorisms running from 4,10 to 4,33. It is worth looking at this bloc and its sub-units in closer detail.

Perhaps a schematic presentation might make the import of this bloc more apparent:

Principle:	4,20	Alienation from worldly behavior
Inverse Statement:	4,21	Priority of loving Christ
Application 1:	4,10-13	Restraint of pleasure
Application 2:	4,14-19	Service to the needy
Application 3:	4,22-28	Personal wholeness
Application 4:	4,29-33	Forgiveness of others

To understand the teaching of the *Rule of Benedict* on separation from the world, it is necessary to see it in this light. Separation from the world is not primarily an act of distancing or detachment, but an act of joining oneself to Christ and to the holy community: an act of attachment. Perhaps this is where some of the medievals went a little wrong with their robust usage of such terms as *fuga mundi* and even *contemptus mundi*. No Christian can scorn the world for which Christ died; he can however refuse to accept its unevangelized standards of behavior. This rejection in itself is not primary in the monastic vocation—anybody with eyes can see how empty and mindless many of the preoccupations of our society are. What is of fundamental importance is rather the desire to attach oneself to Christ and the conviction that this union is achieved through membership in a particular community in the Church.

The reading from St Jerome for the Common of Abbots in the former breviary used to make this point repeatedly throughout the year. "Christ did not say simply 'You who have left all things'. For Krates the philosopher (who went around naked) and many others have despised riches. But he added what is proper to Apostles and believers: 'And have followed me'."[13]

A first definition or description of what Benedict understands as alienation from worldly ways would have to include the rejection of anything that would deny absolute priority to our love for Christ. Anything that would get in the way of our responding to his love, anything that would prevent us from expressing the love that we have for him. This is the ultimate unworldliness, that we do not allow anything in this passing aeon to restrict us to the here and now activities which fall in the sphere of material stimulus and response. The monk is called to break loose from the fetters of time and to live already with free access to eternity.

This is why he takes a vow to live as though in heaven—*conversatio nostra in coelis est*.

The first way in which the monk shows himself distinct from those whose commonwealth is on earth is by his attitude to pleasure. Renunciation is an evangelical imperative which is applicable to all Christians. It is not blind and automatic "nay-saying," but an attempt to eliminate anything that could obstruct, distract from or substitute for the love of Christ. So, Benedict demands abnegation, but to it he adds its purpose: *ut sequatur Christum*. For those who would like to interpret this principle as some harmless, fluffy reality without any bite, he makes the matter more specific. It means disciplining the body and its impulses, on the one hand, and not embracing delights, on the other. Perhaps there is here more than a question of not pampering oneself. Great emphasis was placed in Latin spirituality, especially after the time of Augustine, on the role of "delight" in leading people to God. It is true that sometimes persons are led to God by the goads of fear and remorse. More often they are induced to make a beginning, and are subsequently supported and guided, by their experience of the sweetness of the Lord. To taste this spiritual joy a certain lack of alternative delights is necessary. Hence the injunction to eschew delights is a reminder that if we are to be led and encouraged by consolation (to use a much later word) then we need to become free from the tyranny of the pleasure principle. Thus we are called on to practice fasting and more, to love it—really to appreciate that the way of the desert is a good and noble thing. To walk it is not an achievement but a privilege and gift. Later instruments fill out the picture: not to love food and drink (4,35-36), not to be lazy (4,37-38), to avoid frivolous and emptying gossip (4,52-54), not to fulfill the desires of the flesh (4,59) and to love chastity (4,64). There is no question here of masochism nor of a mindless puritanism, but a clear assertion that if the monk is to make his way to God he needs to disembarrass himself of whatever will slow him down and will have to be abandoned eventually in any case. Whatever helps and supports him on the way is good; whatever disguises the clear options he has to make is bad. There is need here for considerable discretion, and a lot of confidence in the instincts which a healthy community develops over the years so that it can judge what is within the range of acceptable monastic behavior and what is not.

The 25th Chapter of Matthew's Gospel is never far from the thoughts of Christian behavioralists. It is not enough to be a successful ascetic, even if it means that one is single-mindedly seeking God. There is a second commandment which ensures that we do not try to journey alone. Attention to the things of God leads us to tend the needs of our brothers and sisters. Hence, a second group of instruments reminds us of our obligations to the poor, the needy and the unwell. The corporal works of mercy are always a good indication that the ascetic is genuine. The breadth of God's love for us is mirrored in our willingness to give ourselves to the undeserving and unresponsive. We go to be with them, we help them, we give them consolation. Here we have a principle which is as destructive of selfishness as the practice of renunciation and mortification. By offering ourselves in service, by putting ourselves out for others, we are freed from the domination of our own immature need for comfort. This has always been one of the puzzles of the Christian way: why is it that a person makes greater progress on the way to God through self-forgetfulness and service than through teeth-gritting determination? Whatever the reason, it does seem to be a fact. Of one thing there can be no doubt: worldly behavior does not include selfless serving of others; the monk distinguishes himself by his willingness to serve.

The third distinguishing feature of a monk is integrity. He is called upon to renounce all those petty reactions which contradict the truth of his being and the reality of his vocation. Not to allow his anger to rampage uncontrolled. Not to nurse a grudge. Not to be deceitful or untruthful either in himself or outwardly. As we read a little later, not to wish to be called holy before being so in fact (4,62). Not to live a lie through false peace and feigned charity, but to live the truth. It was Bernard of Clairvaux who was to exploit most effectively the idea that real humility is nothing more than a progressive submission to truth, and that it is truth which sets us free, makes us whole, and provides the foundation for a life of genuine peace and love.[14] In a world beset by trickery in so many forms, the monk is called to the practice of integrity and truth—he is not to concentrate on "image" and "packaging" but to give his life to the reality beneath.

The final sub-unit concerns the monk's reactions to the fact that the ideal life is rarely achieved and the consequent existence of conflict, disharmony and even violence. His response is a generous, unflinching patience—quite at odds with the anticipated secular response to being victimized. He does not return evil or initiate it. He bears it patiently and loves his enemies. This is the Christian Gospel; it is not the way of the world. Endurance, gentleness and non-violence are integral parts of the monastic separation from the world.

Looking at these blocs of text it becomes apparent that, for Benedict, separation from the world was not a matter of physical observances so much as solid behavioral adhesion to the principles of the Gospel. It can, of course, be argued that paying too much attention to literary structures can be misleading. So it can. But sometimes the structural analysis of a text does produce significant coincidence, as it does in this case. It may be that the Master and Benedict picked all the instruments of good works "out of a hat" and that what we have here is a completely random listing. It is more than that. There is no overall plan, but there seems to be a number of minor groupings within the whole—sometimes quarried from widely disparate sources. These minor groupings may not represent an explicit, reasoned progression, but they can be the result of an intuitive association of ideas, which causes one bloc to be laid beside another and perhaps a number of blocs put in orbit around a central item. It is an unconscious process, and perhaps all the more valuable for being so, since it enables us to see the whole person at work, rather than merely his head and pen.

There is much more that could be said about separation from the world. One could develop the New Testament teaching to all Christians and see it contained in the baptismal commitment of all the faithful. Or one could develop the creative potential of "evangelical distinctiveness" as I have done elsewhere.[15] Here one concern is paramount: to demonstrate that, for Benedict, separation from the world is of fundamental importance, that it is a matter of values and behavior rather than of precise physical structures, and that there is about his whole approach a strong evangelical character, which accords perfectly with the other elements of his spiritual doctrine.

NOTES

[1] *Pastoral Constitution on the Church in the Modern World, (Gaudium et Spes),* #37.

[2] Cf. Rom 12:2, James 4:4, 1 Jn 2:12, Lk 16:15.

[3] Maximus the Confessor, *Centuries on Charity,* 2.53-54.

[4] "Peculiar" does mean "particular and proper," but it can also apply in a special way to some of the bars, grilles and spikes I have observed in certain non-Benedictine enclosed convents.

[5] Cf. M. Casey, "Ascetic and Ecclesial: Reflections on *RB* 73.5," *TJ* 28 (1985), pp. 14-23.

[6] Cf. M. Casey, "*RB* Then and Now: Principles of Interpretation and Application," *Benedictines* XXXVI.2 (1981-1982), pp. 10-15.

[7] There is no grace to be found in "separation from the Church," no matter how "worldly" the Church may appear.

[8] Victor Dammertz, "St. Benedict, Master of Religious Life," *Consecrated Life* 6.2 (1982), pp. 243-256; p. 251.

[9] Cf. Bernard of Clairvaux, *Hum* 28-30; *SBO* 3.38-40.

[10] Cf. Bernard of Clairvaux, *Conv* 30; *SBO* 4.106.11-12, *Conv* 32; *SBO* 4.109-110, *Conv* 38; *SBO* 4.114.13-14, *Conv* 40; *SBO* 4.115.19-22.

[11] Cf. Bernard of Clairvaux, *SC* 43.4; *SBO* 2.43.21, *SC* 36.1; *SBO* 2.4.4-5, *PP* 1.3; *SBO* 5.189-190, *SC* 41.1; *SBO* 2.29.8-9, *SC* 58.7; *SBO* 2.131.26, *SC* 79.4; *SBO* 2.274.21, *SC* 33.8; *SBO* 1.239.19-22.

[12] Cf. Bernard of Clairvaux, *Apo* 28-29; *SBO* 3.104-107, *Prologus in Antiphonarium, SBO* 3.515-516, *Ep* 398; *SBO* 8.377-379.

[13] Readings for the third nocturn of the Common of Abbots from St. Jerome's third book *On Matthew's Gospel,* commenting on chapter 19, verse 27.

[14] Cf. Bernard of Clairvaux, *Hum* 1.1; *SBO* 3.16.23-24 and subsequently developed throughout the first part of the treatise.

[15] Cf. M. Casey, "The Monk in the Modern World," *TJ* 21 (1981), pp. 5-24.

"COMMUNITY" IN THE BENEDICTINE RULE

This article was prepared in 1980 for the Third International Regula Benedicti Congress in Kremsmünster. It examines the cenobitic credentials of Benedictine conversatio *and concludes that there is much that we can learn from tradition. The essay appeared in* Regulae Benedicti Studia 8/9 (1982) *and was translated in* Monastische Informationem 26 (1981).

To many contemporary readers, St Benedict's model of community life appears rigid and formal. It seems like a system which is governed by innumerable rules and sanctions without any reference to the aspirations and capabilities of its members and liable to generate in them a strong sense of alienation and estrangement. The community seems to exist apart from the persons who are its components, subsisting only through massive recourse to authority and by steadfastly resisting any challenges to change which come to it from the "outside."

It cannot be denied that the traditional Benedictine community is often defective when measured according to modern standards of spontaneity, affectivity and supportiveness. Some communities have tried to remedy this defect by undertaking a program of "building community." Some success has followed such efforts, especially in those cases where a strong community sense pre-existed the projects. Perhaps more solid progress may have been achieved, however, if care had been taken to identify and strengthen those elements in the Benedictine tradition which promote creative communal living, rather than introducing values and practices which have no organic link with the received patterns of Benedictine *conversatio*.

There is a specific Benedictine emphasis on community life which is worth cultivating. It represents a minority viewpoint in society and in the Church. This is so, not because it is not feasible or untrue, but because Benedictines themselves have failed to understand and to propagate their distinctive heritage.

In this paper I should like to touch upon some important emphases in Benedictine monastic life which contribute to the emergence and growth of authentic Christian community.

1. *Unanimity*

To a large extent, monks may be presumed to share a common philosophy of life. All alike desire to live in accordance with the teachings of the Gospel. Fidelity to evangelical principles and personal loyalty to Christ are the factors which lead to a man's becoming a monk. Throughout his life they remain the surest source of unity with his brothers. United with Christ and faithful to the fundamental priorities of Christian life, the monk discovers his deep personal union with those who journey along the same path. To be with Christ is simultaneously to be with all those who share his life.

In this view, the primary dynamic of community is not the result of processes internal to the group itself. It is, rather, the outcome of a relationship with One who stands without. In the words of Antoine de Saint-Exupéry's much-quoted dictum: "Love is not a matter of looking at each other, but of looking together in the same direction." To the extent that monks are animated by true zeal for God's kingdom, communal life poses few problems. On the other hand, when a community recedes from this ideal, divisions and deviations manifest themselves and the community becomes prey to its own politics.

It is in view of this common fund of beliefs, values and standards that formation assumes an importance. Men come to a community from different backgrounds. If they are to co-exist creatively and harmoniously, a certain "fusion of horizons" is necessary. Through its daily life, through its teaching and through the interventions of authority, a community has to provide each of its members with a philosophy of life which is both distinctive to individuals and recognizably communal.[1] The first requirement of community is a comprehensive philosophy: concrete and distinctive enough to serve as a basis for unity, yet sufficiently flexible to accommodate a healthy variety of viewpoints.

It is noteworthy that many of the communities who experience difficulty in communal living are those which have under-estimated or neglected the role of teaching within the community. Specifically, they have failed to take seriously St Benedict's injunction that the abbot buttress his exercise of authority with the creation of a climate of meaning by his example and by instruction. It is not enough to import experts from outside the community or to rely on professional qualifications already achieved. An abbot is obliged constantly and patiently to expound the divine law to his monks, relating it to their changing situations and challenging them to keep responding to it.

A man was asked to make a fundamental decision concerning his willingness to accept the community's concrete philosophy before he became a monk.[2] During his period of probation he was exposed to the life to which he aspired, told of its liabilities and asked to choose between accepting it in its facticity and freely going away. If he decided to remain, it was understood that he accepted to live according to what the community believed.

In a world which seemed more static than ours, such a choice made freely by an adult could realistically be expected to last a lifetime. For us who are subject to greater change, it is important that this initial act of choice be constantly renewed; we need to insure that individual growth does not isolate us from general community development. Being with the community, participating in its tasks, listening to its teaching and accepting its authority afford the possibility not only of drawing from but also of contributing to its common fund of wisdom. To be of one heart we need first to be of one mind concerning the practice of monastic theory. To the extent that such unanimity is lacking, daily life becomes the occasion for self-perpetuating pre-judgments and uncreative conflicts.

2. Solitary Values

Basic agreement about primary principles does not mean that the Benedictine community becomes totalitarian in its demands for uniformity. Ideology and oppression have no role to play. Mindless conformity is not an aid to community, but its denial. Healthy communal interaction is only possible between unrepressed adults who are prepared to grant others the freedom to be themselves. If it is true that "Benedictine monasteries for all their appearance of uniformity and calm, tend to be full of enthusiastic eccentrics,"[3] then it seems likely that community life can be very interesting indeed.

In his description of the abbot's attitude toward his monks, Benedict repeatedly insists that he treat his monks as individuals, modifying his actions to suit their dispositions and encouraging all, irrespective of their degree, to keep responding to grace. "Let him so order all things that the strong may desire more and the weak may not be discouraged."[4] What is important is that the abbot help each monk to keep growing; it is not a question of enforcing a particular series of predetermined actions, but of animating each individual to greater fidelity.[5]

In a stable Benedictine community there will always be a wide range of individual responses. The neophyte cannot be expected to emulate the solid virtue of the seniors. Brothers differ in background, talents, virtues and opportunities. They are severally different men, filling distinct roles in the community. Nothing is gained by reducing them to stereotypes.

> The monastery is truly a paradise, a region fortified with the ramparts of discipline. It is a glorious thing to have men living together in the same house, following the same way of life. How good and pleasant it is when brothers live in unity! You will see one of them weeping for his sins, another rejoicing in the praise of God, another tending the needs of all and yet another giving instruction to others. Here is one brother at prayer and another at reading; here is one who is compassionate and another who inflicts penalties for sins. This one is aflame with love and this one is strong in humility. This one remains humble when everything goes well and this other one does not lose his nerve in difficulties. This one works very hard in active tasks, this other one finds quiet in contemplation.[6]

Variety adds richness to communal life and provides the possibility of creative interaction between brothers. Discipline is not a matter of imposing uniform observance, but of helping each to be free from whatever diminishes the personal content of his acts. The result of discipline is not conformity but complementarity.

Achieving the harmony between social goals and individual goals is never easy in practice. It cannot be decided once and for all, but rather a constant effort must be made to achieve dynamic balance between communal and personal values.[7] Both need to be strongly affirmed if healthy community is to result.

3. Non-Instinctuality

To an age which believes that self-expression, uninhibitedness and spontaneity are necessary aspects of an individual's life in community, the Benedictine tradition of discipline seems strange. In the monastic tradition the greatest obstacles to the growth of love are the instincts, the passions, the emotions. Unless these sub-personal forces are subjugated, personal life is retarded and love, the noblest flower of personhood, becomes impossible.

The greatest obstacle to a loving community life is the presence within the community of uncontrolled emotion. Unless disordinate movements toward self-gratification are subjected to free, personal decision, and unless the community accepts the need for *askesis* and self-discipline, no progress in "building community" is possible.

The first instinct to be confronted is the tendency to *acquisitiveness*. One obvious cause of disagreement and dispute between brothers is the clash of rival claims to the possession, use or disposal of material things. The principle of common ownership of goods is an important foundation of community. If a community has but one heart and one mind it is the effect of none claiming anything as his own. "If he claims nothing for himself, he entirely cuts off the first cause of quarrel."[8] "Monks also maintain a lasting union in intimacy and possess all things in common."[9]

Detachment from material acquisitions is reinforced when the monk allows himself to develop an indifference to his own comfort and convenience. Many breaches of community love result from the resentment caused by unscheduled interruptions, requests for help, disturbances of sleep and disappointment in matters of food and drink. A monk who is substantially detached from his own well-being is less liable to have reason to complain of his brothers.

In the area of celibacy, the monk has to guard himself against using others for the purpose of self-gratification. Associations which are not built upon authentic unselfishness can easily develop sexual connotations and serve as an escape from the demands of concrete community living.

Likewise, the monk has to avoid the transference of his acquisitive instincts into the arena of spiritual striving. It is not good for him to be too interested in what he can get out of serving God. This is to reduce himself to the level of the hireling. The psychocentric approach which has been favored in spirituality for the last four hundred years tends to produce an excessive interest in the workings of consciousness and in spiritual "experiences," which leaves the individual wide open to delusion. The more disinterested and objective approach of monastic tradition is a useful corrective here.[10] Excessive pre-occupation with private religious experiences is not a helpful factor in promoting community life.

A second instinct to be countered is the habit of *manipulation*. Exploiting others for personal advantage, whether fully conscious or not, is incompatible with genuine love. Paternalism, patronage and certain types of "supportiveness" can result in an unhealthy relationship of dependence which, in the long terms, profits neither party—notwithstanding apparent immediate gains. St Benedict seems to have been fully aware of the dangers of such situations.[11] One who helps because it feels good to be a helper is likely seeking his own, and not the other's, well-being.

In the third place, love is also impeded by *violence*. Violence is not limited to aggressive behavior; it is present in any action accompanied by intense sensual experience or passion. Lust, anger, jealousy are clearly violent states, but so too are total absorption in work, mindless enthusiasm and capitulation to depression. In every case the possibility of personal action is diminished because it does not proceed from a pure heart, dedicated to the service of God. "The last temptation was the greatest treason to do the right deed for the wrong reason."

Love is possible in a community only to the extent that individuals restrain their instincts and learn to live from the basis of personal choice, guided by grace. This is not the denial of emotion, but its ordering, *ordinatio caritatis*. *Agape* is not lacking in affective warmth, but it is deeper, more universal and ultimately less destructive than the ready movements of *eros*. And it has to be worked at.

4. Wholesomeness

In Benedict's view, the community is not defined by any specific task to which it is assigned. The quality of community life depends, rather, on its composition at any stage in its history. As a non-functional community, the Benedictine monastery is shaped largely by its present membership. To the extent that authentic variety is fostered, a rich sub-culture results which is unique, creative and eminently satisfying. Talents and skills are discovered and allowed to flower; traditions of art and culture are formed of which mankind as a whole is the beneficiary. It is not that such outcomes are deliberately sought; they are the felicitous by-products of a wholesome life lived in harmony with God and man.[12]

The phrase *ora et labora* in its primitive sense indicates something of the dual movement found in authentic Benedictine life in which neither spiritual nor physical tasks are left undone. The Benedictine monk is not a pure spirit, sustained only by the esoteric practices of the contemplative life. He lives in community, he earns his bread and he improves the world as well as giving himself to reading, reflection and prayer. There is variety; there is balance; there is *humanitas*.[13]

One of the prime requisites for fruitful community life is the absence of excessive communal introspection. A community which happily gives itself to prayer and work, grows into a unity. Over the course of years differences are reduced and where disagreement remains, tolerance and patience intervene. Thus all the brothers can live in peace, *pax*.

5. Patience and Tolerance

St Benedict's ideal of a community permeated by the spirit of the Gospel and translating into a contemporary context, the prescriptions of the ancient Fathers, is one which has attracted men and women throughout the centuries. Yet St Benedict was a realist. He takes for granted that few communities would have the fervor even to reach the "beginning" which he describes.[14] He is aware that scandals and quarrels often occur in monasteries,[15] and makes provision for every kind of human failure from oversleeping[16] to murder.[17] Monks remain sinners, and as members of a community, they are constantly called to bear the weights not only of their own offenses but of the failings of others.

To be able to live lovingly and creatively in community, a large measure of patience and tolerance is required. It is this ability not to be unnerved by the weaknesses of others that demonstrates the reality of a monk's virtue.[18] Anyone can perceive faults and denounce them; it is only the truly spiritual man who can "hate the sin yet love the sinner." Such patience quietly accepts even personal injury,[19] seeing in such hardship a means of fellowship in the sufferings of Christ.[20] Tolerance is less dramatic and demonstrative than gestures of "caring and sharing" but it is long-wearing! Without it community becomes a clique.

6. Friendship

One of the most valuable fruits resulting from a detailed comparison of Benedict's *Rule* with the *Rule of the Master* is evidence of Benedict's concern for fraternal relations. Benedict extends the ascetical ideals of Cassian and the Master, (perhaps drawing on Augustine and Basil) to make provision for interaction and companionship within the community. This "horizontalism" is clearly Benedict's own contribution.[21]

Friendship is an important theme in monastic literature from the earliest times. An initial survey of this vast topic has been published by Adele Fiske and it is to be hoped that others will continue the research.[22]

For monastic writers from Cassian to Aelred, friendship was not merely a sentimental attachment on the basis of felt attraction; it was a mature person-to-person relationship that was both comfort and challenge. A good friend was a guarantee of spiritual progress, a remedy for depression, a stimulus to good action, a correction for evil and a constant reminder of the love of God. Friendship was a goal to aim for since, according to St Aelred, God himself *is* friendship.

These points for reflection only touch upon the wealth of teaching contained in the Benedictine tradition about community. There is much more that could be said besides. Perhaps Benedict spoke little about "community" as such because he took it for granted; it is far more difficult for us who have been raised in a world characterized by individualism, social fragmentation and alienation. But it seems that there is much that we can learn from him.[23]

NOTES

[1] On this, see the papers gathered in *TJ* 14 (1977) under the heading "The Formative Influence of the Benedictine Community."

[2] *RB* 58,1-16.

[3] Dominic Milroy, "Benedictine Education," The Benedictines, supplement to: *The Tablet* (12 July 1980), XI.

[4] *RB* 64,19.

[5] Cf. M. Casey, "Discerning the True Values of Monastic Life in a Time of Change," *RBS* 3/4 (1974/75), pp. 79-81.

[6] St Bernard of Clairvaux, *Div* 42.4; *SBO* 6a.258.16-23; cf. *SC* 22.8; *SBO* 1.135.9-13.

[7] Cf. M. Casey, "'Balance' in Monastic Life," *TJ* 9 (1975), pp. 5-11.

[8] Cassian, *Conl* 16.6.

[9] Cassian, *Conl* 24.6.

[10] Cf. M. Casey, *Saint Benedict's Approach to Prayer*, CS (1980), pp. 327-343.

[11] *RB* 69,1-4; 70,1-3.

[12] Cf. M. Casey, "Saint Benedict and Civilisation," *Australasian Catholic Record* 57 (1980), pp. 359-365.

[13] Cf. M. Casey, "The 'Humanitas' of the Benedictine Tradition" in: J. S. Martin (ed.), *Benedict: A Man with an Idea*, Continuing Education Committee, Faculty of Arts, University of Melbourne, 1981.

[14] *RB* 73,1.

[15] *RB* 13,12.

[16] *RB* 11,12.

[17] *RB* 4,3.

[18] *RB* 72,5.

[19] *RB* 7,35.

[20] *RB* Prol 50.

[21] Cf. A. de Vogüé, *La communauté*, pp. 485-486.

[22] A. Fiske, *Friends and Friendship in the Monastic Tradition*, Cuernavaca 1970.

[23] Cf. M. Casey, "The Monk in the Modern World," *TJ* 21 (1981), pp. 5-24.

DISCERNMENT AND PASTORAL CARE

This article began life in 1974 as an address to the Benedictine Union of Australia and New Zealand with the title "Discerning the True Values of Monastic Life in a Time of Change." It was published in Regulae Benedicti Studia *3/4 (1974/75). Strongly marked by the experiences of the post-Conciliar period it examines the role of abbatial discernment and the special difficulties posed in a time of renewal. This article also appeared with a new title in* Hallel *6.1 (1978) and was translated in* Monastieke Informatie *9 (1977).*

The fact that it is possible to raise the question of "discerning the true values of monastic life" is, in itself, an indication that such a process is not as easy as it would seem. It leads to the conclusion that specifically "monastic" values are not at all obvious; that historical forms—traditional beliefs, values and practices—do not, of themselves, guarantee continuity with genuine monasticism; that there is a need for some manner of supplement to ensure that the heritage of the past retains its proper effectiveness in a much changed world.

The Conflict of Past and Present

On a theoretical level a solution is found in formulating an adequate hermeneutic of monastic tradition, comparable to that widely accepted in interpreting the Bible.[1] It is not sufficient simply to expound the significance a particular text had in its own setting in the past; it is also necessary to see what bearing it has on the present. It is not merely a question of what the text says, but of what it means. The fundamental task in discerning what are true monastic values consists in being open both to past and to present and in allowing both to assert themselves without inhibition. The goal aimed at in such interaction is that more of what is right may be grasped and that the particular aberrations of each period may equally be subjected to the judgment of truth.[2]

It is to be regretted that, to some degree, the vastness of the hermeneutical task defeats its purpose. The extent and complexity of monastic tradition is so considerable that it would require an army of researchers adequately to cover the material it has produced. Furthermore, the prospect of assessing the unwritten, unofficial and even underground traditions found operating in most monasteries is daunting, to say the least. And finally, when it comes to any attempt to bring together inside knowledge and scholarly research, those monks with the necessary experience for the task would generally prefer to *live* monastic life rather than to theorize about it. Some progress in this field is certainly possible but, meanwhile, life has to go on. On a practical, administrative level, short cuts have to be found.

The tension between the beliefs, values and practices of the past and those of the present is often resolved on a superficial level. Firstly, the problem can be reduced to a question of language. On the one hand, legal and historical precedents can be found for a wide range of options, and traditional concepts can be used to buttress almost any novel proposal. On the other hand, very traditional ideas and structures can be dressed up in trendy modern clothes, without any substantial alteration to the realities themselves, and the process called "renewal". Secondly, it is possible for a superior to hold together widely divergent tendencies by a combination of personal prestige and charm. In this case, the emphasis is on a diplomatic balance between conflicting elements in a community and a range of stratagems is employed to keep as many as possible happy most of the time. Finally, a superior might arrive at a working solution simply by keeping his fingers on the pulse of the community, judiciously overseeing the blending of past and present, bringing forth from his storehouses new things and old with an eye to the common good and to the welfare and progress of individuals. The trouble with this approach, otherwise so admirable, is that it tends to sacralize the *status quo*, and may unconsciously discourage any suggestion of change. To a large extent it is dependent for its effectiveness on the correspondence between the facts of life in the community and their official interpretation, and this is something that is not easy to come by. Notwithstanding centuries of exhortation to the contrary, monks are not always keen for their abbots to know too much about their private lives.

Among mature monks, whose experience spans a couple of generations, the clash between past and present is often solved at the level of a personal appreciation of monastic values. Having, in the past, engorged the whole tradition, they have eventually come to an understanding of what monastic life is all about, and how to make it work in their own case. They have developed a certain flair for distinguishing what is important from the peripheral and merely transitory and they feel at home in the monastery. For them, discarding the old and accepting something new takes place in the context of a stable and familiar core. There are fluctuations in fidelity, certainly, and deviations and delusions but, in the main, their lives are lived in conformity with their practical experience of certain perennial values. They have a criterion for evaluating different options, a norm to return to, an ideal to aim at. In all other matters they feel free.

This remains a good working solution for many monks, though it is not without its problems. In the first place, its strength is its weakness; what it gains in catering for the needs of individuals it loses in general acceptability on a community level. It can lead to a divisive individualism and unending discussion about which beliefs; values and practices are "essential." One man's meat is another man's poison! Secondly, such an approach fails to take account of the possibility that part of the tradition absorbed in the past may require adjustment. A certain complacence in past achievement may lead to insensitivity to the possibility of improvement. Thirdly, relying on personal experience and individual insight as a basis for discernment is possible only for those with insight and experience. It is inoperative as far as concerns the growing number of monks who have not been exposed to the beliefs, values and practices of the traditional well-organized monastic system; whose time of formation has coincided with a period of transition and confusion; and who sometimes regard the past simply as an obstacle in the path of progress and common sense.

All of these methods of dealing with the fact of conflict between past and present are, at root, thoroughly conservative. They succeed, to some extent, in ensuring the continuance of the beliefs, values and practices of traditional monasticism. They fail insofar as they concentrate too exclusively on the survival of historical forms and tend to be negative and defensive about innovation.[3] Rightly suspicious of introducing novelties, they fail to recognize when traditional practices have become counter-productive. The value discerned in traditional forms is sometimes measured more generously than that inherent in their alternatives.

To say this is not necessarily to fall into the opposite error of affirming that the past has passed and everything must be changed. It is the recognition of the fact that, for the most part, those who carry influence in the monastic world today were formed under the *ancien régime*. Their occupational hazard is to pay too much attention to the past, not the reverse.

It is at least arguable that this tendency is reinforced by a vision of the abbatial office, which sees him too predominantly as the upholder, and enforcer of the law, as a sort of policeman. In practice, it is thought by some that the abbot's main duty is to see that the rule is kept; to exaggerate slightly, he is seen to be on the side of the rule and the tradition and in opposition to the community, which is constantly prone to backslide.

That there is some element of truth in this conception is no excuse for its being amplified to the point of distortion. It is true that it is the abbot's duty to see that the rule is known and observed, but this is far from being his principal task. The rule, the tradition, exists independently of the abbot; it possesses its own inflexible facticity, and as such is freely accepted by the monks in their act of making profession. The task of the abbot is not to insist on the slavish accomplishment of each detail of the rule, on the contrary—to borrow a phrase of Churchill—he watches the tides and not the eddies.[4] Nor is he to consider his role mainly in terms of correction. His duty is to see that the rule is lived and he does this principally by ensuring that it is, in fact, livable. Through his efforts the past is used to enrich the present, not to dominate it or replace it. It thus becomes, in Margaret Mead's terms, "instrumental" rather than "coercive."[5]

The idea that the function of the abbacy is to apply the rule to the present, to administer it with regard to concrete circumstances, is not new. In the next section some attempt will be made to show that this seems to be the view evidenced in the *Rule of St Benedict*. In addition to personifying the authority of the rule, the abbot is called upon to exercise in his community an active ministry of care.

The Notion of "Care" in RB

Dom de Vogüé has written extensively and well of the interrelation of abbot and rule. There is, he notes, an intrinsic harmony between the two sources of authority insofar as the ultimate legitimization of both is founded on the fact that they each mediate Christ's presence in some way.[6] This concord was evident to St Benedict who saw no contradiction in insisting more than the Master both on a greater fidelity on the part of the abbot in regard to the rule and on a more generous discretionary power to suspend its directives.[7] What is of interest, as far as this present essay is concerned, is how this discretion is exercised,[8] what cardinal principle governs the process of differentiating between alternative courses of action and discerning the "true values of monastic life".

It in the notion of *care* that we find the key to Benedict's vision of the practical functioning of the abbacy. Words like *cura, sollicitudo* and *diligentia* occur more often in this connection. Care for the welfare of his monks is considered to be more important than the abbot's own spiritual life (2,39) and he is frequently reminded of his accountability in this regard (2,6 and *passim*). Although he is able to share his task of caring with others in the community, with the cellarer (31,15), the novice-master (58,7), the infirmarian (36,10), the deans (21,2) and generally with seniors *vis-à-vis* juniors (22,3; 46,6; 70,4) the ultimate and unavoidable responsibility remains his (31,9; 36,10). This care is to take precedence over all other tasks (2,33). The abbot is not to indulge his personal preferences in his dealing with his community (2,16-22) but to adapt his style to suit their behavior, *multorum servire moribus* (2,31) and their needs (2,24-29). In particular his ministry of care extends to those less able to look after themselves, delinquents (27,1), the sick (36,1, 6, 10) and poor people and pilgrims (53,15). His business is to be useful rather than to take first place (64,8) to look after weak souls rather than to institute a reign of terror over the strong (27,6). The care exercised by the abbot is not the same as fretting, for the abbot must ideally be a person not easily oppressed by anxiety (64,16). Rather it is characterized by shrewdness and industry (27,5).

The care envisaged by St Benedict seems to have been more effective than affective and he often uses the verb *gerere* in this connection (2,33; 21,2; 27,1; 27,5; 31,3; 31,9). He sums up his whole approach to this matter in one pithy sentence, "He should so moderate and arrange everything both to save souls and (to ensure) that what the brothers do they do without justified grumbling" (41,5).

The object of the abbot's care is the *total* welfare of his monks. He is to make sure that the monks are adequately clothed (55,3) and provided with everything that is necessary (33,5; 55,18-20), differentiating according to the needs of his monks (34,1-5; 55,20-21); especially concerning the weak (48,25 and *passim*). Likewise, he is to see that the food and drink of the monks are sufficient (39,6; 40,5) and that the hours of meals are appropriate (41,5). On the social level, the abbot is responsible for the smooth running of the monastic day (47,1), the arrangement of the Work of God (11,6; 18,22), and the appointment of officials: the deans (21,3), the cellarer (31,1, 15), the infirmarian (36,7), the two seniors who patrol the monastery to ensure that the brothers are engaged in reading (48,17), the monastery craftsmen (57,1-3), the novice master (58,6), priests and deacons (62,1), the prior (65,15) and generally those in positions of precedence (71,6). Wherever someone in the monastery is in need of assistance in his work it should be given to him (35,3-4; 63,18-20).

There is no evidence to suggest that St Benedict envisaged the abbot's role as merely this combination of humanitarian and administrative tasks. Fidelity to his sources obliged him to see the abbot not only as a provident *paterfamilias* but also as one who mediated Christ and who was a source of spiritual teaching for his monks.[9] By his teaching (2,4-13; 62,2,9) and that of his deans (12,4) the riches of monastic wisdom are made available in the community. Benedict considers it important that the running of the monastery be in the hands of the wise (53,22) and expects the abbot to supply where intelligence is lacking (23,4; 30,1-2; 42,4). The abbot must teach by his actions what he cannot convey in words (2,12). Above all, the abbot is frequently admonished that he ensure that the regimen of the monastery is in effective correspondence with the will of God. "Therefore the abbot should teach, lay down or order nothing that is outside the Lord's precept (2,4)." If the commands of the abbot are considered worthy of the obedience given to God's own commands (5,4), it is only on the assumption that the abbot has already made sure that the two correspond. The abbot is believed to act in place of Christ in the monastery (2,2; 63,13)[10] not because of some ontological transformation but because it is his function to discern the will of God and implement it.

If we are prepared to accept that the religious or spiritual needs of man are as real as his physical and social requirements, we must assert that it is part of the abbatial charge to ensure that these deeper needs are not neglected. St Benedict even cautions the abbot to avoid overconcern about secular and passing realities at the expense of spiritual values (2,33), on the understanding that God's kingdom is his *first* priority (2,35).

Far from being an automatic application of the rule to the situation of the moment, or the abbot's spontaneous reaction, the commands envisaged by St Benedict presuppose a great deal of preliminary activity on the part of the abbot. He is expected to perceive (61,11), to know (2,7; 64,8), to remember (2,30), to foresee (32,1; 41,4; 64,17; 55,8), to be prudent (64,12), to be cautious (61,13), to practise discretion (64,19), to reflect (65,22; 64,7), to consider (10,21; 55,3; 64,17), to weigh (3,5; 65,1), to choose (65,16), to decide (44,3; 65,14), to judge (24,2), to temper (8,4; 41,5; 41,19; 64,17; 64,19), to arrange (22,2; 65,12) and *then* to take action or give a command. It would seem that a lot of the action in discerning the will of God takes place in this preliminary processing of data; *et audiens consilium fratrum TRACTET APUD SE* (3,2). The care and solicitude of the abbot is chiefly evidenced in the seriousness and patience with which he sifts information in order to arrive at the truth.

Care and Discernment

The question of "discerning the true values of monastic life" is, then, not a new one. The difficult and wearing task (2,31) of responding to individual need was considered by St Benedict to be the most characteristic of the abbot's tasks and to constitute a formal principle in the structuring of the concrete life of the monastery. In fact, the art of discernment is the fundamental benefit that a monastery can offer to a prospective member. Without discernment confusion arises and politics take over. The past hardens into an establishment; individual needs are equated with weakness and the slightest failure to conform is regarded as a threat to the survival of the institution. Deviants are punished or dismissed; those who remain are often colorless conformists. Regularity may be maintained but creativity and verve are nowhere to be seen.

This overdrawn picture of the state of monastic life without discernment finds partial realization in many monasteries today. At the risk of laboring the obvious, several reasons might be given for this.

- *Firstly*, the process of discerning the will of God in a multiplicity of options is a demanding task. Ideally it rests upon an easy familiarity with God's ways and an ability to recognize his presence in its most unlikely manifestations. Not only is the discerner required to be a man of some spiritual experience, he must have the rarer knack of disengaging his personal attractions and preferences from those of God. The first reason for the breakdown in discernment is the dearth of spiritual men.

- *Secondly*, in many monasteries it happens that the qualities which govern the choice of an abbot and the concrete demands made upon the incumbent produce a situation in which an abbot may have little aptitude or opportunity for paying attention to alternative options and may, instead, be content with allowing the monastery to go ahead on its own momentum.

- *Thirdly*, when the abbot is viewed principally as an upholder of the law and the advocate of discipline he is reduced to being a cog in the organizational machine with little scope for initiative or flair. Even his capability for ensuring regularity and offering correction is reduced by the fact that these negative interventions occur in isolation; they tend to occur outside the context of a zeal for the realization of the full potentialities of each individual. Instead they appear simply as police action.

- *Fourthly*, the rejection of excessive paternalism has led, in many monasteries, to the position where the abbot is afraid lest he appear patronizing and the monks are resentful should he manifest any interest or solicitude about their individual welfare. It is not that abbots are not caring or that monks do not desire to experience this care. What is wrong is that there are no recognized channels in which this care may freely flow without causing discomfort or embarrassment to both parties. In many monasteries there is a reduced capability to facilitate the creative growth of the monks simply because the structures of care envisaged by St Benedict have become obsolete and have not been replaced.
- *Fifthly*, there is little doubt that the role of the abbot throughout *RB* is far too paramount for modern tastes. As a result, the functions attributed to the abbacy by St Benedict have, to some extent, been redistributed. His powers of legislation and decision have been made over, in part, to committees and chapters, greater opportunity is left for individual responsibility and initiative on the part of the monks and even a limited scope is allowed to freedom and fantasy. In the reformulation of the abbatial office many were anxious to get their hands on its privileges and to bring the abbot back to human scale. But it seems that insufficient attention was given to the effective continuance of his ministry of care, of providing personalized help in self-realization, in acknowledging and responding to need, of discernment. The result is that in some cases something important seems to have lapsed. There are monks and nuns operating at a level of reduced vitality, simply because they are uncared for, no attention is paid to their needs and aspirations and they are not made to feel at home in the monastery. Communal discernment, so fashionable today, is only a partial substitute. Its accountability is too

diffuse to ensure its seriousness whereas St Benedict threatened the abbot with Hell if he were negligent (2,34). Furthermore, the suitability of community discernment for processing data on individual needs, which are not public knowledge, remains to be demonstrated. Finally, it would seem to be easier to find one man prepared to put aside private interests in order to cater to the needs of others than to find the community so disposed.

◆ *Sixthly*, many abbots feel insecure in their role as teacher. Because of the fact that many of the monks may have more knowledge than the abbot about any given subject, many abbots prefer to say nothing. Nor is this situation confined to monasteries. "Today nowhere in the world are there elders who know what the children know, no matter how remote and simple the societies in which the children are. In the past there were always some elders who knew more than any children in terms of their experience of having grown up within a culture system. Today there are none.... There are no elders who know what those who have been reared in the last twenty years know about the world in which they were born."[11] The fact that abbots have shown themselves reluctant to pose as the ultimate repositories of monastic information, and the fact that monks have been even more reluctant to accept them as such, have often led to the position that an abbot's voice is simply one among many and not of particular interest. It seems that there is insufficient appreciation of the fact that teaching is possible without claiming a monopoly of the relevant facts. Accepting life as it is, it is the abbot's task as teacher to interpret experience in such a way that the action of God stands out distinctly. By aiding monks to see Christ's work in their own life-situations and to nurture the ability to recognize this, the abbot really mediates Christ to his monks. Without this discernment, the Lord would have passed by unnoticed.

♦ *Seventhly*, discernment is difficult today because people, as a whole, are presented with a wide range of options in almost every field of human endeavor. For every customary action there is an awareness of a dozen alternatives. Most modern monks have been reared on such pluriformity. Even in monastic matters they know that what is done in their own monastery is not the only course that is available; they have read history, they have contact with monks from other monasteries, they themselves may have traveled extensively, they know that things can be done differently. There is just a danger that the process of discernment in the monastery might get clogged up by the volume of alternatives to be examined and that short cuts might produce a situation in which discernment is effectively excluded from everyday life.

♦ *Eighthly*, there is today a general mistrust of structures and institutions and a feeling of alienation from traditional methods. This sense of anomy has been reinforced by the discovery of rottenness underneath the respectable façades of many institutions. Watergate is only one example. Ideology is everywhere suspect and every science or discipline today contains an element of *Ideologiekritik* as its starting point. The resultant cynicism regarding official pronouncements and their underlying motivations causes much of what is said to be discounted as a matter of course. Distance between official propaganda and truth is not unknown in monasteries. Some cases of disenchantment with traditional teaching on humility, patience and obedience have at their origin the discovery that these values have been used by superiors as a cloak for the defects of their own administration. A clear case of religion being used to tranquilize the working classes! What is important for our purpose, however, is not the examination of the pros and cons of individual instances, but the prevailing climate of suspicion. In so far as this is present in a particular monastery, the abbot's task of care through discernment will be rendered impracticable.

♦ *Ninthly*, social organizations tend to look with disfavor on the manifest needs of their members because their existence seems to level an accusation at the range of need-satisfaction provided by these organizations. Those who act in accordance with their unsatisfied needs may find themselves labeled as deviators and put under pressure to conform. It is arguable, however, that needs are not necessarily the same as willful and irresponsible fancies. It is also credible that bizarre behaviors are more often traceable to the repression of these needs than to the needs themselves and that the needs can be dealt with only in so far as they are recognized as part of reality. Finally the possibility has to be entertained that the needs which impel deviant behavior are experienced by many in the community, but as far as others are concerned, find less visible expression in conduct.[12] The process of discernment is possible only where *all* the data is available. Unless a community feels sufficiently secure in its existence to encourage the manifestation of unsatisfied needs, its awareness of the facts of life will be incomplete. If needs are considered too inappropriate or disreputable to discuss, then no assistance can be provided in dealing with them. To identify the real with the beautiful is to live in a world of dreams. The process of discernment is often frustrated by the belief that God manifests himself in the ideal rather than in the real.

♦ *Tenthly*, discernment is hampered by an inadequate appreciation of the depths of human nature, by the belief that Christianity or monasticism is something added on to man and foreign and unfamiliar to his "real" self. When monastic life is presented as a number of beliefs to be subscribed to, attitudes to accept and things to do, something is lost. Unless it can capitalize on the experienced yearnings of the human heart and see in these attractions and desires God's directives for the life of the community, monasticism will continue to be reproached for superficiality and concentration on externals. To the extent that a monastic community is bemused by its own way of doing things, convinced by its ideology and unresponsive to anything outside itself, it cannot tend to the needs of its members. It is of no help to real people who cannot evacuate their life-situation, because that is where God is.

♦ *Eleventhly*, to the extent that this discernment is part of God's plan to lift the monk up from his natural state of sin to a newness of life, resistance is to be expected. God's presence is often experienced as the diminishment of self and resented. For an abbot or community or an individual monk to submit themselves to the governance of God, sacrifice is required, and there is nothing less agreeable to any of us. In many cases discernment is resisted because it reveals God's will and demands our obedience. Perhaps the most we can do of ourselves to counter this resistance to God is to acknowledge its presence, to call it by its name and to pray that he may overcome it. We are here on the threshold of mystery.

Conclusion

The confusion which we experience at this time concerning what are "true monastic values" is due largely to the fact that past and present or historical forms and contemporary needs have become polarized. To overcome this conflict it is necessary to transcend issues and options and to locate the discussion on the level of personal and communal adherence to truth. Whether the function of the abbot in discerning and mediating God will, remains as exclusive as St Benedict envisaged is not really important on condition that equally effective alternatives can be found. The task of discernment must be done; who does it is secondary. The fact remains that unless the effort is made to englobe past and present in a single perspective, monasticism will be in turmoil. New forms will probably have to be found, but in the meantime, the obligation of care through discernment seems to rest substantially with the abbot.

NOTES

[1] This is not the place to enter into a discussion of the Hermeneutical Movement. For a general survey of J. M. Robinson—J. B. Cobb Jr (ed), *The New Hermeneutic*, New York 1964. Vol. 4 of the *Journal for Theology and the Church*, New York 1967, was entirely devoted to this topic. I would especially like to refer to the work of H. G. Gadamer, especially, *Wahrheit und Methode. Grundzüg einer philosophischen Hermeneutik*, Tubingen 1972; *Hermeneutik und Dialektik*, Tübingen 1971; an *Hermeneutik und Ideologiekritik*, Frankfurt 1971. I have tried in some tentative articles to apply the approach to monastic tradition. Cf. M. Casey, "Variations on a Theme—Approach to the Rule" *TJ* 2 (1972), pp. 5-11; "The Hard Sayings of R.B."*TJ* 3 (1972), pp. 133-143; "Community and Tradition,"*TJ* 5(1973) pp. 39-50. Cf. Also O. du Roy, *Comment se référer à la règle de S. Benoit*

aujourd'hui? and the six articles following it, which apply its general principles, *Moines aujord'hui Une expérience de réforme institutionelle*, Paris 1972, pp. 257-259 and pp. 261-316. A most satisfying approach can be found in several articles by A. Veilleux: "Creativeness and Fidelity to Tradition" *CSQ* 3 (1968), pp. 98-103; "The Technical Requirements of Fidelity (with Special Reference to the Theology of the Abbacy", *CSQ* 4 (1969), pp. 286-298; "The Intperpretation of a Monastic Rule," in *The Cistercian Spirit: A Symposium in Memory of Thomas Merton*, (ed. B. Pennington), Spencer (Massachusetts) 1970, pp. 48-65.

[2] It will be noted that the terms of discussion exclude the obligation of burrowing into monastic history in order to distill from it a definition of the essence or perennial nature of monasticism. The level of discussion is given simply by the fact that many monks are currently experiencing a conflict between monasticism in its facticity and the special needs of this time. Anyone interested in the question of definitipon can find an adequate survey and bibliography in M. Sheridan, "Towards a Contemporary Self-Definition of Monasticism," *ABR* 19 (1968), pp. 452-482.

[3] "To enact literally today what the founder did long ago would be the worst of infidelities. To deny this would be to deny history. What is constant is not the material solutions but the proportion between the conditions of the age and the reaction of the founder." O. du Roy, "Reading RSB Today: With Special Reference to the Chapters on the Abbot," *CSQ* 6 (1971) pp. 239-248; p. 241.

[4] "The general conclusion is that the important thing is to adopt the major orientations rather than to observe to the letter every minute ruling." The statement was made by Jean Leclercq concerning St Bernard's observance of the Benedictine Rule: "St Bernard and

the Rule of St Benedict," in *Rule and Life: An Interdisciplinary Symposium*, (ed. B. Pennington), Spencer (Massachusetts) 1971, pp. 151-168; p. 165.

[5] M. Mead, *Culture and Commitment: A Study of the Generation Gap*, London, 1970. p. 118

[6] A. de Vogüé, "Sub Regula vel Abbate: the Theological Significance of the Ancient Monastic Rules," in *Rule and Life*, pp. 21-64; pp. 46-47.

[7] Cf. *RB* 3,11; 64,20 and such texts as *RB* 40,5; 34,1-5; 55,20-21. "If we associate the two points we have just made we can say that in comparison to the Master, Benedict is both less sure of the abbot and more liberal towards him." A. de Vogüé, *ibid.*, p. 50.

[8] For a general overview of the notion of discretion cf. A. Cabassut, art. "Discrétion," *Dict. Spir.* Vol. 3, 1311-1330. On the differences between Benedict and the Master cf. A. de Vogüé, *La Communauté*, vol. 6, p. 1203. In what follows I have omitted to discuss some nuances of Benedict's own treatment of the abbot's functions. I believe that such source-critical considerations are not completely relevant to an outline of a determinate sociological role and that there is a danger of their deflecting attention to literary problems.

[9] De Vogüé's conclusion is that the notion of the abbacy englobes three ideas, that of the *abbas* in the Desert Tradition, that of *paterfamilias*, and that of head of a Christian community. *La Communauté*, p. 176.

[10] Both texts state that the abbot is believed to *act* as Christ's representative, not that he *is* "the vicar of Christ." For some of the historical background to the ideological development of this conception with regard to the Papacy, cf. Y. Congar, "The Historical Development of Authority in the Church: Points for Reflection," in J. M. Todd (ed.) *Problems of Authority*, London, 1962, pp. 119-156; J. M. Cameron, *Images of Authority: A Consideration of the Concepts of "Regnum" and "Sacerdotium"*;

London, 1966, especially Chapter One, "Vicarious Authority," pp. 13-36; B. Jaspert, "'Stellvertreter Christi' bei Aponius, einem unbekannten 'Magister' von Nursia. Ein Beitrag zum altkirchlichen Amtsverständnis", *ZThK* 71 (1974), pp. 291-324.

[11] M. Mead, *op. cit.*, pp. 101-102.

[12] "The overtly alienative and the compulsively conformative tendencies are most emphatically part of the same dynamic system." T. Parsons, *The Social System*, New York, 1951, p. 283.

THE BENEDICTINE PROMISES

This article is a summary of material used in workshops on the monastic vows. It was published in Tjurunga 24 (1983). It aimed to demonstrate some of the reasonableness and spiritual significance of the commitments demanded by Saint Benedict.

One of the features of existing monastic practice which is sometimes difficult for our generation is the insistent identification of the desire of entering a community and profiting from the life it offers with the willingness to remain in that situation for the rest of one's life. It is not only the issue of whether one wishes to limit one's future journey in a manner so radical which is raised. A more sophisticated awareness of the dynamics of social change renders doubtful the very possibility of making a commitment. Hitherto, there was a visible continuity between the perceived past and the expected future; in an era of rapid change, this assurance of substantial changelessness cannot be given. Changes in society and in mentalities mean that the Church and religious life also change, and it is not unreasonable for a person about to make a commitment today to wonder what form its realization will take in forty years' time.

Furthermore, we have become more sensitive to the notion that human beings themselves undergo change as they develop and that the course of life may involve even major adjustment in one's choice of direction. A complex of factors which may be creative at one stage of growth may be seriously retarding at another. The conclusion immediately presents itself that to commit oneself to a materially defined way of life is immediately to restrict the possibilities of future development to one's present view of reality and of self.

To take such a step is to preclude that transcending of the present which is necessarily involved in ongoing growth. Instead of allowing life's creative possibilities to unfold, one is prematurely strait-jacketing oneself on the basis of far from perfect self-understanding.

Such difficulties are not illusory, nor are they merely the outcome of individual neurosis. It was wrong to under-estimate the force of such arguments not only in the minds of those who give expression to them, but also more covertly in the attitudes and prejudices of others less articulate. Not that it is impossible to give any adequate response to such objections. In fact, a sound case *can* be made in support of intelligent religious commitment, not only on the level of personal resolution of difficulties, but even in a general way. Some of the elements of such an advocacy are the following.

> 1. Commitment is a two-way process. An individual's involvement with a community is related to the force of attraction or holding-power exercised by the group. A social organization with the greatest capacity to impart to its members a sense of belonging is one which generates a sub-culture of high quality, where fundamental beliefs and values are stated and allowed to find expression in rituals, communal activities and priorities and personal work, growth and adventure. An *esprit de corps* is essential.
>
> 2. The distinctiveness of a group's sub-culture seems to be a point in its favor. Where the attitudes and behavior of a community are indistinguishable from those "outside" its membership, morale flags. All religious communities should reflect the distinctiveness of the Gospel way, rather than merely echo the dull vacuities of bourgeois conform-

ism. To the extent that an organization acts on the basis of its own beliefs and values rather than waiting for others to set the precedents, its social forms have the possibility of coalescing into a sub-culture whose power of inner cohesion is substantially independent of external approbation. It need not necessarily be a counter-culture force although, almost certainly, some of its aspects will have this character. It is easier to make a commitment to a group which has such a clear sense of identity and which is able to translate that feeling into modes of action which express and reinforce it.

3. Belonging to a group includes owning its past. The degree of a member's commitment is not unrelated to his acceptance of the roots of present corporate existence. A religious community with a good tradition facilitates commitment by encouraging creative access to the past. If there is a long tradition, so much the better. This provides not only a remedy for the many distortions introduced into religious life in the last century and for their reaction-formations in the present, it also serves as a criterion for evaluating innovations possibly based on equally insubstantial reasoning. The past is not to be viewed merely as a fund of legal precedents; more importantly it affords the possibility of a life-giving contact with men and women of guaranteed spiritual stature. Such an awareness brings with it a sense of perspective in which current threats to commitment appear less overwhelming and more susceptible of creative resolution.

4. It follows that commitment to a religious community is not merely the undertaking to participate in its activities. It goes deeper than that. It involves also the willingness progressively to become at home within its specific climate of meaning; that is to say, to work at fostering those fundamental beliefs and values which are more enduring than the range of activities which express them. Such a pursuit of meaning is a life-long endeavor. Commitment to a religious community is necessarily a commitment to keep growing into that community, to deepening one's grasp of the purpose which informs it. There is no undertaking made nor guarantee given that this will involve doing the same things in the same way indefinitely.

5. Furthermore, it is not so much a question of committing oneself to a system as to a concrete group of persons. The written code is always administered by human beings, whose task it is to see that everything possible is done to facilitate the growth of all. Nor is it very sensible to allow the disenchantment and cynicism which many of our contemporaries have with regard to all social institutions to shape our attitude to religious life. Most religious communities choose as their leaders persons of sensitivity, high intelligence and substantial integrity and it were very foolish to regard them as being on a par with the numbers-men of political lotteries. Far from strait-jacketing individuals, it is possible for a religious community to accommodate itself to many varied expressions of basic values, and not only to tolerate creative innovation, but also to encourage it and to support those involved in it. In fact it is often only the understanding and acceptance given by a community which enables an individual, with boldness and generosity, to try something new.

6. It is also a mistake to underestimate the power of the human will freely to determine its own path of future growth. Such self-determination demands, of course that one has enough maturity to recognize the force and direction of one's instinctual tendencies, and enough experience to judge one's own limits. Granted such an understanding, there is no reason why an individual would not decide to restrict the bulk of his energies to pursuing a particular goal and making the most of it. Nobody can ever be perfectly sure in advance what such a choice will entail; he simply makes a mature judgment about the general orientation of his life and then uses his common sense to compensate for its liabilities and to capitalize on its assets.

7. While it is true that a firm commitment can prove to be uncreative, it is probably a fact that resistance to any commitment, be it to religious life, to marriage or to any long-term avocation, is far more damaging. Fear of the responsibilities and obligations inseparable from adult life is certainly a regressive factor. Far from being an athleticism of mind, a vision so broad that it cannot be contained in any category, it represents a real failure to

perceive the ultimate potential of any authentic human situation. It may also be an indication that one radically doubts one's ability to cope with any change not generated by oneself. In this case it is a withdrawal from the challenge of social living.

It is possible, therefore, on the basis of such reasoning, to conclude that commitment to a religious community remains a meaningful act in individual cases and a not unreasonable requirement for enrollment in the religious state. It is now important to look at the inherent spiritual value in taking such a step, and to do this we need first to understand a little of its history.

1. The Making of a Monk in the Rule of Benedict

The ancient monastic approach to the admission and incorporation of candidates gave birth to considerable variation in matters of practical detail. The elements remain fairly constant. The candidate was not granted immediate admission, but was submitted to various forms of probation to test his mettle. Several different systems were devised to allow for his progressive entry into the community, providing for his instruction and socialization by the agency of those already experienced in the life. On his part, the candidate had to demonstrate his own freedom in making this choice and a willingness to accept monastic life and to persevere with it even when things became difficult. At some point he was required to take a definitive step which was externally symbolized in his being invested with the monastic habit. The rites varied, but the key elements remained: probation, formation, commitment, incorporation. Benedict takes over these components from earlier tradition and forms them into a new synthesis.[1]

In *RB* 58, great care is taken to ensure that the ritual act of commitment is a reality and not merely an empty form, later to be shrugged off with the plea of ignorance regarding its concrete consequences.

Far from proposing that the monastery conduct recruitment drives, Benedict recommends a certain reserve in accepting candidates. This is probably due less to a pessimism about general suitability than to a desire that, in every case, entry into monastic life be as free of superficial motivations as possible. The prospective monk is to be queried about his reasons for coming (60,3), not so much so that a psychological profile can be built up for later use, as to lead the candidate himself toward a great understanding of the inner forces which move him. He needs to be led to isolate the mysterious urge which brings him to the monastery from the range of accidental and even unreal elements which surround it, so that what is essential may be recognized and strengthened and what is transitory may be allowed naturally to pass.

Furthermore, the candidate is expected to demonstrate something of the constancy and stolidity of character which will bear him up through many subsequent storms. The difficulty here is being able to distinguish genuine perseverance from stubbornness, obstinacy and pig-headedness. Perhaps patience is more to be sought than mere tenacity, a certain softness and flexibility rather than a hard, stiff-necked endurance. If patience really is the monastic means *par excellence* of sharing in the Paschal mystery, then it is a completely different reality from the time-serving toughness of a trainee commando. If the prospective monk has the beginnings of an understanding of these things, then it is not likely that he will go far wrong in the future.

One who thus demonstrates the strength of spiritual priorities is permitted to share something of community life. An experienced monk is deputed to look after him and to make sure that he is under no illusions about the obligations he is about to assume. He gives formal instruction about the difficulties of life ahead, stressing that these are to be regarded as par for the course; they are not the accidental results of one's own failings or those of others. Since this senior is chosen on the basis of his capacity to win souls (58,6), it seems to be implied that he is not merely an examiner, but one who has a capacity to help those in his care to surmount the obstacles they encounter.

The object of this period of initial exposure to the monastic way is twofold; in the first place it is to confront the novice with his own spiritual drive and, secondly, it is to make sure that there is a compatibility between this inner movement and the specific means which the community has to offer. Is the search for God furthered by participation in the regular round of communal worship and its supporting practices? Is the way of obedience to a rule and to an abbot a creative means of reining the instincts and self-will? Is there an acceptance of the purifying effects of suffering and the hardship of humble and humdrum living? These means are not for everyone; it is possible to lead a spiritual life outside a monastery. What the novice has to do is to ask himself whether he is not only prepared to tolerate the reality of life as it is lived by the community, but also whether it will be for him a source of life and progress.

There is no blinkering in Benedict's novitiate. The *Rule* is to be read to him repeatedly during his probation to make sure that he knows in detail what is involved when he gives his assent to it. Apparently, Benedict did not think it would become necessary for a novice to be told to leave; he seems to assume that if he honestly confronts the demands of the life he is considering, he will certainly leave of his own accord if he has not the contrary determination. He thinks of monastic life as tolerable only on the presumption of a vigorous spiritual life; in the absence of such, no normal person would want to have anything to do with it.

The reason for this candor about the difficulties ahead is to be found in Benedict's view that commitment once made is irrevocable. The monk promises to be steadfast in his purpose, knowing that there will be hard and painful times which will seriously test his resolve. The promises he makes derive their permanence not only from the fact that he has uttered them in full and aware freedom, but also because he has solemnly invoked God as a witness. (There are, therefore, more in the nature of oaths rather than vows, as this latter term would subsequently be understood.) To reverse his commitment is not only to destroy his own integrity; it is mockery of God—an act of irreligion (58,18).

This act is, however, more than a permanent career-choice. The verse sung by the new monk in the ritual of profession gives a key to its significance. The monk prays, "Receive me, O Lord...." It is a self-offering, a gift of self to God, symbolized by the placing of the deed of profession on the altar. The addition of the word *Domine* to the psalm-verse is, perhaps, an indication that there is a Christological aspect in the monk's act of self-spoliation. By renouncing his goods, his will and his prospects, he reposes all his hope in the promises of Christ that those who die for his sake will find life. Profession is an intensely religious act; its main components are faith, hope and a deep love for Christ.[2]

This act recapitulates all the movements of dedication in the monk's previous life. There is only implicit reference in *RB* to the relation between baptism and profession, but this linkage is assumed and developed repeatedly in tradition. It is also good to see this formal act as the resumption and culmination of all those steps which have led the monk in this direction: the searching that led him to the monastery, the learning and re-learning from experience, the softening effect of suffering endured for Christ. It is, simultaneously, the signature-tune for the rest of his life, whereby he takes steps to ensure that nothing is considered more important than the love of Christ (4,21).

It is only this final promise which is regarded as permanently binding. His promise to persevere in his efforts, made at the beginning of the year (58,9), does not affect his liberty to depart (58,10). The promise mentioned in vs. 14, if it is regarded as distinct from the profession, is probably best treated as an anticipatory expression of a willingness to go ahead with formal commitment.

Benedict takes great care to ensure the juridical character of the promise. The document is drawn up in the name of the saints and of the abbot; it is signed and sealed with an oath and, in the presence of the community, placed on the altar. The document remains forever in the archives as testimony of his gift, even if later the monk reneges on it. Included in it is a disappropriation of all material possessions, even the clothes he is wearing, since he has already signed away his very body (33,4; 58,25), and the greater must include the less. The significance of investiture in *RB* is less as a sign of consecration than a gesture of dispossession and dependence on the community. The focus in the rite is on what *the monk* does, not on what the Church or the community does to him.

What is the content of the promise or promises by which the monk makes a gift of himself? In latter times it has been taken for granted that the monk enunciated three distinct vows: stability, *conversatio morum* and obedience. For good measure, poverty and chastity were understood as implicit. But it seems that such a neat division scarcely corresponds to Benedict's intention: 58,17 does not list the promises made by the monk, but merely surveys the general area covered by them. There is no question of his assuming three distinct and mutually exclusive obligations; what he promises is "to live the full monastic life as was practiced in a particular monastery and defined by a particular rule"³ and abbot. Thus the three items specified overlap; they are not distinct responsibilities newly assumed but three aspects of the unitary obligation assumed by the new monk. *RM* 89,7 states the matter somewhat differently: "I want to serve God, by the discipline of the rule which has been read to me, in your monastery." The triple form may, perhaps, be taken as asseverative; what is twice repeated can scarcely be attributed to a slip of the tongue.

Notwithstanding the fact that, for Benedict, the act of profession is general and all-embracing, there is some meaning to be found in distinguishing three aspects or modes in which what is promised takes practical expression. If one wishes to regard them as "vows" it should be remembered that while they are promises made to God, the content of all the promises concerns the whole of life and not merely one specific department of it.⁴

2. The Promise to be a Good Monk

The meaning of *conversatio morum* is notoriously difficult. There are three fundamental problems in understanding the expression:

> a) The relationship between *conversatio* and the term often substituted for it in later tradition, *conversio*.
>
> b) Is *conversatio* used in its normal sense of a habitual or corporate pattern of action and reaction, a way of life, or is it used specifically as a synonym for the *monastic* way of life?
>
> c) What is the relationship between the two words *conversatio* and *morum*, and how are they to be translated?

At least something must be said about these matters before attempting to understand the meaning of the vow in its contemporary setting. It is possible to make ready sense out of the idea of a vow of conversion. Conversion is the means by which one turns one's back on the slothful disobedience of heedless living and begins the arduous journey of return to God. Each day one allows oneself to be converted a little more, by attending to the Word and allowing it to shape one's options. In this way, the wealth of material in the Scriptures and in tradition is drawn upon and it becomes possible to construct a spirituality of the vow in terms of lifelong conversion.[5]

As regards the original reading, we have to bow to the experts and agree that, indeed, the more obscure text is the more likely, *lectio difficilior, potior*. The fact that succeeding centuries were comfortable with understanding it as *conversio* is certainly an indication that such a connotation is not absolutely foreign to what Benedict had in mind, but this tolerance is not to be interpreted as an agreement that the full meaning of the promise is contained in the idea of conversion. There can be no real doubt that what the monk promises is *conversatio morum*, and that there is more to this term than a permanent state of conversion would imply.

The second preliminary point concerns whether *conversatio* was, already in the sixth century, a semi-technical term for the monastic avocation. There is some evidence in *RB* that it was at least domestic shorthand for monastic life and values, but the security of the linkage is not absolute. A modern community may discuss "life-style" or "pattern of life" in a manner which might astonish an eavesdropping etymologist; it is simply that they have become used to using these generic terms in a specific sense and in a particular context. In the same way, *conversatio* came to be used by monks to mean the only way of life they were interested in, their own. The meaning of *RB* 58 is not at stake, in this matter, and it may be better left loose.

The third area of difficulty is not as easily resolved. What does the curious phrase *conversatio morum* mean and how is it to be translated? The various options are discussed by Ambrose Wathan, and need not be recalled here.[6] There is much value in Basilius Steidle's argument that the term is one of many examples of the epexegetical genitive in *RB*.[7] In this sense, 58,17 could be translated "...he makes a promise regarding his stability, his *lifestyle and behavior* and his willingness to obey" (stressing his attitude rather than performance in the matter of obedience). Thus "lifestyle and behavior" can be seen as the broad area covered by his promise(s). *Conversatio morum* is not the content of the promise but a statement of the spheres in which his new monasticity will be expressed. Obviously this means that he is promising to live a *monastic* lifestyle and to behave as a *monk*. In other words, the basic monastic promise is the promise to be a good monk, with all that will eventually involve as circumstances change and sensitivities sharpen.

The import of the monk's promises is signaled by his investiture. The secular clothes which belong to him are removed and he is garbed in monastery garments. He is assuming a new way of life; there is no continuity between what he was hitherto and what he has become.[8] He renounces the world and self in order to live substantially for Christ. This means that the understanding of one aspect of *conversatio morum* is greatly enhanced by an appreciation of the theme of *fuga mundi*.

Many of the traditional phrases which describe this aspect of a Benedictine lifestyle cause great alarm: *fuga mundi*, flight from the world seems to be escapism; *contemptus mundi*—contempt for the world reeks of elitism. Such a pre-occupation with avoiding the contamination of secular society seems to go against the whole notion of salvation through incarnation and the Church's mission to proclaim the Good News to the limits of temporal existence. This is where it is very important to understand the meaning of the traditional expressions.[9] In particular, the polyvalence of the word "world" must be understood.[10] The monk is not called upon mindlessly to renounce all human values, but to initiate a process of discernment whereby he may distinguish what is good, authentic and beautiful in human life from what is merely appearance; to dissociate himself from the manipulative marketing of products and opinions and submit all things to be assayed according to the standards of the Gospel. It is not a matter of mindless separation from things commonly valued, but an attempt to live at a deeper level of truth, not only for one's own sake but as a service to the Church and to the world. If the monk is called upon "to make himself a stranger to the world by the way he acts," this is to be understood within the context of his intention "to give nothing precedence over the love of Christ"; the juxtaposition of the two aphorisms is not accidental and is of considerable significance.[11]

In fact the monk is called to do no more than any baptized person. St Paul writes unequivocally, "Do not be conformed to this world"[12] and leaves no doubt that those who choose to follow worldly ways are on the road to destruction. St John demonstrates the same concern: "Do not love the world nor anything in the world; if anyone loves the world then the love of the Father is not in him."[13] St James is equally uncompromising: "Do you not know that friendship with the world is enmity with God; if anybody wishes to be a friend of the world, he makes himself God's enemy."[14] St Luke transmits a saying attributed to Jesus which includes the statement, "What is highly regarded by human beings is an abomination before God."[15] There is ample material for reflection even in the New Testament itself.

Christians renounce the "world" in the very ritual of baptism, promising to live innocent of the pomps of Satan. This necessary negativity has its origin in the reality of sin against which the believer must positively wage war, if he is not to be lulled into a lethal decline. Its positive side includes the fostering of all that is noble in humanity, as St Ambrose remarks: "To flee from the world is this: to hold oneself in the image and likeness of God and to stretch one's capabilities in the imitation of God."[16] This fundamental statement of priorities is taken seriously by the monk: to arrive at his goal—the kingdom of heaven—and to achieve his purpose—an undivided and unsullied heart—he must work hard to ensure that he is not the slave of social ideologies which imperceptibly guide him in a different direction.

Another way of describing this aspect of *conversatio morum* is by reference to Phil 3:20, *conversatio nostra in coelis est*, our citizenship (*politeia*) is in heaven. Monastic life was often termed "the heavenly life" or "the angelic life" to highlight this aspect, and devotion to heaven has always been a solid component of monastic spirituality at its most authentic.[17] The monk is "to desire eternal life with all the yearning of his spirit,"[18] to see his life as a hastening toward his heavenly homeland,[19] a return to the Father,[20] a means of sharing in the reign of Christ.[21] It is his hope of the future that enables him to tolerate the hardships and unfairnesses which are the normal concomitant of any adult life.[22]

This independence from the processes of a predominantly unchristian society is particularly important for our generation, since the possibilities of control of the masses through misinformation are so spectacularly expanded. A culture which is predominantly sensate leaves itself open to influence by the selection and presentation of items for it to process. A television screen can be filled with score of demonstrators while hundreds of thousands of supporters are allocated a mere passing glance. Decent and sincere people can be made to look foolish by skillful editing, and constant repetition can give to trite platitudes an infallibility no pope would ever claim. More than ever before, the Christian needs to be on his guard against error, not merely doctrinal misformulations but error in basic beliefs, values and presuppositions. Anyone who thinks himself immune to untruth is already a fool.

The social aspects of *conversatio morum* are complemented by individual striving, *askesis, disciplina*.[23] One has to assert control over one's own sub-personal nature, to bring the instincts into line with the will, to train the body in the habit-formation which is appropriate to the goal being sought and to counter the depressive effect of fears, dependencies and inertia. The images of Christian life are images of action: it is warfare, it is athletic pursuit, it is tirelessness in doing good: its greatest enemy is not misdirection but omission. The monk has, therefore, constantly to struggle against being too tired to do something positive, to avoid postponing his efforts until things seem easier and to refuse to cloak his laziness in a pseudo-concern to determine more fully what is the right thing to be done.

However important self-control, determination and will-power are to *disciplina*, they are not as essential as a willingness to learn, to be formed, to be possessed by the meaning-system of which action is the effect. *Disciplina* is a derivative of the verb *discere* and is related to the noun *discipulus*. It is substantially informed by the idea of learning. It is not merely a matter of performing the "right" actions, without appreciating why they are "right," merely wishing to conform to the expectations of those who advocate them. It is a matter of accepting at a deep, personal level an alternative philosophy of life, with foundational beliefs and values upon which actions and behavior-patterns can be built. Unless one is molded by these beliefs and values, the actions which one performs cannot be free, nor can they respond flexibly to the changing demands of different circumstances.

Therefore, an important part of acquiring that *disciplina* which is at the heart of *conversatio morum* is a building up of a sense of identity and this is done, especially, through having a living *rapport* with other members of one's community and by allowing oneself to be animated and guided by sound tradition. There is a form of solitary behavior which is no more than stubborn self-gratification. It is not fidelity to principle but a sheer unwillingness to be guided by anything outside oneself, or outside the select band of those prepared to acquiesce in one's preferences. No matter how hard such a one lives, no matter what rigors of observance he espouses, he lives an undisciplined life—not because he lacks will-power, but because he refuses to continue to learn from the community in which he lives and from the tradition in which it stands. *Disciplina* is a much subtler and nuanced reality than either obstinacy or mindless perfectionism.

Included in the ambit of *disciplina* are the areas traditionally assigned to the vows of poverty and chastity. It is probably more helpful to see them in relationship with the whole area of *conversatio* than in treating them in isolation, since problems in chastity (for example) are rarely extreme where one has built up a fidelity to grace in poverty, obedience, prayer, community life and in the various other spheres of challenge. On the other hand, almost no permanent advance can be achieved in chastity without the effort to consolidate the more fundamental areas of one's response to vocation first.

Poverty and chastity are simultaneously means by which we challenge the inevitability of instinctual behavior and they are expressions of *fuga mundi*. Poverty negates the instinct of acquisitiveness, both material goods and of less tangible possessions such as status, recognition, popularity, experience, education, convenience and so forth. We are asked, with the poor, to depend on Christ and on our community, not to build empires for ourselves nor to hoard minor treasures for our own enjoyment. It also means that we have less in our lives subject to the sanction of society and dependent on its approval. As one of John Steinbeck's characters remarked, "You can never have enough money. You either have no money or not enough." Chastity has to do with controlling the pleasure-principle within us and also to putting a stop to relationships which are mutually exploitative. It is not pious fantasy to say that it frees us to love—in fact the same dynamic operates in marriage—since not everything which claims that noble name for itself deserves to receive it. It is possible to love by not loving, so to speak, although our sensate nature would often have it otherwise. Because chastity means that we do not belong to a family unit, it further increases the distance between a monk and a suburban householder and establishes a potential for fruitful interaction. Both poverty and chastity are part of a distinctive lifestyle within the Church; they rise or fall according to the evangelical character of that way of life, taken as a whole.

A particular result of such an integrative approach to the vows is that the unhealthy prominence given to chastity is reduced. Not that the quality of sexual life does not remain a significant factor in assessing life as a whole, but that things are viewed in proportion. One could be excused from thinking that many writers of this subject in the not-so-distant past were really advocating an impossible return to pre-pubescent innocence which had the effect of making *everyone* feel guilty. Like most of the virtues, chastity is something that flourishes at the end of many decades of striving; the final product is of sufficient splendor to outshine any patches of darkness along the way. One would wonder whether the concept of virginity as something always better than its opposite can be maintained at all. The glorious illogicality of the prayer of the Missal, *Deus innocentiae amator et RESTITUTOR* (O God, lover and restorer of innocence) would seem to indicate that nothing is irreversible. One could, perhaps, be forgiven for wondering whether a person who prays too fervently for perfect chastity is not lacking both common sense and a genuine confidence in God's willingness to restore.

Conversatio morum is the monk's means of countering the traditional enemies of the Christian, the world, the flesh and the devil.[24] Of the last we will say nothing except that the monk is protected from the delusions and tyrannies normally associated with "diabolic" influence through his obedience to the law of Christ and by his availing himself of the powers of discernment which are available to him in the community. Certainly, in the view of the ancient monks, his fervent living of the life he has promised is already an affront to the demons and represents a reduction in the power of evil and a growth in the world of goodness and truth.

3. *The Promise to Persevere*

The vow of stability works against the immediate gratification syndrome. It is essentially a commitment to the long-term perdurance of a vocation. To promise stability is to submit oneself to the cumulative effects of monastic life—as Benedict himself notes, it gets easier as it goes. Toward the end it is like a second skin; far from being an imposition or a distortion it all comes naturally.[25] This means having the solidity of mind to be able to ride out difficult patches, the *dura et aspera*, seeing them within the greater context of a life which is progressively possessed by God and so creative of genuine humanity.

Such perseverance is more than a thick skin or the ability to endure, it is the sort of constancy which enables one to keep working at one's vocation, responding on a daily basis to the call of grace, and not becoming discouraged or cynical about the tardiness of final perfection. It means submitting oneself to a very prolonged apprenticeship without wanting to break out into independence, recognizing that the spiritual craft can be acquired only in this way. It bespeaks a willingness to keep learning, an openness to others and a relative freedom about one's own fixed ideas. It is also a matter of employing those *means* to perseverance of which mention has already been made, those aids to deepening our grasp of basic beliefs and values such as continuing prayer, reflection and reading. In this way a *stabilitas mentis* is built up which is the only authentic basis for an external expression of stability.

Perseverance is not such an easy thing, a fact to which the numerous references in the New Testament must draw our attention. Since our own age is characterized by a great deal of *mobility*, one could anticipate special problems for our contemporaries. There is, undoubtedly, a great deal of *mobilitas mentis* nowadays, evidenced not only in the amount of travel and moving house, but also in change of opinions, employments and value-systems. In one sense the remote control devices for changing television channels are more eloquent symbols of this restlessness than the motor car. There are many who simply cannot persevere with something as undemanding as watching television; there is a recurrent urge to see whether there is not something better somewhere else.

Such restlessness is parodied in ancient monastic literature and listed among the vices. It was given the name *akedia* (acedia, accidie), a basic condition of being unable to commit oneself to anything, of heedlessness, restless, subservience to the vagaries consequent upon inner inconsistency. *Akedia* is the denial of all that is meant by stability; it is impossible to reconcile undisciplined and purposeless living with the *stabilitas mentis* essential both for prayer and for perseverance.[26]

Of course, *stabilitas* is often interpreted juridically in terms of remaining permanently attached to a particular community or congregation. Occasionally it is even suggested (somewhat agoraphobically, I submit) that it implies a devotion to remain inside four walls. In both cases it seems to me that the practical expressions of stability have been cut adrift from the basic value. Certainly there is no more obvious channel of instability than a refusal to put down roots in a local community or to accept one's membership in a particular congregation. Of course, one who is never at home is not giving the system much chance to produce its effects and there may well be grounds for a charge of escapism. But these are not automatic effects. Any particular act or habit needs to be taken in reference to the basic criterion: does it help or hinder the long-term perseverance of this person in the life which has been promised?

Human life can sometimes be very complicated and, in individual cases, *stabilitas mentis* can admit of very paradoxical expressions, some of which may seem to run counter to the spirit of *stabilitas loci*. It is not inconceivable that in monastic life, as sometimes in marriage, the only way of ensuring the continuing creativity of the bond is to build in the possibility of ensuring that familiarity does not breed contempt. A community which is not a mere shared fantasy system can only profit from any enrichment one of its members receives from outside contacts. Of course, this is a dangerous thing to say and liable to misunderstanding. It is matter for pastoral discernment to establish what courses of action are most likely to further both the growth and perseverance of the individual and the continuing well-being of the community.

It is hard to see how a genuine spirit of love and acceptance can be built up without a great deal of mutual exposure. The particular mellowness of monastic relationships is dependent on a well-weathered trust and a history of many acts of kindness and forgiveness. Such a level of interaction presupposes many years together, many hardships borne in solidarity, many simple pleasures shared. It is such a good thing, even on a human level, that it counterbalances some of the less favorable aspects of *stabilitas loci*; staleness, role-fixity, routinization and lack of challenge. The sort of fraternal life envisaged in *RB* is certainly possible within the context of attachment to a single community, but it has to be worked at for many years and even decades.

Stability or perseverance (it is Benedict himself who states the equivalence) must be viewed not as an end in itself, as though merit were obtained merely by staying around, but in its relationship to *conversatio morum*. It is more than time-serving. It is a matter of courageously continuing to give oneself to monastic life in the concreteness of its everyday demands. Its special feature is that it always has an eye to ultimate perseverance and tempers present behavior to that end. It needs to be possessed by a special sort of prudence, so that it is able to work out in a general way what is likely to help continuing fidelity and what will work against it. It is not possible to live by the book; sometimes too much fervor results in burn-out, foolishly invested efforts at improvement foster frustration. Zeal which is not from God leads to hell.

4. *The Promise to Obey the Rule and the Abbot*

The promise to obedience is, obviously, not unconnected with the other two, but it has its own special significance. It is the least disembodied of the vows, in the sense that its object is not something general or indeterminate, but it represents a concrete undertaking to live in accordance with the dictates of a specific rule according to the interpretation of a specific abbot. This is to say it is a giving of submission and allegiance to demands and obligations which have their origin outside one's own subjectivity. It is the most far-reaching of the remedies for one's disordered willfulness.

If it can, for the moment, be presupposed that the object of submission is worthy, then obedience can have a great capacity for guiding the individual toward greater self-understanding and more complete awareness of the exigencies of vocation. It is not a question of buckling down under *force majeure*, much less of contriving to subvert its application. It is a matter of opening oneself to be guided by the teaching of Christ as this is mediated through the Church, in the rule and in the abbot. It is a sacramental rather than a political affair.[27]

What is communicated through the rule and through the abbot is a particular way of life, with specific emphases—including obligations, recommendations, reservations and prohibitions. These are the MEANS by which purity of heart is obtained and the goal of monastic life realized. Thus, formally and informally one is obliged to live a life in which prayer and reading have a part, in which participation in community activities and standards is enjoined and the observance of norms and customs accepted by the community is pursued. It is not so much a question of which things are to be done on which day and to what extent and how greatly one sins if these are omitted, but of a recognition that unless one exercises a practical fidelity to the substance of common observance one is liable to drift away from the community and from one's own sources of comfort and challenge. This is not to say that in every case one can formulate the limits beyond which effective and affective membership in the community begins to be jeopardized, but simply to aver that belonging to a community is impossible without participating in its activities within the bounds of one's own possibilities.

The promise of obedience involves a conformity with community observance which is substantial, objective and life-long. It is not to an inanimate code that one commits oneself, but to a rule administered by an abbot in the context of a concrete community reality. Such obedience is nuanced and realistic; it is not a rabid literalism or an eclectic antinomianism, but a humble, plodding and sustained effort to ensure that the main lines of one's life fall within the limits of the community's self-understanding—reserving the right to *enlightened* dissent in situations of proportionate gravity.

Of course, obedience also means doing what one is told when the superior insists in the form sanctioned by law. Many religious grow old waiting for their first such injunction, so it were foolish to regard this as the primary focus of the vow. There will certainly be times in which one must put aside one's own plans to accede to the expressed wish of another and maybe even crises of authority, but the real crux of obedience is something broader and more embracing.

In fact obedience introduces us, as St Benedict notes, into the whole mystery of Christ's submission to the Father and thereby to the plotting of human beings. Obedience is really less about taking orders than of allowing oneself to be immersed in the plan of God. It demands a special confidence in divine providence which is able to write straight on crooked lines. It is often a call to us, through imperfect and even aberrant human beings, to maintain our faith notwithstanding serious reversals, to keep moving even when our hopes are shattered and to allow our own plans and projects to be transcended out of love for something better.

In fact, it is not being over-dramatic to assert that it is through obedience, and especially through the suffering which we experience when obedience brings us hardship, that we become participant in the Paschal Mystery. St Benedict insists on this: patience is the ordinary means of attaining the goal of our life. It is not by achievement but by endurance for the love of Christ that we become open to the Spirit's power. This is the final outcome of a life open to obedience. When we promise obedience we give ourselves to the paramount dynamic of the life of Christ himself. If we render what we vow, we will become like him.

The Benedictine promises are broad in their significance, reaching into every aspect of life and seeking to integrate them all in one lifelong movement away from sin and slackness back to the Father. They are not promises made with reference to a number of specific "do's" and "don'ts," but a basic program for a life lived progressively under the influence of the Gospel after the model of a specific tradition. Their precise application grows with the individual and takes its shape from the circumstances in which he lives. It is not an impossible commitment, nor is it unreasonable, but it does demand clear-sighted generosity and a very intense desire to give oneself to God and to live for Christ.

NOTES

[1] A convenient summary of the ancient monastic approach to the incorporation of new recruits is found in Claude Peifer, "Monastic Formation and Profession," Appendix 5 of *RB 1980*, The Liturgical Press, Collegeville, 1981; pp. 437-466. An incisive complement to this traditional approach may be found in Mary Collins, "Rule and Gospel: The Meaning of Benedictine Vowing," in *Benedic* 35.2 (1980), pp. 27-46. A great deal

of detailed information on subsequent developments is found in Jean Leclercq, "Profession according to the Rule of St. Benedict: An Historical Survey," in M. Basil Pennington (ed.) *Rule and Life: A Symposium,* Cistercian Publications, Spencer, 1971, pp. 117-149. Id., "Tradition, Baptism and Profession: The Genesis and Evolution of the Consecrated Life," in *Aspects of Monasticism,* Cistercian Publications, 1978, pp. 71-98.

[2] Cf. Augusta Raabe, "The 'Suscipe': A Benedictine Koan," in *Benedic* 35.2 (1980), pp. 76-81.

[3] Peifer, *op. cit.,* p. 458.

[4] In an unintentionally whimsical article, O. Lottin, following the lead of Bernard of Monte Cassino and Delatte sees the three vows in relation to the three forms of monastic life itemized in *RB* 1. By the vow of stability, the monk renounces the ways of the gyrovagues; by obedience he protects himself from the willfulness of the sarabaites, therefore by the vow of *conversatio morum* he eschews the temptation to eremetism. "Le voeu de *Conversatio morum* dans la Regle de Saint Benôit," *RTAM* 26 (1959), pp. 5-16.

[5] Cf. I. Nowell, "Turning and Being Turned to the Lord: Biblical Foundations of *Conversatio* in the RB," *Benedic* 36.2 (1981), pp. 16-21, 29. Cf. P. Schmitz, art. *Conversatio morum* in *DSp* 2.2206-2212. Both authors accept *conversatio* (and not *conversio*) as the genuine reading of the text of *RB*, but interpret the former in terms of the latter.

[6] A. Wathan, "Conversatio and Stability in the Rule of Benedict," *MS* 11 (1975), pp. 1-44. This article comprises a rich and annotated bibliography as well as detailed textual discussion.

[7] B. Steidle, "'De Conversatione Morum Suorum': Zum philologischen Verstaendnis von Regula S. Benedicti Cap. 58.17," in *Regula Magistri-Regula*

Benedicti, StA 44 (1959), pp. 136-144. The comparative approach of this article is supplemented by a grammatical survey published in the following year. "Der Genitivus epexegeticus in der Regel del Hl. Benedikt," *SM* 2.1 (1960), pp. 193-203.

[8] The literature of monasticism has never quite resolved the problem of how radical monastic beginnings are. There is an ambivalence about the value of a pre-monastic Christian life. Theoretically, there is no doubt that the life of grace begins at baptism which was, perhaps, received in infancy but, in practice, the living out of baptismal obligations for those destined to become monks really only commenced with their "conversion" from worldly ways and their entry into the monastery. It is, perhaps, a pity that nobody thought of the possibility of arguing for the sacramentality of monastic investiture in the period when the sacramental *septenarium* was not fixed. As it is, the ritual associated with it has tended to borrow now from baptismal rites, now from those of ordination and, in the case of women, matrimony. From a scrutiny of the actual rites used, both universally and locally, one could be forgiven for concluding that a great deal of confusion exists concerning what is taking place.

[9] It was with great concern that I read in an article by the Abbot Primate of Benedictines, "Benedict...has no place for *fuga mundi*." But then this is defined as a "contempt for human values," a sense which is not traditional and which I would agree is not something to be cultivated. Cf. Victor Dammertz, "St. Benedict, Master of Religious Life," in *Consecrated Life* 6.2 (1982), pp. 243-256. The quotations are taken from p. 251. On this question, see Jean Leclercq, "Separation from the World and Relations with the World," in *Contemplative Life*, Cistercian Publications, Kalamazoo, 1978, pp. 33-45. Cf. J. -C Guy, "La place du *Contemptus mundi* dans le monachisme ancien," in *RAM* 41 (1965), pp. 237-249.

R. Grégoire and Jean Leclercq, "Saeculi actibus se facere alienum: Le mépris du monde dans la littérature monastique latine mediévale," ibid., pp. 251-290. F. Lazzari, "Le 'contemptus mundi' chez S. Bernard," ibid., pp. 291-304. R. Grégoire, "Introduction à une étude théologique du 'mépris du monde,' *SM* 8 (1966), pp. 313-328. There is also a series of books and articles dealing with this theme by the Dominican Robert Bultot; a summary of his work can be found in "Spirituels et théologiens devant l'homme et le monde," *Révue Thomiste* 72 (1964), pp. 517-548. See also, Emero Stiegman Jr., *The Language of Asceticism in St. Bernard of Clairvaux's Sermons super Cantica*, unpublished Ph.D. thesis, Fordham University, 1973; especially pp. 22-31.

[10] Cf. Jacques Maritain, *The Peasant of the Garonne*, Geoffrey Chapman, London, 1968; pp. 28-63. This line of thinking probably strongly influenced some of the utterances of Pope Paul VI in this matter.

[11] *RB* 4,20-21. The items immediately preceding this couplet refer to the corporal works of mercy, those following it are about aspects of an attitude of integrity, both series manifesting the sort of interior and exterior facets of both the love of Christ and separation from the world of selfishness and sin.

[12] Rom 12:2

[13] 1 Jn 2:15.

[14] James 4:4.

[15] Lk 16:15.

[16] Ambrose, *De fuga saeculi*, 4.17. Cf. R.J. Halliburton, "The concept of 'Fuga saeculi' in St. Augustine," *DR* 85 (1967), pp. 249-261.

[17] J. Leclercq, *The Love of Learning and the Desire for God: A Study of Monastic Culture*, in SPCK, London, 2nd edition 1978, pp. 65-86. Id., "Monasticism and

Angelism," in *Aspects of Monasticism*, Cistercian Publications, Kalamazoo, 1978; pp. 151-162. Garcia M. Colombas, *Paradise et vie angelique: Le sens eschatologique de la vocation chrétienne*, Cerf, Paris, 1961. V. Ranke-Heinemann, "Zum Ideal der *vita angelica* im fruehen Moenchtum," *GL* 29 (1956), pp. 347-357.

[18] *RB* 4,46.

[19] *RB* 73,8.

[20] *RB* Prol 2.

[21] *RB* Prol 50.

[22] *RB* 7,39.

[23] Cf. J. Leclercq, art. "Discipline," *DSp* 3.1291-1302.

[24] Siegfried Wenzel, "The Three Enemies of Man," *MDS* 29 (1967), pp. 47-66.

[25] *RB* Prol 45,50; 7,67-70.

[26] On the theme of *akedia* cf. G. Bardy, art. "Acédia," *DSp* 1.166-169; this is translated and summarized in *TJ* 2. Siegfried Wenzel, *The Sin of Sloth: Acedia in Medieval Thought and Tradition*, The University of North Carolina Press, Chapel Hill, 1967. S. Giora Shoham, *Society and the Absurd*, Basil Blackwell, Oxford, 1974. Mark D. Altschule, "Acedia; Its Evolution from Deadly Sin to Psychiatric Syndrome," *British Journal of Psychiatry* 111 (1965), pp. 117-119. Id., "The Two Kinds of Depression according to St. Paul," *British Journal of Psychiatry* 113 (1967), pp. 779-780. Noel L. Brann, "Is Acedia Melancholy? A Re-examination of the Question in the Light of Fra Battista de Crema's *Della cognitione et vittoria di se stesso* (1531)," *Journal of the History of Medicine and Allied Sciences* 34.2 (1979), pp. 180-199. There is a beautiful article by Jean Leclercq on stability: "In Praise of Stability," in *MS* 13 (1982), pp. 82-98.

[27] Cf. Charles Dumont, "The Mystery of Obedience according to St. Benedict and St. Gregory," in *TJ* 23 (1982), pp. 5-20. The continuations of this series are "The Holy Labour of Obedience," in *TJ* 24 (1983), pp. 4-10 and "The Phenomenology of Obedience," in *TJ* 25 (1983), pp. 36-41. For a treatment of obedience in its reciprocality with the due exercise of monastic authority cf. my "Leadership in a Benedictine Context," in *TJ* 22 (1982), pp. 5-103.

THE VALUE OF STABILITY

This article started life as part of a spiritual commentary on the OCSO constitutions, abandoned for lack of interest. It explores some of the spiritual significance of the first vow prescribed by Benedict, taking as its starting point the dense text of the Cistercian constitutions. This article appeared in Cistercian Studies Quarterly 31.3 (1996).

The content of the first Benedictine vow has always been something of a puzzle. Jacques Winandy concluded that it was "a term and a concept not free of ambiguity."[1] There is, for instance, no article on the spiritual aspects of stability in the meter-long *Dictionnaire de Spiritualité*. Usually the canonical obligation of the vow is clearly enough defined in constitutions according to the nature of particular Benedictine congregations. Even so, it remains difficult to know exactly what value is enshrined in the vow. What animates its observance? To what extent can stability be considered an "evangelical counsel"? Is stability a value that may worthily be embodied in any serious Christian life?.

In this article I would like to reflect on the values inherent in Benedictine stability. My starting point will be the brief text on this vow to be found in the *Constitutions and Statutes of the Cistercian Order of the Strict Observance*. The masculine and feminine texts are the same; here I take the liberty of basing my reflections on the masculine text.

1. General Remarks

We begin with the text on stability and point out some elements of background that give a basic clue to its meaning.

> **C. 9   Stability of Place**
>
> By the vow of stability
> within his community
> a brother obliges himself
> there
> to make constant use
> of the means of the spiritual craft,
> trusting in the providence of God
> who has called him
> to this place and
> to this group of brothers.

This text is little changed from that of draft prepared for the 1984 General Chapter discussion (*Project Three*).

> By his profession of stability a brother obliges himself to persevere in the practice of the spiritual craft in the monastery of his profession, confident in the providence of God which has brought him to this place and entrusted him to these brothers.

Notwithstanding the historical complexity of the question, there was great insistence at the General Chapter that the profession of stability be clearly stated to be a separate vow, this, it was alleged, as a means of placating the Congregation of Religious.[2] Another difference is that the important term "perseverance" has dropped out, **although it is clearly linked with stability in *RB* 58,9. The sense, however, remains the same.**

The basic idea of stability espoused by this *Constitution* is grounded in the conclusion to Benedict's chapter on the instruments of good works. Stability principally concerns perseverance in the practice of the totality of monastic virtues.

> These are the instruments of the spiritual craft. If we will have used them continually, day and night, and handed them back on judgment day, then we will be recompensed by the Lord with the reward he himself promised. "Eye has not seen, nor ear heard what God has prepared for those who love him." The workshop where we must diligently accomplish all these matters is the enclosure of the monastery and stability in the community (*RB* 4,75-78).

The challenging note that the *Constitution* takes from the *Rule* is that stability is dynamic not static. Stability is not to be confused with tenure; a guaranteed future not tied to performance. Stability is not a matter of immobility or resistance to change but of maintaining one's momentum: "to make constant use there of the means of the spiritual craft." Since loss of fervor generally manifests itself in an inability to respond creatively to the challenge of change, stability is its exact opposite. The vow enjoins sustained progress in monasticity, notwithstanding the new challenges that life concretely lays before us.

In this vein Bernard of Clairvaux describes the negative component of the vow in terms of avoidance of anything that would impair continuing progress.

> The contract of stability rules out henceforth any feeble relapse, angry departure, aimless or curious wandering and every vagary of fickleness.[3]

This vow's observance neutralizes opposite threats to monastic *disciplina*. On the one hand it rules out the kind of routine sluggishness that comes from regarding the monastery as a nesting place where survival requires minimal effort. It equally excludes our being driven by instinctive reactions into any withdrawal from the way of life we have embraced. In accordance with the usage of the opening chapter of Benedict's *Rule* we might say that stability keeps us as cenobites, not sarabaites or gyrovagues.

Stability is the first vow in *RB* 58,17 and in the traditional formula of profession. It cannot be separated from fidelity to the monastic means (*conversatio morum*) and obedience,[4] but it has its own distinctive emphasis. This may be summarized under seven headings. A schema may illustrate how the material is related to the different phrases of the *Constitution*.

OUTLINE

By the vow of stability
within his community   # 2: *Aggregation to a Local Community*
a brother obliges himself there   #3: *Localization*
to make constant use
of the means of the spiritual craft   #4: *Commitment to Practice*
                                       #5: *Perseverance in Practice*
                                       #6: *Stability of Mind*
trusting in the providence of God
who has called him   #7: *Trust in Providence*
to this place and
to this group of brothers.   #8: **Lovers of the Brothers**

2. *Aggregation to a Local Community*

The effect of solemn profession is that the candidate becomes fully a member of the community (and, according to *Constitution* 56.2, also of the Order). It is not simply a legal nicety. Nor is it a practical matter of cohabiting the same address, or even sharing a lifestyle and having common ideals. Profession implies a monk being linked by an inner bond to his community until his death.

There is a firm tradition in the Order that one's spiritual physiognomy is determined not only by the Cistercian charism in general but also by the special quality of the local community. There is a lot of anecdotal evidence to support the notion. Perhaps this is connected with the linking of stability with a given community, rather than with the congregation or Order. More subtly, this marking derives from absorbing "the Cistercian spirit" not from books or in an abstract essence, but concretely from persons who each embody aspects of it. The particular grace that each monk and nun lives is communicated to receptive newcomers even beyond contemporary generations. No one can pass on to others what they have not themselves received, but usually the opposite is also true. Those who receive cannot fail to communicate something of their own giftedness. This is why love for the community in its specificity, expressed in a reverence for seniors and a willingness to receive from them, is such a necessary means of being imbued with the character of the local community.

Monastic metabolism is slow. No matter how glamorous, attractive or talented candidates are, they will not win unreserved acceptance from the community in the same way as one who has kept faith over many decades and through many difficult times. There is a special affection, latitude and forgiveness given to those who have steadfastly identified with the community for the best years of their lives. In the ritual of solemn profession the community embraces the newcomer. So long as the newly professed remains substantially faithful to what has been promised, the community will continue to sustain him and be indulgent in regard to his inevitable limitations. The bond is stronger and deeper than a momentary embrace.

Most communities do not demand that monks attach themselves exclusively without any other relationships or interests. But there is a thin and undefined line between what is acceptable as an addition to a fundamental adherence to the community, and what is already becoming a substitute or compensation for a non-existent local commitment. Those who belong and feel at home in the community, are both zealous for its improvement and loyal to the point of being a little defensive about outside criticism. They allow themselves to be formed by local standards and discover an emerging unanimity even with those whom they consider different. On the other hand, those who remain coolly detached rarely pass beyond the politics of abstract ideals. They quickly become alienated and never experience fraternal solidarity in the pursuit of the monastic goal. They may remain fervent in their own eyes, but theirs is often a self-righteous virtue that separates from the community rather than builds bridges.

Solemn profession of stability means that the whole cosmic drama of salvation is transferred to the microcosm of the monastery at least as far as the individual is concerned. Contacts, activities and even apostolate may involve persons in the wider Church but, because of the effects of monastic profession, the battleground remains fundamentally the monastery itself. Other engagements are to be assessed for what they bring to this basic commitment. What anyone has to offer "outside" will depend on the quality of life "inside." Henceforward personal existence is mysteriously bonded with that of one's community.

It is precisely the containment of ultimate events within the human scale that enables the monk to live more intensely. "I am a human being and consider myself no stranger to anything that is human," as the ancient poet wrote. Monastic life is not a means of escape from anything. On the contrary, it has the effect of bringing monastics into sustained confrontation with realities they might otherwise avoid, disguise or deny. Part of the bonding of a monastic community results from the common exposure to the ultimate demands of existence, the frailty of their response, and the working of grace negating their weakness. To experience communion at such a profound level needs the security of lifelong commitment, not only to God, not only to the monastic ideal, but also to the people with whom the journey is made.[5]

3. Localization

This vow is often qualified as "stability of place."[6] The Constitution emphasizes this by the title and, more especially, by its inclusion of the little word *ibi* (there). Thus is clearly localized the rest of the content of stability.[7] This is not to say that the primary object of the vow is enclosure, as this is envisaged canonically. It does mean, however, that the reality of stability cannot be realized without spending a substantial part of one's life and investing one's energies within monastery limits, living in a state of mutual visibility with others in the community, making the monastery one's home and feeling fully at home only in the monastery. Particular excursions can be considered lawful, helpful and productive, but what needs to be considered is the sum total of absences and their emotional content relative to the life lived within the community. When presence in the community falls below a critical point, a sense of belonging evaporates. If outside contacts begin to engage the bulk of one's affectivity, then it would not be surprising to find that relations with the community begin to be unsatisfying. A balance between "inside" and "outside" is not always easy to achieve. The first step in succeeding, however, is to be aware of some of the universal hazards. In my mind there is little doubt that many who leave, disenchanted with the level of affective satisfaction in the community, are those who have, over a long period, sought affirmation and support "outside," without a comparable personal presence "inside."[8]

Such personal presence within the community does not exactly correspond with bodily presence, as even St Bernard notes. One can continue to remain within the enclosure, but roam at will throughout the world by fantasy. This will often lead to the well-recognized monastic vice of *acedia*—an unconcern for community doings, a depressive detachment from what concerns the group and a consequent inability to feel commitment to anything inside the monastery.

On the other hand, one of the beautiful results of spending the bulk of one's life in a single place is that one retains and cherishes the memories of past years, surrounded as one is by so many reminders. We mellow alongside the trees we plant. Like those who spend their lives in the village of their birth, we can never escape from our history. We are always confronted with our past without having it erased by a change of ambiance and company. Not able to leave behind stories of youthful excess or foolishness, necessity becomes a virtue. We are compelled to live in greater truthfulness, serenely experiencing a proportionately deeper sense of acceptance, and having a strong sense of continuity. It can also be said, if St Bede is any example, that geographical limitation need not result in any narrowness of mind. Indeed, depth of understanding is often helped by the lack of distraction consequent upon much movement. Those who are faithful to stability can be truly called, as Stephen Harding was (EP 17), "lovers of the place." Ultimately, loving the place is a facet of loving ourselves and accepting the vicissitudes of our personal history.

4. Commitment to Practice

The first effect of stability is that it brings lofty dreams of spiritual growth down to earth. Present opportunities are to be taken seriously since nothing much is going to change. In this aspect, stability parallels the functioning of Benedict's first level of humility. Once the idea sinks in, there is no excuse for postponing effort under the pretext that opportunities are lacking or that the time is not ripe. In our supermarket culture it is possible to spend a lifetime toying with alternatives, convinced that one is a genuine spiritual seeker, but never committing oneself to anything beyond the first flush of enthusiasm. Stability puts an end to this. The monk accepts to live in a microcosm, where the spiritual combat remains firmly on a human scale. The challenge of this intense channeling is that life is lived more intensely.

Evagrius of Pontus entitled his treatise on monastic life, the *Praktikos*, bringing into focus the active basis on which monasticism builds. Stability ensures that it is more difficult to avoid the twin struggles experienced by all who attempt the practice of a spiritual life: actively to persevere in doing good and passively to withstand the rigors of progressive purification. Both tasks are eminently practical; both demand a lifetime's expenditure of energy.

In particular, when external circumstances are relatively unchanging, we are more frequently confronted with those elements in our being that need reformation. This happens not simply at a cognitive level—by being kept informed of our own liabilities—but also at the level of personal experience. In a mysterious way, stable communal interaction has the effect of burning out the dross precisely by making us aware of the concrete dimensions of our negativity and causing us to agonize as a result. Aspects of the self that could be successfully concealed in looser association assert themselves in a close community and cause pain—to others, certainly, but more especially to ourselves. Stability protects this process of purgation. We are tied down under the surgeon's knife.

A community that is oriented towards contemplation needs to recognize that its goal cannot be realized without members experiencing this pain of passive purification. Such purification is not only the result of mysterious interior states, it also comes about through the blunders and blemishes of social interaction. The hardships and difficulties listed by Benedict in his fourth level of humility are essential to spiritual progress. They cannot be dismissed as mere products of an imperfect community that do not exist where the grass grows greener. They are the ordinary means by which the image of Christ is re-formed in us.

Stability prevents us from running away from necessary development. From this angle, what works against stability is any tendency to delude ourselves into thinking that progress is possible without growth pangs and that difficulties, therefore, are avoidable. This leads us to project our inner dissatisfaction on the community and blame others for the negativity we experience in ourselves. We all know those who spend their lives lamenting the malformation they received and the misunderstandings with which they are everywhere beset. We perceive it in others, but the tendency is also in ourselves. In any conflict it is the other who is wrong, demanding, offensive, unkind. For all of us, much of the challenge of stability is the interior task of learning to sit with our own impairment, allowing ourselves to be hollowed out as the frontiers of dread expand, blaming neither ourselves nor others, but bearing the weight of sin, absorbing its malice and not allowing ourselves the luxury of wilting under the pressure or passing the time devising means of evading the truth.

That this is a purification and not habitual bitterness is shown by a real growth in sweetness of disposition. It is through the willingness to have one's sharp corners rounded that breaks the link between familiarity and contempt. One's appreciation of others increases as obstacles are dismantled and this not only by the friction of social contact but also by changes wrought at a deeper level of personality.

Identification with a local community leads to acceptance, love and loyalty in its regard. It includes a willingness to travel with the community not only in the halcyon days of prosperity but also in times of personal regression or communal difficulty. It means not dreaming too easily of more attractive alternatives. St Anselm has a good description of this in *Letter* 37.

> Just as any young tree, if frequently transplanted or often disturbed by being torn up after having recently been planted in a particular place, will never be able to take root, [and] will rapidly wither and bring no fruit to perfection, similarly an unhappy monk, if he often moves from place to place at his own whim, or remaining in one place is frequently agitated by his hatred of it, never achieves stability with roots of love, grows weary in the face of every useful exercise and does not grow rich in the fruitfulness of good works.
>
> And when he realizes—if perchance he does reflect on it— that he is making progress, not towards good, but towards evil, he unjustly assigns the whole blame for his misery not to his own behavior but to that of others, and hence unhappily works himself up to even greater hatred of those among whom he lives.
>
> Wherefore it behooves anyone taking on the vow of monastic life (*cenobitarum propositum*) to strive with total application of his mind (*tota mentis intentione*) to set down roots of love in whatever monastery he made his profession—unless it is so bad that he is forced to do evil against his will—and to refrain from judging the behavior of others or the customs of the place, however useless they appear to him, as long as they are not contrary to divine precepts. Let him rejoice at having at last found a place where he can stay, not unwillingly but voluntarily, for the rest of his life, and having put away all anxiety about moving from one place to another and, being at peace, let him resolve to

devote himself assiduously (*sedulo vacet*) to pursuing the single-minded exercise of a holy life.[9]

St Anselm reasons that failure actively to persevere in one's life-project leads to emotional instability, frustration and eventually stagnation. Blaming others and moving around are no cure. The only solution for one who experiences the difficulty of maintaining fervor in a holy life is "to strive with total application of his mind to set down roots of love in whatever monastery he has made his profession." To love and serve those close at hand often changes our perception of what they are.

Such texts seem to envisage stability as essential for an individual's spiritual growth. The purpose of the vow is not merely canonical regulation of one's relationship with a community. It discourages us from deferring love until we find a community worthy of it. The barriers to love are within ourselves. Until we dismantle them, no community will meet our standards. Meanwhile progress ceases. And because we fail to recognize how much we contribute to our own unhappiness, we project blame onto the community. Stability is really a matter of learning to love. And this process means staying around long enough for monastic grace to work its magic on us.

5. *Perseverance in Practice*

Perseverance is the essential component of stability. This does not primarily denote the happy accident of dying in the monastic habit, but sustained fidelity to the "monastic means" envisaged in the term *conversatio morum*.

Initially, as is indicated in *RB* 58,9, stability means submitting patiently to the formative process by which a man begins to be changed into a monk: following monastic practices, acquiring the values inherent in them, and gradually being formed in the *philosophia*

Christi so that everything is evaluated in terms of the Gospel of Christ. This is not as smooth a transition as we might imagine. It involves obscure inner conflicts and resistances—a certain deconstruction must take place before much progress is evident. It is important that neophytes learn to stay where they are while the storms rage. "He endures: neither losing heart nor going away"(*RB* 7,36). When the immediate drama is over, there is a degree of clarity: a window of opportunity in which good decisions can appropriately be made. Meanwhile the apprentice monk is told to stand firm.[10]

The struggle of stability does not end with profession. Life presents us with new challenges as we develop, and we need new resources to deal with them creatively. Not everyone who successfully completes initial formation is necessarily equipped to handle the surprises of later years. If these are not to overwhelm us, then we need to ensure that we continue to be formed throughout our middle years. This mature and ongoing formation comes about chiefly by our wholehearted embrace of monastic *conversatio*: liturgy, prayer, *lectio divina*, work, community involvement. These are the unexciting buttresses that support our commitment. To keep practicing them, in turn, involves a fair degree of fidelity to the elements of traditional *disciplina* that safeguard and protect the way of life: regularity, silence, self-denial, and obedience.

As we grow in the monastic way of life, unfortunately, these means often lose their urgency and can be allowed to slip away. Once socialized in a monastic community, it is easy to allow oneself simply to be carried by the corporate momentum. The monastic persona may continue to exist, but it begins to lack the skeleton of regular, personal investment of energy. We are "faithful" to the common exercises, but there is a certain hollowness about our observance. While we are sustained only by external structures interior values begin to atrophy. There is a danger that a single buffet may cause the whole edifice of our life to collapse.

It is for this reason that it is important to identify as significant elements of stability the interior exercises that prevent our monasticity from being an insubstantial shell. Our perseverance is linked especially with personal commitment to prayer and *lectio divina*. These are the means by which the heart and mind are evangelized and thus equipped to live a life based on the Gospel. Furthermore, they cause a shift in the center of gravity away from the notion of a spiritual life based on observances in the direction of Christocentrism. Constitution 3.5 says:

> The organization of the monastery is directed to bringing the monks into close union with Christ, since it is only through the experience of personal love for the Lord Jesus that the specific gifts of the Cistercian vocation can flower. Only if the brothers prefer nothing to Christ will they be happy to persevere in a life that is ordinary, obscure and laborious.

Enthusiasm for monastic practices will quickly evaporate unless there is a corresponding growth in affective experience. Alternatively, monastic observance will become mindless: an end in itself to be performed with military punctilio or mere bureaucratic compliance with accepted routines.

There can be no stability that is not expressed by external fidelity. St Benedict's goal of turning away from evil and doing good (*RB* Prol 17) is not speedily achieved. The vow constantly alerts us to our obligation to keep on rendering the duty of divine service (*RB* 50,4). Perseverance in this noble calling is, however, practically impossible without a nuanced adherence to the value-system that sustains the practices. Stability of place cannot be separated from stability of mind. It is not enough to be keepers of the Rule; we must also be *lovers* of the Rule, as were both Alberic and Stephen (*Exordium Parvum* 9, 17).

6. Stability of Mind

John Cassian defines prayer in terms of immobility of mind. The monk who seeks perseverance in prayer "strives for immovable tranquillity of mind and perpetual purity."[11] Prayer follows on a state of inner quietness that is the result of prolonged exercise in the virtues. This moment of intense mental and spiritual concentration (*intentio cordis*) is only possible on the supposition of a harmonious life, the result of substantial dedication to the *unum necessarium*. Any lack of focus in living produces an uncreative dispersal of energies in prayer. Stability is at the service of contemplation.

Monastic tradition shows itself aware that a multiplicity of thoughts disturbs the steadiness of the monastic *propositum* and destroys the attentiveness necessary for prayer. This concerns not only the entertaining fantasies typical of *acedia*, but also the laudable preoccupations associated with work. This is how Bernard describes the situation.

> I say that psalmody should be performed with a pure heart to indicate that, during psalmody, you should not be thinking of anything except the psalm itself. Nor do I mean that only vain and useless thoughts are to be avoided. At that time and in that place are to be avoided those necessary thoughts about necessary community matters which frequently importune the minds of those brothers who have official positions.[12]

More disturbing than these are thoughts that constantly submit to questioning the basic direction one has given one's life. St Benedict seems to think that once profession is made, after prolonged and serious deliberation, there is nothing further to ponder (*RB*

58,14-16). Even reviewing alternatives becomes a temptation to be avoided—not only because it undermines the permanence of the commitment once made, but also because it is the expression of a fundamental dissatisfaction with the relationship established by profession. Even to entertain the thought of an alternative life undermines the totality of daily self-giving.[13] Deferring a generous effort to live monastic *conversatio* until "the vocational question is settled" is a not uncommon recipe for apostasy.

A great threat to quietness of mind is the suffering experienced as life proceeds. On the other hand the practice of patience, as this is envisaged by St Benedict's fourth level of humility (*RB* 7,35-43), is probably the surest way of experiencing an habitual state of calm that often leads to intense prayer.[14] The key to patience is faith.

7. Trust in Providence

There is an obscurity inherent in any human commitment. When we oblige ourselves to do something, we can never know in advance whether the circumstances in which we are due to render our debt will have changed. Before binding ourselves we make an assessment on the basis of both objective and subjective information, but no practical judgment can be infallible. What we decide comes into being only *after* our decision; we can never know what would have been if we had decided otherwise. Every commitment we make involves an element of risk-taking. On the other hand, once we have taken the step, we are honor-bound to a certain obstinacy not only in keeping our promises but in actively pursuing the purposes for which the promises were made.

The commitment involved in monastic profession is even more hazardous. In effect it is a commitment to self-transcendence. "Self-transcendence" is a very fine phrase and the process itself is easily recognized as the essential component of ongoing adult growth. But the daily reality of allowing our limits to be broached is a ready source of much anxiety. By its very nature self-transcendence involves yielding control of our lives to the apparent vagaries of life-as-it-happens. Sometimes there is turmoil: our sensibilities are affronted by unexpected difficulties, whatever skills we may have developed may seem irrelevant, we have no way of gauging the shape of our future. As we become more experienced we understand that we have no certain guarantee of a comfortable life. We find that trying to anticipate unpleasant surprises can be more unsettling than dealing with the misfortune itself.

This means that we have to develop the firm conviction that whatever comes from the hand of God is good. Instead of blaming those around us for the negativities we experience, we need to develop a robust faith in Providence. Such trust is an important component of stability. If we are blind to the action of God in our daily life, we will reject the value of our concrete circumstances. Instead of growing through difficulties we will probably want to go somewhere else.

The perception that God is truly in this place and that I am called to find communion with God *here* is a very substantial gift of grace. Fundamentally it is what brought me to the monastery in the first place and what continues to sustain my hope when life becomes hard and rough (*RB* 58,8). This is why the *Suscipe* sung at the moment of profession becomes the *leitmotiv* of monastic life in its entirety: "Receive/sustain me, Lord Christ, according to your promise and I shall live; do not disappoint me in my hope."

Trust in Providence is not necessarily a soporific. It can also be energizing in that it enables us to capitalize on a window of opportunity: *Carpe diem*. If we believe that God is truly acting in our lives we will be more inclined to take the "signs of the times" seriously, lest the Lord send us a messenger for a particular reason (*RB* 61,3). Such practical faith is certainly a comfort, but sometimes it can be a challenge as well.

Trust in Providence is the real test of faith. Cassian affirms this clearly in the first conference of Abba Isaac on prayer:

> No one can sincerely say *Thy will be done on earth as it is in heaven*, except those who believe that God arranges all things—whether they seem favorable or unfavorable—for our benefit, and is more concerned and diligent regarding the health and comfort of God's people than we are for ourselves.[15]

If we believe that the present situation is not opaque to God and that it offers the possibility of a real spiritual growth, then we are much more likely "there to make constant use of the means of the spiritual craft." As we grow in monasticity and faith we begin to experience also an expansion in our capacity to love others without self-interest.

8. Lovers of the Brothers

Fraternal love or friendship is one of the great challenges of cenobitic life. Distance seems to make the heart grow fonder. The closeness of communal living can easily make us hard-hearted with respect to others. Daily interaction continuing for a lifetime permits no escape from the exigencies of love. With more exposure, occasions for coolness and conflict multiply, bringing to the surface negativity within myself and within others. It is easy to opt for a substitute association that is no relationship, but merely politeness, lack of interest, institutionalized reserve, withdrawal and distance. With enough escape routes the situation is not totally intolerable, but it is scarcely a challenge to affectivity. In a monastic setting, even a desire for solitude and silence can sometimes mask a fear of the risks involved in drawing close to other persons. "Seeking God" is sometimes the respectable face of avoiding human beings.

Contemplative community is not a denial of human intimacy, but it progressively demands a high level of integrity in relationships. Humility, service and amiability lay the foundations on which good relationships build. Good relationships prepare the soil from which friendship flowers. Monastic friendship is always eminently realistic. It learns to cope with negativity on one side or the other, and keeps coming closer despite the increasing level of demand that this can sometimes evoke. Any effort to be truthful with a fellow human being means risking rejection because, ultimately, there can be no hiding of one's inadequacies. To love another exposes one's own vulnerability. On the other hand, to care for a brother means bearing his burdens: his limitations, his hurts, his mistakes and ultimately, if the relationship becomes truly redemptive, the crushing weight of his sins. In some way, growth in prayerfulness demands a collateral movement towards others and, at the same time, provides the energy to sustain that outward motion by a love that becomes ever more pure and disinterested.

St Alberic of Cîteaux was distinguished by the title "lover of the brothers" (*Exordium Parvum* 9).[16] One supposes that this was a love exercised in the proximity of daily dealings, and not merely a tribute to his capacity to reside in a monastery without ruffling others' feathers. To live monastic profession as a Cistercian, is to be a lifelong learner in the school of love. Stability is an important factor in this development and, on the other hand, without genuine love stability is meaningless.

Conclusion

The spiritual value behind the vow of stability is difficult to isolate from the other components of fervent monastic living. It involves ongoing fidelity to the ordinary monastic means of spiritual growth and stoutheartedness in bearing with inevitable hardships. It is a call to continuing confidence in God's handling of our case, even though our life seems not to be what we previously expected. We may not be called to the heroic stubbornness of Job, but we can at least identify with his sentiment: "Even if God kill me, still will I trust him" (Job 13:25). Gregory the Great comments thus on this verse.

> There is no virtue of patience in times of prosperity. The ones who are really patient are those who are crushed by adversity and yet never bend under its weight; their hope remains upright. It is about the unjust that Scripture says, "They will praise you when you do good to them." In this is the mind (*mens*) of the good distinguished from others that the praise of almighty God continues even in contrary times. The mind is not broken when external things are lost, it does not fall when external glory fails. Rather, whatever it was in the days of riches, it is more so now because it is stronger and remains stable when riches are lost.[17]

Faith gives us fervor when things go well and it is a bulwark for our commitment when adversity comes. It is faith in the ultimate goodness of God that keeps us where we are and keeps us growing. Stability is no more than the expression of evangelical faith.

NOTES

[1] See Jean Leclercq, "In Praise of Stability," *MS* 13 (1982), p. 98.

² There are two distinct questions involved. Did St Benedict intend the *promissio* of monastic profession to be a vow? Does the text of *RB* 58,17 indicate one vow or three vows? See Richard Yeo, *The Structure and Content of Monastic Profession: A juridical study, with particular regard to the practice of the English Benedictine Congregation since the French Revolution*, StA 83 (Rome, Edizioni Abbazia S. Paolo, 1982), p. 328. His conclusion: "We should therefore describe the *promissio* as a *sui generis* commitment. It is not a promise to God, but *coram Deo*; not a promise to the abbot and community, but *coram omnibus*. It is a solemn, binding and public commitment of oneself, and it is made *coram Deo* in order that the monk should know that should he default he will have to answer for his failure to God, not just to men."

³ *Pre* 44; *SBO* 3.284.7-9.

⁴ As Peter the Venerable noted: "If they keep the first vow [stability] they are held by the content of the second [*conversio—sic—morum*]. If they keep the second, they are bound by the constraints of the first." *Ep* 28; Giles Constable [ed.], *The Letters of Peter the Venerable*, Cambridge, Harvard University Press, 1967, vol. 1, p. 55.

⁵ "Stability has the nuance of fidelity and perseverance, and this is related primarily to persons, not primarily to place." Ambrose Wathen, "*Conversatio* and Stability in the Rule of Benedict," *MS* 11 (1975), p.43.

⁶ *Stabilitas loci*. This phrase was rejected by Latinists at the time the Constitutions were redacted, on the ground that it seemed to make the vow concern itself with the avoidance of earthquakes. The expression *stabilitas in loco* was preferred.

⁷ "Contemporary Western society is marked by a loss of the sense of place, and its intellectual traditions, far from controlling this loss, have encouraged it....

Humanity is not fitted to live in placeless communities, the creations of pure human will unmediated through natural circumstances, the communities offered to us by the liberal tradition of political theory." Oliver Donovan, "The Loss of a Sense of Place," *ITQ* 55 (1989), p. 39; 58 (1992), p. 48.

[8] Clearly, the survival of a vocation often involves living in limbo for a while—and more than once. To mix metaphors somewhat, there is a time lag between burning one's bridges to the world and putting down roots in the monastery.

[9] Walter Frölich (trans.), *The Letters of Saint Anselm of Canterbury: Volume One* (CS 96), Kalamazoo, Cistercian Publications, 1990; pp. 134-135. The image of the tree is commonplace, perhaps deriving from *Vitae Patrum* 5, 7, 36: "Sicut arbor fructificare non potest si saepius transferatur, sic nec monachus frequenter migrans potest fructificare" (*PL* 73, 902a). See also *Eynsham Customary* 11.19; CCM 2 (Siegburg, F. Schmitt, 1975) p. 123. 4-5.

[10] In this sense, the verb *stare*, from which "stability" is derived, occurs in *RB* 58,11 and 13.

[11] *Conl* 9.2; *SChr* 54, p. 40. This text is one that Salvatore Marsili identifies as dependent on Evagrius; In this case *De Oratione* 2: "The soul, purified by the fullness of the virtues, strengthens the mind's stance so that it is able to acquire the *katastasis* it seeks." See Giovanni Cassiano. ed. *Evagrio Pontico: dottrina sulla carità e contemplazione* (Rome, Herder, 1936).

[12] *SChr* 47.8; *SBO* 2.66.17-21.

[13] In Henry Purcell's opera *Dido and Aeneas*, Dido thus reproaches her lover for wavering between love and duty: "O feckless man...it is enough whate'er you

now decree, that you had once thought of leaving me." Infidelity begins at the level of thought.

[14] See M. Casey, "The Virtue of Patience in Western Monastic Tradition," *CSQ* 21 (1986), pp.3-23.

[15] *Conl* 9.20; *SChr* 54, pp. 57-58.

[16] Perhaps the phrase *fratrum amator* is drawn from Onias' description of Jeremiah in 2 Mac 15:14.

[17] *Moralia* 11,34,47; *CChrM* 143A, pp. 612-613. I translate as "remains stable" the verb *stat*, from which stability derives. Note that modern versions of Job, such as the *NRSV*, translate the text in the opposite sense, "God will kill me. I have no hope."

SACRAMENTALITY AND MONASTIC CONSECRATION

This article appeared in 1998 as part of a whole issue of Word and Spirit *devoted to the theme of monastic profession. It wished to explore the profound theology inherent in the traditional liturgy for monastic consecration. In particular it reflected on the idea of profession as a "second baptism".*

In a minute addressed to the Roman Curia in 1939 Agostino Gemelli remarked on an imbalance inherent in many treatments of religious life. Most of these tended to give considerable emphasis to the vows as sources of obligation, without paying much attention to the theme of consecration.[1] By the act of profession, the religious was perceived as entering into a series of contractual obligations as specified by the vows. Minimalism marked the definition of the content of the three vows — since inner dispositions were regarded as out of bounds for legal prescription. The result was a two-tiered notion of profession based on the distinction of "vow" and "virtue." Consecration was not considered an important concept for understanding religious life.[2]

1. Confusion of Terms

The use of the term "consecration" in relation to religious life is typical of postconciliar reflection, although it had been in use from the time of Pius XII. There is, however, a duality in the term that is worth examining.[3]

> a) *Active Consecration:* Persons dedicate themselves to God by a specific act of commitment. From this standpoint the consecrated life is viewed in terms of self-offering, fidelity to promises and lifelong perseverance of will. The primary agent of active consecration is the one making profession.[4]
>
> b) *Passive Consecration:* Persons receive from the Church a blessing that imparts a sacred character to those who receive it. This is analogous to the consecration of bread and wine at Mass or the consecration of a church or chalice. The primary agent of the consecration is God acting through the Church and the appropriate ministers. In this sense consecration refers both to the prayer made by the church and the effect of the rite on the person consecrated.

To illustrate the difference one might say that in communities of monks the abbot *receives* the active consecration (or self-offering) as the superior of the community; he *imparts* passive consecration as a priest and minister of the Church. Active consecration is a moral and juridical reality; passive consecration belongs broadly to the sacramental order.

In the *Rule of St Benedict* active consecration is expressed by the writing of the schedule of profession, signing it and placing it on the altar.[5] It is a deliberate act by which novices remove their lives from the sphere of self-determination and relocate them in the sphere of the sacred. Passive consecration occurs through the traditional act of divestiture and investiture. A worldly identity is exchanged for the monastic *habitus*.[6] These two elements are the columns on which the whole rite of profession depends. They are connected by the *Suscipe*, which is simultaneously a prayer for the acceptance of the offering (in this sense *suscipere* is technical cultic usage) and a prayer for the continuance of God's saving action.

Initially the induction of a monk was simply a matter of investiture with the monastic garb. This was considered to be a symbolic act that effected the transition to the monastic state.[7] In the *Rule of Benedict* the ritual is richer. With the passage of time, simple components were considerably amplified. Rites were duplicated and prayers were added to accompany the hitherto silent ritual acts. The most significant change was the addition of collects to be said over the prostrate form of the newly professed, probably borrowing from the rite of presbyteral ordination.[8]

Both aspects of profession remained in view as the rites and the theology evolved. The term *consecratio* and its cognates continued in use, especially for the liturgical act.[9]

Even with the resurgence of the vocabulary of consecration, there is a certain amount of ambiguity in the use of the term, although in both *Lumen Gentium* #44 and *Perfectae Caritatis* #5 the verb *mancipare* (to transfer ownership or rights to another—the opposite of "emancipate") is used for active consecration.[10] Nor is there more clarity regarding the relationship between the making of profession and the consecrated state.[11] The phrase in *Perfectae Caritatis* #1, *vita per consiliorum professionem consecrata*, seems to make consecration a result of the profession of the evangelical counsels, as if to suggest that it is a direct consequence of human action: the heart of profession is the emission of vows and their acceptance by accredited authority. The same formula is repeated in can. 573.1 *C.I.C.* and in the *instrumentum laboris* prepared for the 1994 Synod. This last document states, "the terms 'consecration' and 'consecrated life' are taken here in their precise theological meaning, indicating a life consecrated by means of the evangelical counsels and recognized as such by the Church."[12] Later, the text gives more detail about the nature of this consecration.

> Consecration consists of a grace of election and a particular gift of the Spirit who takes possession of a person and configures him to Christ and enables him to live his proper charism according to the evangelical counsels.[13]

The emphasis, however, remains on self-offering; very little is made of the state of consecration. The postsynodal exhortation, *Vita Consecrata*, precisely because of its admonitory character, dwells mainly on active consecration and the ongoing need for generosity. Furthermore it does this with great specificity, frequently returning to the individual vows of poverty, chastity and obedience in a manner that may feel foreign to those accustomed to the monastic approach to profession. There is recognition that the grace of profession includes a grace of configuration to Christ, but the nature of this conformation is scarcely explored; there is more interest in its effects in mission, in witness and in various activities.

Profession involves both active and passive consecration. There is a distinct danger that too much emphasis on the former may cause us to lose sight of the mystery and giftedness inherent in the grace of monastic consecration.[14] Reflection on the monastic tradition can help us recover a saner balance.

2. Sacramental Connections

In ancient monastic tradition, profession was seen as a rite in which the monk or nun was objectively set apart from God and established in a state of holiness through the ministry of the Church. In an era in which the notion of sacramentality was less rigid, it is not surprising that the understanding of the rite of monastic profession and its effects was influenced by the theology of the sacraments. The rite conferred grace even if the recipient was unable to participate.[15] Innocent II expressly forbade the Abbess of Las Huelgas to consecrate those whose profession she had received, understanding this act as reserved to ordained ministers.[16] Once given monastic consecration was not to be repeated.[17]

a) *The Paschal Mystery*

Profession was seen as the doorway by which the monk or nun entered into the mystery of the death and resurrection of Jesus. Herbert of Clairvaux states this explicitly. "It is clear that the monk's habit [cowl] contains a great mystery for one who is faithful to the monk's way of life. For it is made in the shape of the cross."[18]

Among Benedictines the dramatic impact of this symbolism was heightened. In some places the profession was always held on Friday.[19] The candidate was covered with a funeral pall while lying prostrate. After profession, the monk spent three days entombed in the black cowl, with the hood sewn up so that the garment could not be removed.[20] The silence was so strict that the newly-professed monk was forbidden to make even a necessary confession; in a case of serious sin he was to make an act of contrition, but not to forgo the privilege of daily communion.[21] At the end of this time, there was a resurrection and the monks took his place as a fully-fledged member of the chapter with active voice.

Monastic life is the monk's means of sharing in the paschal mystery. It gives life by inflicting death. Not a ritual death or a relatively painless symbol common to many rites of passage, but a systematic demolition of identity with a view to recombining all its elements in a later synthesis. Some centrifuge and are lost, others are re-incorporated at a deeper level of truth. This deconstructionist aspect of monasticism is not accidental or due to human folly or malice. It is the essence and meaning of monastic *conversatio*. It means that neither the theology nor the experience of monastic life makes any sense without reference to the paschal mystery. Such elements of the rite of profession signal the linkage.

b) Martyrdom

As the writers of the early Church realized that the grace of martyrdom was not given to all and as its possibility waned with changed political circumstances, a theory of substitute martyrdom began to evolve.[22] It was recognized that a life of heroic Christian witness could be lived in embracing an ascetical life or by becoming a monk or nun. In this way the sacramental significance of martyrdom which, in the mind of Cyprian "had the value of 'a baptism of blood', of the eucharistic sacrifice,"[23] was attached to the practical living of an evangelical life. Mundane daily actions were thereby invested with a spiritual potency that came from God and far exceeded any human contribution.

The symbolism is complete only on the understanding that the monk perseveres until and including death.[24] We know from an apothegm of Phocas that there was a connection in the minds of the ancient monks between profession, holy communion, the keeping of the Lord's Day and death.

> The Egyptian Fathers had the custom of keeping until their death the short-sleeved tunic (*lebiton*) and the cowl given to them when they received the holy habit and to have themselves buried in these garments. They wore them only on Sundays for holy communion and then immediately took them off.[25]

The receiving of the habit was the beginning of a process that continued with the lifelong reception of the eucharist and culminated only at death.

c) *Baptism*

From the time of St Jerome, monastic life was referred to as a "second baptism," completing the parallelism between monasticism and martyrdom. The conversion and renunciation typical of entry into monastic life were seen as fulfillment of the potential inherent in baptism. If there were tears of repentance, then these completed the symbolism of washing away post-baptismal sins. From the seventh century[26] the idea of a second baptism was applied also to the act and the rite of monastic profession.[27]

A key text in this matter comes from the *Verba Seniorum* 1,9: "There was once a great man among the seers who affirmed the following: 'The power I saw standing above baptism, I saw also standing over the monk's garment when he receives the spiritual habit.'"[28] The text is quoted by Smaragdus,[29] paraphrased by Odo of Cluny[30] and explained by such expositors as Odo of Canterbury[31] and Alcuin.[32]

There was a strong tradition that monastic profession restored innocence to the monk.[33] His post-baptismal, pre-monastic sins were forgiven since the option for a life of repentance effectively reversed the deviancies of the monk's former life and gave him a fresh start with baptismal graces unimpaired.[34] The monk is, according to Odo of Canterbury, "wholly reformed with the making of profession."[35] Bernard described the relationship of baptism and monastic profession thus:

> We who have clearly experienced the charms of a deceptive world and the perfidy of our own will have need of a second baptism, so to speak, the baptism of our conversion.[36]

> [Monastic life] restores the divine image in the human soul and makes us Christlike, much as baptism does. It is also another baptism in that we put to death the earthly side of our nature so that we may be more and more clothed with Christ, being thus buried in the likeness of his death. Just as in baptism we are delivered from the power of darkness and carried over into the kingdom of light, so likewise in the second regeneration of this holy profession we are refashioned in the light of virtue, being delivered not now from the unique darkness of original sin, but from many actual sins, according to that cry of the Apostle, "The night is far advanced and the day is at hand."[37]

This connection is extremely important for understanding the effects of monastic profession and will be discussed in more detail in a later section.

d) Confirmation

It is not easy to understand the specificity of confirmation in the light of its history and the different practices current in East and West.[38] Like religious profession it brings an increase and deepening of baptismal grace. As a permanent empowerment to express Christian faith by word and deed, confirmation serves as the driving force of religious and monastic vocation and animates both the prayer and the mission of the monk. Monastic profession is not a necessary consequence of confirmation but, going in the opposite direction, the sacraments of Christian initiation are the necessary preliminaries for monastic profession. Monastic *conversatio* draws its energy from baptism and confirmation. As a result, the intensification of the effects of these sacraments usually figures among the benefits prayed for in the liturgical rites of profession. "Profession is a sacramental intended to consummate the sacramental grace of baptism and confirmation."[39]

e) Confession

Monastic profession has been seen by tradition to act counter to personal sin. This assertion has been explained in different ways.

- ◆ Profession remits personal sin.[40]
- ◆ Profession negates the residue left by sin even after repentance and forgiveness.[41]
- ◆ Profession lessens the hold of the vices which are both the causes and effects of sinful acts.[42]
- ◆ Profession absolves from all penalties due to sin.[43]

As is evident, there is a clear consensus on the power of profession to neutralize sin, but there is no agreement about the manner in which this beneficial result is effected.

Granted that the act of profession has been seen in this light, it is not surprising that receiving the sacrament of reconciliation has been considered an appropriate preliminary. In this way is sacramentalized the personal conversion that is the heart of a response to vocation. Often a general confession was recommended.[44]

f) Eucharist

Since the avowed goal of monastic life is communion with God, it is not surprising that the sacrament of holy communion has a particular affinity with the core monastic experience.[45] The rite marking the entrance into the monastic state was usually located at the offertory of the Mass.[46] Communion was to be received during the Mass,[47] and for three days afterwards.[48] So serious was the linkage that, in the pre-concelebration era, a priest making solemn profession did not say Mass on that day, but received communion during the Mass in which he was consecrated.

g) Orders

Without commenting here on the compatibility of monasticism and priesthood, it is possible to note simply that the development of the rite of monastic profession included elements borrowed from the ritual of ordination. This happened either directly or through the intermediary of the rite for the consecration of virgins. The most dramatic innovation on Benedict's provisions was the expansion of the rite of investiture with the cowl (by which a man became a monk) into an explicit consecration.[49] The prayers of consecration were based on Eastern monastic models but the resulting rite began to look more and more like priestly ordination. The addition of other elements such as the use of pontificals, the inclusion of the litany of the saints and the *Veni Creator Spiritus*, reinforced this impression.

We are not permitted to query the wisdom of the Council of Trent's fixing the number of sacraments at neither more nor less than seven. It is not difficult, however to see that, in a theological ambiance less concerned with arithmetic, the rite of monastic profession could be considered sacramental. Certainly where there is indifference to the sacramental order, the view of profession must be reduced to that of simple engagement and the subjective openness to its special graces must be less. This is an impoverishment that runs counter to ancient monastic tradition. By re-establishing the sacramental context of monastic profession, we would give less emphasis to what the monk or nun does in making an offering of self, and more to the efficacy of Christ acting through the Church.

3. A Grace of Sanctification

In an era in which the sense of sin was strong and there was more fear and trembling about personal salvation, it was possible to formulate a marketable theology of monastic profession in terms of the negation of sin and its effects. We have already seen how strongly and how frequently this belief has been stated in the past. Today we are faced with the challenge of expressing more positively the content of the mystery of monastic profession. Perhaps the best starting point for this is a deepening appreciation of passive consecration, understood as gift imparted to the newly professed by the ministry of the Church.

Let us examine some of the themes that occur in the various prayers of consecration and in some of the associated formularies. The following petitions occur in the *Rituale Cisterciense*. The texts used there were not specifically Cistercian, but were found in most monastic rituals dating from the Middle Ages.

- ◆ the gift of the Holy Spirit,
- ◆ interior renewal (as in Rom 12:1-2),
- ◆ the replacement of the old nature with a new source of activity (as in Eph 4:22-24 and Col 3:9-10),
- ◆ the dissolution of the oppressive debts of past impiety (as in Isaiah 58:6),
- ◆ fervor in living out the monastic *propositum*,
- ◆ divine consolation in times of trouble and anxiety, and
- ◆ a happy perseverance in the monastic pursuit.

More modern prayers of consecration are often in the form of a preface, beginning with a recital of the *mirabilia Dei* in Salvation History. The petitions on behalf of the recipient occur at the end. The first text in the *Roman Ritual* (#72) prays for the sending of the Holy Spirit, the deepening of the effects of Baptism and a closer union with the Lord; it asks for a lifelong fidelity to Christ, the Church and to spreading the Good News, and for guidance and protection for the newly professed. The second text (#159) asks for the gift of the Holy Spirit, the revelation of Christ to them so that they become a living icon. It asks for freedom of heart, a willingness to serve, and a capacity to see God's wisdom at work in the world. The monastic ritual in use by French Benedictine nuns concludes:

> Look with favor on our Sister N. Sanctify her, bless her and keep her always. Give to her, Lord the fruit of the Spirit: charity, joy, peace, patience, kindness, generosity, confidence in others, gentleness and self-control. May your Spirit be her life, may your Spirit animate her actions and keep her in love.[50]

The text in use at La Pierre-qui-Vire simply concludes,

> Give them the gifts of your Spirit in their fullness so that their life may be no longer for themselves but for the Lord Jesus who died and rose for the salvation of all.[51]

All these are admirable prayers and worthy petitions. I doubt whether we can deduce from them the specific effects wrought in the newly professed by the rite of consecration. Any theology that attempts to describe profession according to its positive effects lacks absolute clarity. The older approach which concentrated on the notion of a new beginning and the cancellation of the debts of the past was definite and easy to understand. To speak in terms of deepening, renewing and re-activating the grace of baptism is less satisfying. Even in the liturgical formularies there is a vagueness and generality that indicate the need for a deeper theology of monastic consecration.[52]

My own instinct is to think of the grace of profession in terms of configuration to Christ. This is a theme often evoked in *Vita consecrata*. Monastic life exists to deepen the baptismal likeness to Christ that is nurtured and sustained by all the sacraments. This happens in various ways and in different degrees.

- ◆ The monk commits his life to the discipleship of Christ, absorbing the teaching of the Gospel, living according to its standards and, as it were, taking his primary identity from the following of Christ.
- ◆ In his daily practice the monk keeps before him the ideal of the imitation of Christ as a means of choosing between possible courses of action. He strives to be Christlike in what he does.[53]
- ◆ In interpreting the events of his life, the monk develops a sense of solidarity with Christ, viewing what happens from Christ' perspective, especially when life becomes hard and contrary.
- ◆ Living in the presence of Christ allows the monk to develop an intimacy with him that is less the fruit of ascetical effort and more the working of grace.
- ◆ Familiarity with Christ grows into union with him and in this the goal of the monastic pursuit is realized.

These avenues of configuration stem from baptism. Monastic consecration confirms a dynamic process by which these modes of relationship with Christ become real possibilities according to the specificity of an individual's personal history and according to the distinctive charism of the community in which profession is made.

Note the double determination. Common grace is rendered more powerful and intense by being recontextualized within the assets and liabilities of one's character and experience so that holiness is more clearly perceived to be a matter of authentic living, of being oneself. On the other hand there is a burgeoning affinity between personal spiritual needs and the range of opportunities offered by monastic *conversatio*. There is an interior bonding between the person and the elements of a monastic lifestyle that is an ongoing source of fervor and renewal. There is also a grace of return. On coming to one's senses after a period of withdrawal from grace, the way back is always signposted. There is a homing instinct that helps us to regain the momentum we lost through negligence.

The grace of monastic consecration is an ongoing change of heart by which Benedictine or Cistercian *conversatio* becomes for us a way of life (*via vitae*—RB Prol 20), and solidarity with Christ is strengthened by the routine rigors of monastic existence.

As in baptism, none of this happens without our ongoing consent. Monastic rules have generally been fully aware of the possibility of resistance to grace and ultimate apostasy. Prolonged fidelity is never easy. The process of growing in likeness to Christ is not without its obscurities, even for the well-intentioned. Reaching authentic Christian adulthood often makes demands that seem unreasonable and incomprehensible at the time, but without the demolition of a false identity, no creative rebuilding occurs. The art of survival involves learning to live with unavoidable negativity, trusting that the process itself will eventually yield a happy outcome. Meanwhile one continues to say "Yes" more often than "No" and trusts in God's providence. This is one of the effects of stability.[54]

Monastic consecration is more than a ceremony of commitment. It is a mystery in which, by the action of Christ, a bonding takes place whereby what is most true in the heart of the individual is released and enhanced by an ongoing connection with all that constitutes monastic living.

4. *Pointers for a Rite of Profession*

In many places local rites for monastic profession have been cobbled together from elements of traditional ritual and the revised Roman rite with readings and hymns selected according to the preferences of all concerned. In a transitional situation, this is to be expected. It is to be hoped, however, that as monastic theology becomes more aware of its own roots and more confident in its own style of theologizing, there may result a clearer understanding of the nature and effects of the liturgical rite. Just as ICEL is preparing for the sacraments not only a new generation of translations from the Latin *editio typica* but also original English compositions, so it is to be hoped that monastic liturgists might exercise creativity in providing for specifically monastic liturgical events.

Here are some suggestions for a renewed rite.

> a) The possibility of a Sunday celebration to be considered. Although it is pleasant to be professed on a major solemnity, there is often a clash between the profession and the feast being celebrated. Perhaps it would be possible to devise profession rites suitable for the usually favored solemnities: Assumption, St Benedict, St Bernard.
>
> b) An explicit renewal of the promises of baptism in a form recognizably the same as that used in the sacrament. This should replace the usual penitential rite and follow the liturgy of the Word: all are invited to join the candidate in this.
>
> c) A clear recognition of the two distinct moments of the rite: active consecration or the self-offering and commitment of the one being professed, and passive consecration or the blessing of the new monk and nun.
>
> d) The homily or instruction should perhaps refer to the rite being celebrated, rather than a more general address on monastic life or a public relations spiel for the sake of the visitors. It can create an atmosphere of expectancy and wonder, perhaps giving outsiders a once-in-a-lifetime glimpse of the mystery of monastic life, helping those who are being professed to dispose themselves and inviting the other members of the community to renew in their own hearts the grace of profession.
>
> e) A clear distinction of the role of the superior as the one who receives the profession and the priest by whose ministry the Church consecrates the newly professed.
>
> f) Attention paid to the altar (as symbol of Christ) as that which receives the signed schedule of profession and from

which comes the cowl—left on the altar in a way that demonstrates its cruciform shape.

g) Maybe the translation of the *Suscipe* needs to be revised to indicate that it is a prayer for the acceptance of an offering. Perhaps on the final repetition it could move from "Receive" to "Sustain" to preserve the other nuance.

h) A ritual linkage of the act of investiture with the cowl with the prayer(s) of consecration. This is probably best done by silence (as a gesture expressing the act already complete) rather than by adding another prayer.

i) A decision to be made about whether the embrace of the community is to be considered a request for prayer typical of a preliminary to consecration (as in *RB* and most medieval customaries) or whether it is a gesture of greeting and welcome into the community, in which case it is appropriately done after the consecration (as at Cluny).[55]

j) If new prayers of consecration are drawn up in the form of a preface, perhaps the recital of the wonderful deeds of God could also include the sacred events of monastic history. Each Order and even each house could add its own pedigree so that Salvation History is seen to reach right down to the event taking place.

k) The benefits bestowed by the consecration should be amply expressed. Any temptation to moralize or exhort at this stage ought to be resisted. It is at this point especially that a renewed theology of profession will have an impact. It is important to note that the traditional consecration occurred a year after entry and was psychologically linked with it, and so comparisons with a life of non-conversion were appropriate. Today those that come to monastic consecration do so after several years of monastic life and fervent baptismal fidelity, the prayer needs to refer to this changed situation.

l) An anaphora with its own preface could be composed to suit the occasion, including a subtle reminiscence of the self-offering in the epiclesis over the gifts and a reflection of the consecratory preface in the epiklesis over the people. Maybe the newly-professed should have a special place to stand. Perhaps the moment of holy communion can be emphasized in some way.

m) Other prayers could be composed for the sacramentary, perhaps following the example of the *Rite of Funerals*, with the possibility of choice between different collects that suit different situations. It is also to be hoped that all these various elements would be printed in a single book for ease of reference.

n) Where there is only one to be professed it is possible for readings and music to reflect something of the individual's spiritual journey. It is important, however, to respect the fundamental nature and dynamic of the rite. There is a transition from the seriousness of commitment to the joy of consecration. It has sometimes been noted that excessive pomp and circumstance contradict the basic simplicity and austerity of the life that is being embraced.

o) It is not for a Cistercian to comment on the Benedictine use of the funeral pall in the ceremony, except to offer the opinion that the same dynamic can probably find alternative liturgical expressions.

In such an endeavor it is to be hoped that the various Benedictine orders might work together in producing an excellent result, which could then be fine-tuned by each institute and community to provide a range of options for its own situation.

Monks and nuns who follow the Benedictine rule have kept alive a strong tradition of monastic consecration and are said to be possessed of a fine liturgical sense. It would be to the advantage of the whole Church if these attributes were practically translated into a liturgical creativity that would bring to birth a theology and ritual worthy of the mystery of monastic consecration.

NOTES

[1] See Richard Yeo, *The Structure and Content of Monastic Profession: A juridical study with particular regard to the practice of the English Benedictine Congregation since the French Revolution*, (StA 83, Rome, Benedictina, 1982), p. 89. There are entries on Gemelli in *The New Catholic Encyclopedia*, the *Dizionario degli Istituti di Perfezione* and the *Dictionnaire de Spiritualité*.

[2] The frequently revised and reprinted *Catechism of the Vows of Peter Cotel* (New York, Benziger Brothers, 1924) explains the vows entirely in terms of obligations assumed. In Felix D. Duffey, *Manual for Novices* (New York, Herder, 1961), the index leaps from "concupiscence" to "copula, see intercourse" and thence to "constitutions" without any allusion to consecration. P. R. Régamey blames the lack of interest in religious consecration to "a mental outlook limited to empiricism or phenomenology, practical naturalism and some degree of secularism" art. "Consacrazione religiosa," *DIP* 2 (1975), c. 1609.

[3] Julia Upton writing in Michael Downey [ed.] *The New Dictionary of Catholic Spirituality* (Collegeville, Liturgical Press, 1993), defines consecration as "the total dedication of a person or a thing to God" (p. 207). This explanation spans both the following senses.

[4] For an example of the use of "religious consecration" entirely in this sense see René Carpentier, *Life in the City of God: An Introduction to Religious Life*, (London, Burns & Oates, 1959), pp. 58-61. Karl Suso Frank remains in the same line of thought in 1994. "The monastic state eventually became a consecrated state in the Church. What constituted it as such was the public decision to commit oneself in this way....The content of this consecration was a total gift of one's life to God, made possible by God's grace." Translated from the first part of the article, "Vie consacrée," *DSp* 16 (1994), col. 658.

⁵ After the Synod of Aachen in 816, a rite of feudal obeisance was added to the basic outline as found in RB. This consisted in the monk making a promise of obedience to the abbot personally, with hands joined between the abbot's. Such duplication is frequent in liturgical evolution.

⁶ A parallel rite involves the shaving of the head and perhaps, the giving of the monastic *corona*. A prayer accompanying the tonsure in the Cistercian ritual emphasizes its renunciatory character. The novice is exchanging "servitude to worldly habit" for the "habit of religion." He is leaving aside (*deponere*) the self. As Benedict states, "he should know that from this day he no longer has power even over his own body (*RB* 58,25)."

⁷ Thus Romanus acted for St Benedict: *eique sanctae conversationis habitum tradidit* (*Dial* 2,1.4; *SChr* 260, p. 132). There is a rich ambiguity in the term *habitus*, and the verb used in this clause underlines the role of human transmission or tradition in bringing about this transition to a holier state.

⁸ For general information see Placide Vernet, "La bénédiction traditionelle du moine et de la moniale, 'sacrament' de la 'conversion' pour la vie cistercienne," *Liturgie* 38 (1981), pp. 183-243.

⁹ Examples can be found in M. Herrgott, *Vetus Disciplina Monastica* (Paris, Charles Osmont, 1726). *Consecratio* and *professio* are distinguished (p. 88). Various provisions are made for the consecration of novices in unusual circumstances (pp. 378, 402, 439, 444), as if this were a term in normal usage. At Cîteaux, we find in the *Carta caritatis prior* (8,4) that priority is given to the *novitiorum consecratio* over attendance at the General Chapter. A clear example of *consecrare* in the active sense can be found in John of Forde, *Super extremam partem Cantici Canticorum sermones* CXX, 52.2, lines 38-39; *CChrM* 17, p. 367: *Christo animas suas et corpora*

sacro quodam matrimonii iure consecrarunt. Gertrude of Helfta was probably the first to use *consecrare* in the sense of a personal or devotional offering of self. See *Exercises* 2, 80-85; *SChr* 127, p. 98.

[10] In his Apostolic Constitution on secular institutes, *Provida Mater Ecclesia* AAS 39 (1947), Pius XII seemed to regard *consecratio* and *deditio* as equivalent (pp. 114, 117). For him the substance of religious life was *consecratio Deo et animabus,* as Jean Beyer notes: *De Vita per Consilia Evangelica Consecrata* (Rome, Gregorian University, 1969), p. 32. It was in this sense that religious life was termed the "consecrated life." Elsewhere, notably in *Sponsa Christ and Sacra Virginitas, consecratio* is used for the liturgical rite of consecration. Paul VI in his allocution *Magno Gaudio Affecti* addressed to Supreme Moderators on 23 May 1964 followed the stricter usage and reserved *consecratio* to passive consecration, using for active consecration, "se Deo penitus committit ac devovet." See AAS 56 (1964), p. 567. In *Evangelica Testificatio,* however, the active use of *consecrare* appears frequently: *Domino vitam suam consecrarunt (#1), tota vita Deo devota per peculiarem consecrationem (#4), Consilia evangelica castitatis Deo consecratae (#7), vitam Deo consecrastis (#56).* See AAS 63 (1971), pp. 497-526. In the numerous references of Pope John Paul II to the religious life, consecration is most often used in an active sense, often qualified by the adjective "total." The document sent from the Roman Curia to the U.S. Bishops on 31 May 1983 entitled, *The Essential Elements of Religious Life* strongly emphasizes consecration in the lives of apostolic institutes (#5-12), but the value of this text is limited in that its premises were apparently selected to prepare the way for certain pre-decided practical measures.

[11] Jean Beyer's attempts to link the two are marred by decontextualized quotations: *loc. cit.,* footnotes 57-58.

[12] #6, *Osservatore Romano* (English Edition), 27 (6 July 1994), p. I.

[13] #50, *ibid*. p. X.

[14] In the practice of the Roman Curia, it is much easier to obtain a dispensation from solemn monastic vows than to get any relief from the obligations consequent on holy orders, or to receive a declaration of nullity of marriage. Profession is regarded as a complex of contractual obligations which the Church, in its benignity, can dissolve. Previously the dispensation was accompanied by an exhortation to try to find ways of fulfilling what had been promised in the changed circumstances. This admonition is no longer included. It may also happen that the use, in official Vatican documents, of the phrase "consecrated life" as a commonplace expression replacing "religious life" may have the effect of robbing the term "consecration" of its specific meaning.

[15] In the *S. Wilhelmi Constitutiones* I, 1, provision is made for consecrating novices in mortal danger, and this without mention of their making vows: *non solum monastico indumento ibi vestire sed etiam, si tam gravis infirmitas mortis periculum minatur, in monachos consecrare.* (Herrgott, *op. cit.*, p. 378.) For some of the principles from a more recent standpoint see Michael Slussor, "The Ordination of Male Infants," *Theological Studies* 57 (1996), pp. 313-332.

[16] *PL* 216, 356.

[17] Cluny was criticized for blessing monks who had already received monastic consecration elsewhere, claiming a papal privilege. In this vein Geoffrey of Vendôme (d. 1132) wrote to Abbot Pons of Cluny (*Ep.* 4.2; *PL* 157, 147-149: "If the fugitive monk, Peter Goscelin, has received 'the habit of second regeneration' then this constitutes sacrilege and makes him liable for excommunication, refusal of communion and denial of Christian burial." Similarly Bernard did not approve

of remaking vows in the case of a transfer (*Ep* 1.6; *SBO* 7.5.25). Peter the Venerable argued the opposite on the basis of reason, precedent and privilege (*Ep* 28; cf. G. Constable [ed.], *The Letters of Peter the Venerable*, Cambridge, Harvard University Press, 1967), vol. 1, pp. 77-78. The Cistercian General Chapter of 1208 did not allow the *benedictio monachi* to be received twice (Statute 19); Joseph Canivez, *Statuta Capitulorum Generalium Ordinis Cisterciensis ab anno 1116 ad annum 1786* (Louvain, Revue de l'histoire ecclésiastique, 1933), Vol. I, p. 349.

[18] *De Miraculis* 2.35; *PL* 185, 1345d.

[19] See Sir Edward Maunde Thompson, *The Customary of the Benedictine Monasteries of St. Augustine, Canterbury and St. Peter, Westminster* (London: Henry Bradshaw Society, 1904), vol. II, p. 279, # 276.

[20] Originally the covering on the head lasted for a week, imitating the baptismal rite. After the Synod of Aachen it was reduced to three days. See Yeo, *op. cit.*, pp. 347-349, Germaine Morin, *The Ideal of the Monastic Life Found in the Apostolic Age* (Westminster, Newman Press, 1950), pp. 59-60.

[21] See Antonia Grandsen [ed.], *The Customary of the Benedictine Abbey of Eynsham in Oxfordshire* (CCM 2; Siegburg, F. Schmitt, 1963) 4.6; p. 64.

[22] See Edward E. Malone, *The Monk and the Martyr: The Monk as the Successor of the Martyr* (Washington, Catholic University of America Press, 1950). Anselme Stolz, *L'ascèse chrétienne* (Chevtogne, Éd. des Bénédictins d'Amay, 1948), pp. 120-143: "L'Ascète martyr." Olivier Rousseau, "Monachisme et vie religieuse" (*Irenikon* 7; Paris, Éd. de Chevtogne, 1957), pp. 40-45: "Martyre et Virginité." François Vandenbroucke, *Why Monks?* (CS 17, Cistercian Publications, Washington, 1972), pp. 57-59. Margaret R. Miles, *Fullness of Life: Historical Foundations for a New Asceticism*, (Philadelphia, Westminster Press, 1981), pp. 19-61. Peter Brown, *The*

Body and Society: Men, Women and Sexual Renunciation in Early Christianity (London, Faber, 1988), pp. 65-82: "Martyrdom, Prophecy and Continence: Hermas to Tertullian."

[23] Thus Jacques Fontaine, "The Practice of Christian Life: The Birth of the Laity," in Bernard McGinn *et.al.* [ed.], *Christian Spirituality: Origins to the Twelfth Century* (New York, Crossroad, 1987), p. 458.

[24] For examples of asceticism in dealing with illness see Peregrine Horden, "The Death of Ascetics: Sickness and Monasticism in the early Byzantine Middle East," in W. J. Shiels [ed.], *Monks, Hermits and the Ascetic Tradition* (Studies in Church History 22, Oxford, Blackwell, 1985), pp. 41-52.

[25] *PG* 65, 432.

[26] Thus Jean Leclercq, "Monastic Profession and the Sacraments," *MS* 5(1968), p. 71.

[27] See Christophe Vuillaume, "La profession monastique, un second baptême?" *COCR* 53 (1991), pp. 275-292.

[28] *PL* 73, 994b.

[29] *Diadema Monachorum* 79: "De Mortificatione Vitiorum"; *PL* 102, 674c.

[30] *Collationum libri tres* 2,7; *PL* 133, 554c.

[31] Relevant texts are edited in Jean Leclercq, "Profession monastique, baptême et pénitence d'après Odon de Cantorbéry," in *Analecta Monastica: Deuxième Série* (StA 31, Rome, Herder, 1953), p. 130. See also Odo's letter to his brother Adam (a monk at Igny) published in Jean Mabillon, *Vetera Analecta* (Paris, Montalant, 1723), pp. 477-478.

[32] *Ibid.*, p. 137.

[33] "In the mind of ecclesiastical tradition our Profession is truly a second Baptism which, like the first, remits all penalty due to sin." Thus Germain Morin, *op.*

cit., p. 60. Cassian says that the hoods worn by the Egyptian monks were thought to be indicative of the simplicity and innocence of little children. *Inst* 1, 3; *SChr* 109, pp. 43-44. The prayer for the blessing of the cowl used until recently in the Cistercian ritual and dating from the eleventh century speaks about this vesture as "a sign of humility and innocence." *Rituale Cisterciense* (Westmalle, Typographia Ordinis, 1949), p. 244.

[34] In St Athanasius' *Vita Antonii* there is an incident in which the demons taunt Antony about his pre-monastic sins. His mentors rebuked them saying, "As for the things from the time of his birth, the Lord has wiped them away; but from the time he became a monk and promised himself to God, let him be held accountable"(#65). *PG* 26, 936a.

[35] *Sermo* 1, ed. J. Leclercq in "Profession monastique," p. 134.

[36] *Div* 11.3; *SBO* 6a.126.11-13.

[37] *Pre* 54; *SBO* 3.289.5-13.

[38] A clear exposition can be found in the *Catechism of the Catholic Church* (Homebush, St Pauls, 1994), pp. 325-333.

[39] Jean Leclercq, "Tradition, Baptism and Profession: The Genesis and Evolution of the Consecrated Life," in *Aspects of Monasticism* (CS 7, Cistercian Publications, Kalamazoo, 1978), p. 91.

[40] Several authors affirm this from different perspectives in "Théologie de la vie monastique: Études sur la tradition patristique" (*Théologie* 49, Paris, Aubier, 1961). For what seems an early stage in the tradition see Paul Antin, "Saint Jérôme," (p. 198). "It is solidly established in ecclesiastical tradition that Profession is like a second baptism which restores to the Christian his entire purity; at the moment of the emission of vows, God forgets all the past and grants a universal forgiveness to the professed: He sees before Him only a

creature totally renewed." Columba Marmion, *Christ, the Ideal of the Monk* (London, Sands, 1922), p. 115. "To such a 're-activation' of baptism is related the remission of sins, not so much because the individual Christian has accomplished something, but because he or she has been drawn in a deeper manner into the Mystery of Christ, a mystery realized for the first time in baptism as a beginning...." Burkhard Neunheuser, "Monastic Profession as Second Baptism and Present day Theological Perspectives," *Liturgy OCSO* 18.1 (1984), p. 12. The original article dates from 1963.

[41] Vandenbroucke, *op. cit.*, pp. 100-106.

[42] "There is a pardon of sins because there is a confession; it is the confession preliminary to profession that acts as a sacrament. But just as confession deals with sins, profession deals with the vices and so anticipates danger." Translated from Leclercq, "Profession monastique," p. 127.

[43] Morin, *op. cit.*, p. 115: "In the mind of ecclesiastical tradition our Profession is truly a second Baptism which, like the first, remits all penalty due to sin." Thus also Vital Lehodey in the *Cistercian Spiritual Directory* (Dubuque, New Melleray Abbey, 1932), Vol. I, p. 163: "For this unreserved oblation of our purpose and of our goods God compensates by the complete remission of the temporal punishment due to past sins."

[44] Thus Theodemarus, *Usus Casinensis* 2,2 (Herrgott, *op. cit.*, p. 88): "Beforehand let them manifest all their crimes." The eleventh-century Bernard of Cluny *Ordo Cluniacensis* 1, 15 (*ibid.* p. 166) prescribes confession before the blessing is received. The customary of Afflighem, dating from the end of the thirteenth century, thus begins Chapter 48, *De Benedictione Noviciorum*: "Whatever they have committed in secular life against the salvation of their soul, let them manifest in confession to the Lord Abbot." in "Consuetudines Benedictinae Variae," (*CCM* 6, Sieburg, F. Schmitt,

1975), p. 183. The early fourteenth-century customary from Eynsham envisages the same practice. During the year of probation the novice is to be carefully instructed so that he makes, as soon as possible, a pure and integral confession of everything which he did in the world, whether previously confessed or not. (3.1; *CCM* 2, p. 44).

[45] I refrain from discussing the question of frequency. See Eoin de Bhaldraithe, "Daily Eucharist: The Need for an Early Church Paradigm," *ABR* 41.4 (1990), pp. 378-440. This article offers a comprehensive survey of relevant literature on the question.

[46] For the Cistercian usage see Danièle Choisselet and Placide Vernet [ed.], *Les Ecclesiastica Officia cisterciens du XIIème siècle* (La Documentation Cistercienne 22, Reiningue, Abbaye d'Oelenberg, 1989), 102, 24; p. 296. The verse prescribed by the *Rule of the Master* and St Benedict begins with the verb *suscipe*, the correlate of *offere*. I have not seen Benoît Thivièrge, *Le rituel cistercien de profession monastique: Un commentaire historique, théologique et liturgique du rituel cistercien de profession monastique et des formulaires de bénédiction du moine et de la coule* (Rome, StA 1992). Blackwell's informs me that as on 30 June 1996 it is out of print.

[47] For instance, *Rituale Cisterciense*, p. 245.

[48] Thus David Knowles [ed.] *The Monastic Constitutions of Lanfranc* (New York, Oxford University Press, 1951), p. 109. As we have noted above (fn. 21), nothing was to impede this reception.

[49] See Chrysogonus Waddell, "*Sequantur IIII Collecte*: A letter to Brother Aidan about the Cistercian Prayers for the Blessing of a Monk," *Liturgy OCSO* 12.2 (1978), pp. 99-130.

[50] Translated from the text as given in the *Mise au point de Rituel Cistercien*, Chimay, 1982, p. 88.

[51] Quoted in Vuillaume, *op. cit.*, p. 292.

[52] There are certain difficulties that complicate any attempt to formulate theologically the effects of profession. Firstly, the existence of *de iure* temporary profession illustrates that it is possible to make vows with great fervor and sincerity, but without receiving a consecration. (The same was hitherto the case for lay brothers and certain other religious). Secondly, the relative frequency of requests for dispensation from perpetual and solemn vows coming within a few years after profession, creates a doubt about any spiritual profit resulting from the act. When solemn profession becomes *de facto* temporary and reversible, it is more difficult to envisage permanent effects resulting from it. Thirdly, it seems an impoverishment to reduce the effects of profession to the moral and psychological order: for instance, the newly professed feels more secure and stable in the monastic vocation. Finally, there remains the question of whether it is the making of profession and the receiving of the blessing that consecrates or the lifelong living of the profession. As an ancient once remarked, it is not being clothed in the monastic habit that matters, it is being buried in it.

[53] For a profound survey of this topic see Giles Constable, "The Ideal of the Imitation of Christ," in *Three Studies in Medieval Religious and Social Thought*, Cambridge University Press, 1995; pp. 143-248.

[54] See M. Casey, "The Value of Stability," *CSQ* 31.3 (1996), pp. 287-301.

[55] After the blessing and clothing the newly-professed brothers "went the rounds of the whole choir so that they might be kissed by all the brothers, beginning with the Lord Abbot." *Consuetudines Cluniacenses* 3, 27; *PL* 149, 713c.

THE JOURNEY
FROM FEAR TO LOVE:
JOHN CASSIAN'S ROAD MAP

This article is a reflection on the passage in the Institutes *from which the Master and Benedict fashioned their ladders of humility. It was originally read at the symposium on* Prayer and Spirituality in the Early Church *organized by the Australian Catholic University in 1996. It was published under that title in the proceedings of the symposium in 1998. It was part of the background for my book on St Benedict's teaching on humility,* Truthful Living, *first published by St Bede's in 1999.*

The Gospel value of humility is scarcely marketable in modern Western culture. Speaking about humility today is like proclaiming resurrection in the Areopagus, notwithstanding the fact that its contraries—arrogance, assertiveness and self-indulgence—are commonly reprobated in polite society. Humility is tacitly seen as passivity, self-degradation and compliance and, as a result, it is robustly relegated to the graveyard of outdated practices. Alone among the virtues it seems easier to practice than to preach!

It is precisely because of this cultural blind spot that we need to identify and suspend our own prejudices and submit ourselves to the discipline of listening to ancient tradition. It may be that there is something missing in our expurgated view of spirituality that is causing us to waste our limited energy to minimal effect. If the spiritual giants of yesterday were correct in seeing a connection between humility and divinization then, maybe, our willful exclusion of the former will disqualify us for the latter.

In this paper I would like to examine an influential text on humility by the fifth-century monastic writer, John Cassian. To some extent this is a practical exercise in hermeneutics. At first sight the teaching seems stern and forbidding and we are inclined to reject it out of hand. If, however, we unlock its meaning by disengaging the text from language that triggers a negative response, we will probably be surprised to discover a message that is not only relevant but urgent in our contemporary context.

1. John Cassian

John Cassian (360-435) was born in Scythia, on the Black Sea in present-day Romania.[1] He began his monastic life in Bethlehem, but seeking further formation went off to Lower Egypt where he and his companion went the rounds of certain monks of high reputation. This stage of his life lasted at least seven years. By 400 Cassian was in Constantinople with John Chrysostom who ordained him deacon; he was ordained priest in either Antioch[2] or Rome, and is known to have been in Marseille by 415.[3] There he founded two monastic communities—one for men and one for women—for whom he wrote the *Institutes* in 420 and the *Conferences* in 425.[4] He died about ten years later.

Cassian is credited with a twofold achievement: translating the experiential teaching of the Egyptian Desert together with its Eastern theory into a Western form[5] and, secondly, adapting its eremitical doctrine to suit cenobites.[6] His writings were widely propagated in the fifth and sixth centuries, substantially influencing the *Rule of the Master* and St Benedict's *Rule for*

Monasteries, as can be seen easily in a comparison of our text with *RM* 10 and *RB* 7.[7] As a result, his subsequent authority was considerable.[8]

2. The Text of Institutes 4.39

It is in this order and by these stages [or steps] that one arrives at this state of perfection.

The beginning of our salvation and its guardian is the fear of the Lord. It is through this that those who give themselves to the way of perfection acquire the beginning of conversion, the cleansing of vices and the safeguarding of the virtues. When fear of the Lord penetrates someone's mind it brings to birth a contempt for all things, forgetfulness of family and a drawing back from the world. The fact is that humility is acquired through contempt for and privation of everything.

[The presence of] humility can be verified by the following indicators:

1. If [the monk] mortifies himself in all the movements of self-will.
2. If he reveals to his senior not only his actions but also his thoughts.
3. If he allows nothing to his own power of discernment but entrusts everything to the judgment [of the senior], thirsting for his advice and gladly listening to it.
4. If in all situations he maintains the meekness that is obedience and the constancy that is patience.
5. If he not only does no injury to anyone but is not grieved when another inflicts on him an undeserved injury.
6. If he does nothing and presumes nothing except what is encouraged by the common rule and the example of the superiors.
7. If he is content with whatever is of little value and in all that is given him to do he regards himself as a wicked and unworthy workman.

8. If he not only outwardly declares himself to be inferior to all but believes it in the very depths of his heart.

9. If he controls his tongue and [also] does not speak loudly.

10. If he is not inclined to ready laughter.

By such and other similar indicators true humility can be diagnosed. When it is possessed in truth, humility will speedily lead you to the higher level which is the charity that has no fear. Through such charity you will begin to observe effortlessly, as if by nature, everything that you used to perform with some hardship and trepidation. [You will be motivated] no longer by contemplating punishment or by any fear but by the love of goodness itself and delight in virtue.[9]

3. Beginning with the Negative

The first four books of the *Institutes* deal with the basic external forms of monastic life and the formation of newcomers; the remaining eight books are dedicated to a detailed treatment of the vices, latent in everyone and eventually to be confronted.

At the end of the fourth book Cassian has inserted a discourse of Abba Pinufius given to mark the entry of a novice into the monastery.[10]

Pinufius begins with the theme of renunciation as being appropriate to the occasion of a rite of passage. Elsewhere it is stated that this renunciation is effective in three areas: it involves poverty in material goods, a change of lifestyle and a disenfranchisement from this present age.[11] This external renunciation, however admirable, will not bring freedom to the monk unless he also purifies the interior affections. "Even one who has no money can be a victim to the disease of avarice so that his impoverishment yields no benefit to him."[12] It is the *affectus possidendi* that is the problem rather than the *facultates mundi*.[13] Renunciation is the visible form (*indicium*) of the cross (4.34). And since the monk's cross is fear of the Lord (4.35), this means that the renunciation is the ordinary expression of fear of the Lord. This is the beginning of the spiritual process (4.39).

Perhaps the biblical term "fear of the Lord" is not without obscurity. In the circles in which Cassian moved, it was not primarily seen as psychological terror at the prospect of judgment, nor even awe and reverence in the presence of the Holy. Fear of the Lord was a more pragmatic attitude of seriousness, relative to one's concrete obligations. It less involves an inner sensation of being afraid of God than a disposition that is evidenced in external acts, such as:

1. Submission to God's law, subordinating desires and acts of will to the law of the Lord.
2. Interpersonal harmony, separation from pride, contentiousness and rivalry.
3. Purity of heart, putting to death all disorderly carnal feelings and desires.
4. Having eternal life as one's goal, having no care for past, present or future, but fixing one's desire on heaven.[14]

If these requirements seem exigent, it is not only because of the hyperbolic rhetoric of exhortation. Cassian himself admits that he found them incomprehensible and amazing.[15] Such prescriptions are grounded on an insight into the depth of universal and innate resistance to grace. Cassian presupposes that all the vices are alive and well within even the most blameless beginner.[16] Those who are serious about the spiritual pursuit must first discover the extent of their unconscious liabilities, and then find ways of neutralizing their impact. The practice of *timor Domini* is paramount among the traditional means by which liberation from this fundamental spiritual inertia is attained.

The first stage of spiritual development is marked by the latent presence of all eight vices, each waiting an opportunity to attack: gluttony, fornication, love of money, anger, sadness, acedia, vain glory and pride.[17] This period of latency in the early stages of spiritual development is very dangerous; it is easy to think one is already close to perfection. Complacency follows delusion and prepares the way for temptation's victory and the probable end of the spiritual adventure. This outcome can be avoided by preparing the neophyte for the onslaught of the vices by bringing into consciousness the reality of the dark forces within. By their spiritual conversations the elders hoped to provide their disciples with antidotes that would prevent problems, by teaching them about the sources of passionate behavior and how health may be attained.[18] In particular they wanted beginners to appreciate that the vices sustain one other.[19] To attempt to fight a limited war that would leave even one vice unconquered is useless.

This is the traditional function of the desert.[20] Like Christ, the monk enters the wilderness to do battle with the demonic. The wilderness is not a place of tranquillity and peaceful retreat, but a *locus horroris et vastae solitudinis*.[21]

Let us focus on the novice as he begins this journey. The period of the "phony war" is ended and the time has come for battle to be joined. Warfare is a good thing; not a signal that something has gone drastically wrong. "The grace of the Savior is good to us and gives us a greater reward of praise because we have fought with temptations than if he had dispensed us from all need to do battle."[22] That is why Cassian considers eunuchs to be lacking in fervor,[23] and those without any troubles are to be pitied.[24]

If the novice seriously considers his future, his disposition is necessarily one of trepidation at the battles ahead, timorousness because of the unfamiliarity of the weapons he must use, and uncertainty regarding the outcome. He knows that he must remain alert, ready to receive any instruction from those more experienced than himself and prepared for hardship, exertion and suffering. This is the price that every soldier pays who goes to war. The first experience of authentic spiritual growth is a multi-layered fear, not of God but of his own vulnerability in the battle ahead.

The clearest exposition of this is in the eleventh conference which deals with the nature of Christian perfection. There three phases of spiritual development are distinguished. First in terms of experience, then in terms of the theological virtue corresponding to each, and finally by means of a traditional set of images.

EXPERIENCE	VIRTUE	IMAGE
Fear of hell or earthly laws	Faith	Slave
Hope and desire for heaven	Hope	Mercenary
Attraction and love for virtue	Charity	Son

After elaborating these stages, Abba Chaeremon continues, "If anyone is tending to perfection let them begin with this first step (*gradus*)."[25] In Cassian's mind it is not wise to leapfrog the negative in order to find a more marketable entrance to spirituality. For him there is not only sequence but also causality: earlier negative experience prepares the ground for later positive experience.

> The beginning of our salvation and of wisdom is, according to the Scriptures, fear of the Lord (Prov 9:10).
>
> From fear of the Lord is born wholesome compunction.
>
> From compunction of heart proceeds renunciation, that is nudity—the contempt of all possessions.
>
> From nudity is humility produced.[26]

Alongside our warfare with the vices, we are obliged to attend to laying the foundation of humility,[27] for this is the disposition that allows God to act freely upon us. The various manifestations of humility indicate a progressive willingness to be formed by God in the perfection of love. "They experience the insufficiency of human strength, weighed down with the burden of flesh, to obtain the desired goal...they fly to the grace of God, who justifies the wicked."[28] Humility is receptivity of grace. It consists "in an intimate abasement of the mind, not in bodily or verbal affectations."[29] The elder must know how to distinguish genuine humility from its spurious alternative.[30]

4. Signs of Progress

Cassian has framed a diagnostic tool for spiritual progress similar to others found throughout the *Conferences*.[31] "By such and other similar indicators true humility can be diagnosed."[32] The signs he lists are not exhaustive, but collectively they give some idea of what changes occur in a person who is advancing. The itinerary seems to envisage the prospective monk beginning as adult, autonomous and assertive. He might even be described as brash and boisterous. The spiritual awakening that marks the onset of his conversion undermines the values on which his previous life was built and gradually substitutes different priorities. He is attracted to living from the principles of the Gospel and this involves attaching himself as an apprentice to one already experienced in this.[33] Being under a master leads to the understanding and eventual control of both irascible and concupiscible emotions and a deep inner attachment to God that is expressed by disengagement from issues that others consider important.

Let us examine the syndrome Cassian has proposed, describing the reality using language that is less weighted. The monk who is progressing from fear to love is:

A: OPEN TO DIRECTION
1. Not self-willed.
2. Ready for disclosure about self.[34]
3. Trusting in the guidance of an elder.

B: MEEK
4. Obedient and patient.
5. Non-violent and not aggrieved.

C: LOW PROFILE
6. Invisible.
7. Easily pleased.
8. Happy with the lowest place.

D: QUIET
9. Taciturn and soft-spoken.
10. Grave.

a) Open to Direction

Those who appreciate the length and complexity of the spiritual journey and understand how compromised is their own integrity, are willing to be helped by others more experienced. After the initial awakening to grace and the first faltering steps along the way, the neophyte is faced with a choice. To allow life to continue substantially unchanged, or to move towards a more radical self-transcendence. If the latter option prevails, then a halt must be called to the self-perpetuating policies of the past and effective control must be ceded to another. This involves declaring a moratorium on "spontaneous" acts of will that have not yet been submitted to the Gospel, and seeking means by which these may be assayed.[35] *Discretio* or discernment was a highly valued gift.[36] It involves being prepared to discuss not only one's behavior but the thoughts and desires by which it is determined. Cassian probably expected of his novices a higher degree of spiritual literacy than is commonly encountered today. Although he uses different language, he is really talking about neutralizing the effects of unconscious self-destructive tendencies.

> The cunning enemy cannot circumvent the young man, no matter how inexperienced and ignorant, and has no means to lead him astray if he trusts in the discernment of the elders and if he cannot persuade him to conceal from the elder his suggestions that he introduces into his heart like fiery darts.[37]

To some extent the non-institutional character of desert monasticism facilitated such self-revelation. Façades disappear quickly in such a situation.[38] When it is accepted that no one is immune from the vices, it is easier to talk tactics for their elimination. We who begin with the assumption of innocence are burdened with a double difficulty. It is harder for beginners to raise matters that may seem dishonorable. On the other hand, elders may be reluctant to draw on personal experience, lest they be discredited in the eyes of the apprentice because of their more ample familiarity with sin.

Being comfortable with an increasing degree of exposure, even though it is acquired at the cost of a certain level of embarrassment, is not only evidence of progress, but a guarantee of its continuation. Seeking guidance for a journey through uncharted territory is not a sign of immaturity or excessive dependence. It is common sense. Where there are no secrets, acceptance is stronger and fear is diminished. A lot depends, of course, on the elder being worthy of the trust and experienced enough to act as a guide. In Cassian's view of things this is the monk's own responsibility: he approaches the one for whose advice he thirsts and to whom he is glad to listen. There is question of personal choice, not an institutional appointee.

b) Meek

Much depends on what view we have of the evangelical quality of meekness. William Barclay's description is appropriate.

There is gentleness in *praus* but behind the gentleness there is the strength of steel, for the supreme characteristic of the man who is *praus* is that he is the man who is under perfect control. It is not a spineless gentleness, a sentimental fondness, a passive quietism. It is a strength under control.[39]

As Cassian says: "Generally the monk who submits his will to that of his brother is stronger than one who obstinately defends and clings to his own way of doing things."[40] The fact that we commonly equate meekness with cowardly acquiescence probably says a lot about the culture we have absorbed.

It is a sign of progress that the monk's social dealings become more marked by equanimity[41] and a spirit of cooperation, that he is able to maintain momentum in difficult times, and that he lacks both aggression and an exaggerated sense of victimhood. One who is genuinely meek does not need to establish an identity by negative relationships. This is because at a deep level of experience there already exists a confidence in one's own identity that is not shaken when others are overbearing or hostile. As he grows, the monk becomes more reluctant to be an accomplice in the games others play, or to allow his inner state to be determined by the onrush of others' emotions.[42] There is a firmness in the refusal to become a participant in someone else's disorder. In the case of objective injustice, one who has advanced in the spirit of the Gospel may, with a quiet mind, choose not to protest or retaliate but to absorb evil in the hope of neutralizing it.[43]

c) Low Profile

Because of a habitual state of contentment, the advancing monk is less likely to engage in attention-seeking behavior. He does not rebel against what is prescribed by custom nor demand preferential treatment regarding what is allocated to him. In contrast to the narcissist he does not think that the world owes him anything. Quite the contrary, he is increasingly aware of his own limitations and liabilities and marvels at the generosity and indulgence shown him. In the light of his own honest guilt he cannot bring himself to condemn anyone.[44] Because his needs are few, such a one is free of the fear of deprivation. He cannot be coerced into inconsistent behavior by anxiety about possessions, positions and public esteem. Being content with little, means that he has nothing to lose, and he begins to understand why Jesus call the poor "blessed."

d) Quiet

Noisiness and compulsive conversation do not favor growth in wisdom. Aimless speech consumes more time than most of us are prepared to admit. Almost every religious tradition recognizes this. It is equally certain that imposing external silence is not necessarily the answer to the problem. This is why it is important to understand that Cassian is not talking about enforced silence, but of a certain gravity of demeanor and restraint of speech that stems from an inner richness of experience. It is similar to the intent concentration of an artisan absorbed in a task. Its opposite is not incommunicativeness but acedia.[45]

Such quietness of mouth and manner presupposes a certain level of serenity at the level of thought. It is not enough to live a noiseless existence while fantasies run riot. Cassian is thinking of someone who has toiled long to overcome the dividedness of his heart and, as a result, is gifted with an inner peace that both profits prayer and eliminates the need for mindless chatter.

The profile of a monk in whom the grace of God is active is of one marked by a tendency to become honest, meek, quiet and easily pleased. These are not the only gifts, but in the situation Cassian addresses, his recommendation makes a lot of sense.

There are several points that make this text remarkable.

1. Cassian regards humility as the effect of spiritual progress rather than its cause. These behavioral manifestations are the fruits of an effective assent to the evangelization of one's lifestyle and commitment to a process of spiritual maturation. Merely aping the behavior without an inner basis is fraudulent.

2. The behavioral content of these *indicia* is not an external code but an attempt to portray changing inner states and experiences. The profile is descriptive rather than prescriptive. The essential change takes place at the level of fundamental dispositions.

3. To some extent Cassian offers us a sequential account of the different challenges that spiritual progress provokes. Although not strictly chronological, there is a certain logic in the ordering of the signs. This is the basis for the conversion of the scheme into a ladder, as found in *RM* and *RB*. He is very interested in the etiology of experience: nothing happens without a cause. Falls may seem sudden, but this is only because the operative causes have been hidden.[46]

4. Cassian understands the various manifestations of humility as milestones in the journey from fear to love. Notice the statement at the end: "When it is possessed in truth, humility will speedily lead you to the higher level which is the charity that has no fear." The monk has attained *apatheia*.[47] He is liberated from the tyranny of sub-personal forces; he passes beyond struggle. He freely embraces goodness and finds his delight in it. Love is no longer a commandment, it is the habitual source of his activity; he can do no other. Thus is attained the immediate goal of the monastic enterprise, purity of heart, singleness of purpose, the perfection of charity.[48] In such a state the monk is ready to receive the ultimate gift—entry into the kingdom of heaven.[49]

5. The Positive Outcome

Cassian's view of the end of the journey is a life that is characterized by charity. For him this consists especially in three qualities:

> a) liberation from the coercion of fear in the conduct of life and the upbuilding of a fund of experience that, by God's gift, permits more victory over sin than defeat.
>
> b) the recession of alienation so that spiritual striving becomes as second nature; a sense of feeling at home with goodness, without violent attraction to its opposite. One who has come to love goodness is almost beyond the thrall of sin.
>
> c) the capacity—once the obstacles are removed—to love others without self interest. To be a friend.

The Master and Benedict will each have a different angle on how the journey ends. Benedict seems more confident that the goal will be achieved this side of eternity. Another nuance that Benedict makes explicit is to bring out the Christocentric character of the final result. For him all the contributing components of the spiritual ascent derive their power from the fact that what is done in imitation of Christ is itself union with Christ. And so at the end the monk acts not out of love for goodness as in Cassian, nor out of love for good habit, as in the *Rule of the Master*, but simply for love of Christ. That is probably what Cassian would have liked to have said. The various forms of humility are simply external indicators that a monk is growing from within towards likeness to Christ. Perhaps in reading these authors we can often substitute for humility another concept: Christlikeness.

NOTES

[1] See Henri-Irenée Marrou, "La Patrie de Jean Cassien," in *Mélanges G. de Jerphanion II (Orientalia Christiana Periodica* 13, 1947) pp. 588-596.

[2] See E. Griffe, "Cassien a-t-il été prêtre d'Antioche?," *Bulletin de Littérature Ecclésiastique* 55 (1957), pp. 240-244.

[3] See Henri-Irenée Marrou, "Jean Cassien à Marseille," *Revue du Moyen Âge latin* 1(1945), pp. 5-26.

[4] I am using the critical text of the *Conferences* edited by Dom E. Pichery for *Sources Chrétiennes* and published in Paris by Cerf: Jean Cassien, *Conférences I-VII* (#42, 1955), *Conférences VIII-XVII*, (#54, 1958) and *Conférences XVIII-XXIV* (#64, 1959). For the *Institutes* I follow the text revised by Jean-Claude Guy in the same series *Institutions Cénobitiques* (#109, 1965). There is no complete English translation of Cassian's works. I have profited from what is included in the *NPNF* and the *CWS* series, but have opted to translate my texts independently.

[5] "[I]l a offert à l'Occident, repensé, clarifié par un cerveau latin, l'enseignement traditionnel le plus assuré de l'Église orientale, de saint Athanase au Cappadociens et à saint Jean Chrysostome." Henri-Irenée Marrou, "Le fondateur de Saint-Victor de Marseille: Jean Cassien," *Provence Historique* 16 (1966), pp. 297-308; p. 308. On the indebtedness of Cassian to Evagrius of Pontus and thence to Origen see Salvatore Marsili, *Giovanni Cassiano ed Evagrio Pontico: dottrina sulla caritá e contemplazione* (Rome, StA, 1936). On the other hand, Marcia Colish states, "[I]t was Cassian more than any other single figure who monasticized Stoicism in the west and produced one of its most original and durable reformulations in his period." *The Stoic Tradition*

from Antiquity to the Early Middle Ages: II. Stoicism in Christian Latin Thought through the Sixth Century (Leiden, Brill, 1985), pp. 114-115.

[6] See Julien Leroy, "Le cénobitisme chez Cassien," *RAM* 43.2 (1967), pp. 121-158 and Philip Rousseau, "Cassian, Contemplation and the Coenobitic Life," *Journal of Ecclesiastical History*, 26 (1975), pp. 113-126.

[7] Bernard Capelle, "Cassien, le Maître et saint Benoît," *RTAM* 11 (1939), pp. 110-118. François Masai, "Recherches sur le texte originel du *De Humilitate* de Cassien (*Inst.* IV 39) et des Règles du Maître (*RM* X) et de Benoît (*RB* VII)," in J. J. O'Meara and B. Naumann [ed.], *Latin Script and Letters: Fs. Ludwig Bieler* (Leiden, Brill, 1976), pp. 236-263. A critical note on the latter article appears in *COCR* 39 (1977), #383, p.[214]. Terrence Kardong, "Benedict's use of Cassianic Formulae for Spiritual Progress," *SM* 34.2 (1992), especially pp. 243-248.

[8] For the customary recital see Michel Olphe-Galliard, "Cassien: Influence," *DSp* 2.1 (1953), col. 267-274.

[9] *Inst* 4.38-39; *SChr* 109, pp. 178-180.

[10] Thus *Inst* 4.32; *SChr* 109, p. 170. He averts to the circumstances of this exhortation in *Conl* 20.2; *SChr* 64, p. 59.

[11] See Abba Pafnutius, "The Three Renunciations," *Conl* 3.6; *SChr* 42, p. 145.

[12] *Inst* 7.22; *SChr* 109, p. 322.

[13] *Inst* 7.27; *SChr* 109, p. 330.

[14] *Inst* 4.35; *SChr* 109, p. 174.

[15] *Conl* 20.2; *SChr* 64, p. 59.

[16] Abba Sarapion understands the vices as prefigured by the seven tribes with which Israel had to contend at the time of the Exodus (*Conl* 5.16; *SChr* 42, p. 207). The eighth vice is symbolized by the pursuing Egyptians (*Conl* 5.18, p. 210). To reach the promised land, each of these must be confronted and overcome.

[17] Cassian ascribed the presence of these inner movements to the Creator, but denies that this acquits the person of culpability for assenting to them. *Inst* 7.4; *SChr* 109, p. 296.

[18] *Inst* 11.17.2; *SChr* 109, p. 444. It is easy to recognize the causality of passionate behavior when it is explained, but before that it is not known. *Inst* 5.2; *SChr* 109, p. 190.

[19] *Inst* 5.11; *SChr* 109, p. 206.

[20] Although Cassian also describes the desert in terms of contemplative possibilities; see *Conl* 19.5, *SChr* 64, p.42.

[21] This is a much-used quotation of Deut 32:10. The poeticisation of the desert has also led to the misinterpretation of biblical texts such as Hos 2:14 and Jer 2:2-3. See Michael de Roche "Jeremiah 2:2-3 and Israel's Love for God during the Wilderness Wandering," *CBQ* 45 (1983), pp. 364-376. See also Michael Kabel, *"Alleen ik en God op de wereld": een onderzoek naar de betekenis van het woort* solitudo *in de Collationes van de presbyter Johannes Cassianus*, (unpublished dissertation, Nijmegen, 1959).

[22] *Conl* 24.25; *SChr* 64, p. 198.

[23] *Conl* 4.17; *SChr* 42, p. 181.

[24] *Conl* 7.31; *SChr* 42, p. 272.

[25] *Conl* 11.7; *SChr* 54, p. 105.

[26] The list continues: "From humility mortification of acts of will is generated. By the mortification of acts of will all the vices are uprooted and wither. By the expulsion of vices the virtues bear fruit and grow. By increase of the virtues purity of heart is acquired. By purity of heart the perfection of apostolic charity is possessed." *Inst* 4.43; *SChr* 109, p. 184.

[27] "First the strong foundations of simplicity and humility must be laid in the solid and living ground of our inner being—the rock of which the Gospel speaks (Luke 6:48)." *Conl* 9.2; *SChr* 54, p. 41. "It is clearly demonstrated that no one can attain the goal of perfection and purity except by genuine humility. He shows this first to the brothers and then to God in the secret chambers of his heart, since he believes that without the protection and help of God at every moment, it is impossible for him to obtain the perfection he desires and towards which he runs with so much effort." *Inst* 12.23; *SChr* 109, p. 484.

[28] *Conl* 23.10; *SChr* 64, p. 153.

[29] *Conl* 18.11; *SChr* 64, p. 24.

[30] *Inst* 4.9; *SChr* 109, p. 132.

[31] *Conl* 20.11; *SChr* 64, p. 70.

[32] Adalbert de Vogüé plots the history of the change of sense witnessed in the title to *RM* 10, where there is question of acquiring and conserving humility and not merely manifesting its presence. "Sur un titre de la Règle du Maître portant des traces de Cassien non encore repérées," *Revue d'histoire de la spiritualité* 51 (1975), pp. 305-309. He returns to the question in "De Cassien au Maître et à Eugippe: Le titre du chapitre de l'humilité," *SM* 23.2 (1981), pp. 247-261.

[33] The neophyte learns not merely from his reading of the text of Scripture, but from his willingness to interact with the living Gospel, incarnated in the lives of spiritual giants. Relevant for understanding this whole area is Douglas Burton-Christie, *The Word in the Desert: Scripture and the Quest for Holiness in Early Christian Monasticism* (New York, Oxford University Press, 1993).

[34] See Columba Stewart, "The Desert Fathers on Radical Self-Honesty," *Vox* 8.1 (1991), pp. 7-53.

[35] *Conl* 1.20; *SChr* 42, pp. 101-105.

[36] Abba Moses' second conference is dedicated to this topic; *Conl* 2; *SChr* 42, pp. 108-137.

[37] *Inst* 4.9; *SChr* 109, p. 132. See also *Conl* 16.11; *SChr* 54, p. 231.

[38] *Conference* 12 "On Chastity," *Conl* 22 "On the Illusions of the Night," *Conl* 2.23 and *Inst* 6 "On the Spirit of Fornication" manifest a degree of sexual frankness that was too much for the nineteenth-century editors of the *NPNF*, and so the texts were omitted. See Kenneth Russell, "Cassian on a Delicate Subject," *CSQ* 27.2 (1992), pp. 1-12. Terrence Kardong, "John Cassian's Teaching on Perfect Chastity," *ABR* 30.3 (1979), pp. 249-263.

[39] William Barclay, *New Testament Words* (London, SCM, 1973), pp. 241-242. See also *TDNT*, vol. VI, pp. 645-651.

[40] *Conl* 16.23; *SChr* 54, p. 242.

[41] See *Inst* 8.5; *SChr* 109, p. 344.

[42] "We ought not to make our improvement and peace of mind depend on another's power." *Inst* 8.17; *SChr* 109, p. 358.

⁴³ See *Conl* 18.12-16; *SChr* 64, pp. 24-36. I have developed this idea in "The Virtue of Patience in Western Monastic Tradition," *CSQ* 21.1 (1986), pp. 3-23. This is reprinted in *The Undivided Heart: The Western Monastic Approach to Contemplation* (Petersham, St Bede's, 1994), pp. 95-120.

⁴⁴ "If he sees someone commit murder he says, 'He has committed a single sin, whereas I sin every day.'" *Apothegmata patrum*, Poemen 97; *PL* 65, 345.

⁴⁵ See *Inst* 10; *SChr* 109, pp. 382-424. Cf. M. Casey "Acedia," in Michael Downey [ed.], *The New Dictionary of Catholic Spirituality* (Collegeville, Liturgical Press, 1992), pp. 4-5.

⁴⁶ *Inst* 9.6; *SChr* 109, p. 374. *Conl* 6.9; *SChr* 42, p. 227. *Conl* 16.17; *SChr* 42, p. 240.

⁴⁷ See M. Casey, "Apatheia," in *The New Dictionary of Catholic Spirituality*, pp. 50-51.

⁴⁸ Evagrius often couples *apatheia* with *agape* and Cassian explicitly identifies the two terms in *Conl* 1.7; p. 85: ... *propter principalem scopon, id est puritatem cordis, quod est caritas.*

⁴⁹ See Richard Byrne, "Cassian and the Goals of Monastic Life," *CSQ* 22.1 (1987), pp. 3-16. Terrence Kardong, "Aiming for the Mark: Cassian's Metaphor for the Monastic Quest," *CSQ* 22.3 (1987), pp. 213-220.

TAKING COUNSEL;
REFLECTIONS ON *RB* 3

This short essay reflects on some of the dynamics inherent in St Benedict's chapter on taking counsel. It emphasizes that this is a process of spiritual discernment rather than an exercise in democracy or a mechanism for reaching consensus. It appeared in Tjurunga 37 (1989)

The third chapter of St Benedict's Rule is one which has come into some prominence in the period after Vatican II as the notion of dialogue began to find a place in religious communities. It is sometimes referred to breezily, and in general terms, in support of a particular viewpoint, whether this leans toward "democratic" options or the opposite. The chapter is, however, finely nuanced and repays close attention.

St Benedict thinks in terms of two levels of consultation, important matters should be opened to the whole community, whereas routine questions may be referred simply to the seniors. The latter practice seems to have clear historical precedents in both Pachomiam and Basilian monasticism.[1] The idea of consulting the whole community seems to derive from the *Rule of the Master*.

> Whatever the abbot wishes to do or have done for the good of the monastery is to be done with the counsel of the

brothers. When all the brothers have been called together, let there be a general discussion about the good of the monastery. However, it is not on their own initiative or against the will of abbatial authority that the brothers happen to engage in deliberation, but by command and direction of the abbot. The counsel of all is to be sought because sometimes there are as many diverse opinions as there are people—all at once the best advice may well be given by one from whom it was least expected, and this may redound most to the common good—and from the many opinions the one to choose will be easy to find. But if none of the brothers can give apt counsel, then let the abbot, after explaining his reasons, decide as he wills, and it is right that the members follow the head. This is why we have said that all the brothers are to be called to the deliberation, according to the monastic maxim that the affairs of the monastery are the concern of all and not of any one person. Of all, because the brothers expect to go on replacing one another in the monastery in the course of time. Of no one person, because there is nothing in the monastery that any of the brothers can claim exclusively as his own, and no one determines or does anything by his own authority, but all live under the command of the abbot.[2]

Benedict devotes a separate chapter to the theme of seeking counsel. He combines the two streams of monastic tradition on the subject and sharpens the focus considerably so that the nature of consultation and its relation to decision-making becomes clearer. The principles he enunciates here apply both to universal consultation and to the more usual functioning of a superior with a legally constituted "council."

In English the discussion can sometimes be clouded by the fact that the group of advisers enjoined by canon law, commonly called *consilium* in Latin and *conseil* in French is generally labeled a "council" in English, although "counsel" is used in other contexts. This adds confusion since the word "council" often refers to bodies which have more than an advisory capacity, bodies which act collegially or make decisions or execute policy. A *consilium* properly has no power. It has rights: in certain circumstances it must be consulted or its consent must be gained as a condition to act but, typically, it does not act itself.[3] This inaccurate usage has probably contributed to the fact that the specific character of asking and giving counsel is not always well understood.

I. Taking Counsel

In the ancient world the search for meaning was a corporate enterprise. It was not considered an agonized stumbling through the labyrinth of individual consciousness towards a unique, personal solution, but the disciplined march of a vast company toward a common goal, undeterred by the loss of stragglers and deviants. Truth was understood as objective and universal: the meaning of life was something necessarily shared by those who live together. Even the most autocratic leaders and dogmatists claimed to do no more than expound and implement traditional universal doctrines, to defend it against the *idiotoi*, those who were unskilled in finding the truth and so wandered off on their own, "enclosed in their own sheepfolds, not the Lord's" (*RB* 1,8).

Although the abbot is paramount in Benedict's *Rule*, he has no monopoly of truth. He is subject to the authority of the church (64,4) and its judgments about orthodoxy (9,8; 73,4). He is bound not to go beyond the teachings of Christ (2,4). He is subject to the *Rule* in all things (3,7; 64,20). Even within these boundaries he is to work hard at the task of discovering, communicating and putting into effect the will of God. Far from being an automatic application of the *Rule* to the situation of the moment, or the abbot's spontaneous reaction, the commands envisaged by St Benedict presuppose a great deal of preliminary activity on the part of the abbot.

He is expected to perceive (61,11), to know (2,7; 64,8), to remember (2,30), to foresee (32,1; 41,4; 55,8; 64,17), to be prudent (64,12), to be cautious (61,13), to practice discretion (64,19), to reflect (64,7; 65,22), to consider (10,21; 55,3; 64,17), to weigh (3,5; 65,1), to choose (65,16), to decide (44,3; 65,14), to judge (24,2), to temper (8,4; 41,5; 41,9; 64,17; 64,19), to arrange (22,2; 65,12) and **then** to take action to give a command.[4]

Benedict's faith-viewpoint is summarized pithily in his chapter on monks who come as guests: "If he happens to make some reasonable criticisms or observations in a spirit of humility and charity, the abbot is to reflect prudently on them, **in case the Lord may have guided him (to the monastery) for this very purpose.**"

It is only in the last verse of *RB* 3 that St Benedict states clearly his underlying promise. He invokes the text of Ecclesiasticus: "Do all things with counsel and afterwards you will not be sorry" (Sir 32:24). A typical pragmatic Roman sentiment, but also one seasoned with humility and faith.

There are three stages envisaged by St Benedict in asking counsel:

1) **Proposing the Topic:** The abbot presents the question, thus defining the scope of the meeting. It is a deliberate, restrained exercise in which cross-discussion between members is not a necessary part. It is important that each one hears what the others say,[5] even though it is not meant to be an occasion for debate. This restriction of the area is a significant component in creative dialogue. If consultation of the community is not working it is probably because the abbot is not asking the right questions at the right moment. There are some aspects of important questions on which members of the community cannot be presumed to have any expertise and it is useless "consulting" the whole community about these. It becomes a charade which ultimately undermines the credibility of the whole

process. Sometimes a community is asked to give its counsel before sufficient data has been generated and, as a result, the meeting is irrelevant, since everyone knows that any suggestion has to be hypothetical and the whole question will be reviewed when information subsequently becomes available. On the other hand, it is possible to consult too late, when thinking has progressed too far along a particular route to turn back. If part of the data is that a million dollars has already been irretrievably invested in a particular project, there may be protests, but not many will seriously suggest taking a new tack. An open forum may yield such a variety of suggestions that division and inaction are almost inevitable; a workable basis for communal action is arrived at only by a sustained and systematic attempt to extend the area of consensus by rigorously excluding irrelevancies.

2) **Listening:** The abbot is to listen to what is said. This ordinary word has in recent decades assumed an almost sacred character: it connotes openness, respect for the person and a sincere humility. It means that the abbot listens earnestly, mindful that each brother is a potential channel of divine guidance in the same way as a visiting monk. There is a strong faith dimension here and an extraordinarily spiritual assessment of the worth of each member of the community. It may happen that the abbot may need to ask questions or to feed back an opinion to the speaker to ensure that he has really grasped the point. When this is done simply and in a friendly manner it becomes an overt statement that every point of view is valued. Jokes, raised eyebrows and nudging a speaker over the edge of extremity are thinly disguised reactions of ridicule and hostility. They signify that, in reality, the issue is already decided, it is only a matter of selling it through a pretense of general participation.

3) **Processing:** Having listened to all (3,3) the abbot is then to withdraw in order to process matters for himself: *tractet apud se* (3,2). The same verb is used in 61,4. There is no doubt that listening and processing are two distinct moments in the taking of counsel, separated by whatever time is necessary for the superior to review what has been said and to be formed by it. Benedict who sees most things in a faith-perspective does not rule out that in prayer and reflection the abbot may become aware of a "higher counsel" (63,7) which should govern his actions. For this reason he needs space after hearing the brothers.

This is the end of the process of taking counsel. After it comes decision. A separate matter which belongs to the abbot alone and for which he will have to render an account at the awesome judgment of God (3,11). The course which he follows is to be that which is "more useful" (3,2), "better" (3,3) and "more wholesome" (3,5). The use of the comparatives seems to indicate that it is a question of searching out the more perfect of two good options, not a matter of making a choice between black and white. Inevitably, opinions will differ and divisions will result unless everyone has antecedent willingness to submit to whatever course the abbot decides, having done his best to weigh matters prudently, with foresight and justice (3,6), in accordance with the *Rule* (3,7) and not merely following the whims of his own heart (3,8). Part of the specificity of the role-description of the abbot is his capacity to decide questions disinterestedly, caring for nothing else but the will of God (2,33-36).

It is particularly instructive to see St Benedict making room for innovative solutions and lateral thinking by reminding the abbot that the best ideas often come from the younger members of the community. The *juniores* are those who are younger in age or profession, not middle-aged mavericks looking for a justification for their obstructionism. Although Samuel and Daniel were mere boys when they passed judgment on their elders (63,6), St Benedict is surely not saying that as one progresses in monastic life and in faith one automatically becomes less likely to know what it is better to do. Later in the chapter he sets up a smaller advisory body composed only of seniors.[6] What he is probably saying is that those who are less socialized in conventional monastic thinking may often generate original suggestions which prove to be helpful. The effect of what we call "experience" is that we view every new situation in the light of what has gone before: it is a part of learning that we do not repeat the mistakes of the past. But there is always a danger that we run too quickly to precedents without really grasping the particularities of the case before us. Approximative solutions are faster and less painful for us but they do not always produce the desired result. The *juniores* are often free from such routinised perceptions. The key word is "often." It happens neither rarely nor inevitably, but frequently enough for the abbot to listen earnestly to what they say. It is to be remembered of course, that there is question here of responses given to an abbot's asking for counsel on a particular subject. It is not a necessary hallowing of every bright idea that emerges from the ranks of the juniors.

II. Giving Counsel

It is important for the understanding of St Benedict's mind on this subject that the separation of functions be appreciated. There is no question of a collegial decision by the community, except in the matter of the election of an abbot (64,1).[7] It is not a data-gathering exercise in which everyone present contributes relevant items of information. Each member of the community is expected to make a conscientious judgment about the issue and express it simply and irenically. There is no question of advocacy, but a straightforward appraisal, offered in a spirit of respect for the views of others and without an inflated view of one's own wisdom. Above all St Benedict sees fit to warn monks that the giving of counsel should not become an occasion for expressing aggression and hostility toward those in authority. We all know that this happens, although we are too polite to mention it.

Church law is just as emphatic in this regard. From paragraph 14 of *Perfectæ Caritatis* through to canon 618 (*CIC*) reminders are issued that superiors make the final decision. This emphasis should not be seen as a selling short of the whole process of consultation. Taking counsel and taking a decision are different operations, the first being preliminary to the second. Separating the two functions has the effect of facilitating the giving of counsel. If everyone attempts to deliver a sober, balanced judgment on every issue, the result of the consultation will likely be predictable and boring. There is a kind of freedom in being able to speak frankly without the burden of facing the practical consequences of what one is suggesting, and knowing that somebody else will try to incorporate the valid point one is making in the final synthesis. The wild card (which Benedict identifies with the *juniores*) presents a new angle and may open the way to a more creative solution.

For a consultative body to be successful there are a number of conditions which need to be accepted by its members. St Benedict mentions some of them. Others are the following:

1) **Patience:** Almost every matter on which counsel is sought will have a degree of complexity about it. This means that there are no facile solutions. Listening to others and waiting while a superior struggles to find some harmony among discordant voices requires both time and a detachment from one's own committed opinion. Most issues require several meetings in which tentative solutions are re-assessed and further steps are

planned. One has to be willing to keep monitoring situations and adjusting one's own viewpoint to suit reality.

2) **Freedom:** One must be able to submit to the movement of a meeting. To consider oneself merely as the representative of a particular viewpoint and, therefore, beyond influence, is a denial of the grace and purpose of sharing wisdom. The consultative body is at the service of the whole community even though, in larger groups, its members may be deliberately chosen to represent special interests within the totality. It is important that those who serve as counselors allow themselves to assume a more global viewpoint and not keep harping on particular concerns, like union representatives chipping away at management. Serving in this capacity should, in fact, have the effect of broadening one's horizons.

3) **Confidentiality:** Nobody is fit to be part of a consultative group who is not prepared to observe appropriate secrecy. This is not the secretiveness which turns everything into a mystery, but the reticence necessary when a matter is still *sub iudice*, or when personal rights to privacy are involved. There is a time for communication; there is also a time to hold one's peace. Because knowledge is power and its possession confers a certain status, some persons find it difficult not to drop hints that they are privy to restricted information. This can have disastrous effects, particularly because it does not allow people to be prepared pastorally for decisions which they may find it difficult to accept. There is also a temptation when one's own view is not shared by other counselors to seek solace by breaking solidarity. When an advisory body leaks, nothing sensitive can be entrusted to it and so it becomes useless.

The qualities required in counselors derive from an appreciation of their proper function. Most practical problems stem from a misunderstanding of the nature of counsel. When this is clear, those who accept to serve as counselors are aware of what is expected of them. If they feel unwilling to comply, they should decline.[8]

III. The College of Seniors

St Benedict recognizes that seeking counsel from the whole community is not always necessary or practicable. The principle of consultation remains intact. For ordinary matters he recommends recourse to the advice of the *seniores*. In history this has been interpreted in terms of a relatively stable group of those who are not numbered among the *juniores*.

The college of *seniores* is a fascinating component of Benedictine administration. Its boundaries are not sharply defined. It is not part of the formal organizational structure.[9] Membership in this group comes from their years of experience of monastic life, thus they are also termed *priores*: those who came before or those who are ahead. Age is not a factor (63,5) nor background (2,20). St Benedict is very cautious about promoting people above their natural rank in the community (63,2-3), even in the case of priests (60,6-7, 62,6). If someone is to be advanced, it should only be a little (61,11).

The *seniores* are models of observance for the *juniores* to emulate (7,55). Honor is owed them (4,70, 63,10-17). They serve as spiritual directors (4,50; 46,5) and are able to instruct (23,1), and admonish (23,2). The abbot may use them to maintain discipline in his absence (56,3), to prevent abuses (22,3, 22,7), to act as policemen (48,17) and formators (58,6) and to complement the abbot's pastoral ministry in difficult cases (27,2). Above all they are to set the tone of the monastery by surrounding those who come after them with nurturing and affirming love (4,71; 63,10; 72,3).

It is from this smaller group that the abbot seeks counsel regarding the ordinary decisions which have to be taken in governing the community. These men form the stable nucleus of the community and at least some of them will have more monastic experience than the abbot himself. And there is the likelihood that they may be in contact with some areas of community reality from which the abbot will find himself excluded.

Perhaps the years of life together gives this group a sense of solidarity and makes it a friendly circle whom the abbot can consult frankly without feeling threatened. It is hoped that the atmosphere is secure enough for the abbot to be challenged if he really goes off the track.[10]

If we take the step of identifying this college of *seniores* with the *consilium* required of religious superiors by canon law, then certain functions are automatically assigned to it. The abbot is obliged to consult it in certain matters and in some to obtain its consent. It is important to note that even when consent is obtained, the abbot is not obliged to act. Except in the instance where it decides collegially, the act of consent gives the abbot the green light to go ahead with a project, but does not oblige him to do so. He is, for example, under no strict obligation to profess one who has been accepted unanimously. He cannot act without the consent, but the consent itself is by way of counsel: it does not interfere with his total responsibility of taking the decision.

There will be many other matters wisely referred to this body. Appointments, for example (65,15). General policy on certain matters can be appropriately hammered out at this level. Pastoral problems can be dealt with confidentially. The group can use its varied contacts as a means of assuring a more efficient data-gathering, especially when minority voices need to be heard. Its members can also serve in the marketing and administering of decisions, once they are made, explaining the background and making sure that channels of communication remain open. All this has become a significant part of the work of counselors, especially in larger groups. They are part of a team which has examined a problem and implemented a solution, but the actual decision itself belongs to the abbot. It is to be hoped that to the extent that they have participated more actively in the decision-making (as distinct from decision-taking), they would be more inclined to accept the measures upon which the superior eventually decides.

Conclusion

The search for truth and the quest for creative solutions in particular situations can be conducted along pragmatic lines of consensus and compromise in which the key element is to convince all parties that they have been granted the substance of what they desire. Techniques to achieve this kind of agreement have only a limited value in religious communities.

If we approach the religious community in terms of a miniature church, an *ecclesiola*, then other priorities emerge. The will of God is absolute, irrespective of whether it is popular among the ranks or yields demonstrable profit to the community. The question that becomes important, in this case, concerns how the will of God is to be found.

One of the attributes of the church as a whole, and of each member in communion with the reality of the church is **counsel**, traditionally numbered among the seven gifts of the Holy Spirit. It is a corollary of Christ's promise to his disciples that the Holy Spirit would lead them into the fullness of truth. Counsel is like a higher form of prudence. It indicates which courses of action are to be followed, but it operates not from the standpoint of human welfare but **supernaturally**—to use an old term. It is like an intuitive instinct for the things of God—the ability to perceive the divine content in a particular course of action. One who is influenced by this spiritual gift speaks as a prophet and should be listened to. Nevertheless, as St Paul reminds us, all prophecy is subject to the discernment of the church.

Seeking counsel depends on the conviction that each church has within itself sufficient resources to uncover God's immediate will. For this reason a thorny problem can be considered as an invitation to search more profoundly for the way ahead, knowing that the quest will not be fruitless.

Because it is a spiritual matter, counsel is best sought and given in the context of prayer. Politics and contention, as St Benedict recognized, subvert the process. Perhaps fasting is indicated. There is no need to be contrived in this matter, but whatever concerns the ultimate welfare of the community is better understood in terms of spiritual discernment than merely as an exercise of corporate decision-making. It is this conviction, expressed in different terms, that animates the whole of St Benedict's third chapter.

NOTES

[1] Documentation on this point is found in Adalbert de Vogüé, *Community and Abbot in the Rule of Saint Benedict*, Volume One, Cistercian Publications (CS 5/1, Kalamazoo, 1979); p. 163.

[2] *RM* 3.41-50. Luke Eberle (trans.), *The Rule of the Master*, Cistercian Publications (CS 6, Kalamazoo, 1977); p. 114.

[3] Cases such as dismissal (can 699.1 *CIC*) in which a *consilium* acts collegially are rare and exceptional.

[4] M. Casey, "Discerning the True Values of Monastic Life in a Time of Change," *RBS* 3/4 (1974/75), pp. 75-88; p. 81.

[5] Even canon law seems to recognize that a certain momentum is built up which guarantees freedom of expression. In cases where taking counsel from a group is a pre-condition to action, this cannot be done legally without the members coming together. Individual consultation on a one-to-one basis is not considered to be the same thing (Can 127.1 *CIC*).

[6] In St Benedict's mind important matters were handled by the whole community and minor questions were treated by the smaller group. Strangely in many communities, the opposite practice holds. Only harmless issues are opened to community consultation.

[7] Even there an alternative method of selecting the abbot is provided.

[8] A conference given by Dom Ambrose Southey to the OCSO General Chapter of Abbesses is most useful for understanding something of the dynamics of council.

[9] St Benedict is adamant that the deans are not chosen on the basis of seniority (21,3) and there is no mention of seniority as recommending itself in the naming of cellarer or prior.

[10] One thinks of St Bernard being forced to withdraw an impetuously issued excommunication. If **he** could make mistakes of judgment, then anyone can. This is not adolescent opposition to authority or a case of personal hostility or envy. It is the prevention of the undermining of authority by the sort of occasional blind spot which everyone has.

COMPASSION: THE MAINSPRING OF MINISTRY

This simple article is a summary of some sessions given to the Sisters of the Good Samaritan of the Order of St Benedict in 1989. It was published in Tjurunga *38 (1990).*

There are many angles from which ministry may be considered. In these reflections I would like to focus upon one of the various subjective dispositions which govern the quality of the service rendered, one which is not dependent on the availability of specific opportunities, external resources or personal skills.[1]

I. The Mind of Christ

If ministry is seen as a sharing in Christ's mission from the Father to work for the salvation of all, it involves operating from the same standards as Christ himself. This means that whatever is undertaken is done in the power of divine love. Human affectivity is so transformed that whenever human need is encountered the response of compassion is elicited. Two texts may be considered which illustrate this reality:

◆ **Mark 6:34:** "And coming out, he saw a great crowd and he felt compassion for them because they were like sheep which have no shepherd; and he began to teach them many things." I have translated *esplanchnisthè* as "felt compassion." The word has a strong physiological basis: it means to feel something in one's innards. To be moved or touched at the level of feelings. The later Synoptic Gospels attach the compassion of Jesus to the crowd's hunger. Mark, on the other hand, relates it to the people's lack of leadership. It is this **feeling** of compassion which triggers Jesus' response: he becomes their teacher. It is not only the imparting of doctrine, but the establishment of a continuing personal relationship: master to disciple. This image is expanded considerably in Luke 15 and John 10.

◆ **RB 28,8-9:** "[The abbot] is to imitate the loving example of the Good Shepherd who left the ninety-nine sheep in the mountains and went in search of the one sheep that had strayed. So great was his compassion for its weakness that he mercifully placed it on his sacred shoulders and so carried it back to the flock." Sometimes concealed by administrative tasks, the heart of Benedict's ideal abbot is soft, generous and self-forgetful. Instead of the authoritarian prince-abbot so admired by the nineteenth century, he is rather a "hands-on" pastor whose prime characteristics are an understanding of human weakness and a willingness to work gently to remedy it.

II. A Spirit of Service

Not everyone remembers that "ministry" and "service" are interchangeable terms. Nor is it always appreciated that rendering service necessarily means not being the boss.[2] The evangelical notion of authority as service involves a complete reversal of many of our accepted beliefs about leadership. St Benedict presents the abbot as one who possesses vicariously the authority of Christ. But the authority which he exercises is one to which he himself must first submit. "And so the abbot should not teach or establish as a policy or command anything which is outside the Lord's instructions" (*RB*

2,4). In repeatedly evoking the prospect of judgment, St Benedict gives us the impression that the abbot is more burdened than anyone else with the task of avoiding self-will.

Extending this teaching into more general principles leads us to the conclusion that, in practice, acts of ministry will depend less on personal moments of creative illumination than on such expressions of God's will as the following:

- ◆ The intrusion of human need (cf. Mt 25).[3]
- ◆ The calling of a local community or the cry of a prophet (cf. Acts 13:1-3).
- ◆ The clear mandate of religious or ecclesiastical authorities.
- ◆ The expression of charism embodied in Constitutions and Chapter documents.
- ◆ The dawning conviction from reflection on the Scriptures and patrimonial texts, amply discerned.

The *status quo*: in the absence of any clear sense of new directions, it may be that the present situation offers the best opportunity for ministry, realistically available. "What everyone has is what the Lord has given them. They should continue as they were when God called them" (1 Cor 7:17).

There is, of course, no guarantee there will never be conflict. Long periods of searching for a resolution may be indicated. The teaching of Christ is not an endorsement of romantic mindlessness. It is not a short cut which enables us to prefer the immediate and urgent to what is long-term and important. No exclusion of planning and calculation is implied. Nevertheless, in weighing the options, we need to keep in mind the directness and simplicity of the Gospel challenge. The chaplaincy of a football team **may** yield abundant pastoral fruits, but it seems a little further from the Gospel than feeding the hungry and tending those whom life has wounded.

It is good to think concretely about men and women who have powerfully served in the spirit of the Gospel. How often we find that they were humble in themselves and in their ministry. On the other hand, if we reflect on our own experience as recipients of "ministry" we will often find that mostly we are left indifferent by those who are arrogant, self-interested and bossy. The service rendered by the saints respects those to whom the service is rendered; they are willing to decrease so that others may grow. Externally the service need not be dramatic or publicly esteemed. There is a humdrum quality about the life of a servant/minister which does not leave much room for self-exaltation. It is "ordinary, obscure and laborious" as was that of Christ himself. It is a mistake to measure a ministry by its quantitative impact. To submit to the plan of God means accepting to operate in an arena in which human assessment is often defective. Criteria of success and failure become irrelevant. The genuinely spiritual character of a work is often invisible to those who operate from non-spiritual assumptions (1 Cor 2:14).

It would seem that the lowlier the task, the more likely it is to be done in the spirit of service. This is why we are invited by the Gospels to ask ourselves continually "Whose feet do you wash?" We have to be careful about distancing ourselves from humble tasks by concentration on administrative concerns. The fact is that our ministry is more truly evangelical when we are dealing with people. When compassion for those who have less is the motive force, the service is purer still. The powerful, charming and interesting easily generate the attention they need. It is in the nobodies that Christ is more effectively served (*RB* 53,15). Even St Benedict knew about "the preferential option for the poor"![14]

III. Function-mindedness

To follow Christ it is not sufficient to serve in the sense of performing the service, getting the job done. If we are truly "servants of Jesus" (2 Cor 4:5) and our service is to be a carrier of life, then we need to look to the quality of the interaction between the servant and the one to whom service is rendered. The mystery is located in the meeting of persons: the performance of the task (be it leadership, teaching, nursing or something else) is purely instrumental. It offers the occasions for service.

For ministry to be revelatory of Christ's love, there must be this personal encounter. In so many cases it is the human contact which is the most important element of the service rendered. Those who are experienced in nursing patients in intensive care know that touches and physical reassurance are essential in sustaining the spirits of those exposed to such a barrage of hi-tech medicine. The technology is important, but there are other factors that must not be neglected.

Sometimes concern for personal presence in service may lead to a preference for maintaining a human scale in what we do, even though it is done more slowly and less efficiently. A dish-washer may enhance community life by removing an unsatisfying chore. On the other hand it may be the loss of an occasion for generosity, collaboration and therapeutic banter, which could deprive a community of one of its safety valves. This is not to say that all technology is to be rejected in life or in ministry. It is simply the reassertion of the primacy of personal presence. There are many tasks in which improved efficiency enhances human contact by freeing a person from routine exercises. But we all know that technology and the use of bureaucratic methods can stifle relationships and impair the quality of the "service" rendered.

Because genuine personal encounter is habitually demanding, one who concentrates on "getting the job done" may find that things go more smoothly by instituting measures to keep people at a distance or, at least, confined to authorized channels of approach. In this way energies are conserved and the chaos of life is somewhat constrained. Whether any service is rendered is extremely doubtful. Nobody would admit it so starkly, but the fact is that many people who desire to serve others actually do it by sterilizing their service of human content. They feel that they can cope with others' mess only by remaining clinically clean themselves.

This is particularly true in those ministries which do not involve direct interpersonal ministration. Liturgical ministry can degenerate into ritualism or music, temporal administration merely a variant of bookkeeping, and teaching the impersonal communication of facts. Those who invest their energies in these fields have to keep asking themselves how what they do can be an expression of the compassion of Christ. Otherwise the end effect is dehumanization. Whatever humane or Christian instincts animated them at the beginning, are consistently frustrated and atrophy sets in. The minister becomes more isolated, concentrating on the job instead of people, removed from potential feedback and cut off from the enrichment which necessarily comes from dealing with people.[5] A priest may become simply a liturgical practitioner, a visitor of hospitals, a parish administrator. Invisibly he has ceased to be a man for others. No wonder he gets lonely. No ministry is so holy that it operates *ex opere operato*.[6]

By looking at an opposite extreme we can see the importance of compassion. Where there is a genuine feeling for others, even vast projects are no barrier to contact. But when ministry has degenerated into an institutional routine, even the most intimate moments may lack warmth and humanity.[7]

IV. Neo-Narcissism

If we are to believe the pundits, the years since the Second World War have been the playground of the "Me-Generation."[8] Let us reflect on what consequences this might have for the theory and practice of ministry. I am not trying to pillory a particular age-group but I hope that, by exaggerating certain possible deviations, the influences which undoubtedly affect us all will become clearer.

For the narcissist, talk about the quality of ministry or interaction is often understood in terms of the way in which it impinges on the self. A ministry is modulated less by criteria such as an objective mission or the needs of others than by the perceptions, needs and resources of the individual. A service needs to be upgraded when it feels bad to the one performing it. At times one is unkindly reminded of St Benedict's parody of the sarabaites: "Their law is what they like to do, whatever strikes their fancy. Anything they believe and choose, they call holy; anything they dislike, they consider forbidden" (*RB* 1,8-9).

The practical effect of overripe narcissism is that reality is interpreted and ministry defined in terms of inner urgencies on the part of the individual. An ex-religious who became a social worker, was surprised to be criticized for helping others because he needed to be a helper rather than for any need of assistance on their part. In over five years of religious life no one had ever pin-pointed this tendency. What happens in this and in similar cases is that sympathy develops between the person and certain others who seem to suffer the same deprivations. In tending them one attempts to assuage the affronts which life has inflicted on one's own inner needs. It can be secretly angry service. The more I minister to others, the more outraged I become that no one ministers to me. Meanwhile, there is an insensitivity to other forms of suffering and envy toward those who do not seem to be similarly deprived. There is often a tempestuous zeal, reminiscent of what St Benedict writes about in *RB* 72. Sometimes real good is achieved, but the principal agenda is within, where the situation remains unchangeable. Good is done and battle is joined with the forces of evil. But everything that happens is instinctively interpreted in terms of one's own deep (and maybe pre-conscious) needs.

When ministry is measured according to its impact on self, an appreciation of its sacramental aspect is forfeited: the presence of Christ within both minister and ministered. This can lead to an exaggerated sense of the minister's own contribution. In such a case a minister can become so self-conscious that a sort of paralysis sets in. It becomes impossible to operate in situations where human resources are unavailing. It is easy to forget, for example, that a dying person may be more interested in seeing a priest *qua* priest than in the personal reactions of Fr. Bloggs.[9]

In a family situation, the utter dependence of the next generation can facilitate the displacement of self by concern for the helplessness of another. This does not seem to happen easily in religious or in those who choose not to have a family. Where there are no fledglings to be cared for, resources are inevitably lavished on oneself. Fulfillment and the quality of present experience become paramount concerns.

The "Me-Generation" makes unprecedented demands on life and devotes to its own gratification a disproportionate share of human and material resources. It is articulate in making its needs known and skilled in making life miserable for others until it gets what it wants. But there is a sadness here also. Perhaps it is a case of what Eugene Boylan called "the curse of a granted wish." Getting one's own way does not always bring with it the sense of well-being for which one hoped. The anger remains.

When it comes to ministry, the needs of the minister often assume a considerable importance and a lot of energy has to be devoted to finding an avenue of "service" in which these needs can be catered for. Sometimes a long (and expensive) period of training is necessary. If after this, the experience of ministry does not live up to expectations, no qualms are felt in searching for a more fulfilling alternative.

Nobody is suggesting that one ought not to look after oneself and try to ensure that one's ministry accords with one's nature and needs. But perhaps it is worth pointing out to this generation that the fulfillment which often seems so elusive is to be found in forgetfulness of self, in allowing the needs of others to draw from us a response which goes beyond our assessment of our capabilities, in breaching the limits fixed by our consciousness of self so that full richness of what we are may blossom and bear fruit.

V. Ecstasy

It has been recognized for many centuries that the way of spiritual growth is one of progressive self-transcendence:

> Man must at times pass through this bodily feeling to a spiritual feeling which is rational, and through the spiritual feeling pass to a divine feeling which is above reason, and through this divine feeling sink away from himself into an experience of motionless beatitude.[10]

So great is the goal that it cannot be grasped until the capacity of the mind is enlarged. The ultimate destination and purpose of human existence is only perceptible to those who have long passed beyond the beginnings. The immediate goal which animates at the outset, itself points to a further stage. Only one step is visible at a time. The God-ward orientation of life reveals itself only gradually. Each phase of growth exists only to be transcended.[11]

Bernard of Clairvaux was emphatic in assigning a key role to compassion in helping us to pass beyond a self-centered existence.

In his treatise *On the Steps of Humility and Pride* he speaks of compassion as the bridge that leads beyond a personal discipline of life to the total experience of God. Those who discover for themselves how much effort is needed to live a life worthy of their vocation are inclined to be a little less prompt in condemning others; they develop a sense of fellow-feeling for those who endure the same burdens as themselves, which makes them patient and tolerant on the one hand and, on the other, motivates them to do what they can to make their neighbor's life easier. It is the opposite attitude to that of the Pharisee in the Gospel. Compassion is a sense of solidarity which makes us forget ourselves in order to do good to others. It is not calculating philanthropy. It is a spontaneous zeal for justice which springs from a feeling of identity with the other.

Perhaps his conclusions come as a surprise. We are accustomed to the neo-Pelagian assumption that the spiritual life is a matter of sustained personal discipline, maintaining our sense of values while all around us standards crumble, reluctant to be numbered among those who cannot achieve salvation on their own merits. What he is saying is that, although personal discipline is an indispensable first step, a point is quickly reached beyond which it cannot take us. To the extent that our native selfishness has been purged, we begin to experience the fact of our union with the other members of the human species. We begin to feel for them, to be affected by the things which impinge on their lives, to rejoice with those who rejoice and to grieve with those who sorrow.

This connatural sym-pathy or com-passion is not irrelevant to our "spiritual" life. It represents a process whereby our hearts continue to be purified, but in a manner different from that experienced in active asceticism. We are being softened up, rendered more human so that progressively we may become more capable of experiencing the attractiveness of God.

In his slightly later treatise, *On the Necessity of Loving God*, Bernard explains the same point differently. Here he thinks of the natural expansion of love from total self-absorption towards total absorption in the other—God being the only one capable of holding human affections so completely. The primal energies of love remain the same: it is a matter of allowing them to find the direction (*Ordinatio caritatis*) in which the mutuality implicit in love can be experienced most fully. The self is powerless to bind love to itself: in attempting to do so it distorts both love and its own nature. Inevitably love needs to go beyond self if it is to find gratification. So it becomes attached to external reality: at first objects and then other persons. In Bernard's view this leads to only moderate satisfaction, and so love begins to seek fulfillment in transcendent reality. Again compassion or human love is seen as an intermediary attitude: richer than selfishness but lacking the full measure of an absorbing love for God.[12]

The important point about this line of development is that it emphasizes the central role played by compassion in our coming closer to God. Many persons experience a tension between their work for people and their desire for prayer and union with God. If Bernard is correct—and experience tends to support him—then there is no dichotomy. Soft-hearted fellow-feeling for other human beings is not only the soul of ministry, it is also the beginning of that self-forgetfulness which is at the heart of mysticism. In fact, it is because there is a certain God-consciousness in the minister, that the works undertaken to meet human needs have something of a divine content, which is often perceptible to those who are being served. On the other hand, without compassion there is neither deep prayer nor worthwhile service of others. None of the substitutes has any right to the name "ministry."

NOTES

[1] Text prepared for Sisters of the Good Samaritan, 25 April 1989.

[2] There are three corollaries from this fact. Firstly, one does not have the luxury of drawing up master plans for one's own future ministry. Secondly, one is obliged to render the service promptly, without waiting until it is convenient for oneself. Thirdly, one is constrained to continue with a task even after it ceases to be gratifying. Sometimes titles such as "servant" or "minister" seem to be more honorary than real. The reality of service involves a considerable limitation on personal freedom.

[3] The fact that compassion for human need is one of the factors which is meant to break through rigid mind-sets and lead to liberation is demonstrated amply in the parable of the Good Samaritan. To the question "Who is my neighbor?" Jesus responds that **anyone** in need is potentially a neighbor, a brother, a sister. Pity for the plight of the wounded is the means which allows us to transcend prejudice and self-interest and become mirrors of the generosity of God.

[4] It is important to note that our attitude to those who are deprived must be one of love and respect. If culture-shock at a lower standard of living, or a false sense of guilt animates our work for others, our minis-

try may appear as intrusive and accomplish no unambivalent improvement. We may achieve some material amelioration but, because we fail genuinely to bear another's burden, we do not much reduce the sum total of pain in the world around us. All we do is to replace hunger by humiliation, ignorance by loss of self-respect and loneliness by dependence.

[5] Often we are surprised to find in ministry to those who are externally most indigent that we are the ones who receive. We come away from the encounter revived, encouraged and enlightened by the powerful presence of Christ in the least of his followers. I think that compassion itself is not merely a self-generated attitude towards others or a natural disposition. It is a gift that is received when we are invited by brothers and sisters to enter that most private sphere which is suffering. So long as we have never been drawn into the pain of others we will never learn compassion.

[6] Of course I am not rejecting the Council of Trent's doctrine on sacramental efficacy.

[7] It is hard to escape the conclusion that even such a great figure in the Western Church as St Ambrose may have been fairly cool in his relations with others. He seems not to have reciprocated Augustine's ardent admiration for him. Perhaps reflecting his days as an imperial administrator, one of his most important works is *De Officiis* ("On Duties"), apparently modeled on Cicero's work of the same name. What is even more tragic is that this mold of churchman has endured through the centuries, unrelieved by the holiness which may have provided a foil in St Ambrose's own case.

[8] According to an article in *The Age* on 6 March 1989, "Narcissism is Booming," this includes those born between 1947 and 1963. Obviously, the trend is not confined strictly to this age group.

⁹ The same could be said of many situations in which the personal needs of the minister are objectively speaking, far less urgent than the exigencies of the other. If I were lying half-dead on the roadside after being mugged, I would like to believe that the rendering of material assistance would take precedence over how the "experience" would be processed in the other's intensive journal.

¹⁰ Jan van Ruusbroec, *Boecksen der Verclaringhe* ("Little Book of Enlightenment"), lines 280-283; text and translation in *Studiën en Tekstuitgaven van ons Geestelijk Erf*, Deel XX.1 (Leiden, E.J. Brill, 1981), p. 136.

¹¹ This is why faith/belief/trust is necessary. I cannot correctly order my life according to its ultimate purpose if I am not at a stage when I can be influenced directly by the goal. Instead I have to trust the experience of others who can see further than I. At times faith has to supplant judgment based on previous experience if forward movement is to result: *Iudium fidei sequere et non experimentum tuum*: Bernard of Clairvaux, *Quad* 5.5; *SBO* 4.374.20-21.

¹² I have written about this in an article entitled, "In Pursuit of Ecstasy: Reflections on Bernard of Clairvaux's *De Diligendo Deo*," *MS* 16 (1985), pp. 139-156.

INTENTIO CORDIS (*RB* 52,4)

This article, published in Regulae Benedicti Studia 6/7 *(1977/78) reflects on the meaning of the phrase* intentio cordis *used by St Benedict and other monastic authors and found to be so difficult to translate. It is argued that the phrase has several levels of meaning, but that its primary sense is that of concentration of the energies of the heart on God.*

In Chapter 52 of the *Rule of Saint Benedict* we find provision made for the monk who wishes to pray privately. In the intervals between the segments of the *Opus Dei*, a recollected atmosphere of reverence and quiet is to prevail in the oratory, so that if a monk feels drawn to prayer, the simple act of entering this sacred place is sufficient to introduce him into an environment already permeated by a spirit of prayerfulness.

In his preference for silent prayer, Benedict gives two features of such an exercise. It is characterized by tears and by *intentio cordis*. The notion of prayer with tears is widely attested throughout monastic tradition, but *intentio cordis* is not a familiar idea, as can be seen by the varying explanations given by translators and commentators.

In this article I shall attempt to show that at least some of the difficulty experienced by interpreters of *intentio cordis* in *RB* 52,4 stems from the intrinsic richness of the term. I hope to demonstrate that the phrase itself is evocative of a tradition of prayer current within Western monasticism from before Benedict's time until the twelfth century or later, and accordingly that it must be translated in the light of this tradition.

Intendere and Intentio: Their Range of Meanings

To understand something of the variety of contexts in which *intendere* and its cognates are used, Nielson's entries in the *Thesaurus Linguae Latinae* are most helpful.[1] We begin with a summary of the appropriate articles inasmuch as they bear upon our topic. References and documentation can be found in the *Thesaurus*.

The basic meaning of *intendere* revolves around the notion of movement. This is, perhaps, already indicated by its formation from *in* and *tendere*. Further confirmation can be found in the fact that προσεχω and επιτεινω are regularly used as equivalents. The movement qualified by *intendere* can be either ordinary external motion, or it can be the inner activities of perception and feeling. There is however, nearly always question of some form of movement, and habitually of movement in a particular direction.

Intendere is often used with the same meaning as *extendere*; a single action being viewed from slightly different viewpoints. Both verbs can describe, for instance, the action of a person holding out his hand in greeting or in gesture. Furthermore, it is not unusual for *intendere* to have the connotation of expanding, distending, stretching or stretching forth. In this context it is used of bending a bow in preparation to shooting an arrow. It is also used of unfurling the folds of a tent. On occasion, this idea of extension takes on the sense of an internally generated movement, a motion dictated by an inner tension, the opposite of which is a state of relaxation, *remissio*. This usage is not unusual in a physiological context; occasionally, as the *Thesaurus* coyly notes, *sensu obscaeno*.

As well as describing the movement from the point of view of the *terminus a quo*, *intendere* can envisage the *terminus ad quem*. Most frequently it signifies motion in a particular direction and, as such, it is suitable to describe the dispatch of arrows and other missiles toward their targets. Topologically it can signify any movement which is marked by finality. Hence it can mean efforts made to expedite motion in a particular direction, whether this involves the elimination of possible deviations or the intensification of the movement itself. It often has energetic overtones. The Vulgate rendering of the Psalm, *Deus in adiutorium meum intende*, provided a model for using *intendere* in the solicitation of divine intervention and influence.

In a parallel development, *intendere* is internalized; it serves to characterize the inner movements of desire and instinct or of perception and understanding. In this context, *intendere* and its cognates are used in association with terms typical of the internal faculties, such as *anima* or *animus, cor, mens, sensus* and *spiritus*.

On a first plane, *intendere* signifies the aim, goal or direction inherent in a particular action and foreseen and willed by the doer of that action. In this usage, the external motion is seen to be a reflection of the will of the agent; when he communicates movement to an object, he does so with a particular end in view. He gives it its direction. Hence there is an intrinsic correlation between what he "intends" and what is, in fact, achieved. His "intention" is embodied in the resultant movement.

But *intendere* often means more than this mere initiation and direction of outward action. It also denotes the motivation, purpose or personal project of the doer of the action. The agent not only "intends" that the arrow arrive at its designated target; by extension, he simultaneously "intends" to slay his enemy, to win honor for himself and to save his country. Hence the verb *intendere* can also be used to indicate something of the person's basic values, and can even give some information concerning his fundamental purpose or orientation in life.

Intendere is able to describe both the impulsion which initiates and sustains the movement and the direction imparted to it. The doer "intends" the movement when he gives it direction with a specific outcome in view. He equally "intends" the movement when, by an expenditure of energy, he causes it to become a reality. His "intention" has, therefore, two complementary aspects: concentration and intensification. The first limits the motion to the pre-determined pattern; the second, profiting from the elimination of wasted energy, speeds the motion to its goal.

When used in a more reflexive sense, *intendere* concerns efforts toward attention, vigilance and the avoidance of distraction; it also signifies affective involvement, occasionally qualified by such adverbs as *vehementer*, with an end result of something close to "enthusiasm." These are complementary significations, in no way to be thought of as mutually exclusive.

A late development is evidenced by the interest of ethicians in the possibility that what is "intended" may not correspond with what is actually achieved. From being the effective determinant of events, what a person "intends" becomes a mere proposition of the will, something which remains within the agent rather than is embodied in the action. In later writing, to "intend" to do something often indicates an *action manquée*, as it does in current English. "I intended to write you a letter" means that, in fact, no letter was written.

There is a loose chronological evolution visible in the verb *intendere*, though it is not to be taken too seriously. There seems to be a shift in emphasis from movement to causation of movement and from causation of movement to the psychological processes preceding any

INTENTIO CORDIS/339

outward activity. Interest swings from objective to subjective realities. It is to be noted, however, that the evidence manifests little uniformity and therefore it is probably best to examine each particular occurrence on its own merits.

The noun *intentio* (or *intensio* as it was sometimes written), duplicates the fluctuation in meaning of its parent verb though, predictably, it seems that abstract significations are relatively more frequent. A number of quasi-technical significations developed which may be noted here and then omitted from further discussion. In musicology, *intentio* was often used to describe what determines the tone of the sound. In forensic documents, the *intentio* was a designated part of a formal presentation (the statement of the grounds of a complaint or of the author's purpose, according to the nature of the text). From this usage, *intentio* borrowed connotations of controversy (as did *intendere* and, more especially the derivative verb, *intentare*), and was occasionally used interchangeably with *contentio*.

The use of *intentio* in epistemology and logic, signifying mental contents as distinct from facticity, became widespread in the philosophical schools of the West, especially after the translation of *Avicenna* into Latin. Its use continued long after the Middle Ages and is, perhaps, reflected in Franz Brentano's coining of the term "intentionality" and its subsequent use in phenomenological circles.

On a more regular basis, *intentio* means, firstly, the action of paying attention to something and the resultant state of attention. Secondly, it can signify a decision taken either in judging issues (*consilium*) or initiating activity (*propositum*). Thirdly, *intentio* sometimes denotes finality; it is used to translate σκοπός, in the *Vetus Latina* rendering of Phil 3:14 and elsewhere. It is used in parallel with *spes*, and its equivalence with ἐπίτασιν is affirmed more than once. Finally, *intentio* used epexegetically has the effect of intensification as in Ambrose's *intentio devotionis*. Elsewhere it describes a heightened state of feeling, fervor or involvement. The same is true of *intentus* and of the adverb.

Ecclesiastical Usage

There is, however, a much wider use of *intendere* and its cognates in the writings of the Church Fathers than is indicated by the comparatively few references to them in the *Thesaurus*. It is obviously not possible to attempt a comprehensive survey here, but it may be feasible to indicate by a few examples how *intendere* retained a wide range of meanings throughout the period under discussion. If we can demonstrate this fact, then we will be amply protected against viewing the occurrences of the term in the ancient monastic writings through the narrowing prism of later Scholastic categories.

The only use of the noun *intentio* in the Vulgate occurs at Heb 4:12. *Et discretor cogitationum et intentionum cordis* renders καὶ κριτικὸς ἐνθυμήσεων καὶ ἐννοιῶν καρδίας. Of the 45 instances of the verb *intendere*, 22 (plus the only use of *intente*) revolve around the idea of being attentive to or giving attention to something; 8 texts expand this idea somewhat by the addition of a note of urgency and an appeal for intervention and aid. Seven times the meaning is to look upon, scrutinize or inspect (plus the single use of *intentator*); five times the verb refers to the action of bending the bow; twice it means giving direction to something and once it seems to mean to advance or prosper. *Intendere* and its cognates are not used often in the Vulgate; their overriding meaning is to pay attention to, but other significations are not totally excluded.

Ambrose of Milan, taking the cue from Origen,[2] placed considerable importance on the distinction between *intentio* and *actio* as respectively the internal and outward components of behavior. In his first exposition *On the Gospel of Luke,* Ambrose makes an extended comparison of *actio* and *intentio* and comes to the conclusion that both are necessary elements in Christian behavior. But what exactly does Ambrose mean by *intentio*? After noting the difficulty of finding a single expression which renders all the meanings assumed by *intentio* in this context, Dom Gabriel Tissot continues: "*Intentio* correspond à tout ce qui est de l'ordre spéculatif: idéal, désir, regard attentif, contemplation, étude."[3] Interestingly enough, later on in the same exposition, Ambrose discusses what later would be called "purity of intention," but he does not use *intentio*. Instead he uses a series of generic terms such as *mens, cogitatio* and *cordis occulta*.[4]

For Ambrose, *intentio* describes the whole gamut of interior movements which precedes and prepares for outward behavior. The following montage amply demonstrates this.

> Gemina virtus est in homine perfecto, ut et intentio sit et actio...Finis autem intentionis est actio, principium actionis intentio...Sed non statim in intentione actio...neque enim in omnibus rebus simul et intentio et actio est, sed cum sit rei alterius actio, alterius adhuc intentio est...Est autem nonnumquam plus in intentione quam in actione aut plus in actione quam in intentione...Est etiam nonnumquam maxima intentio, cassa actio...Est etiam in nonnullis uberior, aliquando actio, exilior intentio...Ideo ergo utriusque virtutis plenitudo quarenda est, quam consequi potuerunt apostoli...ut per id quod viderunt divinae cognitionis intellegatur intentio, per id quod ministri fuerunt eorum actio declaretur.[5]

Later in the commentary, Ambrose reverts to the notion of *intentio* in the sense of attentiveness, when he applies to Mary of Bethany the felicitous formula, *religiosa mentis intentio dei verbo.*[6]

Intendere and its cognates are found occasionally in the Augustinian corpus but not, apparently, with any particular emphasis. The several references to Augustine's writings in the *Thesaurus*, for instance, cover a broad spectrum of meaning and application. An important example as far as subsequent thought is concerned, occurs in his commentary on the First Epistle of Saint John. In the discussion leading up to the much-quoted epigram, "Love and do as you will," Augustine clearly points to intention as the principal moral determinant in behavior: *Diversa ergo intentio diversa facta fecit.*[7] But it is the development of the thought as a whole which is significant here, rather than the single use made of *intentio*.

Intentio occurs often in the writings of Gregory the Great and in a wide variety of senses. A preliminary study of his *Homilies on the Gospel Texts* reveals the presence of many different nuances in his use of the word. In the first place he sees *intentio* as the invisible complement to external, observable behavior,[8] the voluntary content of an action, not traceable to chance or coincidence,[9] but resulting from a firm act of the will.[10] *Intentio* is used also in the sense of attention, for instance, in the expression *tota intentione cogitate,*[11] and to designate the object of a person's interest or concern.[12] In one case it is identified with an immediate goal or purpose in acting and contrasted with the ultimate end which is the object of *spes*,[13] but it is also used to describe the movement of the Christian toward heaven, *pro intentione supernae patriae,*[14] and employed in parallel with *coeleste desiderium*.[15] An unusual occurrence is where *intentio* designates the cause of a dispute in a sense close to that of *contentio*.[16]

The same pattern emerges in the first two books of the *Moralia in Iob*. There is a long excursus in the first book about the ways in which the "ancient enemy" subverts man's efforts at accomplishing good. He does this by casting a blight either on the *intentio* or on the actual doing of the good deed or on its ultimate end.[17] We note that he here distinguishes between *intentio* and *finis*. In this section *intentio* seems to refer to the internal processing (*cogitatio*) or motivation which is, in fact, the real beginning of the action,[18] or to some fundamental orientation which undergirds all virtuous behavior.[19] In this last sense the phrase *intentionem cordis dirigere* is used with the apparent meaning of checking on one's basic priorities, re-affirming one's personal direction in life.[20] In another instance, *intentio* refers to an overall motivation which is opposed to the pursuit of temporal glory.[21] Elsewhere it describes a decision taken at a deep level of personal involvement,[22] and the last shred of godliness when faith, hope and charity have disappeared is designated a *recta intentio*.[23] In one case *intentio* seems to indicate the whole active power of the mind, with perhaps something of *attentio* included in its meaning.[24] Finally, in an interesting similitude, later taken up by Gilbert of Swineshead,[25] Gregory compares *intentio* to a hair ribbon which binds together all the freely flowing strands of hair; *intentio* has a unifying role with regard to the *defluentes animi cogitationes*; when the word of God is preached, *quasi ad unam se intentionem colligant*.[26]

Intentio is an emphatic word in the writings of Gregory the Great, but no effort is made by him to restrict its meaning. One gains the impression that *intentio* is an internal movement which is deeper than the superficial fluctuations of thought and emotion because it stems from close to man's personal center and appropriately has in view ultimate rather than immediate reality. There are, however, numerous exceptions to this general pattern.

John, abbot of Fécamp from 1028 until 1078, an eleventh century "master of the spiritual life" was much influenced in his vocabulary by the writings of

Augustine and Gregory. For him, *intendere* and its cognates are used exclusively with respect to desire or movement toward God, a theme that was very dear to him.[27]

Bernard of Clairvaux's use of *intendere* and *intentio* is rich and varied and will be discussed in greater detail in another place. For the purposes of this article it is sufficient to note that even in the twelfth century, *intentio* retains a measure of flexibility. For Bernard it can mean looking at, scrutiny, inspection.[28] By extension, it can mean attention or carefulness.[29] The contrast between *operatio* (or *exercitium*) and *intentio* is not uncommon.[30] Bernard seems to understand *intentio* as a voluntary principle interposed between the *affectiones animae* and the actual activity.[31] In at least two places he uses *intentio* in parallel with *anima* or *animus* with the apparent meaning of a non-specific inner principle of experience or reaction.[32] *Intentio* can be used in tandem with *votum* and *propositum* to signify desire or yearning, *intentio cordis mei*.[33] It can refer to a particular motivation,[34] or to a more general attitude toward life.[35] There is often question of a "pure intention"[36] and Bernard frequently insists on effort being expended in the process of purification.[37] Finally, there are many texts in which the subsequent technical sense of the word begins to appear. Bernard is, in fact, one of the first to place great emphasis on intention as a determinant of the moral quality of behavior and on the consequent importance of verifying the integrity of a person's intention before attempting to assay the moral content of an action. *Colorem operi tuo dat cordis intentio*.[38] In writing to Guy about the incident of the consecration of an empty chalice, Bernard enunciates a succinct ethical principle. "It is intention, which is the cause of events, that determines whether there is question of fault or of merit, not the components of the acts nor their outcome."...*rerum causa, non materia nec exitus actuum, sed intentionis propositum culpas discernit et merita*.³⁹ On a more general level, intention is the *facies animae*⁴⁰—the mode of a person's concrete self-presentation which, in his stance before an issue, manifests his real inner quality. To appreciate a person's *intentio* is to go beyond appearances and to make contact with the inner dynamic principle which animates all action. Two elements comprise the constitutive principles of *intentio* as far as Bernard is concerned: the *res*, which is the possibility which the doer of the action wills to come about, and the *causa* which is the reason, purpose or motivation behind his endeavors.⁴¹ For an action to be virtuous both components must be free from all taint of malice and lower desires.

In a general way, *intentio* seems to mean an inward principle of behavior, as far as Bernard is concerned. It is the role of this internal disposition to orient a person in the direction of God. It is both universal and particular. It remains under the control of the will both in its permanent orientation and in its concrete application. Its opposite is aimlessness, carelessness or unfeelingness. It is capable of purification which is usually understood in terms of the elimination of inauthentic or unworthy motivations and desires and progressive simplification in one's turning toward God.

This brief sketch of the historical evolution of *intendere* and its cognates might be concluded with a brief mention of Thomas Aquinas, the master theologian of the thirteenth century. In many instances, both in ethical and logical contexts, *intentio* is used as a technical term, nevertheless, Aquinas remains fully aware of the wider implications of the term and of the way in which it had been used in the preceding centuries.⁴² His was not the mistake of the writer responsible for the article "intention" in the *Dictionnaire de Spiritualité*, who skips blithely from the scriptures to Thomas Aquinas in a few vacuous sentences.⁴³

* * *

This sampling of the variety of signification assumed by *intendere* and *intentio* gives us the possibility of formulating a list of *a priori* possibilities for the translation of *intentio* in *RB* 52:4. Eliminating certain technical and rare usages from consideration, the following words severally translate the many nuances of *intentio*.

1. Movement, tendency
2. Thought, idea, notion
3. Decision, determination
4. Motivation
   a) Intention
   b) Orientation, ideal
   c) Disposition, attitude
   d) Aim, goal, plan, purpose, priority, direction
5. Fervor
   a) Desire, yearning
   b) Stretching, stretching forth
   c) Enthusiasm, zeal
   d) Feeling
   e) Intensity
6. Attention
   a) Attentiveness, alertness, vigilance
   b) Diligence, concern, carefulness, industriousness
   c) Concentration, application
   d) Interest
   e) Scrutiny, inspection, contemplation, gaze, look

There is, of course, considerable overlap between the alternative renderings offered, but since there is no single equivalent for *intentio*, perhaps we were well advised to keep several options in mind each time we encounter the word!

Cassian and the Master

Because the most important immediate sources of the *Rule of Saint Benedict* (RB) are the *Conferences* and *Institutes* of John Cassian and the *Rule of the Master* (RM), it is obviously useful to examine their usage a little more closely.

In the writings of Cassian the noun *intentio* and the past participle *intentus* (habitually used adjectivally) appear relatively frequently. Once again, we must note that *intentio* carries a considerable number of different connotations, a fact which often proves to be an embarrassment to translators. Furthermore, Cassian uses *intentio* interchangeably with a large number of alternative expressions and in a variety of verbal contexts—points of style which clearly demonstrate the flexibility of the word.

To demonstrate the difficulty often encountered by translators, we have made a comparison of the renderings of 40 representative instances of *intentio* in Cassian. The basis for the comparison were the translations in the *Sources Chrétiennes* series (SC) and the more traditional and literal rendering offered by Edgar J. Gibson in the *Nicene and Post-Nicene Fathers* series (NPNF).[44]

	SC	NPNF
Intention	3	2
Attention	5	7
Application	10	2
Effort	4	2
Fervor	11	5
Gaze, regard	2	1
Purpose, goal	3	16
Other	2	5

The matter is further complicated by the fact that particular translations diverge far more than can be shown by a statistical table. The pressing obligation to find a single word to render *intentio* has often forced translators into choosing a particular word and thereby eliminating all alternative connotations.

In Cassian's writings, *intentio* means the opposite of relaxation.[45] It denotes an active application of the faculties, expenditure of energy, effort.[46] This energetic involvement may take the form of close attention to detail,[47] for instance, to the text of a reading.[48] On the other hand *intentio* may qualify an intense effort which is closely akin to fervor, ardor or enthusiasm.[49]

On a more cognitional plane, *intentio* refers to the aim, goal, purpose or "intention" inherent in a particular action or in a pattern of behavior;[50] it can denote the animating vision,[51] or the actual path taken.[52] By extension, it connotes movement toward God and becomes something very close to desire or aspiration.[53]

The past participle *intentus* is often used more as an adjective than strictly as a past participle. As a rule it duplicates the alternative renderings of the noun. It can mean vigilant or attentive,[54] or intense (where it is used in parallel with "pure"—*puras intentasque preces emittere*[55]) or again, applied, intent, concentrated.[56]

Three special uses of *intentio* are particularly noteworthy: *intentio spiritus*,[57] *intentio mentis*[58] and more especially, *intentio cordis*. The last occurs at least eleven times, apart from four quotations of Heb 4:12. Twice there is question of a close and prayerful attention to the chanting of a Psalm.[59] Once the expression is qualified by the addition of *sollicita* and used in tandem with *cum sudore vultus sui* to signify laboriousness and effort.[60] In the same sense it is used in parallel to *industria*.[61] The expression *intentio corde* is combined with *muto ore* to denote a monk's attitude in prayer; this is perhaps the closest parallel to our phrase in *RB*.[62] The phrase is used three times in a final sense, meaning goal, purpose or aim; in two of these occurrences the addition of the word *tenacissima* seems to endow the phrase with greater urgency.[63] There are also three places in which it seems likely that the phrase *intentio cordis* has connotations of intensity, zeal or fervor.[64]

The excellent concordance to Dom de Vogüé's edition of the text of the *Rule of the Master* indicates four instances of the verb *intendere*. The instance in the Preface means either to be attentive to or to take care to.[65] Both examples in the chapter on the reader at table seem to mean to pay attention to the reading.[66] The other use occurs in the chapter on work and it seems to mean interest in, engagement in, perhaps even absorption in.[67]

The single use of the noun *intentio* occurs in the chapter about the installation of a new abbot. *Sed hoc tota mentis intentio adsumat et diligenti observatione custodiat....* There is question of a determined and sustained effort to avoid pride; the new abbot is instructed to engage all his inner resources in avoiding this pitfall.[68]

The parallel to *RB* 52 (*RM* 68) contains no statement comparable to the one we are investigating, nor, for that matter, does the other source the *Rule of St Augustine* (*RA* 7).

In *RB*, apart from two uses of *Deus in adiutorium meum intende*,[69] there is one use of the verb in the chapter on the reception of the brothers. The novice master *curiose intendat*; he is supposed concernedly to watch over his charges.[70] The past participle is used once, adjectivally, concerning those who are not intent on their reading, that is to say those who are inattentive or failing in application or effort.[71] *Intentio* is used only at 52:4.

This examination of the immediate monastic sources of Benedict's *Rule* affords no incontrovertible solution. The range of meanings allocated to the word *intentio* is wide and particular translations are easily challenged. It does seem arguable, however, that all the employments of *intentio* which have been examined lead to the conclusion that an appreciation of the meaning of *intentio cordis* in *RB* 52:4 is not to be arrived at through a process of analysis with a view to arriving at a single semantic equivalent. The word is to be understood by appreciating all the alternative connotations, noting the various linguistic fields in which it is used and the additions and parallels which qualify its meaning. In other words, we are liable to fail to understand what St Benedict is saying in *RB* 52:4 if we do not take into account the intrinsic richness of the expression itself. The very multiplicity of meanings is itself part of the data.

Simple, Heartfelt Prayer

The first thing to be remarked concerning the *intentio* which St Benedict includes in his notion of prayer, is its connection with the heart. Generally Benedict understands by the word "heart" an undifferentiated inner aspect of man,[72] though he also uses the word in the stock phrase to designate the memory.[73] It is at the level of the heart that man responds to spiritual stimulation,[74] since it is the seat of his ability to understand, to love and to decide.[75] Two important traditional phrases signal the importance of the heart in Benedict's spirituality: purity of heart and compunction of heart.[76]

One of the aspects of *intentio cordis* that needs to be examined carefully is the relationship between the two words *intentio* and *cordis*. Although it is possible to interpret the phrase simply as meaning a movement of the heart, originating in the heart or engaging the powers of the heart, there is some ground for suspecting that something more is involved. One of the things which can be observed about *intentio* is that it often refers simply to a non-specific internal movement. Frequently when it is qualified by the genitive of some internal power or faculty, the meaning of the word becomes somewhat more precise, but nothing substantial is added to the signification of the expression, taken as a whole. In many cases there seems to be question of hendiadys, or perhaps, more accurately, of the inherent genitive (*genitivus inhaerentiae*). It seems entirely possible that in many of the instances discussed above, *intentio* refers simply to the bringing into operation of some inner potency. Accordingly, the movement characterized by the word *intentio* is not to be considered apart from the heart (mind or spirit, as the case may be) but refers to an overt exercise of a power which is, at other times dormant or latent. It is true that Dom Steidle does not include *intentio cordis* in his ample listing of epexegetical genitives in RB, but he does, at least, demonstrate that this construction was far more familiar to Benedict than it is to us.[77]

A decision on whether *intentio cordis* is an example of the inherent genitive depends largely on one's definition of that construction. Whatever solution is adopted, it is important to see that the movement referred to by the word *intentio* is not understood as external to the heart. The *intentio* proceeds from the heart immediately. It is something that flows from a person's center. It is the expression of a voluntary choice freely made. If we understand the phrase simply to mean attention, in the sense of freedom from distractions, there is danger that we are locating *intentio* too close to surface behavior. *Intentio* is externalized, but its source and origin is in the profoundest depths of the human reality. There is not question simply of manipulating the "organs" of consciousness to achieve attention or concentration, with a specific object in view. *Intentio* is the means by which the deepest stratum of human being seeks embodiment: in consciousness, in behavior, in identification with an object external to itself. It represents an outward movement from the center, energized and given direction by a personal act of election. From one point of view it might almost be said that the proper function of the heart is precisely "to intend."

We can understand something of what Benedict wishes to signify by the phrase *intentio cordis* by noting that its opposite is external clamor. In both contexts where Benedict speaks of the quality of prayer, he contrasts it with exterior tumult, on the one hand with *multiloquium*[78] and on the other with the disturbing restlessness characteristic of those not ready to pray.[79] For Benedict prayer requires a certain external inactivity, a *vacatio*,[80] so that inner potentialities may freely be activated. Prayer is first and foremost a movement from within.

Is it possible to specify this movement of the heart more closely? Certainly, it has nothing to do with methods or programs of prayer. What is envisaged by St Benedict is predominantly the elimination of alternative activities. A monk will pray if he stops doing other things. This attitude of emptiness is mirrored externally by the starkness he requires of the place of prayer. It is reinforced internally by a life of renunciation. Prayer is a recession from the multiplicity of ordinary life; it is a movement toward simplicity. It demands a transition from the variety and interest of external happenings to the intense unity of inner reality. The monk who wishes to pray must be prepared to accept a superficial monotony first. He needs to apply himself diligently to a process of quieting down, purifying his mind of vagrant thoughts and curiosity and seeking to fix his attention on the one thing necessary.

This movement toward a low-keyed simplicity has the effect of producing in the consciousness of one thus dedicated to the practice of prayer a consequent intensification of his relation to God. With alternative pursuits restricted and other thoughts and desires eliminated from consciousness a person is more possessed by the power of prayer which resides permanently in the heart of the Christian but which goes unnoticed in the tumult of daily living. He becomes more responsive to the Spirit leading him to the Father in company with the Son. A monk who follows Benedict's advice and simply "enters and prays" is creating a space in his life for the indwelling dynamism of prayer to fill. The intensity of his prayer will be in proportion to abandonment of other possibilities of occupying himself. What he experiences is what constantly takes place beyond the limits of consciousness, the inevitable stretching forth of the human heart toward its God.

Prayer for St Benedict, therefore, is a matter of concentration of heart: concentration in the sense of an active effort to restrict other activities, thoughts and desires; concentration in the sense of strengthening one's awareness of the reality of the heart's movement toward God; concentration in the sense of returning to one's center. By putting aside substitute goals and allowing oneself to become one-pointed (or *ekagra*, as the Hindu masters insist) one's movement to God is intensified and one's life is progressively stamped by the intrinsic character of the heart rather than by the diversity following upon involvement with the world.

The two most important elements of *intentio cordis* are indicated by two other fundamental monastic expressions: *puritas cordis* and *compunctio cordis*. Purity of heart is very close to the ideal of simplicity; it means to set one's heart on a single object and to allow nothing to cause one to deviate from the pursuit of that goal.[81] The pure prayer, often spoken of by the ancient monks, is one which rises from a heart which has been cleansed of vices, passions, worldly cares and their residues and which holds itself aloof from any thoughts or notions which might limit it to the sphere of human affairs and so prevent it from being lifted up to God.[82] Compunction was, for the ancient monks of the West, not merely a question of grief for sin, and sorrow and regret due to personal transgressions. It was, from the time of Cassian and Gregory the Great, a question of being touched (pierced) by God. It was a matter of feeling, experience, of being moved by the presence of God right to the depth of one's being. So intense was this experience that tears spontaneously flowed, expressing love for a God who had so revealed himself, disgust and sorrow at one's own non-responsiveness and ardent to experience the full inheritance, pledged and proclaimed in this fleeting adumbration.[83] In these two concepts are given the key to what is meant by *intentio cordis*. It is a question of a heartfelt personal response to the presence of God and the progressive purification from all that is not him.

Prayer for St Benedict is not a matter of external involvement or of tumult of mouth or thought. It is something which flows naturally from a life of generous dedication to God. It is characterized by a move away from noisiness, novelty and narcissism and an unshakable contentment in an austere and simple life. *Intentio cordis* is a matter of discipline, quietness, concentration and tenderness in the presence of God.

NOTES

[1] *Thesaurus Linguae Latinae,* editus iussu et auctoritate consilii ab academicis societatibus diversarum nationum electi, Leipzig, 1918; Vol. VII, cols 2112-2124.

[2] On what follows, see Daniel A. Csányi, "Optima Pars: Die Auslegungsgeschichte von Lk 10:38-42 bei den Kirchenvätern der ersten vier Jahrhunderte," *SM* 2 (1960), pp. 5-78; especially pp. 54-58.

[3] Ambroise de Milan, *Traité sur l'Evangile de saint Luc,* (G. Tissot ed.), Paris, Cerf (*SC* 45) 1956; p. 51.

[4] I: 18-21, *loc. cit.* pp. 55-57.

[5] I: 8-9, pp. 50-52.

[6] VII: 85, SC 52, p. 36.

[7] Augustin, *Commentaire de la première épître de Jean*, (P. Agaësse, ed.), Paris, Cerf (SC 75), 1961; VII:7, p. 326.

[8] *Hom in Ev* 11:1, PL 76, col. 1115B; 22:7, 1178B.

[9] *Ibid.* 12:5, 1141B.

[10] *Ibid.*, 3:4, 1088B.

[11] *Ibid.*, 1:6, 1081C; 7:4, 1102B.

[12] *Ibid.*, 17:14, 1146B-C.

[13] *Ibid.*, 12:2, 1141B.

[14] *Ibid.*, 9:1, 1106C.

[15] *Ibid.*, 11:1, 115B.

[16] *Ibid.*, 8:2, 1104D.

[17] Grégoire le Grand, *Morales sur Iob*, (Introduction et notes de R. Gillet; traduction de A. de Gaudemaris), Paris, Cerf (SC 32), 1952; I, 34:47-36:53, pp. 170-176.

[18] *Ibid.*, 36:50, 51, 53, pp. 172, 173, 175-176.

[19] *Ibid.*, 35:49, p. 172.

[20] *Ibid.*, 34:47, p. 170.

[21] *Ibid.*, Praefatium 7:16, p. 138. An interesting expansion of the thought occurs further on (I, 26:36, p. 163): Quisquis aeternam patriam appetit simplex procul dubio et rectus vivit; simplex videlicet opere, rectus fide; simplex in bonis quae inferius peragit, rectus in summis quae in intimis sentit.

[22] *Ibid.*, II, 15:27, p. 201.

[23] *Ibid.*, 49:79, p. 238.

[24] *Ibid.*, 48:75, p. 233.

[25] *In Cant* 30:3-4. Gilbert's commentary can be found in J. Mabillon (ed.) *Opera Omnia Sancti Bernardi*, Paris, Gaue, ⁴1839; Vol. V, cols 208-209.

[26] *Loc. cit.*, II, 52:82, p. 240.

[27] Jean Leclercq and Jean-Paul Bonnes, *Un Maître de la vie spirituelle au Xie siècle: Jean de Fécamp*, Paris, Vrin,

1946; Cf. *Confessio Theologica* I, line 231; II, line 371; III, line 931; Conclusio, line 1263; *Lamentatio* lines 187-188. These texts are edited in the volume cited.

[28] For the works of Saint Bernard I am using the critical edition established by Jean Leclercq and others (Rome, Editiones Cistercienses, 1957 ff.); I give the reference to the saint's writing, using the standardized abbreviations; this is followed by reference to the volume, page and line of the *Sancti Bernardi Opera*, SC 32:6, 1.230.4-6.

[29] SC 30:6, 1.214.7; 30:7, 1.214.19; 69:7, 2.206.14,22.

[30] *IV HM* 14; 5.66.10.

[31] *Quad* 5:7, 4.375.21; *V HM* 4; 5.71.17-22.

[32] *Pasc* 2:9, 5.99.16; *O Pasc* 1:7, 5.116.24.

[33] *QH* 2:3, 4.391.14.

[34] SC 30:1, 1.210.10-11.

[35] Ideoque maxime opus est etiam puritate intentionis qua soli Deo mens vestra et placere appetat et valeat inhaerere; SC 7:7, 1.35.5; *Pasc* 3:3, 5.105.12.

[36] *QH* 9:2, 4.436.25; *V Nat* 3:6, 4.216.10.

[37] *Adv* 6:2, 4.192.1; *O Pasc* 1:7, 5.116.24.

[38] SC 71:1, 2.215.2-3.

[39] *Ep* 69:1, 7.169.14-16.

[40] SC 40:3, 2.25.11.

[41] SC 40:2-3, 2.25-26.

[42] This can be seen especially from ST 1-2, q. 12; something of the various contexts in which Aquinas uses *intentio* can be gleaned from the 28 entries *sub voce* in the *Tabula Aurea* of Petrus de Bergamo.

[43] H.-J. Fischer, *art*. "Intention," in *Dictionnaire de Spiritualité* Paris, Beauchesne, Vol. VII (1971) cols 1838-1858.

[44] Jean Cassien, *Conférences* (Tr. E. Pichery), 3 vols, Paris, Cerf (*SC* 42,54,64), 1955-59. *Institutiones*

Cénobitiques (Tr. J. -C. Guy), Paris, Cerf (*SC* 109), 1965. *The Works of John Cassian* (Tr. E. Gibson), in *A Select Library of Nicene and Post-Nicene Fathers of the Christian Church*, Second Series, vol XI, pp. 161-621; photographic re-issue by the Wm. Erdmans Publishing Co, Grand Rapids (Mich), 1964.

[45] *Conl* 9:30, *SC* 54, pp. 65-66.

[46] *Inst* VI, 5; *SC* 109, p. 268; XII, 14:1; *SC* 109, p. 468. *Conl* 9:6; *SC* 54, p. 46; 10:8; p. 83; 10:9; p. 84; 14:3; p. 185; 14:4; p. 185.

[47] *Inst* III, 8:4; *SC* 109, p. 112. *Conl* 7:6; *SC* 42, p. 253; 10:14; *SC* 54, p. 95.

[48] *Conl* 10:14; *SC* 54, p. 96; 14:12; *SC* 54, p. 195.

[49] *Inst* V, 18:1; *SC* 109, p. 220. *Conl* 9:36; *SC* 54, p. 72; 7:23; *SC* 42, p. 266.

[50] *Conl* 9:34; *SC* 54, p. 69; 19:1; *SC* 64, p. 38.

[51] *Conl* 9:14; *SC* 54, p. 51.

[52] *Conl* 9:35; *SC* 54, p. 72.

[53] *Conl* 9:6; *SC* 54, p. 46; 9:14; p. 51; 10:7; p. 81; 10:11; p. 93.

[54] *Inst* II, 14:1; *SC* 109, p. 84.

[55] *Conl* 9:15; *SC* 54, p. 53; 9:26, p. 62.

[56] *Conl* 9:35; *SC* 54, p. 71.

[57] *Inst* V, 32:3; *SC* 109, p. 242. *Conl* 9:36; *SC* 54, p. 72.

[58] *Inst* III, 8:4; *SC* 109, p. 112; V, 18:1; p. 220; VI, 5; p. 268. *Conl* 10:11; *SC* 54, p. 93; 10:14; p. 96.

[59] *Omni cordis intentione, Inst* II, 5:5; *SC* 109, p. 68; II, 12:1; p. 80.

[60] *Conl* 23:11; *SC* 64, p. 154.

[61] *Inst* V, 34; *SC* 109, p. 244.

[62] *Conl* 14:9; *SC* 54, p. 193.

[63] *Conl* 1:7; *SC* 42, p. 85; 7:3; p. 247; 9:6; *SC* 54, p. 47.

[64] *Conl* 4:4; *SC* 42, p. 168; 9:7; *SC* 54, p. 48; 9:12; p.50.

⁶⁵ *La Règle du Maître* (Tr. A. de Vogüé), 3 vols, Paris, Cerf (*SC* 105, 106, 107) 1964-65; Pr 8; *SC* 105, p. 289-290.

⁶⁶ *RM* 24,35; 37: *SC* 106, p. 130.

⁶⁷ *RM* 50,38; *SC* 106, p. 230.

⁶⁸ *RM* 93,49; *SC* 106, p. 432.

⁶⁹ *RB* 18,1; 35,17.

⁷⁰ *RB* 58,6.

⁷¹ *RB* 48,18.

⁷² *RB* 4,50; 7,44; 5:17; 7,51, etc.

⁷³ *RB* 9,10; 12,4.

⁷⁴ *RB* Prol 1.

⁷⁵ *RB* 3,8; 4,1; 4,28.

⁷⁶ *RB* 20,3; 49,4.

⁷⁷ B. Steidle, "Der Genitivus epexegeticus in der Regel des Hl. Benedikt," *SM* 2 (1960), pp. 193-203.

⁷⁸ *RB* 20,3.

⁷⁹ *RB* 52,3; the nature of this unreadiness becomes clear from an examination of the sources.

⁸⁰ For a rich development of this theme in monastic literature, see Jean Leclercq, *Otia Monastica: Etudes sur le vocabulaire de la contemplation au moyen âge*, (StA 51), Rome 1963.

⁸¹ See the extensive treatment and bibliographical indications in J. Raasch, "The Monastic Concept of Purity of Heart and its Sources," *SM* 8 (1966) 7-33, 183-213; 10 (1968) 7-55; 11 (1969) 269-314; 12 (1970) 1-41.

⁸² Cf. G. Bekes, *Pura oratio apud Clementem Alexandrinum*, in StA 18-19, pp. 157-172; especially p. 162.

⁸³ It is hoped that the idea of compunction as it appears in Cassian and Gregory the Great will be treated more amply in another place.

Monastic Formation

MODELS OF MONASTIC FORMATION

This article is a summary of a program given to the Cistercian superiors and formators of Latin America in 1993. Following the example of Avery Dulles' Models of the Church, *I sought to distinguish different ways of envisaging and practising monastic formation and to assess how they might work together harmoniously. The text appeared in* Tjurunga 45 (1993).

From the amount of attention given by most religious orders to the matter of initial formation one might reasonably conclude that this is an area in which the inadequacies of the existing process are more evident than creative outcomes.[1] This is especially true of smaller groups that do not have large access to resources and personnel or the kind of experience that comes from dealing with higher numbers of entrants. Such is commonly the situation in autonomous monasteries. In these cases formation can lack a sense of reality. The process can fail to appreciate the generational specificity of those arriving and/or it can be out of touch with the facticity of religious life as it daily evolves. In either case, instead of serving as a bridge on which to make a transition from one lifestyle to another, formation can become a reality-substitute: an independent kingdom, a limbo-like phase of un-connectedness and indirection—something to be survived in the present and transcended in the future. The fact that it is easier to recognize the problem than to prescribe a remedy does not invalidate the diagnosis. It is simply an invitation to a more thorough corporate reflection.

Beyond this failure to appreciate the end towards which "formation" is a means, there is another complication in that the process of formation itself is sufficiently exigent and absorbing to make it difficult for formators to accept external appraisal of their work. It is not easy for them to appreciate the message to be found in the malaise that others honestly feel about the quality of the formation being given. That inexperience, ignorance and undesirable subjective dispositions may color the expression of dissatisfaction compounds the difficulty. The fact remains, however, that among the rank and file of many religious orders there is a vague unease about formation that needs to be addressed directly.

Sometimes this incomprehension about the ways and means of formation derives from an inattention to generational change. Most of us appreciate the fact that religious life and monasticism have undergone substantial modification in the last thirty years. We need to remember that people are also different. Those who belong to the school of thought that insists that "human nature never changes" sometimes underestimate the extent to which society and human consciousness have undergone alteration in the generations following World War II. Massive swings have taken place at the level of perception, belief and valuation over which individuals have no control. The effects must be accepted as part of reality and steps taken to create a fusion of horizons between this bold new world and accepted monastic theory and practice. "Formation" begins with the recognition and valuing of the particularity of the recruits whom Providence sends. It cannot be grounded on a naïve persuasion that it is sufficient to do for today's newcomers what was done for us twenty, thirty or forty years ago.

The so-called "baby-boomers," came to maturity under the tumultuous influence of the 1960s.[2] They operate out of perceptions of selfhood different from those of the previous generations. As a result, their manner of relating to others and to organizations is also distinctive.[3] It follows that any attempt to "form" newcomers to monastic *conversatio* needs to be inspired by a genuine respect for what they are. The capacity of novices to embrace "monastic values" is not a moral issue; it is a matter of communication. Perennial monastic wisdom needs to re-express its giftedness in terms accessible to its recipients. The onus is on those already formed to bridge the gap. The obverse is also true. Mature monks must equally be ready to receive from their juniors that by which the monastic patrimony will be enriched and secured. The future can come only from the new generation. If the future is to be in continuity with the cherished past, effective dialogue between the generations is crucial. At the risk of tautology it must be said that in such a dialogue traffic is necessarily two-way.

The concrete means of formation cannot today be the same as those considered successful in previous decades. To some extent, the new emphases will stem from the changed dispositions of those entering. Moreover it is important that the community understand not only the details of the modified process, but also appreciate some of the reasons for making changes.

It is in this context of arriving at a common language to describe formation and a common will to implement policy that I offer these reflections on models of formation. Obviously the idea behind this approach comes from the work of Avery Dulles,[4] but my isolation of the models is, in fact, not dependent on his work. It derives more from my own observations and discussion with others. You will remember that it is one of Dulles' assertions that disagreement within the Church often stems from people using a single word to describe different realities. They are operating out of different models. One who sees the Church primarily as an institution will judge situations differently from those who perceive it predominantly in mystical, sacramental or eschatological terms. In the same way, I would ask: When we talk about "formation" are we using the term univocally?

1. Initial Description of the Models

Before presenting models of formation, I would insist that in distinguishing different approaches I am not suggesting that they are incompatible. It is more a question of emphasis and priority. I am aware that there are other functions associated with novice masters and novice mistresses beyond "formation," such as the control of the novitiate regimen and the important task of discernment of vocations and the probation or testing of candidates. For the purposes of the present discussion, I shall concentrate on initial "formation," without trying to read too much into the term itself nor, for the moment, confronting the possibility that formation might, in certain circumstances, become deformation.

The five models can be classified according to their perceived principal agent: whether this be God, the community or the formator (Diagram 1, page 367).

An alternative way of showing the relationship of the models would be to see the agents of formation in three concentric circles: the formator operating within the context of the various community functions and agencies and all alike embraced by the pervading action of God.

Let us examine each of the models briefly before passing on to a more detailed analysis.

Diagram 1.

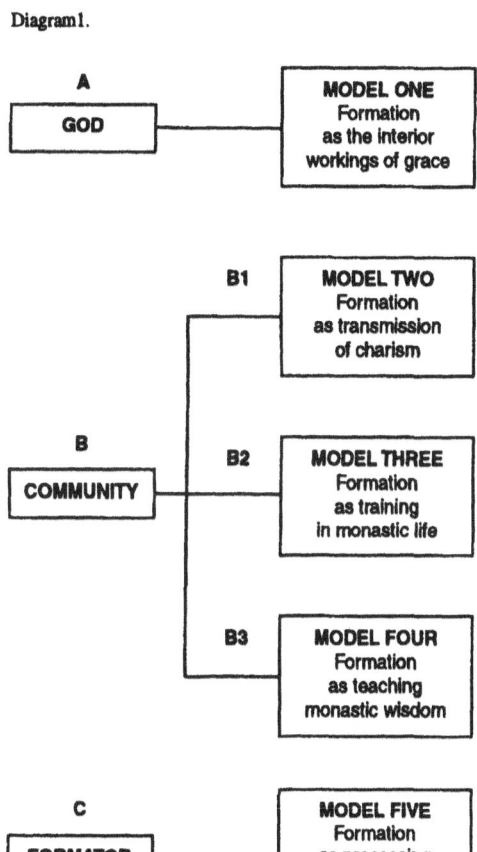

A. Formation as the Invisible Divine Work

It is God who is the principal agent of all sanctification; whatever monks and nuns become by reason of their vocation must be attributed primarily to grace and not to the work of any human agency or institution. The reformation of a soul deformed by sin and the restoration of Christ's likeness is beyond human control; it proceeds at its own pace and according to its own reasons. In the end, granted a basic receptivity, it produces the result that God intended. Paul Claudel's dictum that God can write straight on crooked lines is relevant here. In so far as divine formation is concerned, human recommendations do not apply; and so documents on formation usually do no more than mention it. Most attention is given to what can be analyzed and, where necessary, upgraded.

B1. Formation as Transmission of the Monastic Charism

A person is drawn to monastic life by the radiance and example of an existing community. Those who enter entrust themselves to this community and are formed by it in ways that are often unconscious. Many Benedictine-based monasteries have a strong tradition of local identity; sometimes we are able to determine a monk's monastery of origin simply by looking at him or hearing him speak. The community imprints its character on the receptive monk or nun and imparts a specific spirit. The result is a kind of connaturality. In mature years the person knows from within, without needing continual external instruction. There is a common basis of beliefs, values and symbols that grounds a unified range of actions and reactions, at least in important matters.

This cenobitic form is complemented by an older, more eremitical pattern in which a single "charismatic" individual is the means by which the monastic character is imprinted. Sometimes communal and personal forms coexist and mutually enhance. There is no doubt that some abbots and abbesses exercise this form of influence over some of their monks and nuns, usually those younger than themselves. It should be remembered, however, that this is the result of personal qualities and is not an automatic effect of their office. More often their impact on formation is indirect; it comes from the influence they exercise on the quality of the community's life.

Charismatic formation is usually the work of a particular elder by whose influence it happens that a man is transformed into a monk, or a woman becomes a nun. The task of elders is to initiate candidates into the specificity of monastic life and to impart their own spirit to them, working especially at the level of personal attraction. A typical mode of communication in charismatic formation is the aphorism; pithy sayings can be made to carry the weight of deeper insight and are often passed on from one generation to the next. Folklore and interpreted history carry the message in a different form. Sometimes there is simply a profound mutual presence. It is not an institutional or hierarchical relationship, but one based on deep affinity and on the willingness of the junior to be influenced. It is the relationship that matters; the content of the exchange between senior and neophyte is less important than the bonding and "reincarnation" that results from it. Symbolism is often important. In the case of a cenobitic elder, less personal sparkle and originality is necessary. The role of the elder is to transmit the accumulated wisdom of the community; the elder embodies the spirit of the community and acts as a conduit. They may often hide personal experience behind the phrase "X used to say..." It is generally not a reciprocal relationship, even though there is a measure of mutual exposure and the bond may develop into friendship. The elder remains forever senior. This disparity is reflected in St Benedict's injunction that seniors are to love juniors and juniors to reverence the seniors (RB 4,70-71; 63,10, but 71,4). In fact, a measure of distance may enhance the elder's standing, since familiarity breeds contempt and mystery often disappears upon close examination.

B2. Formation as Living "the Life"

In this conception the formator is a master (or mistress) and the newcomer is considered as an apprentice. The work of formation is socialization; the novice is trained through participation in concrete activities to fit in with the other members of the community. The primary field of formation is the following of the common life. It is presumed that interior experience is shaped by external behavior; by common work, liturgy, adherence to community standards and style and submission to community structures, the newcomer eventually begins to think, feel and act spontaneously as a "monk" or "nun" of a particular community. Since formator and novice are both *sub regula et abbate* there is a certain equality or fraternity. Once trained in monastic *conversatio* novices become adept at the common life and, as such, apart from the matter of perseverance, the peers of their former master. After profession they are able to relate as equals, the formator being simply a more senior practitioner of a craft that the junior has now also mastered. In this perspective, during the novitiate the formator is especially concerned with outer behavior. Good example is important and many corrections may be necessary since novices are expected to do first and learn by their mistakes.

B3. Formation as Learning

In some languages the word "formation" is used almost as a synonym for "education." A person in charge of formation is one who, above all, gives instruction. The formator is seen as a teacher. This teaching is not limited to academic instruction or theory; it is especially concerned with communicating information about the practicalities of living a monastic and spiritual life. The formator's role can be exercised by conducting classes, in personal interviews (which can become like tutorials in living), by guided observation in which novices are trained to learn from what they see about them and by personal example and testimony. In all of this, however, the point of entry is cognitive. The teacher possesses that which is communicated to the novice. The main function of the novice is to receive what is transmitted, to assimilate it and then live it. In such a conception "good" formation is marked by comprehensiveness and depth in the material communicated. As a result, idealistic programs are drawn up to ensure that no species of knowledge is neglected that has the potential of eventually enhancing monastic life.

C. Formation as Help to Living Fully

Here formators act as counselors; they help the novices to process their experience of community life, prayer and vocation, as well as deal with other personal agenda. This is especially a matter of the internal forum. The privileged moment of the relationship is the regular interview. The interaction may be "client-centered" in the sense that it is the novice who determines the direction and pace of discussion while the formator remains somewhat non-directive: a challenge and stimulus to reflection, re-evaluation and reframing, but not an enforcer of monastic mores. The formator may prefer not to exercise leadership, but simply to "accompany" the novices in their induction into the mysteries of monastic life: to be there for them. The method may be loosely termed "Socratic" or heuristic; issues are usually dealt with as they surface; answers are not sought where the questions have not arisen. The formator's role may approximate either that of a therapist (if it veers towards psychological factors) or that of a spiritual director (if it concentrates on spirituality) depending either on the skills and background of the formator or, perhaps, on the needs of the novice. In some sense there is nothing specifically "monastic" about this kind of relationship except that the experiences being processed are those of someone moving deeper into monasticism. This type of assistance is as meaningful if novices leave as if they persevere. Because it concentrates on helping them to clear the obstacles to a full human (or spiritual) life, less is invested in their specifically monastic future. Some contact may continue even after a novice withdraws.

Another possible model is worth broaching here, at least for the purpose of discussion.

D. Formation as Spiritual Friendship

Spiritual friendship is another channel of monastic formation, and one that plays an important role in the lives of some. I have excluded such friendship from my listing, because we are mainly concerned with the institutionalized structures set in place for initial formation. Monastic and spiritual friendship is a powerful means of growth in likeness to Christ, as St. Aelred brilliantly demonstrated, but it cannot be achieved by legislation. There is a whimsical Providence about friendship that defies human prediction. The beginnings of friendship are unplanned and often give no indication of its future intensity. Its course is long and is marked by painful vicissitudes as each tests the other's trustworthiness. Its term is a level of truthfulness that sometimes stretches conventional structures. A solid level of maturity is demanded. Mutuality is its soul. It is unrealistic to assume that such a deep adult relationship will exist between formators and novices. Indeed it would be a delusion for a formator to act on this basis and may even constitute a serious dereliction of duty.

I have tried to present these oversimplified models as sympathetically as possible. Each has its own persuasiveness and distinctive contribution. It must be obvious, however, that someone who strongly favors one model will be less sensitive to some of the benefits that accrue from other models and, perhaps, critical of those whose preferences are different. The fact is that each approach has its limitations which render its exclusive use inadvisable. In addition, there are too many inconsistencies in the whole area to permit the hope of a single "super-model" which would happily combine all the best features of each.

What tends to happen in official documents (such as formation statements, including the 1990 text from CRIS) is that the novice master or mistress is described indiscriminately in terms of all the models. The end product is a role-description which is totally implausible. It is important that we recognize that there are different functions to be performed in the task of formation and that these functions need not necessarily fall to the lot of a single functionary. They can be spread more broadly afield.

Let us now examine each of these models. Not only do they tell us about formation itself, they also inculcate certain expectations about the role of the formators. Inevitably formators will respond to situations according to the manner in which they perceive their own function—be this as policeman, guru, hierarch, friend, therapist, representative of the status quo, consoler or intercessor. Knowing the models out of which we operate is an important stage in upgrading the operation itself.

2. Formation as a Supernatural Process

All monastic development builds on the foundation of baptism and takes place within an ecclesial and sacramental context. It sometimes seems to me that we have to re-sacramentalize monastic life. There is a danger that psychological factors will begin to carry excessive weight. Emphasis on the quality of experience, personal appropriation of values, consistency of behavior and the growth and fulfillment of individuals and communities can obscure the sacramental elements of our life and the importance of explicit faith. This, in turn, can lead to a certain slipping away from the idea of participating in the life and death cycle of the Paschal

Mystery. As a result the alternation normal in spiritual experience becomes more difficult to endure and more liable to generate crises of faith in God or trust in one's community. The themes of sacrifice, atonement and reparation have been somewhat abused in recent centuries, but there is something irreplaceable about them in the contemplative life if monks and nuns are going to be motivated to keep giving and to stop measuring the efficacy of the life in terms of what they receive from it at any particular moment. Monastic life is a call to share fully in the divine mysteries not only in the liturgy and in our prayer-related activities, but also in the rhythms of our daily life. Without self-emptying (which always feels bad) there is no solidity in our following of Christ. I wish by this to assert the primacy of theological faith in monastic formation. There needs to be formation to a lively sacramental life, to an awareness of the monastery as Church, the work of grace and the Holy Spirit, and to a sense of the sacred (and therefore mysterious) character of all that happens *infra saepta monasterii*.

Beyond the sacramental dimension is the need for the monk to live a fervent life of faith. This means, specifically, developing a personal and interpersonal devotion to Jesus Christ and to Our Lady.

No amount of abstract conviction, cosmic good-will or generous striving can take the place of this. The words of the Cistercian Constitution 3.5 are worth recalling.

> The organization of the monastery is directed to bringing the monks and nuns into close union with Christ, since it is only through the experience of personal love for the Lord Jesus that the specific gifts of the Cistercian vocation can flower. Only if the sisters and brothers prefer nothing whatever to Christ will they be happy to persevere in a life that is ordinary, obscure and laborious.

An important word occurs twice: "only." Personal devotion to Christ is the one means of internalizing and thus realizing the Cistercian charism. Each one of us could probably write an anecdotal commentary that would demonstrate the truth of this text. Attention to the specifically monastic values and practices should never be allowed to diminish the importance of this affective Christocentrism—so important at any period when Benedictinism flourished. Indeed, much of the work of formation should be to allow such devotion to develop according to its own rhythm—recognizing the truth of what Bernard says in *De Diligendo Deo* about its progressive spiritualization. We need to take care that newcomers do not fall into a "piety void" such as many experienced in the wake of the liturgical reforms of Vatican II.

Devotion to Our Lady varies among individuals and cultures. It is of sufficient importance that the monk or nun will eventually come to it, so long as development continues. There is a time to promote such devotion and a time to be discreet. I cannot imagine that her maternal solicitude is less for those who are not yet ready to perceive it. The day they do will be one of great consolation. When it exists already as an element in the devotional life the formator will need to be very prudent in scraping away any rust lest the vessel be holed. For the time being fervor may be more important than strict ideological purity.

Grace has its own rhythm and season. "The anointing that you received from God abides in you, and you have no need that anyone should teach you, since this anointing teaches you everything and it is true" (1 Jn 2:27). The power of the Spirit's interior direction is not to be underestimated at a practical level. It is not enough to recommend docility and abandonment to the novice: the formator likewise must listen and submit to the Lord's voice. This "obedience of faith" is strongly recommended in *The Cloud of Unknowing*.

> Let that thing do with thee and lead thee whereso it list. Let it be the worker and thou but the sufferer; do thou but look upon it and let it alone. Meddle thee not therewith as though thou wouldst help it, for dread that thou spill all. Be thou but the tree, and let it be the carpenter. Be thou but the house and let it be the husband dwelling therein.[5]

Great respect must be given by the formator to the action of God both in present promptings and in the previous phases of the novice's salvation history. Providence is never under human control; spiritual wisdom consists in recognizing its traces and then having the humility to adapt ourselves to accord with its imperatives.

Calendar-Time or Kairos? The problem with programs is that they usually envisage a time-scale. Sometimes it can be very hard to reconcile salvation-time and the fixed demands of policy or law. This may be an issue at entry: a candidate may be *a priori* refused as too young, too old, too feeble or stupid, without reference to the freedom of God to call indiscriminately. Again, attention to the immediate interior agenda may postpone or compress elements of monastic initiation that should be dealt with within a fixed period (e.g. the novitiate). Perhaps our programs need to be loose and leisurely in order to avoid strait-jacketing God's action. Even the 1990 *Instruction* seems to recognize this. "It should be noted from the outset that the course of formation among contemplatives will be less intensive and more informal because of the stability of their members and the absence of activities outside the monastery" (#75).[6] We are talking here about following the lead of grace; it is not a question of advocating or legitimating disorganization or procrastination that may be a function of the formator's inability to fit things into prescribed limits. A practical corollary of this sensitivity would be a certain flexibility about incorporation: not setting dates far in advance and not putting pressure on those who entered together to remain yoked as they pass through the various stages.

God remains always in control. This means that formators always feel that their work with novices is out of their control. Humble intercessory prayer is an important component of any pastoral relationship. In the light of *RB* 28,4 it can be said that a sense of helplessness coupled with fervent prayer is the greatest contribution formators make to the spiritual growth of those in their charge. Sometimes a situation may be so difficult that all a formator can do is to sit prayerfully with the novice in the presence of God. All is not ashes however. Assuredly there will be other moments in which wonderment at the gifts of God will predominate, a sense of privilege and joy for the formator to share and a source of deep gratitude and praise. The important thing is that the novices are in God's hands; all we can do is to guide and support them leading those in their care to submit to Christ's magisterium (*RB* Prol 40).

We need constantly to remind ourselves of the goal of all monastic striving. It is, through imitation of Christ, to be conformed to the Word. It is a question of putting on Christ (Gal 3:27, Rom 13:14), of having the mind of Christ (2 Cor 2:16, Phil 2:5), of entering into the subjectivity of the Word so that we no longer view things from a merely human standpoint. We are called to share in Christ's awareness of the Father and in his compassion towards human beings. There is a new creation: a level of activity beyond human calculation or control. There is a fundamental foolishness in trying to offer monastic formation to others if we do not appreciate that what we seek can be accomplished only by God.

What is specific to this model is the primacy attributed to a "supernatural" ambiance. Fundamental is the confidence that God is active both through and despite human interventions. When a community exudes such an aura, its principal means of formation are its theocentric vision of life, its symbolic or sacramental embodiment of this, its power of attraction that draws and sustains commitment and its fidelity in giving a good example of a life that is fully human and fully divine.

The privileged means of formation in this perspective are lectio, liturgy and prayer. There is not much emphasis on habitual spiritual direction. In crises and in exceptional situations counsel will be sought. In issues involving the community the superior will be approached. Generally, however, this approach sees the monks and nuns as fundamentally on course towards their goal, all they need are relatively minor course corrections; these Providence supplies through the normal channels provided in the monastic day.

In one sense a whole program of monastic formation could be built using this model. The qualities to be sought in a formator would probably be a certain placidity or even passivity, a non-interventionist stance, and a genuine seeking of God's mysterious ways. As the Cistercian *Ratio* says: "Those responsible for formation will always be attentive to the Spirit of God working in those they are called to train" (#57). Such formators need not necessarily be good teachers, skilled counselors or deft organizers of novitiate activities. They may be lacking in their judgment of persons. In one sense even their ability to communicate well with the younger generation may not matter much. The primary requirement would be that they be deeply spiritual. They are prepared to stand aside and let God do the work.

Life would be comparatively simple if we operated from one model only. At least we could pursue it to its ultimate logic. As it is, we demand rather more than this from our formators. This is what complicates their ministry.

3. Formation as Transmission of the Monastic Spirit

It is one of the characteristic emphases of Catholic theology to insist on the importance of human mediation in God's communication of gifts. The inner stirrings of the Holy Spirit are not the only source of guidance and support, nor is our mystical communion in the Church entirely without comprehensible content. God's action forms a visible community that bonds persons together in such a way that outward realities are not irrelevant to those interior depths that only the Spirit plumbs (Rom 8:27). Human beings and human acts can, therefore, become channels of divine grace and energy. Not only that: these necessary aids to holiness are often denied to those who are unwilling to receive them from human beings. What God offers through the Church (including the monastic Church) is generally not given except through the Church. God does not do directly what can be done through others.

Why is a person attracted to the monastic life and even to a particular monastery? How is it, then, that a person entering a local monastery and persevering there comes to be imprinted with a character that is clearly identical or in continuity with that borne by the great figures of the past? How is it that they feel drawn to the sources of monastic spirituality and find expressed in them so much of what belongs to their own intimate spiritual history? How is it that they become recognizable members of a particular community, manifesting some of its special traits and endowments? To answer these questions we have to explore a second model of formation, one which pays special attention to the sharing of spiritual gifts within the monastic family.

In concretely forming a monk or nun the Holy Spirit uses the instrumentality of an existing community to perpetuate the spiritual gifts proper to its form of life. The medium of communication is an orientation or vision which interacts with everyday situations facing the community at this time to produce an authentic version of the charism expressed by a blend or balance of the principal observances. A very subtle force, akin to style, is operative here. It is not a question of outward performance, since different monasteries have always had distinctive spirits even when observances were rigorously uniform.

The key to understanding this charismatic continuity is to be found in the Preface to the Cistercian Constitutions (#1). "A substantial spiritual heritage was engendered through the lives and labors of innumerable brothers and sisters…" The spiritual charism of the Order is not abstract. It is concretely incarnated in the lives of men and women who receive the talent with joy and pass it on with interest added. They may be famous or obscure; what matters is that they have kept alive in themselves the gift they received and by their unstinting efforts have passed it on to the next generations. Religion, they say, is caught not taught. Each person in the community receives the inheritance differently—according to their capacity. Each embodies it in a distinctive—but not discordant—manner. Each transmits it uniquely: by word, by creative work, through selfless fidelity, by example. The power of the community to form newcomers is based on historical continuity; it is the life-blood of tradition that flows from one generation to the next, carrying with it the accumulated riches of centuries of humble fidelity. Our tradition is, in fact, strong enough to leap-frog generations and able to revive itself in communities where it seems to have died. Partly this is the result of cross-fertilization which provides for mutual support and encouragement in difficulties, partly it flows from the fact that the tradition is also embodied in writings, in liturgy and in the structures of *conversatio*.

What is received in this charismatic formation is a sensitivity and attraction to particular beliefs within the Christian totality as well as a certain reluctance to be drawn in alternative directions. There is a certain quality of instinctive certainty about the way to live, about what to read and how to pray that predates formal instruction in these matters. A certain feeling-at-home in the spiritual climate of the monastery—work, *lectio*, liturgy, devotion—that makes one disinclined habitually to seek spiritual nourishment elsewhere. There is an inner resonance with the outward expressions of the monastic charism. The monk or nun acts from inner principles.

All this is the fruit of others' fidelity. Goodness participates in the being of God, whereas evil is defined precisely as non-being. What is good is essentially enduring. A residue of goodness clings to the vestiges of a holy life that facilitates goodness in those who come into contact with it. This is why saints usually appear in clusters! A holy life is not merely a matter of individual perfection; the saint is a means by which divine life is made concrete and, therefore, available in human community. The love of God comes to us through the transparency of those whom it has transformed— and it comes to us mysteriously imprinted with something of their uniqueness. We are not always conscious either of the holiness of others or what we receive from them. Perhaps as we advance in closeness to God the connection becomes more obvious.

Most of us are more particularly open to the spirit of the community as it is manifested in persons whom we especially revere. These are they who manifest God's love to us. Often the most senior members of a community exercise this important function. One of the less useful effects of the period immediately after Vatican II was to disenfranchise or discredit the old, and attribute undue importance to middle-aged mavericks. Ideas and verbal proficiency became more important than gentleness and tolerance; appearances outweighed realities. A certain amount of the harshness sometimes evident in communities where this has happened, as also in new foundations, derives simply from an absence of venerated elders.

The spiritual counselors and those who serve as trusted confessors may well serve as cenobitic elders capable of transmitting the spirit of the Order and of the local monastery to others. Those assigned to formation have the same opportunity and, to some extent, they are to be chosen for their aptitude in this sphere. Most descriptions of the formator of novices includes St Benedict's phrase about a senior who is able to hold novices by a personal power of attraction (RB 58.6). This means fundamentally that formators must be content in their own monastic life, appreciate the other members of the community and have a reverence for the various aspects of monastic tradition. In this way they will have access to a wisdom broader than their own experience and will have something solid to communicate to those in their charge. Formation well done will effect in its recipients a deep inner bonding with others in the community that will be a source of comfort and strength in the years to come.

What can be said, then, about the task facing formators in this model? The word that comes to mind is passion. They need to be lovers of monasticism, the Order, the monastery, the place, the *conversatio*, the brothers/sisters. Perhaps they need to be enthusiasts, able to communicate their own love for these things to others. For this communication to take place they must first have been able to convince those in their charge that they also are loved, accepted, and respected. Formators will never market their own passion until they can win the prospective buyers. In this case, as in so many others, you catch more flies with a spoonful of honey than with a bucketful of vinegar.

If formation is approached from this point of view humility becomes important for formators. Their task is not the assertion of personal preferences but putting the novices into contact with the resources of the community: its patrimony, its living treasures, its spirit. Formators act as mediators in this process. To the extent that the introduction is successful their presence is no longer needed. Like John the Baptist they must fade away; their work is done.

4. Formation as Apprenticeship in Monastic Living

To the extent that monastic *conversatio* is seen as the prime human agency in monastic formation, the task of formators becomes one of introducing novices to the various elements of monastic life, instructing and supporting them in their efforts to come to grips with the observances and offering corrections where necessary. Sanctification is seen as socialization. The formator's principal task is to oversee this predominantly external process.

There is a radical transition to be made on entry from one way of life to another that—despite some apparent continuity—is distinctive and disjunctive in its totality.[7] In some ways this is harder to appreciate now than it was in 1960. Then the Cistercian lifestyle was unlike anything hitherto experienced. Entry was like diving into cold water; all previous habits and preoccupations were shocked out of awareness and it was relatively easy to accept that new ways of doing familiar things had to be learned and accustomed habits abandoned. Nowadays monastic customs are less medieval and, hence, less dramatically different; in addition newcomers are prepared for the changes by periods of observorship. Because they are generally more mature, a certain leeway is allowed for the exercise of responsible choices. They are introduced gradually into the lifestyle. The danger is that they may be led to attend piecemeal to disparate duties without undergoing a substantial evacuation of their previous identity. This will lead to mere conformity. The development of the bonding needed for life-sustaining nourishment is delayed, and undue suffering is caused later on by this omission. The "kindness" that allows many existing networks (family, friends, profession, hobbies) to remain in place during the time of formation may be, in the longer term, unkind. At some stage the monastic option has to be made in all its radicality; it is usually easier when it is made earlier. The first task a formator faces is to ensure that the novice does not bypass this significant experience of liminality. It may require a certain firmness, but it is to the novice's own ultimate advantage that the break with the past be as clear and decisive as possible.

This model of formation has a very objective tone. The goal of the process is for the novice to become proficient in the monastic lifestyle in both its positive and negative components. It is not mere external uniformity, though it does envisage a substantial commitment to the major elements of *conversatio*. It envisages, however, that sustained exposure to the "monastic means" will eventually nurture a monastic philosophy of life. The beliefs and values inherent in daily practices will be internalized.[8] The end product is substantially the same for everyone, even though some allowance is made for individual differences. Subjective dispositions and personal history are not disregarded, but they are seen as realities to be dealt with, almost as obstacles or impediments, rather than as offering anything positive to the process of formation.

This view of formation is probably the one most commonly held within monastic communities as a whole,[9] especially by those not directly and immediately concerned with the training of novices. Aspirants are in the novitiate to be trained in monastic life: bows, vows and all the rough and tumble that "we" also had to pass through. It is feared that concessions made at this stage may end up being the beginning of a lifetime of making demands for special treatment.

This is a traditional, robust, take-it-or-leave-it (*RB* 58,10) approach to formation. "The life" pre-exists the entry of the novice and will probably survive his or her departure or death. In the interim there is a space for mutual testing. If all agree at the end of the period of probation that the basic skills for living "the life" are present, then the novice is permitted to make an engagement and to receive monastic consecration. The master/mistress has the task of presenting monasticism in all its truth to the novice: including the *dura et aspera* (*RB* 58,8). Novices are expected to handle *opprobria* (*RB* 58,7) since there is no guarantee that fidelity to their future commitment will not stretch their limits and seriously try their endurance. Discernment depends on the novice's informed willingness to live monastic *conversatio*.[10] The assumption is that perseverance in this course will automatically nurture the requisite qualities and, by the grace of God, straighten out any kinks that bedevil subjective dispositions—though not without persecutions!

The formator, in such an approach, is one who is content and relatively uncompromising in living the monastic lifestyle. Candidates for monastic life are not scrutinized very closely; it is believed that "the life" itself will sort them out. Contact with the novices involves instruction, supervision and approbation or correction. Interviews often begin with questions such as "How is your *lectio*?", "Are you able to work with X?", "How are you coping with Lent?" and the like. Included in the task of practical initiation is occasional lubrication. St Benedict understood that monks implement precepts best when they understand the reasons for a course of action or are otherwise motivated. A good master/

mistress will know that external performance is not everything. The novices need to know why some things are done: their questions require responses and (at least some of) their objections must be anticipated or answered.[11] Sometimes obligations can be suspended, on the understanding that too much of a good thing is counter-productive. Too much fasting, not enough sleep and too much heavy work cannot be dumped immediately on newcomers. They need time for their bodies, emotions and good habits to come online. Hence the perennial monastic emphasis on discretion (*RB* 64,17-19). Approval or praise and correction (reward and punishment in behaviorist terms) are important means of stimulating the continuance of good behavior and discouraging aberrations. In this a benign master/mistress may be more persuasive and certainly less misery-making, but this quality is not absolutely necessary. We can be as well trained by an exacting tyrant as by a prince of patience and forbearance.

In this situation the novices who persevere are often those who get into the most trouble and are most often reproved. To be left uncorrected is often a sign that not much is hoped for. On the other hand, those without the kind of visible "faults" which merit rebukes sometimes compensate by inner poverty. This may be why many "good" novices leave. It is too easy to dissemble; those whose energies are devoted to staying out of trouble or winning the approval of their formator never develop the inner freedom without which there is no real joy in a monastery. Learning to stand on one's own feet and to relate directly to the *conversatio* is a skill that stands one in good stead throughout life. Without it, monastic life becomes a charade. It is this widely-accepted model that best induces such an attitude of independence of both approval or blame.

5. Formation as Education

The model of a formator as one who educates novices in the theory and practice of monastic life is very enduring. It could be traced back to *RB* 58,8—if one regards *praedicentur* as deriving from *praedicare* rather than from *praedicere*. In this conception the master or mistress provides an overview of spiritual and monastic life by word and example, giving classes or "repetitions" to emphasize publicly the principal themes. Individual sessions then help the novices to slot their own experiences into the general schema. It is hoped that what is communicated is of sufficient quality to serve throughout monastic life both as guide and incentive to continual growth. Usually, however, novices absorb only as much as they need for the moment and leave the rest aside. I have heard many mature religious claim that certain points were never covered in their formation—notwithstanding the fact that their contemporaries (and sometimes the formators) clearly remember the opposite.

The impression given by many official documents on formation is that teaching is an integral part of formation. It is, however, the work of a group wider than the "formators." Formators give conferences, but others also are involved in teaching. The range of topics to be treated makes this a necessity. It is at this stage that some confusion exists in many texts. Formal studies, especially theological studies, are regarded as formative, but are not to be identified simply as "formation." Studies and courses are part of the material content of formation, but are secondary relative to more existential work to be done with the novices at a personal and communitarian level.

At the same time it is important to affirm the immense contribution to later living that is made by a sound monastic education, especially if solid foundations have been carefully laid. It not only makes it possible for the monks and nuns to profit from the ample leisure of the monastic day by a broader search for wisdom, it also enhances the quality of their monastic vision and thereby upgrades their input into chapter discussions and decisions. The vocation of a western monk or nun is well summed up by the title of Jean Leclercq's famous book: *The Love of Learning and the Desire for God.*

Comprehensiveness and depth are the qualities most sought in a monastic education. For this reason there is tendency to multiply courses, so that eventually juniors, even if they remain in their own monasteries, have to suspend their monastic life to become students. In the eyes of the community they may appear to be in limbo—professed members and yet not fully available to share the community's life. When the first draft of the Cistercian *Ratio* appeared with its illustrative programs of studies (as existing in different monasteries and regions), many superiors and formators were horrified at the number of units described. There is a dilemma. It is vital that "young" monks and nuns be well educated, yet it is also necessary that the integrity of their burgeoning monastic lives be maintained as much as possible. Perhaps we need, once and for all, to dissociate ourselves from the seminary or university mentality and try to devise a system of monastic education that is truly monastic—and truly educational. Everyone knows about the disadvantages involved in trying to do solid study in a monastery. Perhaps we should start by assessing what our advantages are and then designing an educational approach that capitalizes on our specific benefits. At the moment there is a dreadful mediocrity about many courses given in monasteries, notwithstanding the considerable investment of resources that they represent. Having been a monastic teacher for 25 years, I must include myself in this stricture. There is a lot of ambiguity about the place of monastic studies within formation that needs to be resolved before the situation can be much improved. Perhaps we also need to look at a wider range of educational methods. When the 1968 *Report of the Formation Commission OCSO* stated that a course "should take account of the emotional, intellectual and spiritual elements if it is to bring a vocation to maturity" (p. 18), it seemed self-evident. How this is to be done in the eleven 45-minute segments allotted to the Gospel of John is not clear to me. After that it will be Deuteronomy. And the juniors have to cope with other courses simultaneously....

There is much utility in monastic education both in initial formation and throughout life. More needs to be done in bringing this about than merely proclaiming its necessity and outlining its desired content. In particular it needs to be recognized that since entrants are now habitually older and often more qualified than hitherto, we need to employ some system of taking into account the resources and skills they bring with them.[12] The fact that numbers are generally lower makes this personal attention even more appropriate and certainly much easier. Methods and means need to be creatively developed, especially for those communities that are not well-endowed educationally.

6. Formation as Personal Development

Most monastic formators since Vatican II have become aware of the importance of human development in the process of stabilizing a vocation. For this to happen, it is not sufficient to initiate a novice into a static program of material observances. One has to make contact with the deep, interior sources of personal identity in order to ensure that good works stem from understanding and lead to love. The formator accompanies the novices in their monastic adventure, helping them to process their experiences and serving as an interpreter of life when events make it difficult to decipher.

It becomes quickly evident that every person is unique. Personal history shapes the present in such a way that the same event resounds differently in the hearts of those participating. The meaning of an act cannot be deduced simply from its external features. Novices must be asked about their behavior and whether it harmonizes with their fundamental beliefs and values. Appearances are often deceptive. Furthermore, sometimes people unconsciously act out scenarios that owe nothing to their avowed philosophy but derive from causes that are completely hidden.

A long time is needed to come to know the heart. A formator requires substantial personal integrity, skill in entering such delicate areas and a solid investment of generous effort. Sometimes one needs to make appropriate use of psychologists, either to mark out the route to greater wholeness for the novice or, on a more prolonged basis, to attempt through therapy to clear some of the larger obstacles.

Much depends on first contacts. In particular, the novice should be encouraged to tell his or her story.[13] So much depends on the empathy communicated by the formator. This is not so much an official history-taking, such as is necessary before entry. It is a global willingness of the formator to enter the world-as-experienced-by-the-other. Usually the recital will be circular. It may begin with a chronological presentation, but progressively it will become thematic, with events being linked sometimes surprisingly. Not everything will be stated baldly; the formator will need to read between the lines, to provide closure where there are gaps, to keep nuancing impressions as trust deepens. Above all, formators are called to share the other's way of seeing things without intruding themselves or precipitately judging the quality of the other's perceptions. The first task to be done is to find the heart or soul of the novice, thence to accept, appreciate and love what is unique in

God's creation. Then this positive appraisal can be reflected back to the novice so that the formator becomes a mirror of the deepest self.

Respect for the other is paramount. To enter this sacred space without reverence is sacrilege and the person will forever feel violated and abused. More than the preservation of confidentiality is involved. The attitude to be desired covers not only the metaphysical core of the other's being and the content of secrets, but more especially it embraces all the practical details which attach themselves to concrete personality: family, upbringing, gifts, education, profession, experience, choices, mistakes, philosophy of life, personal history.[14] To be invited to enter this private zone is to move towards intimacy. Any abuse of this hospitality will engender mistrust and may cripple the victim for life. Even more worthy of respect is the other's spiritual and religious life. Sometimes there is a tendency not to take seriously a novice's post-baptismal, pre-monastic life. Not only is this theologically unsound, it is practically wrong. The candidate lived such a fervent Christian life that it brought him or her to the advanced state of being prepared to give up everything to follow Christ. How many people even think about becoming Cistercians, much less get to the point of doing something practical? This means that—however formators may flatter themselves as "molders of young souls"—they are, in fact, dealing with persons who have already invested years of their life in seeking God and living the Gospel. If children's spiritual experience is to be taken very seriously, how much more that of those who come to us with years of adulthood as well, particularly in the case of those who have been actively involved in spiritual living, ministry or religious life?[15] Whatever is done by way of spiritual guidance must build explicitly on this foundation; it absolutely cannot be disregarded. To do this is to diminish what God's grace has done through the years. It is an attempt to begin afresh according to one's own conceptions without reference to the fact that God is already halfway through the work.

This model raises the point of multiple formators. Is it wise to pass a candidate from one to another, like a baton in a relay race? Especially when the flow of candidates is greatly reduced. Positively it means that those who felt ill at ease with the first formator may be more comfortable with another but, negatively, the transition will be hard for those who have found a soul-friend already. No doubt there will always be, in addition, some who will deal with the whole series of appointed guides strictly at a business level. They will play their cards close to the chest; not having learned to trust (or having learned not to trust). Perhaps they will find someone outside the structures (although this can be hazardous since many communities regard openness with formators as a prerequisite for profession).

In this model the period of initial formation is a time of intense spiritual direction. Most monasteries now expect those in formation to present themselves frequently for personal interviews with their formators. What transpires during these interviews seems to depend on the individuals concerned. Obviously much will depend on what model of formation predominates in the mind of the formator. Sometimes these sessions are so informal that they are more like a friendly chat. In other cases they may be like an examination of conscience on the elements of daily life. Some begin with the question, "How do you feel?" And the agenda develops from there; others never ask this question. Formators who take seriously their role as counselor find themselves somewhere on the continuum between therapist and spiritual director. Even though they would prefer to operate as spiritual director, and the novice may also be seeing a professional therapist, there are often unavoidable issues that demand a basic level of psychological expertise—at least to be able to make a specific referral in situations that clearly demand another competence.

Experience helps. But training is also necessary, especially so that others are not damaged while formators are learning their craft.

> 1. On a cognitive level, one needs to know something about human development and have a median degree of psychological sophistication, well integrated with theology. A knowledge of spirituality, including its transitions and deconstructions is vital. Furthermore, one needs to know from reflection on experience and from others' testimony, some of the classical features that mark the unfolding of a monastic vocation. All this will help the formator to discern what is happening in the other's life and avoid the trap of thinking that others merely reproduce the pattern of one's own experience.
>
> 2. There is also a need for interpersonal skills and the ability to communicate. The art of listening is of crucial importance. Knowing when to be silent in a way that communicates love and encourages further disclosure is even more vital. A certain habitual serenity is necessary if one is to welcome the truth even when clothed in ugly vesture. Body language so often gives to the other a message that distances and condemns. A disinterested concern for the other's welfare will demand much self-denial and often involve the renunciation of many hopes and laudable projects. In addition "they will be helped by having a clear knowledge of themselves and of their [personal and emotional] needs. At some stage it may be useful to seek the assistance of specialists towards acquiring this knowledge" (Cistercian *Ratio* #57). In this way power plays, unhealthy dependencies and various affective disorders may be recognized in a relationship and scuttled before too much harm is done.
>
> 3. For many the art of making the leap from discussion into a prayer-like atmosphere is very difficult. Certainly the asking and giving of counsel, as a gift of the Holy Spirit, implies some awareness of God's presence in the encounter. If it comes naturally to the formator, then it will

be easier for the novice to move towards God-inclusive discourse. This in itself is an incentive to a more integral truthfulness and continually opens the area under discussion to reframing and—sometimes—resolution. In such a setting, the opening up of negative situations is not seen as asking "advice," but as an invitation to share the discovery of God's love and providence in them. Emphatically it is not a matter of denying pain, uncertainty or responsibility by theologizing them out of existence. It begins by accepting what is real—not only events but also, for example, the outrage they provoke—and humbly searching in them for the epiphany of God. And this not without groans and prayers.

4. A further range of skills involves looking after oneself. Beyond time allotted for interviews there needs also to be leisure to reflect on what has transpired and to recover from its rigors. Manual work can often help in the displacement of uncreative tensions. Formators (and communities) need to recognize the ravages inflicted on equanimity, prayer and even health, by being constantly exposed to the anguish of others. Precautions need to be taken to ensure that formators do not become so fragmented by their work that they damage themselves and do no good to those in their charge. Superiors need to keep an eye on this. Formators with an ordinary measure of common sense are generally open to receive some form of supervision in their task. This is especially important because it is not always possible to maintain a professional distance in the way that social workers and psychiatrists do. There is no limit to mutual exposure. One encounters the other constantly, not only in the privileged forum of the interview, but also in other roles and activities, including some that may demand close co-operation. It is not easy for the warmth of brotherly or sisterly affection to be seen to coexist with clinical coolness, and this difficulty can cause a certain chronic strain within the relationship. The demands of other aspects of the formators' task can, likewise, impose severe restraints on their effectiveness as a counselor—in the strict sense of the term.

It is in the sphere of counseling that formators most often feel the necessity of training, and the need for a forum to process their experiences without violating confidentiality. Often their work with the novices raises issues for their own development with the result that they recognize the desirability of therapy for themselves, or a more intense spiritual direction or supervision of their ministry. All this is good, but their zeal for the remedying of their own defects should not be allowed to consume so much time and energy that the novices are relegated to a secondary position. Doing their best in good faith and accepting their own limitations are more important than attempting to become perfect formators.

When formators see themselves primarily as counselors, there is the possibility of misunderstandings between them and other members of the community. Because the transactions involved are private, this is an area that is little known or appreciated by the community. The corollary of this can be stated in two ways:

1. The community should trust those chosen as formators.
Or
2. Those chosen as formators should be persons whom the community trusts.

In situations when significant community concerns seem to be treated as secondary "for pastoral reasons" and no explanation is generally offered, the community needs to believe that it is not done lightly or out of disdain for what the community cherishes but (to use canonical language) only for a proportionately grave cause. If this confidence does not exist then the superior (as ultimately responsible), the formator and the novice may have to bear the silent (and sometimes not-so-silent) disapproval of some or many. The friction thus caused sometimes militates against the success of the initiative and failure results—sometimes to the delight of the critics. This is another example of the complications which follow incompatible perceptions of the nature of formation. This is why explaining formation policy to the community and being willing to accept suggestions and occasional criticism are so important.

Formators chosen with this model in mind tend to be younger. Usually they have a good grounding in theology and some training in the requisite skills. The isolating effects of this emphasis need to be offset by regular contact with the superior, wholehearted participation in a formation group and, at a different level, a genuine zeal to relate with the rest of community, sharing their joys and sadnesses and being involved in community activities. In this way the formator will be kept in touch with the reality of community life and also establish an infrastructure which will permit members of the community to offer desires and suggestions about formation. Contact with ordinary monks or nuns may also provide relief from the hothouse atmosphere often found in novitiates and monasticates. Every tendency to becoming a virtual recluse is to be resisted.

7. Conclusion

The beginning is also the end. We began with different paradigms of formation and this is also where we finish. There is a certain amount of overlap in the different models I have described, especially at the practical level, but the approaches themselves are fundamentally irreducible. The best candidates for amalgamation are "B1" and "B2," "formation as handing on the charism" and "formation as apprenticeship," but there are good reasons for keeping them separate.

Since it is impossible to combine the benefits of all the different approaches and issue the result as a role-description of a formator, some choice has to be made. All the functions described are ideally present in the community's impact on newcomers. How this works in practice needs to be codified, and the specific task of "formators" and the complementary task of others can be clearly spelled out. The "others" mentioned would be the superior, the officials of the monastery, confessors, therapist, work-organizer, academic teachers and instructors in practical matters. Probably the community needs to be involved actively but not intrusively. If they are relegated to the role of ignorant bystanders while the "experts" get on with the job, resentment will result.

Perhaps such a distribution of roles can be explained schematically by modifying the diagram already used (Diagram 2, page 398).

This needs to be explained to the community. The whole process of formation also needs to be laid out for the novices so that there is one less monastic mystery to be mastered. Doctors and dentists nowadays usually explain each step of a procedure to their patients, sometimes inviting them to monitor its progress. One of the criticisms aimed at the whole language of formation is that it gives the impression that, all the while, the novice is passively under the process. To break this impression can. 652.3 *CIC* recommends that the novices give "active co-operation." The theme is repeated in *Cistercian Constitution* 45.3 and in the 1990 *Instruction* (#53). The respect due novices as persons of committed spirituality demands that they be constantly invited to be actively and intelligently involved in the work of monastic initiation as it is concretely realized in their particular case.

Much of the hardship experienced by formators comes from the conflict of different expectations within their office. The problem becomes even more intense when formators hold several important positions in the

Diagram 2.

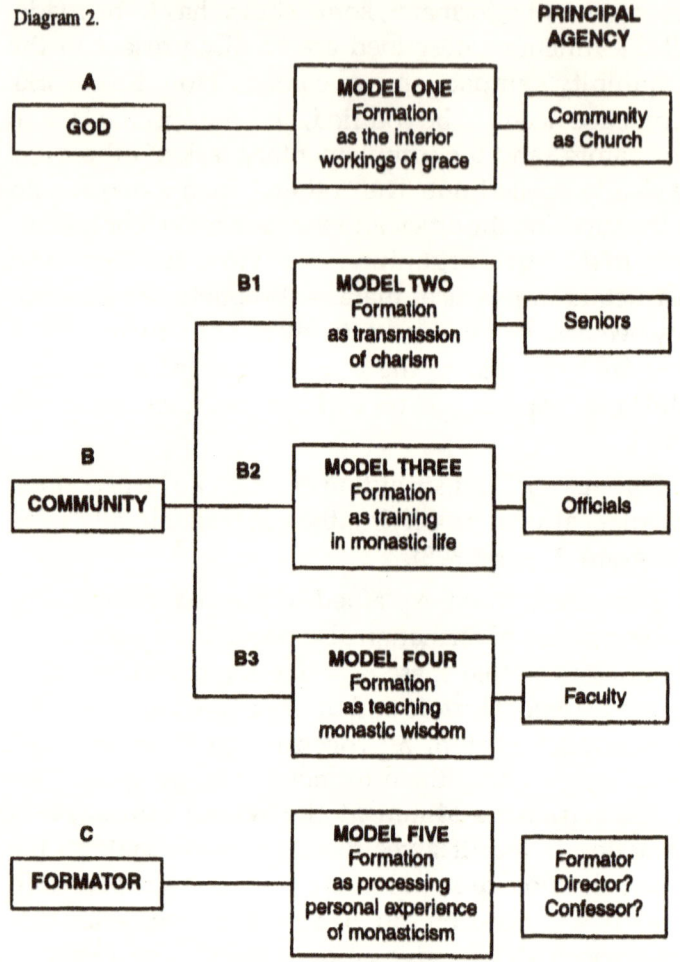

community. The distinctive purview of a prior, cantor or cellarer easily clashes with what is required of a formator; the novice may be confused—as also the formator. It is hard to find alternative office-holders in many communities, but all need to be aware of the dangers of pluralities.

Perhaps it would be easier for everyone if it were accepted that formators are not paragons: they are weak human beings with many liabilities, working hard at a sensitive and demanding task and trying to avoid doing irremediable damage to others. Perhaps they need to be more accepting of their own limits, more open in admitting these to their novices and frankly avowing them in the presence of the community. In such a climate of honesty perhaps it will become possible for the community to close ranks and to work out practical ways to do the best they possibly can for those whom the providence of God has called to this particular place and community.

Appendix: Formation in the Cistercian Ratio Institutionis

Following are some extracts from the *Cistercian Ratio Institutionis* that illustrate the different models we have examined. Taken together they illustrate the truism that a patchwork "consensual" document often embodies perspectives that are difficult to reconcile in practice. All the ideas are good but the cumulative effect of such role-descriptions seems beyond ordinary competence.

A. Formation as God's Work

The goal of the monastic journey is a gradual transformation into the likeness of Christ through the action of the Spirit of God...aided by the maternal solicitude of Mary, Mother of Jesus and of the Church, and our model in the following of Christ...Those responsible will always be attentive to the Spirit of God working in those they are called to train...Finally all must be aware of the fact that, whatever the means used in the work of formation, it is ultimately the Holy Spirit alone who can accomplish in us the necessary transformation—though this is something which will not take place without our co-operation.[16]

B1. Formation as Inspiration/Inspiriting

As a school of the Lord's service, each community is called to maintain and to transmit the Cistercian patrimony and a faithful version of its charism to those who enter...The community is the ambiance where the transforming action of the Spirit of God takes place...It is in the particular and delicate balance of *lectio divina*, liturgy and work that the Cistercian charism most directly manifests itself...All who live in the community share responsibility for its unity [and] its dynamic fidelity to the Cistercian charism...A community's ability to form new members depends largely on its having a unified spirit so that it can impart a single orientation to the upcoming generations...so that practical everyday questions can be located within a shared vision of the Cistercian ideal. This vision must be one that is rooted in the experience of monastic living and which spans the several generations which together form the community.[17]

B2. Formation as Training in Monasticity

It is essentially by living out the various aspects of Cistercian *conversatio* that a person gradually becomes ever more truly a Cistercian. The community is the ambiance where the transforming action of the Spirit of God takes place. Through the daily practice of monastic disciplines and under the pastoral care of the superior and those who share in the superior's ministry, this *conversatio* provides the means for personal and communal growth. The various elements of Cistercian *conversatio*...lead, each in its own way, to the interior freedom through which purity of heart and an abiding attention to God are attained. But it is in the particular and delicate balance of *lectio divina*, liturgy and work that the Cistercian charism most directly manifests itself...[The formator] will be responsible for introducing the candidates to the Cistercian *conversatio*...The postulancy is a period of initiation and progressive adaptation to the monastic life...[The formator] helps [the postulant] surmount the difficulties which are proper to this stage. Often these are connected with the physical and affective separation from the activities and relationships that were part of the postulant's life before entering the monastery...The novitiate is a time for a personal integrating of the Cistercian way of life...the novices are led to a more intense personal experience of what is involved in the living out of the Cistercian *conversatio*...Careful attention must also be given to ensure that the fruits of the juniors' vocation are becoming manifest in their lives through their regularity and through their application to prayer, *lectio*, the divine office, work, and the acceptance of corrections...The primary characteristic of those appointed [as formators] is that they be imbued with love of Cistercian life...[18]

B3. Formation as Monastic Education

Those with insufficient knowledge of Christian doctrine will be invited to complete their catechetical preparation...The novice director...gives regular conferences...A program of monastic studies begins in the novitiate. The courses of the novitiate are under the control of the novice director and are oriented to the spiritual needs of this stage of formation. They are also however coordinated with the program of the monasticate. Among the topics to be presented are the following: Sacred Scripture, in particular the Psalms; the Liturgy, especially the Liturgy of the Hours, with practical instruction in singing and public reading; the *Rule of St. Benedict*; Monastic History and Spirituality, especially the Cistercian Patrimony; instruction in Prayer and *Lectio*, on the Vows and the meaning of Religious Life, an introduction to the Christian Mystery and Christian Doctrine and to the Constitutions and

Statutes of the Order...[The formator of juniors] gives conferences...Through their participation in a program of monastic education the juniors are led, on the one hand, to a more conscious awareness [sic] of the content of the faith and of the monastic patrimony; on the other hand, they are invited to a deeper reflection on their own beliefs and values. In this way it is hoped that they will be able to construct a broader context in which to locate their personal experiences and to have some objective means of checking their judgments and opinions...While the conditions of each monastery are to be taken into account, communities are to be generous in providing time for juniors for classes and personal studies...The core courses of the monastic curriculum are: Sacred Scripture, Cistercian Patrimony, Philosophy, Systematic Theology, Moral Theology, Patrology and Liturgy. These courses must be presented along with the basic themes of Cistercian Spirituality whether in classes, or with the help of audio or video cassettes, or in some other manner. Other courses in some of the following subjects may also be offered: Methodology, Church History, Theology of Monastic Life, Spirituality, History of Religions, Canon Law and the various human sciences. An introduction to the original languages would be of the greatest value in reading the Scriptures and the writings of the Fathers. A knowledge of modern languages can also be of great help for the study of any of the above-mentioned disciplines...A program of ongoing formation available to everyone is to be developed in each community...The goal of such ongoing education is a deeper penetration of the mystery of Christ and of the Church. A good assimilation of the patrimony of the Order, a real familiarity with the contemporary teaching of the Church, and a better understanding of human experience as a whole will contribute greatly to the development of a solid and objective basis for faith and practice...Competent teachers contribute to the proper formation of new members and to the quality of the intellectual life and monastic culture of the community...¹⁹

C. *Formation as Accompaniment*

These aspirants will be helped by those who receive them to discover the working of God in their lives and the nature of the attraction they experience...All candidates will be encouraged to give themselves totally to God in whatever way he is calling them...[The formator of novices will be responsible for] accompanying them on their spiritual journey until the moment when they leave the novitiate. Apart from this individual guidance...The novice director and those who assist him or her need to have a real love for persons and a reverence for the grace of God present in each individual...They need to be persons who possess the ability to listen...The novice director helps [the postulant] surmount the difficulties which are proper to this stage...In order to profit from this period the novices will strive to develop from the beginning an open and confident relationship with the novice director and the superior who in their turn will help the novice by pastoral care, prayer and example...The novice director shows understanding and sympathy for the hesitations and soul-searching of those who are doubtful in their vocation...The [junior] director reviews with [the juniors] their experience of monastic living in the community, prayer, vocation, the vows, study, work and the acceptance of responsibilities. Because the monasticate is such a critical time of growth, it is important that the juniors receive understanding, acceptance and encouragement from the director, as well as being encouraged by him [or her]...[Through monastic education] they will be able to construct a broader context in which to locate their personal experiences and to have some objective means of checking their judgments and opinions...The superior will see to it that [the formators]...are given the means to acquire the knowledge and skills needed for the guidance and direction of souls and for the understanding of the young. This applies especially when there is question of appointing a novice director.[20]

NOTES

[1] This article is a reworking of a program given to the Cistercian superiors and formators of Latin America in April-May 1993. This is the explanation for the predominantly Cistercian focus to my remarks.

[2] An article in *The Age* of 6 March 1989, "Narcissism is booming," identifies the baby-boomers in Australia as those born between 1947 and 1963. Doubtless, the frontiers of this sub-class are fuzzier than this specification allows. Those born in this period constitute 27.5% of the population.

[3] For example there is a real anti-institutional and anti-ritual bias; a more "personalist" approach to common life is preferred, marked by equality, informality, spontaneity, subsidiarity, responsibility. For some relevant observations in this general area see M. Francis Mannion, "Monasticism and Modern Culture: II. The Cultural Conversion of Monks—Liberalism and Monastic Life," *ABR* 44.2 (1993), pp. 125-142.

[4] *Models of the Church*, (Garden City: Doubleday, 1974). *Models of Revelation*, (Garden City: Doubleday, 1983), *Catholicism and American Culture*, (New York: Fordham University Press, 1990).

[5] Chapter 34. See Phyliss Hodgson, *The Cloud of Unknowing and the Book of Privy Counselling* published for the Early English Text Society by Oxford University Press, 1944; p. 70.

⁶ It is clear that this is one of the texts in this document that is verbally dependent on the first draft of the *OCSO Ratio Institutionis*, since the relevant text (2.022) was not retained in subsequent redactions nor in the official text.

⁷ See Gerald A. Arbuckle, "Planning the Novitiate Process: Reflections of an Anthropologist," *Review for Religious* (July/August 1984), pp. 532-546. "Now is the crucial time for the candidate to grasp more deeply the overall root paradigm for the novitiate—the death resurrection paradigm. If there is to be a continuing response to the call of the Lord to closer intimacy, the 'price' must be paid. There must be death to self, death to false worldly attractions" (541). "All initiation rites necessarily involve suffering in one form or another— the pain of separation from the comfort of one's immediate family, the dramatic rupture with one's past style of living, the restrictions of community living, the uncertainty of what will happen next in the process, the loneliness and boredom of isolation. Candidates must learn to accept such suffering without complaint if they are to be accepted into the adult world" (542).

⁸ This was the subject of the Advent 1982 Circular Letter of Abbot General Ambrose Southey, OCSO. Following the Rulla school he distinguishes three ways of bridging the distance between past habits and monastic practice: compliance or conformity, identification, and (ideally) internalization.

⁹ The most common criticism of formation one hears in communities is "Why are the novices doing (not doing) X?" Becoming involved in "unmonastic" activities and the omission of "monastic" activities seem inappropriate to community members when novices are considered to be in a state of apprenticeship—even though the same activities or omission may be accepted as permissible for the seniors. Nor is an appeal to

subjective need or "pastoral" factors found very convincing by those who make the criticism from this perspective.

[10] The willingness and capacity to make a positive decision to adopt or persevere in a religious vocation is itself part of the data to be weighed in discernment. Procrastination and hesitance are often signals that a person is acting not from the strength of grace but from the emptiness that comes from mere bright ideas, fantasies or delusions.

[11] One of the unpleasant aspects of the formator's role in this model, is being morally compelled to act as a defense attorney for the community (even though sometimes formators may themselves disapprove of what happens there). Since the bonding between novice and community and fidelity to its way of life are so important, the formator is naturally anxious to minimize any distance between the novice and the concrete expression of Cistercian *conversatio*. As a result, any attempt to respond to criticism may be marred by hasty defensiveness. It needs to be recognized that some negative remarks have objective bases; in offering them novices need not be attacking community solidarity or belittling the lives of individuals. Sometimes such questions merely express the marginality of newcomers to the community. Alternatively the novices may simply be struggling with the unreality of their own ideals or, alternatively, trying to develop a conscientious stand relative to monastic values. Genuine questions or criticisms should not be staunched by bluster or counter-attack. In most cases a less institutional response will be more helpful.

[12] It should be noted that in the educational systems of many countries there has been a new emphasis on "retraining" and consequently on what is termed the "recognition of prior learning." Instead of forcing older

persons through the treadmill designed for youth, an attempt is made to assess the skills/knowledge already acquired so that vain repetition might be avoided. For a general survey, see Alan Brown, *Valuing Skills: Recognition of Prior Learning: Changing the Delivery of Education* (North Melbourne: The Victorian Education Foundation, 1992).

[13] I have a chapter entitled "A Story to Tell" in *Towards God: The Western Tradition of Contemplation* (Melbourne: Collins Dove, 1989), pp. 133-147.

[14] The listener has to be aware of the insider-outsider paradox. Sometimes insiders are allowed to disparage or denigrate themselves; if the same criticism comes from outside it is experienced as belittling and resented, especially if it is repeated to third parties. I may say (and believe), "My relatives are all fat and ugly," but I do not want to hear you agree, and I will find it demeaning if you were to repeat the description to others.

[15] One needs to learn that the gifts of God are sometimes expressed in original ways that may seem, at first sight, bizarre, since they have not formed part of the formator's own history. With a little experience one begins to appreciate that genuine spiritual content can be uncovered in the most unusual events.

[16] Nos. 2, 4, 57, 73.

[17] Nos. 3, 6, 7, 11, 12.

[18] Nos. 6, 7, 24, 27, 29, 31, 41, 56.

[19] Nos. 20, 24, 32, 37, 40, 41, 43, 48, 58.

[20] Nos. 20, 21, 24, 25, 27, 30 33, 40, 56.

MARKETING MONASTIC TRADITION WITHIN MONASTERIES

This article is a summary of a program given to male Benedictine formators at St Joseph's Abbey, Louisiana in 2001. It is practical in orientation, discussing concrete methods of selling the wisdom of tradition to an upcoming generation of monastics. It was published in Tjurunga *60 (2001).*

In the contemporary world of religious seekers, monastic spirituality has a high reputation. Monastery guesthouses are enjoying a boom. Lay associations are thriving. Academic interest in aspects of the monastic phenomenon has led to a profounder knowledge of its history and context. Meanwhile, the *Encyclopedia of Monasticism* has been published[1] and many books written by monastic authors are purchased and read with gusto.

It must be seen as a bit of a tragedy that this external success is not matched by a comparable intra-monastic enthusiasm. Even though the amount of monastic literature available in English has increased tenfold in the last quarter-century, it is sometimes difficult to convince monks and nuns of the utility and sheer delight inherent in becoming devotees of their own tradition. Many who are exposed to a representative sampling of monastic writings during their years of formation somehow lose interest later on—unless there is a sermon or conference to prepare. Their interior life becomes quarantined from this vast storehouse of wisdom and guidance. There is danger here! What was too much to take in during the early years and is set aside, becomes urgently relevant as we pass through the different situations and changes of the spiritual journey. It is an unkind perversity that, in hard times, makes us look elsewhere for guidance, when the sort of help we need is close at hand.

This means that superiors and other persons with pastoral responsibility for the community, need to see themselves as advocates of monastic tradition. Not as hecklers of modernity or enforcers of particular "traditional practices," but as those who, in their lives and words, embody and communicate the cumulative wisdom of 1500 years of monastic experience. This must be what St Benedict means when he suggests that all such officials should be chosen because of their capacity to "teach" both by their acts of governance (*disciplina*) and by their words (*doctrina*). In the latter case, this may well mean introducing or reintroducing the monks or nuns to the sources and encouraging them to keep going deeper.

1. A Love of Letters?

The two characteristics of Benedictine monachism indicated in the title of Jean Leclercq's book, *The Love of Learning and the Desire for God* generally evoke an unqualified assent. Whereas "desire for God" has an ontological basis and eventually can be unearthed in even the most disordered life, "love of learning" seems less universal today even among the followers of St Benedict. On the one hand we note the preferential option for rusticity preached by many highly literate reformers — and there are still those who are bewitched by the dream of a "simple" life. On the other hand, and more to the point, there is a tendency towards lukewarmness in personal reading which causes many monastics to abandon books. This dereliction may be traced to an excess of work—especially intellectual work—activity, hobbies, conversation, pulp novels, newspapers and easy-read periodicals, together with their electronic cousins, talk-back radio, television, videos, computer games and surfing the Internet. And perhaps there are extramural activities that are enthusiastically embraced as culture but might be more objectively described as entertainment. We are talking here of a general drift towards the besetting sin of acedia, long known in monasteries and recognized by some as typical of contemporary western culture.[2] There are some counterweights to this tendency. The cultural level of many monastic communities remains high and many monastics have a good theological education. The practice of communal reading, particularly during meals, affords a good exposure to a wider and wiser world. Apostolates and activities involve a certain bookish involvement. And, of course, *lectio divina* remains as a privileged means or adjunct to prayer. Such inbuilt reading sometimes disguises the underlying alienation from a genuine "love of letters." The joy and profit from such traditional contact with books comes under threat if it is not supported by a wider literacy. Many monks and nuns no longer find enjoyment in worthwhile reading. Such indifference is not due to work having become more imperious in its demands on our time, but derives from the fact that our notion of leisure no longer includes solid disciplined reading. For many, periods of vacation or recreation scarcely ever include giving oneself to the enchantment of a good book.

I wonder what manner of reply we would receive if we were to quiz the monastic population for the titles of serious books recently and gratuitously read from cover to cover. In an article published in *The American Benedictine Review*, I discussed the different reading habits of "black" and "white" Benedictines.[3] An anonymous pre-publication reader opined that the distinction was nugatory, since nobody read books anymore. When visiting libraries in poorly-endowed monasteries, I am often struck by the fact that their few resources seem to be much better patronized than the serried ranks of unused volumes accumulated in richer monasteries. Many monastic librarians will confirm this impression; holdings continue to increase but borrowings are down, and books tend to remain out for longer periods—presumably unread.

Both personal experience and what I can glean from history incline me to believe that a serious love for reading plays a *crucial* role in the formation of a Benedictine heart and of a Benedictine ethos. I am not talking about mere egg-headedness, a gluttony for information or the acquisition of some marketable expertise. I am advocating the medium rather than the message. Reading that becomes a significant component of a personal lifestyle bespeaks a certain *gravitas* which would delight the heart of Benedict. Solitude, silence and reflectiveness surround the act of reading. Absorption in the printed page can calm the anxious heart and soothe the bruises inflicted by discordant interaction. It can allow the great Benedictine qualities of reasonableness and moderation to re-assert themselves when tranquillity is endangered. Reading teaches us to listen and receive. Viewing matters more energetically, we can see that the adventure of taking up a book and remaining in its spell exposes us to alternate ways of viewing the world, and perhaps gives us new keys to understanding ourselves. If I read a book unread by others in my community, not only may I be invited to original thoughts, but I can act as channel by which the community renews itself from outside without losing its distinctive identity.

Reading is described as a cool medium. Instead of immobilizing the imagination and pre-empting logical thought, it gives us the constant possibility of gently pausing to consider critically the implications of what is said. It facilitates the transition from knowledge to wisdom. By contrast, electronic media wields a greater impact over consciousness, but they are less potent in encouraging creative thoughts. Some say they immobilize the brain as surely as a snake hypnotizes a rabbit. More darkly, electronic media have been described as the instruments of a new colonization, disenfranchising traditional beliefs and values, notwithstanding their self-proclaimed role of enlargers of consciousness.[4] And meanwhile the antidote has been abandoned: our reading has become less regular, and less substantial. We begin to falter in the practice of the kind of autonomous thought that can balance the hail of not-disinterested opinion with which we are pelted. We are too often undiscriminating in our conformity with ideology and the latest modes of political correctness. "The failure to read good books both enfeebles the vision and strengthens our most fatal tendency—the belief that here and now is all that is."[5] Reading transports us to another world, one that may have been horrible enough but was, at least, less drenched in *current* propaganda. When we return it is often with a judicious sense of perspective and proportion.

Hermann Hesse wrote somewhere that we live in an age with a comic-strip mentality. To say the same things in more contemporary terms, our attention span scarcely exceeds the 22 seconds allocated for a "sound-bite." As a result we find it more and more difficult to read, to follow a logical argument and to make a judgment on a solid philosophical or theological treatise. This means that in complicated issues we have to rely on others to navigate the evidence; even our most important judgments are often mere pale reflections of the conclusions that others have reached. The most-used tactic I hear in discussion is an appeal either to an authority or to an anti-authority, depending on the speaker's location on the scale of compliance. Are we losing the capacity to think for ourselves?

The disappearing art of solid reading has consequences not only for the serious side of our life. Alienation from books separates us from a noble source of comfort and self-realization. The contemporary world finds it incredible that a wounded soldier would spend a whole day in a shell crater reading Aeschylus's *Prometheus* in Greek.[6] How many of us have never acquired or have latterly lost the capacity to be charmed and consoled by good literature! I have often thought that monks and nuns with a good habit of reading fit in more readily with the restrictions inherent in any serious monastic life. Without being a burden to others they can access whatever they need to make life both more livable and more creative.

My book *The Art of Sacred Reading* is dedicated to a confrere, Brother Kevin Burke, who died after the manuscript was finished but before publication. Kevin came from the Dublin slums of the 1930s, and with a minimum of education had lived more than 50 years as a monk in Ireland and Australia, many of them spent milking cows. He was always a solid reader. Three days before he died he brought me one of his great treasures: his personal anthology of bits and pieces taken from books he had read over the years. After his death, as I paged through the large notebook, I came to see how extensive his habit of reading had been, and began to suspect that the solid books to which he had applied himself had been the keel that kept his yacht upright as he sailed through the many stormy seas typical of any monastic existence.

As I ponder this age blessed by an abundance of available information, I am reminded of an unsourced axiom attributed to Seneca. "A large library is apt to distract rather than to instruct the learner; it is much better to confine yourself to a few authors than to wander at random among many." A few things at depth are more useful than a whole world of superficiality. Monasticism at its best is a call to profundity. The habit of serious reading, although not absolutely necessary for salvation, is a valuable adjunct to any monastic existence. I say this not in an excess of anti-modernist pique, but simply in recognition of how much old-fashioned reading habits still can contribute to contentment, intellectual alertness and growth in wisdom.[7]

2. Humana lectio et divina

The usual response to any jeremiad about the declining quality of reading is countered by the assertion that — despite increasing book prices and taxes—books are selling on an unprecedented scale. The question is: "What books?" Often enough they are tie-ins with famous films or successful television programs; coffee-table extravaganzas and travel guides; books with useful information: gardening, self-improvement or cookery books, business guides and computer manuals; novels to read at airports and aloft: pulp fiction by the ton.

I have nothing against such books, as such, except that they generate about reading expectations of instant gratification that make denser volumes seem less worth the effort. Such reading has two harmful effects. First it encourages us to skim through a book or magazine until we find something that grabs our interest; we read that and ignore whatever is outside our immediate purview. Otherwise we become obsessed with an exciting plot and we race through the book to find out what happens, caring little about whether we grasp the finer points of plot, scenario or characterization. Blurbs boast that a book is "unputdownable." This means that we get ourselves helter-skelter into an affair with the book without ever taking the opportunity to withdraw a little and consider its implications. We swallow everything and digest nothing. On a more ponderous level, university courses which demand that students skim rapidly through large masses of largely indigestible material, may lead us to conclude that speed reading is the sign of an educated person.

Perhaps we need to reconsider the value of slower reading. This means that we will cover less territory, but that we will have a greater chance of adding to our knowledge and understanding by interacting more consciously with what we read. As a writer, I know that my message has to be condensed into the relatively few pages of a book. Sometimes there are levels of meaning and experience below the obvious. I am often painfully made aware of how much of this slips unnoticed past an inattentive reader. And I know that, as a reader, I do not always grasp everything that an author intends to communicate—both at the level of message and that of meta-message.[8] On occasions when I have been marooned in an alien environment and forced to read and reread whatever is at hand, I have often been astonished by how much can be found in a simple source, if we abandon our reluctance to delve deeper. Unless we take the time to ponder what we read, to view it from different angles and to enter into active dialogue with it, much of what is expressed will pass us by.

In many ways effective reading demands skills parallel to those necessary for good listening. Today we are conscious that there is a difference between picking up the auditory signal and accurately receiving the message that the words are meant to communicate. To read well we must give ourselves totally to the task of hearing what the author has to say, suspending for the moment our own beliefs and immediate responses. We need to be relaxed, silent and in a non-intrusive environment. Only when we have fully digested what the author is saying—and this may involve rephrasing the message in our own language — can we afford to analyze and respond. If we jump in too quickly with an immediate reaction, it is more than likely that what we hear is quite different from what the author intends. In the same way, we will have a better chance of perceiving the insight embodied in a text and learning from it if we take our time and give ourselves fully to the task. Part of our motivation will come from our respect for the author, so that we are prepared to grapple with the difficulty of coming to terms with a distinctive viewpoint. Those who go to hear the Dalai Lama do so out of a sense of reverence: they are not dismayed by his thick accent or halting delivery; the abstruseness of Tibetan Buddhist terminology is no discouragement. These difficulties simply mean that the audience has to listen harder. This they do happily. In the same way, the fact that close reading a particular text is difficult does not mean that it should not be undertaken. The extra effort is the price paid for the non-immediate gratification of growth in wisdom.

It sometimes occurs to me that our *lectio* is less *divina* because we have not developed the art of engaging seriously enough with what we read. Many factors are involved in this. Choosing to read worthwhile authors is an obvious first step. Reading whole books, as St Benedict enjoins for Lent, would probably offset our tendency to disengaged browsing, and invite us to practice not only *stabilitas loci* but also mental steadiness: *stabilitas mentis*.[9] Allocating an appropriate amount of time can serve as a means of verifying the seriousness of our reading: a solid text cannot be well grasped if we read much more than ten pages an hour. To remain at that rate requires that we slow down our thinking and restrain its wild or woolly impulses. We have to concentrate more fully on the text before us. By sustained application we begin to acquire the art and the habit of **close reading**.

I suppose the fewness and awkwardness of medieval books would have discouraged speed reading, and a different approach to literacy would have encouraged attention to style as well as content. Certainly one of the tasks that confronts monastic educators today is to help the next generation to rediscover for themselves how close reading can add a sparkling dimension to their interaction with books. We all laugh at those tourists who cannot afford to spend quality time with the works of art they visit so compulsively, yet we are no better if we merely skim the surface of a text of which so much must be sought at a deeper level.

The author of *The Closing of the American Mind* describes close reading in these well-chosen terms:

> A line-by-line, word-by-word analysis must be undertaken... The hardest thing of all is the simplest to formulate: every word must be understood. It is hard because the eye tends to skip over just those things which are the most shocking or most call into question our way of looking at things... The argument or example that seems irrelevant, trivial or boring is precisely the one most likely to be a sign of what is outside one's framework and which it calls into question. One passes over such things unless one takes pencil and paper, outlines, counts, stops at everything and tries to wonder.[10]

Beyond the obvious point about reading and understanding every single word, he makes the bold assertion that in rapid perusal we tend not to see elements to which we are habitually blind; it is only when we slow down that we become aware of truths that are normally invisible. We are not obliged automatically to agree with such contrary insights, but there is much profit to be found in entertaining these unfamiliar guests, entering into dialogue with them and gaining from them a precious complement to our existing sum of wisdom. The writings of Peter Singer, the maverick philosopher and animal rights activist, could scarcely be considered as music to the ear of a career theologian; perhaps that is why they would profit more from reading them than from continuing blindly on their familiar treadmill. As a devotee of twelfth-century Cistercianism I am professionally obliged to be familiar with the unsympathetic writings of Adriaan Bredero and Constance Berman, even though I believe that on many points they are in error.[11]

It would be a shame, however, if we concluded that close reading is a contentious affair involving only discipline and self-control. In fact, the slow savoring of a text adds much value to the time already devoted to reading. Because we become alert to all manner of nuance that otherwise would have been invisible, our experience of a piece of writing becomes more delightful. It makes a greater impact on us and stays more easily in the memory. Many who have been re-introduced to this practice have remarked that their tendency to fall asleep has been greatly diminished.

Close reading serves not only analytic diligence with respect to the text, it also gives time and space for intuitive synthesis to emerge. This is especially true in reading texts which embody "monastic" as distinct from speculative or "scholastic" theology. These works are akin to poetry, they need room to breathe. In reading the monastic patrimony, we have to be as much influenced by the style or medium as by the message. In creating an atmosphere of scriptural reminiscence, these authors steer us into a zone of calmly energetic acceptance—whether the overt content be words of confident assurance or practical challenges about the quality of daily life. Close reading enhances our unbiased reception of what the author intends to communicate. Instead of just re-thinking familiar thoughts we receive something new that has, at least theoretically, the potential to revolutionize our whole outlook on life, on self, on God.

If we are successful in convincing others of the necessity of reading in general, and the advantages of applying ourselves closely to this task, then we are faced with the additional challenge of persuading them to spend time with the classical monastic authors. In the early years of formation some propaedeutic is usual to bridge the gap between us and these ancient writers; it is much to be desired that a taste or even a passion for monastic literature would be transmitted in the process.

What has to occur if we are to communicate an enthusiasm for patrimonial authors is to take practical steps to ensure that they are perceived as knowledgeable about what the upcoming generation is experiencing in their monastic life and in their prayer. Not just supporters of the party line propagated by those currently in authority, but as possessing an expertise in mirroring the inner landscape of those entering the tradition. This means, first of all, ascertaining what are the entrants' abiding questions at the level of experience. Then we, as instructors or formators, use our familiarity with the authors to initiate a process whereby ancient wisdom and contemporary conscious-ness interact.

There are specific dynamics in the task of teaching in a monastery, where the numbers are lower and the relationships are multi-layered and more enduring. A method of instruction needs to be found that respects the horizontality of intra-community relationships. An alternative needs to be found both to the "jug and mug" model of learning and to the mere sharing of ignorance that results when formal instruction is abandoned. This means being aware of some advances in educational theory appropriate to the society in which we live, in particular the possibilities that are offered by methods based on specifically adult-oriented programs.

There are three concerns that should characterize any structured approach to monastic education:

Person-centered. Formation courses have no other goal apart from the personal growth of the participants. It is not a question of qualifying newcomers for a particular job, but of helping each to be able to tackle intelligently the demands of a monastic lifetime. In that context, education needs to take the "students" as they are and lead them further, without pre-defining too closely in objective terms what everyone is expected to master. There is scope in a monastery for a more heuristic approach to learning.

Value-oriented. Facts are undoubtedly useful, but they need to be subordinated to the communication of values. Since monastic *conversatio* is counter-cultural, every effort must be made to submit to scrutiny values passively absorbed in the process of prior socialization, and then to make explicit an alternative perceptual horizon in which the practices and abstinences of monasticism make sense.

Text-based. Group interaction with a well-chosen text is a valuable means of leading participants into a discussion of values based on their own experience. Their questions, as they probe the meaning of the text, provide an opening for the one leading the group to provide background information. Alternatively, obscurities can lead the participants to search out answers for themselves. In such a situation teacher and students alike yield precedence to the tradition — before it all are disciples, though with different resources. Here is a means of initiating an unequal group of adults into the monastic patrimony without some of the resentments that sometimes thwart the process, and in a manner that will serve them well throughout a lifetime.[12]

Introducing monastic texts to persons living the monastic life is different from giving an academic course. One does not have to drone on at length about the intricacies of long-dead controversies "moving bones from one graveyard to another." To monastic juniors it can be said "This is your life! Here are the outward features of your vocation. Here is a language suitable for describing the many unspoken experiences of your deepest self."

To help the newcomers engage with the text, Bloom's advice is worth following. "One passes over such things unless one takes pencil and paper, outlines, counts, stops at everything and tries to wonder." I have found it useful to distribute working copies of texts. This way it is not possible for people to slip into the habit of speed reading, they must concentrate on the block of text before them. They are encouraged to use highlighters and to write notes in the ample margins I have allowed on the copies. Key words are indicated and counts encouraged. Bits and pieces of information that surface during discussion can be written directly adjacent to the part of the text to which they refer.

In the treatment of a selected text there are five distinct processes that engage different skills in different people and, when used together, bring a great richness to the common reading of a text. For the sake of a mnemonic, I call this the **CARDS** method.

> **Comparing** one text with another—Bernard's treatment of humility and Benedict's, Anselm's meditations with Guigo's or those of William of St Thierry. By making comparisons and choices between two authors "out-there," students are able to adopt one option as the more appropriate expression of their own thought or as a vicarious carrier of their own unique experience.
>
> **Analysis**: breaking up the text into individual words and phrases and aiming at a precise understanding of every element in the whole. This forces readers to pay attention to details, to become aware of obscurities and to find solutions to their questions. A teacher can help here, explaining—as an ancillary resource—what is necessary to understand the meaning of the text.
>
> **Repetition**: On the understanding that "nobody ever lost money underestimating the public" there is an advantage in reading each text several times. At different stages of the discussion, especially when there seems nothing more to say, it may be useful to reread and to begin on a fresh tack. It seems wise never to hesitate to say the

same thing more than once. Points of clarification repeated using standard phrases often stick in the memory more effectively.

Dialogue: Getting participants to contribute their own research and reflection and to draw on their particular fund of experiences is very helpful in making a text come alive—and in enhancing the solidarity of the group. Dialogue about texts presupposes solid preparation on the part of all—otherwise the exchange degenerates into an airy impressionism that is no more than the sharing of ignorance.

Synthesis: The knack of pulling together divergent insights needs to operate at several levels. A particular text will often need to be located within the author's whole literary *corpus*, and perhaps tied in with the general emphases of monastic tradition. Practical application to the experience of the group will often generate a sense of harmony between past and present. Finally, there may be profit in crystallizing the experience of the group as they encounter the text, asking the participants to reflect on the dynamics and draw some conclusions from it.

Text-based, person-centered and value-oriented programs are not a lazy option. They work only in so far as teachers themselves continue to struggle and to learn. In this way each session is an adventure. Great care is needed in the selection of texts to be studied. The items selected should faithfully represent the tradition as a whole, their degree of difficulty should not surpass the students' present level of competence, and their message should be relevant to the general situation of those participating in the course. The great danger is to attempt to do too much, so that the quality of attention given to each text declines. In a way, close reading is a wondrously inefficient means of surveying tradition. But it can be very formative, if it is done well. After all, the task of monastic education is no more than a sampling intended to prepare the way for a lifetime of banqueting.

3. Integral Benedictinism

The pivot of western monastic tradition is Benedict's Rule. It is both a summary of antecedent tradition and a charter for a variety of future developments. It is a wonderful document, but it cannot stand alone. Its author recognized this when he added a final chapter sending us to seek a fuller practice of monastic virtue in a wider world of wisdom. Benedict's "little black book" is not a free-standing program of life, but an introduction to a dynamic tradition into which the fervent monk will continue to delve throughout the changing decades of his life.

Nowadays any decent program of monastic formation includes not only a gentleman's survey of the *RM-RB* question, but also a grounding in the desert tradition and the system of spirituality that evolved from the writings of Evagrius and John Cassian. Augustine, Basil and the other "Catholic Fathers" who were Benedict's teachers may also merit a mention.

The more closely we read such a text, the clearer it becomes that we need not only to learn another language, **we must somehow find a way of entering into and coming to grips with a completely different world.** The recognition of the linguistic and historical distance between ourselves and an ancient text reveals the real depth and breadth of the interpretative task. It suggests that we must not only familiarize ourselves with the basic geography of that other world, we must also find a way of translating meaning from that world to our own. Such a translation, if it is to be viable, must find a way of bringing our world into dialogue with the other world, so that we can experience growth and new understanding. [Emphasis added.][13]

The first task we encounter in recommending monastic reading is that of contextualisation. Once the first romantic flush has faded we need to get down to the onerous business of attempting to lead others into a different time and culture where the extent of what they learn will be dependent on their ability to read the tradition in its own terms, and to impose a moratorium on rapid conclusions and judgments prompted by their native culture and mind-set.

Already Friedrich Schleiermacher knew that no reading of a complex text will ever be able to claim to have exhausted the text. Hence a total adequacy of reading is impossible and it would be wiser to work for a 'relative' adequacy. Such a relative adequacy, then, we could define as being achieved **when a text is read through perspectives which seem appropriate to its generic and stylistic identity**, and when the reader aims at responding critically to the text as far as possible without claiming to have exhausted the text. [Emphasis added.][14]

Here is a program that could last a lifetime, but is it enough? I have long been convinced that we can never understand the intrinsic dynamism of Benedict's *Rule* if we study only the antecedent tradition. What Benedict wrote is important not only for the ideas and issues that he consciously and directly addressed. It serves a function in the transmission of life that continued long after he laid down his quill. The full implications of the *Rule* become visible only in subsequent history. In any tradition there are certain latencies which manifest themselves when conditions are ripe. Involvement with education or pastoral care, a more self-conscious pursuit of contemplation, giving evangelical witness in an unjust society, even martyrdom: these are not universal facets of Benedictine life explicitly propounded by St Benedict. In certain circumstances, however, good zeal expressed in inculturated fidelity means that these also are to be numbered among the tools of good work.

From the typically Cistercian field of animal husbandry, I would like to introduce into the discussion the notion of **hybrid vigor** or heterosis. This is the explosion of energy that results from the mating of unrelated parents expressed in a growth-rate improved by up to 25%, thrift, fertility and resistance to disease. Within the unity of the species the more distant the parents, the greater the hybrid vigor. Pure-bred cattle, on the other hand, are not necessarily the best in many situations; they can be precious, highly-strung and less adaptable.

It is, at least, arguable that the most vigorous expressions of the Benedictine charism have been those in which the historical tradition stemming from Benedict's *Rule* has suppressed its tendency to inbreeding and has interacted creatively with the situation in which it finds itself. The search for an authentic embodiment of the Benedictine spirit cannot, therefore, be equated with a "neo-primitivism" which aims at re-creating the cultural ambiance of sixth-century Italy. Such a project makes good television, but it is not what monastic life is about. The most exciting expressions of Benedictinism have all been accused of playing with the dangerous fire of innovation. Benedict would, no doubt, have been astonished at Charlemagne's Synod of Aachen and the measures associated with Benedict of Aniane. The Cistercians and other reformist orders in the twelfth century tapped into contemporary veins of vitality to produce a form of monasticism unknown and even foreign to the historical Benedict, but attractive to their own contemporaries and fruitful for the Church, as later did the Trappists and the Maurists. The same could be said about many of the nineteenth-century monastic adventures and the interaction of monastic philosophy and observance with non-European cultures. And surely, none of us believes that monasticism can flourish in the twenty-first century in any other way than by combining attention to the signs of the times with fidelity to our ancient and more-than-honorable tradition. Yes, there is a certain allure about selective anachronism but it is ultimately self-indulgent. The past cannot be reconstructed, even if we eschew refrigeration and modern plumbing. Our collective consciousness has been irreversibly changed. Our concepts and sensibilities have been refined. The Goths no longer threaten and the Internet is here to stay. It seems to me that our vow of stability obliges us to make the effort to become not only lovers of our place, but also lovers of our times. Living in the present is always a more "Benedictine" goal than dissipating our energies in maundering about an idealized past.

As the Benedictine ideal was embodied in different situations, it evolved to meet the challenge of conditions beyond the purview of St Benedict. Church, society and consciousness have changed—for the tradition of the Rule to have a role in successive generations, it also must undergo some level of transformation. What was implicit was forced by circumstances to become explicit; what was contained only in germ needed a fuller development.

To my mind historical Benedictinism is fundamentally a *conversatio*: a complex of key values and observances, interpreted by reference to the *Rule*. It belongs to the sphere of *praxis*. Between the sixth and the eleventh centuries, progressively a period of dominant Benedictinism, there is comparatively little written about Benedictine philosophy, or about the experience of living according to the *Rule*. Commentaries on the *Rule* were written. There was legislation and attempts at standardization. Customaries were composed describing and prescribing what was done, but the inner face of observance was relatively neglected. It was only in the twelfth century, when an interest in personal experience began to develop, that more attention was paid to the interiority of monastic life.

Twelfth-century Europe witnessed the emergence of a new and irreversible level of self-awareness, termed variously "the discovery of the individual,"[15] "the discovery of the self,"[16] or "consciousness of self."[17] There is a new emphasis on subjective experience—it was recognized that there is significance not only in objective reality, but also in its reception or perception by individuals.[18] This new trend is exemplified in many treatises written according to the literary genre of the mirror (*speculum*), and in the increasing emphasis on self-examination.[19] This person-centered emphasis, already somewhat evident in the works of Evagrius and John Cassian, was enthusiastically embraced by later monastic theology. Medieval monastic thinkers were more concerned with the recipient and the reception of grace, than with its abstract definition. Not only do these masters seek to provide pastoral assistance by enunciating the essence of *conversatio* and its concrete demand, they also demonstrate a facility in discussing how a monk or nun **feels** in passing through the various stages of monastic growth and/or regression. Many monastic teachers wrote treatises of pastoral anthropology with a view to exploring and explaining the complex componentry of human behavior. This preoccupation often gives to many of the writings of the twelfth century a semblance of modernity absent in more antique sources, without loss of the sense of otherness due to their provenance in a century distant from our own. This sense of immediacy is less evident in the writings of the thirteenth-century mystics, partly because the experiences they describe are more uncommon and partly because even they were not untouched by contemporary preoccupations more commonly associated with Scholasticism. Later the window closed altogether as rampant Aristotelianism conquered the western world and theology attempted to become an objective science.

Writing from a Cistercian perspective, it is almost impossible for me not to view the monastic tradition of the West through the prism of twelfth-century Cistercianism. My study of Cassian and the *Rule of the*

Master certainly helps me to understand Benedict's chapter "On Humility" but I am, perhaps, more influenced in my interpretation by Bernard's thoughts about humility as truth and his practical examples of what happens when humility is deficient. The contextualisation of monastic practice in a theological anthropology seems to me a vast enrichment. Likewise, the addition of an explicitly mystical layer to monastic *conversatio* seems to fill a gap and to provide the sort of approach for which many of our contemporaries are grateful. For me the great achievement of the early Cistercian giants was to develop a coherent and self-aware spirituality derived from the monastic way of life and inseparable from it. It offers a theology and practice that supports and guides fidelity to a Benedictine vocation. Cistercianism is not a sect apart from Benedictinism. This is why Cistercian works were so freely copied and circulated in the monasteries of the Black Monks, and why an author like Peter of Celle speaks with a voice almost indistinguishable from the prevailing literary torrent that emanated from Cîteaux. It also explains why it has been recently queried whether there is such a thing as "Cistercian Spirituality"—since, it is clear that there was a certain porosity in the defining Cistercian boundaries, and even inside them a large degree of variation existed.[20]

In the process of trying to understand the *res monastica* or the *res benedictina*, it seems valid to me to be open to the teaching of masters such as Bernard of Clairvaux, Aelred of Rievaulx, Guerric of Igny, Isaac of Stella and Beatrice of Nazareth. The fact that they have progressed far beyond the limits of the "small rule for beginners" signifies little, since they all lived and wrote in the context of fidelity to the ongoing tradition of which the *Rule* is part.

The same is true (though perhaps less dramatically) of writers of other centuries and of our own generation. Gregory the Great has much more to offer Benedictine spirituality than the second book of the *Dialogues*. Their specific cultural standpoints sometimes give them access to aspects of the monastic patrimony not found in the *Rule* itself, and also somewhat invisible to us. Being snobbish about relying only on the *Rule* itself, is not unlike a species of fundamentalism in that it leads to a concentration on a single, manageable text instead of confronting the wild confusion of a long-lasting and unwieldy tradition of which the *Rule* itself is simply one privileged expression.

5. Fusion of Horizons

Of King Henry VIII's theology, Diarmaid MacCulloch has remarked recently that it was "like a jackdaw's nest." I fear, alas, that the same can be said of those of random reading habits: without training or grounding in any discipline, they seek to "pillage the Egyptians." In attempting to produce a result that may dazzle the simple-minded, they allege an array of brilliant references that is marvelously decorative, but adds nothing to any deeper understanding of their own tradition, and builds no bridges towards dialogue beyond it. The tragedy is that it can be easy to get away with such superficial erudition in a monastery where, it may be hazarded, nobody knows any better. Even Thomas Merton was not immune from such slick antics. For instance, I am sure that no reader ever dared to question the data on which he based his assertion that there was in Philoxenus of Mabbug "a striking affinity with the epistemological bases of Zen Buddhism,"[21] or that certain verses in the *Bhagavad-Gita* "can easily be harmonized with St Augustine, due allowance being made for divergences in ontological theory."[22] There is no doubt that Merton was better-qualified than most to indulge in inter-disciplinary displays. But do they serve any useful purpose unless a reader can match his expertise?

There is something to be said for restricting oneself to a palette of authorities and not wandering too widely or wildly afield, especially in the beginning. If we understand one tradition in its integrity then, gradually, we become qualified to go beyond it, and to point tentatively to "echoes" in other traditions. The acceptance of a literary "canon" and its embodiment in a social organization results in the constitution of a "textual community" that, in turn, allows the development of a specific vocabulary which empowers the members of the monastic group to find meaning in their experiences and to transmit it to others.[23]

Having said this it is important to note that the hermeneutic by which we move into a tradition involves a double reverence: for the texts which embody the tradition and for the beliefs and values that constitute our own implicit philosophy of life. "Every conversation presupposes a common language or it creates a common language."[24] The act of interpretation is not the mute transmission of a fixed body of material from one location to another. Genuine communication is always conscious of the gulf it has to span; some translation is always necessary. Therefore there is scope for creative approximation. We have to take risks.

Tradition is not an object that can be examined with professional disinterestedness and eventually mastered. Hermeneutics is more than mere exegesis. As monks or nuns we are part of monastic tradition; the process of understanding monastic texts necessarily involves also an advance in self-understanding. We approach the text, not objectively, but full of implicit prejudgments. We think we know what a "scapular" is, or how much is a *hemina* of wine. We think we know what the text is about to say and so we dispense ourselves from really listening. We need to be aware of how our own perspective shapes our perception.

"Every assimilation of tradition is historically different ... This means that assimilation is no mere repetition of the text that has been handed down, but is a new creation of understanding."[25] This means that no final or definitive interpretation is possible, but only an interpretation for the situation in which the text is read—in other words, an application. We understand the Sermon on the Mount by living it; we can understand the words easily enough, but without experience the reality behind the words is absurd. The *Rule of Benedict* yields its full meaning only to those who lovingly keep it.[26]

The interpretation is for the moment. Tradition continues to flow onwards. Like a river it carries with it something of all the places it has been. The family access that monks and nuns enjoy with regard to monastic tradition can never be an excuse for a lack of diligence in constantly re-reading the patrimonial texts in the light of changing events. Surely it is a common experience that the Rule we heard read as novices is no longer the same that we hear as older, and presumably wiser, persons. As our experience grows so our interpretation is deepened and enriched.

It is important, especially for those who enter a monastery in mature years, that they are able to bring their adult experience to bear on the understanding of the texts they read. Education is a matter of educing answers they already have, drawing forth wisdom and knowledge from latency into consciousness. All that the Spirit has accomplished in them since Baptism can and should be harnessed to drive their monastic vocation further. To treat a monastic neophyte as a *tabula rasa*, and to think only of pouring in knowledge from the outside is a significant failure in respect for a person's particular salvation history, and, because of that, a sure means of educational calamity.

Monastic instructors must face the question of **how** the resources of their students can be fully engaged in the process of their education. This means initiating lines of discussion that are absent from an academic treatment of the same material.

Feelings: Sometimes it can be helpful to invite not only intellectual responses to a text, but also to make the transition to a more experiential level. Monastic texts, in general, belong more to the sphere of rhetoric than dialectic. There is usually an element of advocacy about them. Because the most ordinary channel of persuasion passes through the emotions, these texts will achieve their desired results only if readers feel moved by their arguments, so moved that they will want to translate what they read into some degree of behavioral change. The usual progression is from text to feeling to behavior. To read the texts in the spirit in which they were written involves paying attention to what happens at an emotional level and not to restrict reflection to its rational content.

Selection of Texts is, as always, of key importance. Experiential writing is more immediate than theological speculation or juridical prescription. The ability to choose texts of some relevance to those participating in a course presupposes both a wide acquaintance with the patrimonial literature and a sensitivity to what it is like to be at the beginning of a monastic life.

Magic: Good magicians don't confine themselves to producing eggs out of their own ears — the trick works much better when the eggs are discovered in the otic apertures of a member of the audience. In the same way the best way to demonstrate, for instance, that St Benedict's presentation of humility is wise and reasonable, is to show that it agrees with what the participants already believe. This can be done, as St Bernard does, by asking them to think about the opposite of humility.[27] The best way to do this is by stories or parables.[28] In modern parlance, we can call these "case studies." By prescribing remedies for the problems of a fictional monk, many are led to formulate, in different words, suggestions that approximate some of the things Benedict recommends. In this way some of the alienation caused by cultural and linguistic differences is eased, and it becomes possible to have a good discussion not only of the points of agreement but, more especially, of instances of divergence.

Difficulties need not be swept under the carpet. In fact, dealing with obscurities in the text, unacceptable presuppositions underlying the text or any other contentious issues is often a speedy way to greater understanding. A tradition that liberates cannot be merely an echo of our own cherished prejudices. It must contain elements of challenge.[29] "Questions always bring out the undetermined possibilities of a thing."[30] Nor should a harmonious resolution be anticipated within a day or a week. The process of exposing participants to a credible alternative viewpoint involves the sowing of a seed that will germinate only when conditions are right.

The aim of every initiation into the literature of monastic tradition is to achieve a progressive fusion of perceptual horizons, so that newcomers begin to perceive and evaluate things in a context compatible with our monastic past, true to their own experience and convergent with the vision of others. This result means a liberation from rampant individualism towards greater communion with the past and a deeper solidarity with the present. In theological terms it can be seen as ongoing conversion at the level of seeing, perceiving and evaluating.

There is no such thing as an "objective" meaning of a text. To ascertain this, we have only to contemplate the plurality of meanings proposed for any particular text. The subjective is always an essential element in the interpretative act; but we need to be conscious of its influence, so that true dialogue ensues and the reading of ancient texts becomes more than antiquarian amusement —it transforms itself into a exercise in self-knowledge.

Communicating the charism inherent in monastic tradition demands more than an expertise in historical and literary questions. Nobody should try to initiate others into the patrimony who does not have a good measure of self-awareness, a broad experience and a knowledge of psychology. Training in speculative theology or engineering is probably a recipe for disaster. Having said this we have to admit that we live in an imperfect world, and more often than not these theoretical criteria will be unmet. At least, let us be aware of what is desirable, how to maximize the meager resources we have and, perhaps, how to share among many the limited resources and expertise that are available.

6. Pathways

The sheer volume of monastic authors means that more than a lifetime is required to build solid friendships with all of them. As readers, we will certainly have favorites to which we constantly return, but as initiators into a tradition we need to expose those in our care to as broad a spectrum of writing as possible. In this way they may be helped to make their own choices. Time needs to be spent on many major authors, nonchalantly flinging open the door of each treasury, indicating something of the richness within and then passing on to the next. This process involves exposing the juniors to a representative sampling of texts that is both attractive and accessible. It may seem easy, but it requires many hours and much love to put together a mini-anthology that grips.[31]

A practical means of displaying what is available in monastic tradition is to find a pathway through the forest of possibilities that makes possible a representative sampling of what is available. Individual instructors will probably develop their own methods, but here are a few ways that I have found useful.

Selected Texts: A good way of introducing a particular author is to develop a collection of texts that are likely to speak to the students with a certain immediacy. These can be of different lengths and densities and touch on a variety of topics. Thus to present John Cassian, a small booklet could be prepared with texts on prayer, the vices, the monastic goal, renunciation, friendship. The goal of such exposure, is that a neophyte gets something conducive to understanding present experience, and becomes disposed to categorize Cassian as a likely source of worthwhile monastic reading for the future. Another example. Instead of attempting to read all 54 of Guerric's *Liturgical Sermons*, it is possible to take one from each of the major solemnities and offer an exposure to a mere dozen—leaving the rest for the students' enjoyment in the course of a lifetime.

Tracing a theme as it evolves through the centuries is another way of encountering the vast cloud of monastic witnesses as they speak of inner experience in a manner that still remains vibrant. Again it is the contact with the patrimonial texts that matters. This allows the ancients to speak in their own voice—as far as translation permits—instead of compressing many different approaches into a single distillation, which may sound to the students little different from the teacher's own voice.

Close Reading of a Dense Text: Cassian's ninth *Conference* (on Prayer), Bernard's 74th Sermon *On the Song of Songs*, the third part of Aelred's treatise *On the Twelve-Year-Old Jesus*, or some sections of William of St Thierry's *Golden Epistle* can be taken usefully as a key text around which the wide world of monastic wisdom can be assembled. This can offer opportunities for initiation into the spiritual vocabulary of western monasticism, the complementary approaches to fundamental observances, and the value-system undergirding the whole enterprise. In this way a text becomes the gateway to the whole tradition. Of course, the text to be studied needs to be carefully chosen and very well prepared.

In all these strategies a certain amount of photocopying is necessary and since the purpose of the exercise is to lead people into having recourse to the complete volumes, such copying may be regarded reasonably as coming under the category of permissible "fair dealing."

7. Seduction

If Karl Rahner is correct, the future of religious life will depend on its owning more emphatically its **mystical** dimension. This is a word that terrifies many, since they associate it with an interest in certain paranormal manifestations of spirituality that they regard as being either pathological or fraudulent. If we regard mystical experience simply as the experience of the Mystery inherent in our being created to God's image, in our pre-elective yearning for God, in our adoption as God's children through Baptism and in the grace of prayer, then mysticism would seem normal for the Christian and an essential component of the monastic vocation.

There is still some relevance in Friedrich Schleiermacher's 1799 views that organized religion is wrong to emphasize morality and metaphysics at the expense of feeling connected to God.[32] We could easily apply his critique to monasticism. It is not enough for a monk or nun to have orthodox views on theology and to embrace monastic standards of behavior. They must **feel** something or eventually, when an opening presents itself, they will leave. More is demanded. They must be able consciously to review their experiences and, according to a traditional image, assay how much gold is present and how much dross. Access to a spiritual tradition enables us more communicatively to describe what we are feeling and to sense solidarity with the innumerable monks and nuns who have walked the same path before us.

There are certain key events in any monastic life that cannot be explained without reference to an interior horizon: conversion, vocation, crisis and its resolution, growth, perseverance. Nobody ends up in a monastery by accident and almost nobody stays for want of more attractive alternatives. Especially today, joining a monastery is a massively disjunctive action that demands much of mind and will. It does not happen without some interior revolution, even though the level of drama differs from person to person. Bernard reminded his monks of this:

> It is clear that each one of you has knowledge of God. If anyone says, "I know him not," he is a liar like the seculars. For if you have no knowledge of him, who is it that led you here? How else could you have been persuaded to renounce of your own free will the affection of your friends, the pleasures of the body and the vanities of the world? How else could you have been led to cast all your thoughts on the Lord and to make over to him all your concerns since, as your own consciences testify, you merited nothing good but only punishment? I repeat, who could have persuaded you all this unless you know that the Lord is good to all who hope in him, to the heart that seeks him, unless you had recognized for yourself that the Lord is gentle, kind and full of mercy and faithfulness? How else could you know these things unless the Lord had come not only to you but into you?[33]

Many of the terms used in describing what we **sometimes** experience in our monastic journey are familiar to us, but we do not think of the realities they denote as "mystical." Perhaps it would be better to speak of "meta-experience" in the sense that in each case there is discontinuity with ordinary sense-based, thought-driven experience. It is a matter of transcending the limits imposed by spatio-temporal existence and being touched by the invisible, intangible reality of the spiritual world. The test of genuineness is not the experience itself but its effects. An experience is likely to be genuine if it gives us a sense of being nourished spiritually, if it helps us to bear darkness and pain, if it energizes us to more evangelical living, if it changes our perceptual horizons in a way that leads to conversion.

I have discussed elsewhere some of the traditional terms that are used to describe the variety of monastic experience: compunction, desire, seeking, alternation, visitation, conformity of will, ecstasy.[34] I tried to demonstrate that in each case a new and unexplainable element is introduced into consciousness that begins a process of transformation. There is nothing here that is divorced from the ordinary heroism of daily fidelity: our efforts to pray, to be chaste and charitable, to forget self and be obedient. These are the outer contributors to an interior state that transcends our control.

Monastic mysticism is the hidden face of an external observance. The monk or nun does not jump through the hoops of a rigorous regimen simply as a perfor-mance. What matters is what is going on inside. The goal of all outward observance, as Cassian reminds us, is that inner simplicity that allows us to live lives that are connected to God. The modes of connection are legion; they vary from person to person and within the unity of a person's life, from season to season. We came to the monastery not only to seek God, but also to find God. And most of us do, even though we cannot control the relationship nor find words adequately to describe it.

The ancient masters of prayer provide us with concepts to grasp what we experience in a zone of our being which is beyond concepts; they give us a vocabulary that enables us to reflect on our experience. It is not a scientific language that constrains and confines within boundaries, but a poetic, intuitive language that maintains reverence of the mystery. For the most part it is the language of the Bible, interpreted somewhat allegorically.[35]

Most of us inhabit a culture which does not encourage us to refer to interior states in our ordinary conversation. Even in more privileged situations, we find ourselves stumbling for words, dissatisfied with our clumsy efforts to describe the mysterious and perhaps feeling a little guilty for betraying the secrets of intimacy. The biblical mysticism of the monastic authors enables us to overcome these restrictions and thus more able to give and receive life-giving counsel.

Ultimately when men and women join a monastic community "to seek God" it is in the hope of finding God. It is important that we humbly display before them how richly this aspiration is contained in the monastic texts, how we can find in them guidance, encouragement and inspiration that enable us to endure and profit from the hard and difficult things that we will certainly meet as we journey towards God. To those who knock on our door we can say, "Here is a tradition that, under grace and with time, will help you to realize the dreams that God has sown in your hearts." If that does not sell our product, I don't know what will.

NOTES

[1] Chicago: Fitzroy Dearborn, 2000.

[2] Thus S. Giora Shoham, *Society and the Absurd* (Oxford: Blackwell, 1974). In his first chapter, Shoham defines acedia as an individual's state of mind that progressively becomes more disconnected from personal identity and detached from social structures. The most evident sign of this is lack of commitment.

[3] M. Casey, "The Dynamic Unfolding of the Benedictine Charism," *ABR* 51.2 (June 2000), pp. 149-167, especially pp. 153-157.

[4] In arguing thus the controversial film-maker John Pilger quotes Edward Said: "The threat to independence

in the late twentieth century could be greater than was colonialism itself.... The new media have the power to penetrate more deeply into a receiving culture than any previous manifestation of Western technology." *Hidden Agendas* (London: Vintage, 1998), p. 9.

⁵ Thus writes Allan Bloom, in *The Closing of the American Mind: How Higher Education has Failed Democracy and Impoverished the Souls of Today's Students* (New York: Simon and Schuster, 1987), p. 64.

⁶ As the future British Prime Minister, Harold Macmillan did during the First World War. Harold Macmillan, *Winds of Change* (London: Macmillan, 1966), p. 88.

⁷ The prerequisite of a life characterized by good reading is well described by Diane Ravitch as *a genuinely functioning intelligence with a sufficient stock of information to provide a person with materials for reflection and enjoyment.* See Alan Ryan, "Schools: The Price of Progress" (A review of Diane Ravitch's *Left Back: A Century of Failed School Reform*), in *The New York Review of Books*, February 22, 2001, p. 21.

⁸ On this subtle and more intuitive level of communication see Deborah Tannen, *You Just Don't Understand: Men and Women in Conversation* (New York: Ballantyne Books, 1990), p. 32.

⁹ I reflected on St Benedict's idea of sequential and integral reading in *The Art of Sacred Reading* (Melbourne: HarperCollins, 1995), pp. 3-15.

¹⁰ Allan Bloom, "The Study of Texts" in *Giants and Dwarfs: Essays 1960-1990* (New York: Simon and Schuster, 1990), pp. 306-307.

¹¹ Adriaan Bredero, *Bernard of Clairvaux: Between Cult and History* (Edinburgh: T. & T. Clark, 1996); Constance Hoffman Berman, *The Cistercian Evolution:*

The Invention of a Religious Order in Twelfth-Century Europe (Philadelphia: University of Pennsylvania Press, 2000). On the latter see Chrysogonus Waddell, "The Myth of Cistercian Origins: C.H. Berman and the Manuscript Sources," *Cîteaux* 51 (2000), pp. 299-386.

[12] "If we want a community of truth in the classroom, a community that can keep us honest, we must put a *third thing*, a great thing at the center of the pedagogical circle.... True community in any context requires a transcendent third thing that holds both me and thee accountable beyond ourselves.... The subject-centered classroom is characterized by the fact that the third thing has a presence so real, so vivid, so vocal that it can hold teacher and students alike accountable for what they say and do. In such a classroom there are no inert facts. The great thing is so alive that teacher can turn to student or student to teacher, and either can make a claim on the other in the name of the great thing. Students have direct unmediated access to the subject, and they can use their knowledge to challenge my claims...the teacher's central task is to give the great thing an independent voice—a capacity to speak its truth quite apart from the teacher's voice in terms that students can hear and understand." Parker J. Palmer, *The Courage to Teach: Exploring the Inner Landscape of a Teacher's Life* (San Francisco: Jossey-Bass, 1998), pp. 116-118. See also Carney Strange and Harry Hagan OSB, "Reading the Signs of the Times: A Benedictine Pedagogy for Creating Community in Higher Education" in *Reading the Signs of the Times: The Good News of Monastic Life* (The Proceedings of the American Benedictine Academy Convention, August 10-13, 2000), pp. 47-60.

[13] Douglas Burton-Christie, *The Word in the Desert: Scripture and the Quest for Holiness in Early Christian Monasticism* (New York: Oxford University Press, 1993), pp. 16-17.

[14] Werner G. Jeanrond: *Theological Hermeneutics: Development and Significance* (New York: Crossroad, 1991), p.117.

[15] Colin Morris, *The Discovery of the Individual: 1050-1200* (Toronto: University Press, reprinted 1987).

[16] Caroline Walker Bynum, "Did the Twelfth Century Discover the Individual?" in *Jesus as Mother: Studies in the Spirituality of the High Middle Ages* (Berkeley: University of California Press, 1982), pp. 82-109.

[17] John F. Benton, "Consciousness of Self and Perceptions of Individuality," in Robert L. Benson and others [ed.], *Renaissance and Renewal in the Twelfth Century* (Toronto: University Press, reprinted 1991), pp. 263-295.

[18] On the importance of *experientia* in the writings of Bernard of Clairvaux, see Ulrich Köpf, *Religiöse Erfahrung in der Theologie Bernhards von Clairvaux* (Beiträge zur historischen Theologie, 61; Tübingen: J.C.B. Mohr, 1980), and more briefly, "Die Rolle der Erfahrung im religiösen Leben nach dem hl. Bernhard," *ASOC* 46 (1990), pp. 307-325.

[19] See Margot Schmidt, art. "Miroir" in *DSp* 10.2 (1979), col. 1291-1295, where important distinctions are made. The purpose of the mirror was, according to the *Speculum ecclesiae* of Honorius of Autun, so that the Church "might see what in her displeases her spouse, and that she might thus arrange her acts and behavior in his image" (col. 1293).

[20] David N. Bell, "Is there Such a Thing as 'Cistercian Spirituality'?" *CSQ* 33.4 (1998), pp. 455-471.

[21] Thomas Merton, "Inner Experience: Some Notes on Contemplation," *CSQ* 18 (1983), p. 122.

[22] "Inner Experience," *CSQ* 18 (1983), p. 132.

[23] See Brian Stock, *Listening to the Text: On the Uses of the Past* (Philadelphia: University of Pennsylvania Press, 1990), pp. 140-158. Also, *The Implications of Literacy: Written Language and Models of Interpretation in the Eleventh and Twelfth Centuries* (Princeton: University Press, 1983). The middle section of the book (pp. 88-240) deals with textual communities. Later (p. 405) Stock writes, "As Bernard of Clairvaux's sermons were circulated throughout the expanding Cistercian Order, they not only provided the century's outstanding example of a 'textual community'. They also brought them together in one group of writings and gave a stylistic imprint to feelings, perceptions, and practical ideas that were the antithesis of the scholastic, informational or objectifying approach.

[24] Hans-Georg Gadamer, *Truth and Method* (London: Sheed and Ward; 2nd edition 1979), p.341.

[25] Gadamer, *Truth and Method*, p. 430.

[26] See "Orthopraxy and Interpretation: Reflections on Regula Benedicti 73,1," in *RBS* 14/15 (1985/86), pp. 165-171.

[27] For example, in *The Steps of Humility and Pride*, *SBO* vol. 3.

[28] The parables of St Bernard in *SBO* vol. 6b, outline the stages of monastic progress by telling, in terms familiar to those being addressed, of the adventures and vicissitudes of a young knight. The same dynamic can be found in St Anselm's *Similitudes* (*PL* 159) and in the *Parables* of Galand of Reigny (*SChr* 378).

[29] "Every encounter with tradition that takes place within historical consciousness involves the experience of the tension between the text and the present. The hermeneutic task consists in not covering up this tension by attempting a naive assimilation, but consciously bringing it out." Gadamer, *Truth and Method*, p. 273.

[30] Gadamer, *Truth and Method*, p. 338.

[31] Sometimes a published anthology is suitable for introducing a particular part of the tradition; for example, Pauline Matarasso, *The Cistercian World: Monastic Writings of the Twelfth Century* (Harmondsworth: Penguin, 1993).

[32] "Wherefore, my friends, belief must be something different from a mixture of opinions about God and the world, and of precepts for one life or two. Piety cannot be an instinct craving for a mess of metaphysical and ethical crumbs..." Friedrich Schleiermacher, *On Religion: Speeches to its Cultured Despisers*, translated by John Oman (New York: Harper and Row, 1958); Second Speech, p. 31.

[33] Bernard, *Adv* 3.3; *SBO* 4.177.6-16.

[34] "Mystical Experiences: The Cistercian Tradition," *TJ* 52 (May 1997), pp. 64-87.

[35] The prospective advocate of monastic tradition will have to explain and ease many difficulties encountered by those unused to ancient modes of thinking and writing. One of the more frequent impediments to be encountered is the seemingly cavalier manner in which the Church Fathers interpreted biblical texts. This means sympathetically exposing the rationale behind the so-called "senses of Scripture." Henri de Lubac's classic is now appearing in English under the title *Medieval Exegesis: Volume I: The Four Senses of Scripture* (Grand Rapids, Eerdmans, 1998).

THE RULE OF BENEDICT AND INCULTURATION: A FORMATION PERSPECTIVE

This article is an expanded version of a conference given in 2001 at the formation week organized by the Benedictine Union of Australia and New Zealand. The point of the article is to illustrate the idea that there is a special difficulty in formation when cultural diversity has not been addressed. It was published in Tjurunga 62 (2002).

The secret of survival is adaptability. Human history is such a complex interweaving of diverse and self-interested forces that no institution can last long if it does not have the capacity to harness external momentum to serve its own purposes. Without the knack of being able to absorb and socialize outside influences, the organization will become like a declining empire, weakened to the point of exhaustion by repeated barbarian incursions and uncreative inner conflicts: unable to restore its vigor.

The Church has demonstrated a remarkable aptitude for self-reinvention in different cultures, earning stern reproofs from purists for its baptism of elements from antecedent paganism. Yet it has been the hybridization of Christianity that has facilitated its growth, not only in terms of geography but, more importantly, in uncovering and proclaiming the latent content of the unbounded Mystery contained within it.

Benedictine monasticism has survived creatively for nearly 1500 years. The reason for this is that it contains within itself a capacity for ongoing re-definition in the context of a changing world.[1] Far from being a *tableau vivant* of ancient or medieval history, monastic life, of its nature, needs to be constantly re-attuned to the signs of the times. We can see this clearly by a glance at history; those Benedictine groups have been most successful in transmitting their ancient charism to their contemporaries who were themselves profoundly "modern."[2]

1. Inculturation

"Inculturation" is an ecclesiastical neologism dating from the early 1970s and rejected in standard spell checks. Applying this ecclesial term to monasticism takes the word a step further. Within the context of an inculturated Church, monasteries take up the challenge of entering into substantial dialogue with local culture in the creation of a new monastic sub-culture that is both faithful to its sources and responsive to the signs of the times and places in which it evolves. Before we can assess the compatibility of Benedict's Rule with the challenges facing an inculturated Church, perhaps some clarification of terminology would be helpful.[3]

a) Enculturation is the process by which persons are socialized into the group to which they belong; the group accepts them and then initiates them into its social and cultural heritage.

Individual   Group/Culture

b) Acculturation is the dynamic process by which a person comes under the influence of another culture, for example in the meeting of cultures through trade or travel or in the westernizing impact on traditional societies in a colonial or post-colonial situation. The process may be more or less bilateral.

Individual with Culture A   Group with Culture B
or
Individual with Culture B   Group with Culture A

c) Inculturation is a theological term used to designate the insertion of Christian faith into a particular pre-existing culture and the consequent unique interaction between the word of God and this culture.[4] Implied in this term is a certain mutuality and not merely adaptation to local conditions. Local culture is respected to the extent that it begins to have an influence on the Church as a whole.[5]

Evangelization, Culture and Universal Church, Local Church

A recent Vatican document, *The Church in Oceania* gives a clear description of inculturation.

> The process of inculturation is the gradual way in which the Gospel is incarnated in the various cultures. On the one hand, certain cultural values must be transformed and purified, if they are to find a place in a genuinely Christian culture. On the other hand, in various cultures Christian values readily take root. Inculturation is born out of respect for both the Gospel and the culture in which it is proclaimed and welcomed.[6]

To these basic terms we can add another: **multiculturalism**. This describes the situation of a community in which several cultures coexist, usually with one culture dominant. In terms of recent history, *one* of the signs of a calling to make a foundation in a young church is the presence of recruits from that region coming to join an established monastery.[7]

Monasteries are not self-generated; they radiate from originating houses. Progressively, new communities are located in regions and cultures far distant from where the movement began. Those who carry the charism to faraway places arrive with an already inculturated form of monasticism—remodeled to suit the place from which they came and not necessarily attuned to the needs and opportunities of their new location. This is obvious in terms of furniture and artifacts brought from the "mother-house." When it comes to customs, local newcomers are often confused about what is "monastic" and what is merely "foreign." Even more subtle are the unspoken expectations regarding modes of relationship, the boundaries of personal space, communication, and such everyday aspects of personal behavior as modesty, hygiene and table manners.[8] This is especially true in communities who view themselves as relaxed and informal; in such groups there are often invisible frontiers, the crossing of which results in silent reproofs.

Such cultural baggage is inevitable. Monasticism is transmitted only in a pre-inculturated configuration. Since that is the only form in which founders have known it, it cannot easily be shed. The concrete network of values, beliefs and behaviors is not a garment to be left aside without regret. In the history of each person, this particular *conversatio* has been the living skin of their monastic experience, the matrix according to which their search for God has been shaped.[9]

No matter how self-sacrificing the founders attempt to be, they cannot generate an inculturated lifestyle. In any case, as the novelty wears off and, especially, as they grow older, there is a strong tendency to revert to their own original culture. All that they can do is to empower those who come to them to recognize and own their particular culture, to submit it to monastic discernment and, in time, allow it to influence the *conversatio* more amply. When we say "culture" in this context we are speaking of the totality comprised of common beliefs and values, corporate memories, solidarities, customs, modes of communicating and relating. It is more than a matter of food, clothes and household *decor*. Many of the most significant elements of the local culture will not be immediately evident, even to those who have been formed by it. More often than not it is by foreign travel or by living with people of other cultures that we discover our own.

There is, in any situation of foundation, an initial period of transition during which those formed in a foreign culture have control of the common lifestyle and, thereby, of the degree of inculturation. It is important that the movement towards inculturation be actively supported by all members of the community and that it not be politicized. Benedictine moderation favors a rate of inculturation that is not so fast that the monastic values embedded in a foreign culture are missed, and not so slow that the monastery becomes an outpost of quaint foreign ways — to the delight of tourists and the chagrin of the younger generation.

2. Benedict's Intrinsic Adaptability

Despite its literary genre as a rule, *RB* is remarkable for its flexibility throughout the ages. Sometimes this has led to tepidity and decline, but more often than not a reforming impulse has rectified the deviation and a newer vision of Benedictine life has resulted. Part of the reason for this adaptability is that Benedict's Rule does not attempt to legislate by defining boundaries and having them enforced. It operates rather at the level of beliefs and values. The functioning of authority in a Benedictine monastery is different from military hierarchy. Instead of just giving commands and demanding compliance, the abbot and the monastic officials are expected to teach, to communicate values, to establish a climate of meaning.[10] In fact Benedict establishes three levels of intervention: to teach, to establish as policy, to give instructions or orders: *aut docere aut constituere aut iubere* (2,4). In like manner, the Rule is concerned principally with imparting a monastic philosophy of life together with indications about how this might be embodied in a lifestyle. As the title of Chapter 73 indicates, not all right living is to be found within it. It is a guidance system rather than detailed legislation.[11]

In pursuance of his policy of listening, Benedict wanted the community to be open to conscientious reframing and not locked into a self-perpetuating system that was designed for different conditions. Thus God is considered to speak *often* through the younger, less socialized members of the community, (3,3), visiting monks may arrive as the Lord's emissaries (61,4), and bishops and lay people may have a better view of what sort of abbot the monastery needs than the monks themselves (64,4-6). Once the basic principles are accepted, there is a flexibility about food (39,6-7) and drink (40,5-6), work (48,7-9), liturgy(18,22-23) and even the administration of the monastery itself (65,12-15). The most explicit example of Benedict's flexibility can be seen in his regulations regarding clothing.

Figure 1: RB 55.1-8

Clothing
is to be given to the brothers
according to **local circumstances**
and the **climate**...
what is **available**
in the province where they live,
and what **costs less**.
The abbot is to take care
that they are not too short
for the wearers
but **measured to fit.**

In Chapter 55 we see multiple adaptability: to fit the individual wearer, to suit the local climate, to reflect regional usage and to accord with the monastic value of poverty; concerning these values the abbot should be diligent. On the other hand, secure in the knowledge that their clothing will cover their *needs*, the monks are to accept that not all their *wants* will be gratified. The clothing may be coarser than they prefer and of the wrong color, but the monks are not to let their freedom from care be compromised by concern about this.

Benedict's openness is never at the cost of essential monastic values. He is always clear about this, as the texts noted above demonstrate. There is a certain flexibility so long as basic monastic requirements are not sidelined. Such fine-tuning permits the details of the monastic lifestyle to become invisible: they are not an issue. That way the monks can concentrate on the purpose for which they came to the monastery: to seek God. It would be far from Benedict's intention to use such tactical flexibility as a rationale for mindless ameliorism, constantly seeking to upgrade the monastic standard of living without any respect for the principles without which monastic life loses its character. It is to prevent this kind of laxism that reform movements generally advocate such means as regular visitation and provide for appropriate supervision through general chapters.

The Rule, as Benedict makes clear in his final chapter, is merely a compendium of monastic wisdom designed to form the incipient and presumably incipient newcomer in basic goodness and monasticity (63,1). The Rule is the mouthpiece of ancient monastic tradition and, under Benedict's system, is to be constantly updated by the abbot in accordance with the community's contemporary experience of the reality of monastic life. The interaction between a written text and ongoing experience may be represented as circle or spiral in which tradition and life interact to guarantee a fidelity that is not only in continuity with its sources, but also responsive to what the Spirit is saying to the churches (Prologue 11). This is represented schematically in Figure 2.

Figure 2: The Cycle of Tradition and Life

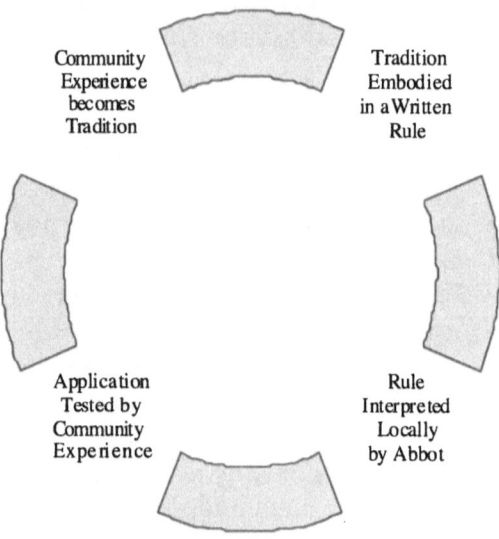

Community Experience becomes Tradition

Tradition Embodied in a Written Rule

Application Tested by Community Experience

Rule Interpreted Locally by Abbot

It is clear from this consideration that the Benedictine tradition is sympathetic to the call for inculturation and that it supports the enterprise of finding new channels by which the monastic charism can percolate through non-European cultures and new media by which the prophetic voices of the young churches can be heard summoning the ancient institution to continuing reformation and renewal.

An inculturated interpretation of the Rule of Benedict must desist from a fundamentalist reading of the tradition. This means a nuanced appreciation of the merely relative importance of some of Benedict's injunctions, even when they seemed very important to him. His extreme attitude to laughter, for example, does not need to be taken literally.[12] Benedict's proscription of the use of proper names (63,11) was his way of ensuring good relations in community. On a different continent in a different century, such usage may seem impersonal, institutional and excessively formal and thus an element in undermining good relations in a community. Another prescription where serious reservation is appropriate is his attitude to bathing (36,8): "Baths may be offered to the sick as often as it is appropriate. For the healthy, and especially for the young, baths should be allowed reluctantly." Fraternal charity dictates that some derogation be made from Benedict's hygienic legislation, especially in tropical countries. It is hard to see that Benedict himself would have been very upset by this.

The monastic prohibition of bathing is first documented among the Egyptian monks, where the extreme dryness of the desert heat was unfriendly to odor-causing bacteria and the scarcity of water made frequent bathing less feasible. The Roman bath was one of the principal means of distinguishing its citizens from the increasingly powerful barbarian hoard. It was a significant element in urban culture, characterized by fine architecture and developed manners. Maybe because "the Roman baths were public gathering places, more like our present shopping malls than later 'Turkish baths' and a strict decorum was expected there,"[13] Augustine had few problems with monks and nuns frequenting the public baths, despite the nudity and the crowds.[14] On top of Monte Cassino there were no public baths, so that was not a problem. Benedict gives no evidence of concern about the sort of homosexual activity that worried Pachomius,[15] so the only issues were the cost of providing baths, the pleasure they gave and the time they occupied.[16] There was a strong monastic tradition against bathing.[17] According to Kardong, Benedict of Aniane was opposed to it,[18] whereas Cluny made provision for bathing two to five times a year. The custom of bathing four times a year declined at Westminster Abbey after a "reform" in the late-twelfth or early-thirteenth century.[19] There is no evidence that the healthy Cistercian bathed at all. Mainly the bath came under the heading of health services. The plan of St Gall shows a bathroom with four tubs in the infirmary, next to the kitchen of the sick.[20]

In the light of this strong history of prohibition it is surprising that few contemporary Benedictines advert even to its existence. Common sense, social expectations and the modern plumbing have all contributed to making Benedict's position untenable and even unthinkable. None of us even has any scruple in going against such a clear injunction, because we sense that we are better judges of the contemporary situation in this matter than the long-dead author of the Rule. Referring back to Figure 2, we can describe the situation in the following terms. Benedict expressed the tradition in a way that was valid in his situation. Constituted authority has decided, on the basis of common experience, that in our situation conditions demand different behavior; this in turn becomes a new and revised tradition which shapes our expectations of how people are to act and may, someday, even be committed to writing.

3. Discontinuity with Folk-Cultures

Most newcomers to a monastery are surprised to find that many of their customary devotional values and exercises are not part of the community's official spirituality. They may be practiced covertly, as it were, by individuals or even small groups, but generally do not find public expression in the prayer life of the community.[21] This is no accident. Benedictine *conversatio* is designed for a lifetime. It is stripped down to accommodate itself to the imperatives of a long, hard, journey (58,8). In this way it is able to serve a community drawn from different backgrounds, with different levels of sensitivity and intelligence and at different stages in the spiritual life. The way of life provides a skeleton; each monk must fashion a fleshed body within its possibilities. It is precisely its relatively "pure" spirituality that makes Benedictine monasticism adaptable to many different cultures. The core of the spirituality that has emerged from living the *conversatio* described in the Rule may be characterized thus: an affective Christocentrism formed by participation in the liturgy and by assiduous *lectio divina* and expressed concretely in fraternal communion and integral monastic observance.

Figure 3. Core Elements of Benedictine Spirituality
>Liturgy
>Community
>Christocentrism
>Scripture
>Conversatio

It is important to notice that these core aspects of the Benedictine approach are almost always accompanied by other elements that vary from time to time, place to place, and person to person. It may be that sometimes these additional devotional additives drawn from popular religion have greater immediacy for persons and are more visible to observers. This is especially true at the beginning. What is important is that a symbiotic harmony is progressively achieved between what is common and what is particular. A personal devotional life, no matter how eccentric it may seem to others, can be the means of bringing to full flower what may otherwise seem to be an excessively bare Benedictinism. Especially in times of transition when a person may experience a fair amount of difficulty and temptation, there needs to be some counterbalance on the feeling level, "lest the heart become hardened through too much sadness and so become even more lifeless through despair."[22] "These expressions were for a long time regarded as less pure and were sometimes despised, but today they are almost everywhere being rediscovered."[23]

At the same time there needs to be some discernment, especially when exercises and practices derive from or are influenced by non-Christian sources and when they have been so thoroughly internalized that they are completely invisible to the person. Here are some examples of specific seasonings we find in the spiritual lives of those entering monasteries today. Cultural background determines which among them are paramount.

- **Animism:** Belief or half-belief in ghosts, spirits, fairies, capri, leprechauns, sacred trees, taboos, various superstitions, even including elements of Christian folklore, for example, overuse of holy water.
- **New Age:** Secular belief or half-belief in pyramids, crystals, astrology, numerology, zones of potency.
- **Alternative:** Lifestyle choices that, when followed seriously, implicitly express a particular philosophy of life such as yoga, Zen, vegetarianism, a certain zeal for a "correct" system of diet or exercise.
- **Devotional:** Too much attention paid to the extraordinary: miracles, visions, apparitions, novenas. Sometimes there is some compulsiveness about particular practices.
- **Apocalyptic:** A fundamentalist approach to Scripture, creationism, belief in imminent disaster.
- **Rigidity:** An expectation that everything will be defined, regulated and codified, and a corresponding suspicion of free choice, pluralism or light-

heartedness. This tendency is often associated with *Vaticanophilia*.

Some of these approaches are rooted in the psychological history of the entrants; others either have a religious origin or are post-Christian substitutes for religion. In most cases problems arise only with excess; in the normal process of growth, time will cause any potential dissonance to ease. The question faced by formators is this: What do we do about the "un-monastic" content in the spirituality of those who enter?

When Benedict moved to Monte Cassino he encountered there the remnants of paganism. Far from trying to dialogue with this folk religion, Benedict is presented by Pope Gregory as following the example of Saint Martin of Tours in destroying the resident cult and attempting to convert or re-convert the local population to a more mainline Christianity.

The stronghold called Casinum is situated on the side of a high mountain, where a broad shelf of land forms the site. Behind this the mountain rises steeply for a distance of three miles, as if to rear its summit to the skies. On the top there was a very old temple and there, according to ancient customs among the heathens, Apollo was worshipped by the poor foolish natives of the rustic population. Sacred groves dedicated to demons grew all around the temple where a horde of pagans still took great pains to offer their sacrilegious sacrifices.

As soon as he arrived, the man of God [Benedict] smashed up the idol, overturned the altar and felled the sacred trees. In the temple of Apollo itself he built an oratory to Blessed Martin, and on the site of the altar to Apollo he built an oratory to St. John. He then began calling all the surrounding people to the faith by his continual preaching.[24]

There are different ways of reading this narrative, remembering always it is Gregory who is writing the account for his own purposes.[25] On the one hand it could be said that Benedict was intolerant of lingering paganism and anxious to avoid any syncretism. So he smashes the idol and overturns the altar. An alternative interpretation of Benedict's actions is to see them as accepting popular religion, even in its debased form, and baptizing it. Benedict does not destroy the sanctuaries or burn down the sacred grove. Instead he removes from them the explicit expressions of paganism and redirects the devotion of the rustic people into Christian channels; supporting this change by persuasive preaching. In the history of the Church this broad-minded approach was far commoner in dealing with prevailing religious practice than hard-line prohibition. The spirituality Benedict proposed to his monks was pure and biblical; but he was able to envisage that a transitional stage of imperfect purity may be necessary, at least for "the poor foolish natives of the rustic population."

It is easy to become intolerant and elitist in a monastery, perhaps forgetting the ways by which we ourselves have come. It is better to allow the elements of popular religion to remain alongside monastic practice and not to make an issue of them. In time, what most favors the person's monastic progress will become apparent and other elements will fall away. Sometimes they will endure, but in a "baptized" form, integrated into a monastic way of life. Alongside Schillebeeckx's remarks about tearing off the living skin of religious experience, we need to be mindful of St Benedict's warning lest we become so zealous in scraping off the rust that we put a hole in the bucket (*RB* 64,12).

4. Transcultural Permanents

History leaves us in no doubt that not all Benedict's provisions have been regarded as equally important and therefore sacrosanct. Practical prudence demands that we discern and distinguish between what is central to Benedictine *conversatio* and what is peripheral. The chapters detailing Benedict's penal code seem to have been honored mainly in the breach. We are still in doubt as to how much wine is indicated by a *hemina* (40,3), what exactly the garment named *scapulare* (55,6) is, and whether it is the same as a *bracile* (55,19),[26] or what is involved in chanting *in directum* (12,1; 17,6). Different congregations have, through history, proposed and followed different interpretations with equal certitude. It is unreasonable, therefore, to regard every detail of what Benedict proposed as immutable and valid for every time and place. Beyond these details, however, there are elements of the Rule which must be considered to be essential everywhere.

St Benedict's criteria for assessing the reality of suitability for a monastic life is a strong indicator of what he considers to be the crux of authentic *conversatio* and, as such, something that transcends cultural boundaries. In addition to the experimental component of the novitiate process and the fact of the novice being willing to continue, Benedict proposes four or five areas that the formator is to scrutinize in order to learn something of the inner face of a potential vocation.

1. Is the novice **really** seeking God?
2. Is the novice zealous for the Work of God?
3. Is the novice zealous for obedience?
4. Is the novice zealous for *obprobria*?

Five qualities are indicated by these four questions. Firstly, there is a mystical prerequisite for every monastic vocation, an inner search for God that is not satisfied by the possibilities of secular life so that the candidate is prepared to renounce everything — including his own body (57,25) — and embrace the hard and rough ways of the mysterious Godward journey (57,8). The combination of prayer and renunciation is a good indication of a monastic call. Secondly there is zeal, passion or even enthusiasm for the concrete, everyday reality of *conversatio* that translates into practical action. The monastery is not a country club for nesting, where one can while away one's hours and years in inactivity and non-commitment (*acedia*); it is a place of intensity — *intentio cordis* (52,4) — that demands not only the expenditure of energy, but its practical channeling into the way of love (72,2-3).[27] This novitiate fervor (1,3) differs from person to person in its expression, and almost always mellows with time; but its absence is not a good sign. Thirdly the novice must love the structured daily prayer of the **Opus Dei**. The novice is not just to be there or even merely to participate wholeheartedly in the Liturgy of the Hours, but to prefer to be there. Fourthly the novice contentedly begins a lifelong process of living in subordination to the will of God (7,31-32), as this is expressed through visible sources of authority, the rule and the abbot (1,2), the other brothers whether corporately or casually (Chapter 3, Chapter 71 and 72,6; note the forceful verb *impendant*), and even through outsiders (61,4; 64,4). The novice is called to go beyond mere external compliance, adolescent rebellion or transference and to order his life by a systematic search for God's will, most often revealed through imperfect and ambiguous human mouthpieces. Finally the novice needs to be zealous for *obprobria*. This difficult term certainly covers those everyday humiliations typical of any human life and the inevitable sense of shame felt in growth beyond the past and in the process of coming to self-awareness and practicing self-disclosure. However, *obprobrium* probably means more specifically the loss of social status and power that comes about by entering a monastery, where a person is expected to accept a junior position, to regress to a less-than-fully-adult role in community and to relate as an equal even to those of a less privileged background (for Benedict this included former slaves) and those less intelligent or virtuous than oneself (2,20).[28] In particular this criterion asks for a pro-active willingness to be involved in the activities of the community, especially those that might be considered as demeaning or more appropriately done by slaves (7,49). This is indicated by a text from Rufinus' translation of Basil's *Asceticon*, known to and recommended by Benedict (73,5).

This can easily be discerned if he bears all the bodily labor enjoined on him, and he tends more zealously for a disciplined life. Also, if he is asked about some sin he is not ashamed to talk about it and to willingly take on the usual remedy for the sin. Also if he tends towards humility without any shame and he does not take it too badly if he is reasonably asked to give himself to mean and servile tasks. If from each of these areas it can be ascertained that he is of firm mind, stable counsel and has a generous soul, then let him be received. But before he is incorporated in the fraternity he should be given some laborious task, one that seems to be held by seculars as *obprobrium*, so that it can be observed whether he fulfills it freely and confidently, without shame or grave difficulty; and whether in this labor he is energetic and generous.[29]

It is obvious that while these requirements are universal, the way in which they are expressed is not. I would like to examine two areas where cultural differences need to be taken into consideration in the process of formation: the attitude to the common life and the art of facilitating self-disclosure.

5. Inherited Attitudes to Social Living

The Rule of Benedict proposes a specific model of community that evolved in its author's lifetime to bring a particular group of monks into a more intense conformity with the Gospel message.[30] We who live in the postmodern West are faced with widespread alienation and with ingrained beliefs and attitudes that make community living very difficult. The term used for this contemporary western disposition is "individualism." This word indicates more than mere eccentricity, showing off, attention-seeking, or outrageous behavior. Individualism involves an implicit rejection of the social element in human nature. It refuses to others any right to provide input about how I live my life. In the encounter of cultures brought about by monastic implantation or by individuals from less westernized countries entering an existing monastery, it may be the "old" establishment has to learn something from the "new"—or perhaps to unlearn some of the cultural attitudes that have become standard since the Industrial Revolution. In this case the dispositions of those raised in traditional societies may be closer to that esteemed by St Benedict than those formed in western cultures.

Let us begin with an example. One practical area in which Benedict's notion of community becomes visible is in the arrangement of common meals. The Rule has many provisions to ensure that eating is a communal affair, a solemn expression of fraternity and not merely the occasion for gratification of the appetite. The *hemina* of wine may have been permitted as a positive reinforcement of this celebration of togetherness. This, we may note, is in contrast with the ascetic regimen adopted in the early Cistercian monasteries, where divine intervention was sometimes necessary to make the food palatable.[31] Even today, especially in the Trappist tradition, the *humanitas* of table fellowship is undervalued as an everyday means of advancing that fraternal communion that finds its fullest expression in the Community Eucharist. Each meal can be a summons to leave behind individualism and to open oneself to others. That is why it sometimes seems that those whose commitment to their community is waning are often irregular in their participation at the common table.

Figure 4: Rules for Meals
THE MEAL AS COMMUNION
[ad mensae communis participationem. 43,15]
avoiding its subversion by individualism

No absences	
No late-coming	43,13-17
No private conversations	38,5
No private snacks	43,18
No outside meals	51,1
No indiscipline	56,3
No murmuring	40,9; 41,5
No overeating	39,7
No drunkenness	40,5-7
Exclusion of guilty	24,3; 25,1
All eat common food	40,1-5
Self-Denial possible	49,7
Mutual service	38,6
Care for the sick	36,9
Care for the young and old	37,2

It is clear from Benedict's injunctions that monks ate only as a community. A recent survey in *Asiaweek* revealed that in most countries in Asia, family meals were considered to be a value worth preserving. In the West this is no longer so; eating out and buying in mean that individuals may have different meals in different places; separate activities (even television) make gathering difficult. Even in monastic communities technology steps in to subvert eating together:

microwave ovens and food-warmers cater for those who eat at other times, snacks are always available, buffet lines and self-service make designer meals possible, and portion-control serves provide each with an individual, untouched-by-human-hands, predetermined quantity of edible substance. In some monasteries common meals are kept to a minimum; at other times each prepares a personal meal whenever it is convenient to eat.

A sanitized and privatized meal can be taken as a symbol of the attitude many westerners have towards community—it is a practical necessity to be endured and survived, not a boon. Affective needs are satisfied beyond the community in a smaller, select circle of friends. Thus community meals are reduced to the intake of food; with no ulterior significance. This is a logical consequence of individualism. Meals are not, however, the only areas of common life which are found repugnant by those who allow themselves to fall under the influence of an individualist culture. What results is an indifference to community life, and an instinctive hostility to any structure that has been formulated by others. In personal projects and self-chosen endeavors great generosity is possible, selective relationships can run very deep. Meanwhile the call to community goes unheeded.

We are called to a double ideal: encouraging others to entrust themselves fully to a community and simultaneously encouraging the community to prove itself trustworthy. Mistrust can lead to a resistance to any attempt by a community to offer nurturance. Equally it contributes to a denial of any necessary involvement in the welfare of others. Each will have a personal list of what causes the decline in "community spirit," but perhaps it is worthwhile listing some of the factors that contribute to this disposition.

- **Dysfunctional families**, in which those growing up never experience mutual love and respect and learn to look for nurture and support to a chosen group of friends outside the family.
- **Abusive educational systems** in which a sense of inferiority is communicated and natural cognitive tendencies and skills are suppressed.
- Social contexts in which **authority** is negatively regarded; where coerced compliance may be shadowed by unobserved subversion.
- Career environments where ambition, **competition** and rivalry are essential for "success."
- Economic environments where the attainment of material goals is given priority over the welfare of persons: workaholism or **economic rationalism**.
- Lack of self-awareness, whereby a person transfers experience from one situation to another, **projecting** onto others attitudes and responses that come from inside the person, not from others.
- An **inability to commit** oneself to a determined course of action and to persevere in it, especially if it entails a general indebtedness or particular obligations to others.
- An excessive need for **personal space** in which no outside claim can be made on time or energies. This may sometimes be linked with various levels of compulsive or addictive behavior, including substance abuse.

Perhaps it is worth remembering that for all its technological savvy, the West is close to bankruptcy when it comes to humane values. Often enough we are not even aware of our deficiencies and we certainly have few strategies to reverse the trend away from any depth of community. Maybe it is only through contact with other less dehumanized cultures that we in the

West can begin to recognize and reverse some of the attitudes and practices that retard our growth as persons and as monastics. On the other hand, in bringing monastic life to non-Western cultures we want to make sure that we do not package it with the sort of corrosive individualism that eats away the heart of monastic community and leaves only a hollow shell.

6. Self-Disclosure

In describing the progress of his monks from fear to perfect charity, Benedict takes over from the Master a ladder of signs that demonstrate growth. With the ascent, there is a movement from inner attitudes in the direction of specific behaviors on the understanding that the prescribed actions flow from beliefs and values that have been already internalized and appropriated in the earlier stages. A difficulty arises if we immediately identify particular manners of acting with the virtue they are supposed to express. It is clear from St Gregory's *Pastoral Rule* that even in those distant times there was an awareness that the same actions do not always have the same meaning; much depends on the temperament and character of the person concerned. We are even more conscious that interpretations vary from culture to culture.

It follows that what might be called the "upper" and outer levels of the monk's ascent to perfect charity need to be interpreted (or re-interpreted) from a culture-sensitive standpoint. Here I am particularly concerned with the fifth step of humility which is, as it were, the bridge between inner disposition and outward activity. This step envisages the monk getting to the point where he is able to acknowledge his inner ugliness in the presence of another human being and thus putting himself in the situation where he is no longer able to deny his woundedness to himself, or act as though there ought always be a presupposition of blamelessness.[32]

How is this necessary self-disclosure affected by cultural diversity? In the case of a monastery where all (theoretically) participate in a single national culture, people will find suitable ways of implementing Benedict's recommendation, despite its inherent difficulty. In multicultural monasteries, especially in the decades of transition as the monastic sub-culture moves from the culture of the founders to that of local entrants, substantial problems are likely.

Benedict speaks about revealing "all the thoughts of the heart." This demands a language suitable for such expression, one far more subtle and intimate than that used for discussing everyday events or intellectual topics. It is a "language of the heart", the mother-language (*la langue maternelle*), perhaps a local accent or a childhood dialect. It often happens that this intimate language is voluntarily left aside in pursuit of a career or barred from official use.

No matter how proficient one is in a foreign language, something intimate is lost when it has to be used exclusively. A person moves away from the region of the heart into that of the head, from poetry and song to prose. "How can I sing the song of the Lord on alien soil?" Progress is made to better levels of fluency, but the link with the heartland, with the soil of primal experience is broken. There is a certain heaviness or artificiality in all that is said, dexterously contrived but never authentically spontaneous.

Those who join a monastery where they have to live in a foreign-language ambiance may not necessarily feel fully at home with the language they have learned. It may be, for example, that I, for whom English is my first language, do not take seriously enough the words of one whose English is rudimentary. Often one's standing is measured by competence in language; if one speaks the language like a child, one is thought to know no more than a child. Implicitly the deeper realities of maturity are considered to be beyond one's grasp. When it comes to intimate dialogue, it is easy for a stranger to feel unheard even by an attentive listener, if one is not satisfied with how one has expressed oneself.

It is hard to feel at home in a community that speaks a different language; the nuances of everyday exchanges are lost, jokes are misunderstood and the emotional content of words and phrase can easily be misjudged. Spontaneity dries up. There is a tendency to be constantly on one's guard against inadvertent malapropisms, and this may lead to a certain reserve in conversation. It gets worse when this withdrawal is judged to be a monastic virtue.

When I entered the monastery in 1960, Latin was used in the liturgy and in community prayers, and sign language was used for daily converse. Its effect was, I believe, to separate a newcomer from his familiar spiritual environment and his roots and to induce a sense of being almost a stranger in a foreign land.[33] That this served a purpose in creating a frontier-to-be-crossed, I cannot deny. To that extent it served a useful purpose. But it also left one feeling stranded, cut off from tried and trusted means of vitality. Inevitably in a such a situation one is at a loss for words to describe inner experience: a new language has to be learned. How much greater when, in addition to all the other separations involved in entering a monastery, one is cut off from using one's first language. At a time when it is important to process one's experience by sharing with another, a radical restraint is introduced. It is like trying to express one's intimate feelings in Morse code or semaphore.

It is not only a matter of translating words; there are attitudes embedded in language that cannot cross the linguistic divide, even in the case of simple words like "Yes" and "No." Some Asians appear to Westerners to be accepting a proposition when in reality they are not; they may be merely registering its content while subtly dissociating themselves from it. In a formation situation this is going to lead to misunderstandings. Different peoples have different unspoken rules governing a conversation: body-language, touching, eye-contact and other non-verbal means of communication are culturally conditioned. Some are happy to get to the point immediately or to proceed by a direct logical approach; others prefer to circle around. In particular, pastoral interventions involving some element of correction will require a great deal of humility and learning from both sides.

In self-disclosing dialogue across cultures a different dynamic of guilt and shame is encountered that sometimes leads to serious miscommunication.

In Hinduism, Confucianism, Islam and all the "rest" of the world's value-systems, moral behavior is based on shame; that is, on manners or habits enforced by external social pressure. In a guilt culture like Christianity, by contrast, morality is based on an inner state of intentionality and backed by an individual's belief in a God who can know and judge that inner state.[34]

Such a difference in fundamental morality is a challenge for both sides. A formator who is concerned to ensure that monastic values have taken root in the heart may be frustrated that the dialogue seems unable to go deeper than external behavior. Novices or juniors, on the other hand, may be puzzled and even affronted by robust inquiries about intimate feelings and motivations, and they may experience discomfort at being tongue-tied in trying to provide the information the formator is seeking. What may appear as secretiveness may be the effect of an instinctive respect for the elder and the elder's good opinion that makes it doubly difficult to talk about the seamier side of one's private life.

What can be done to ease the situation and especially to ensure that those in formation are not deprived of valuable means of assistance for their journey through life? First and foremost is needed an **awareness of the difficulty** of the situation. There are certain normal barriers to communication such as the distance between any two persons, the generation gap, and the power gap between formator and formatee (more strongly experienced by the formatee than by the formator). These still exist but they are supplemented by the difficulty of communication deriving from a different culture and a different language. Secondly, **sensitivity to the other** is required on both sides. Respect and humility are strongly indicated. Thirdly, all need to **resist the temptation** to withdraw from dialogue under the guise of tolerance and an all-too-facile acceptance. This means continuing to invest time and energy in attentive listening, and in checking one's understanding through a feedback process. Finally, we are called to assert what we have in common, **our humanity,** our humus-based condition, our proneness to bumbling hurtfulness, our capacity for sin. This asks two things of us: an ongoing commitment to forgiveness and reconciliation and, just as important, an unshakable sense of humor.

At the level of tactics, we have to be inventive. The use of a patrimonial vocabulary can offer a means of fusion of horizons. When personal experiences are associated with monastic terms, through a process of reflective initiation, then it is possible to break through some culture-based constraints. Young monastics may feel more at ease discussing their private life in terms of Cassian's eight vices than in using a psychological or moral vocabulary. In this way, the monastic tradition, belonging to a different world, can be a bridge between the cultures. We are aware that keeping a journal can often facilitate sharing, since it brings material to the surface without any sense of pressure. A journal kept in one's own language can help too, since in reviewing what one has written, it becomes possible to reflect also on how this can be communicated in another language so that one has something to say that really communicates.

The difficulties of multiculturalism are the result of the growth of monastic life. They are not something to be regretted, they are blessed challenges to growth. All the Church documents that touch on inculturation make the point that it is a bilateral process; old-timers are as much called to change as newcomers. Such adaptation is a means of building a more creative future and not merely a matter of perpetuating the ever-stagnating past. It is not an optional extra. When God sends to our communities people of a different culture, we are being called not only to welcome them into our own culture, but also to embrace aspects of their culture as part of our future, even at the price of a new detachment. They can be for us God-sent means of monastic renewal, just as we can be for them channels of sacred tradition.

We do not think of failure to inculturate as particularly harmful; yet it is this deficiency that is at the heart of so many examples of monastic decline throughout history. Perhaps this might become clear by examining one particular case, that of the Cistercians in Ireland from the twelfth to the sixteenth centuries.

7. A Case Study: The Cistercians in Ireland

Occasionally one encounters a moralistic view of monastic history that loves to distinguish "Golden Ages" from their baser succedents. Decline in fervor is regarded as an all-inclusive explanation for every departure from this hallowed standard. The interplay of circumstances resulting from wars, plagues, political unrest, social change and intellectual ferment is minimized to emphasize ethical and spiritual failure on the part of the monks and nuns. A downward scale is constructed leading from fervor to mitigation, and thence to abuse and generalized decadence. Blame is assigned to those deemed responsible for the backsliding. Such heavily interpretative historiography serves a cautionary rather than informative purpose.

Perhaps this facile moralism underestimates the impact of social and cultural factors on the monastic project. A flourishing monasticism transplanted to a different time and place without adaptation quickly withers. In such a perspective, individual or corporate morality is less important for understanding the reality of the situation. In many cases structural failure of the institution occurs because the system has been unable to accommodate itself to changed conditions. An unenculturated monasticism cannot thrive. Examples of this are legion. Let us examine one case in detail: the Cistercians in Ireland from their establishment in the twelfth century to their suppression in the sixteenth.[35]

One of the reasons for the "success" of the Cistercians in twelfth-century France was that the Cistercian philosophy suited the temper of the times and appealed to an important sector of the population from which recruits could be drawn. The Cistercian ideals of simplicity and rusticity were wildly attractive to the literate, urbane and upwardly mobile members of what today we would call the "upper middle class" and it was they who formed the demographic core of Cîteaux's expansion.[36] The primitive austerity of reformed monasticism was a creative foil to the relatively high level of culture in French knightly circles and incipient universities, and provided a fruitful ambiance for spiritual growth. Meanwhile, these adult recruits were probably unaware that they were living off the resources of their previous life and education as much as from what they received in the monastery.

In 1140 Bishop Malachy O Morgair, formerly Archbishop of Armagh, invited the abbot of Clairvaux to make a foundation in his territory. Two years later, Bernard sent across the seas a mixed community composed of mature French monks and Irishmen who had been deposited by Malachy at Clairvaux. These were augmented by a second wave of Irish monks who had completed their novitiate at the mother house. From the beginning, therefore, multiculturalism was a potential source of tension. Not all the French monks stayed and, on hearing about life in the distant western regions, few suitable men could be found at Clairvaux who were willing to go to Ireland.[37] It was not long before conflicts arose—possibly about the style of building to be followed in the new monastery.[38]

Despite its distinguished monastic past, Bernard regarded Ireland as a *terra nullius* as far as monasticism was concerned. "There is need for much vigilance, since this is a new monastery and it is located in a country that is unaccustomed to and unskilled in monastic discipline."[39] It is also clear that Bernard wanted Mellifont to mirror Clairvaux. He had earlier written to Malachy: "According to the wisdom given you by the Lord and according to the disposition of buildings that you have seen in our place, make provision for and prepare a place for them that is far from the disturbances of the world."[40] In Bernard's mind the lifestyle which had worked so well in Burgundy was to be reproduced exactly in Ireland.[41]

The foundation was made because of Bernard's admiration for Malachy, and despite his low opinion of the Irish. Of Malachy he later said that "he tamed the beastly barbarity of his fellow-Irishmen."[42] This same judgment is amply illustrated in the *Vita sancti Malachiae* written between 1148 and 1152, from which it is clear that Bernard viewed the Irish as uncultivated barbarians.[43] The prime example is the following description of Malachy's flock at Connor:

> Once [Malachy] began to exercise his office, then the man of God understood that he was addressing not human beings but beasts. He had never experienced people so

immersed in all manner of barbarism, so twisted in their morality, feral in their rituals, so lacking devotion in their faith, barbarians as far as the law was concerned, obstinate in matters of discipline. and Christian in name, pagans in reality.[44]

It is clear that Bernard did not envisage any attempt at what we would term "inculturation." It was not even an encounter of cultures, but the meeting of culture with what was perceived to be non-culture. What the French monks brought was meant to replace whatever had pre-existed their arrival.[45]

Mellifont did well, but it remained a Gallic outpost. The situation in the country was greatly politicized after the Anglo-Norman invasion of 1169, when Ireland began to be ruled by French-speaking governors and ecclesiastics. Although only eight or ten of the 40 odd Cistercian houses eventually established in Ireland were "of foreign parentage,"[46] the necessary French connection through the structures of the Order[47] plus certain privileges granted or confirmed by the invaders were enough to engender malaise among the natives. As a result, there was in the Irish monasteries a high level of resentment at foreign intervention that may be regarded as a kind of pre-nationalist sentiment. This found expression in eccentric observance, independence and various levels of rebellion. Difference there certainly was, but not necessarily decadence—at least in the beginning. Barry O'Dwyer's sober conclusion is that "in the midst of much evidence relating to the moral state of the monasteries there is little that suggests the existence of serious moral fault."[48]

It was only with difficulty that the Irish monks could be torn from early Celtic customs.... Not long after their arrival, the Anglo-Normans endeavored to gain control of Irish abbeys in districts which came under their influence, causing friction and loss of discipline among the monks, and some of the Irish abbots began to ignore instructions of the General Chapter of the order. From 1216 to 1231 it became virtually a struggle between the Anglo-Norman abbots, who supported the chapter general, and the Irish abbots who did not."[49]

Unsurprisingly such manifestations of Irishness did not find favor with foreign Visitators, nor with the General Chapter, By the fourteenth century such attitudes were perceived as hostile also by the civil authorities in England who adopted legislative measures to preserve the Anglo-Norman character of the principal monasteries—to the point of eventually excluding Irishmen completely.

Midway in the process some attempt was made to deal with the deteriorating situation which had come to a head prior to the General Chapter of 1216 with the "conspiracy of Mellifont" involving armed resistance to any attempt at regular visitation. In the General Chapters of 1227 and 1228, Stephen of Lexington, Abbot of Stanley, was appointed, by way of exception from the general practice, to act as delegate for the Father Abbot of Clairvaux in making the regular visitation of the Irish monasteries.[50] It was a task involving not only spiritual and disciplinary firmness, but perceptiveness, negotiating skills and a large measure of physical courage.[51]

The evidence seems to indicate that the Irish monasteries were in a parlous condition having neither accepted in full the discipline of European monasticism nor fulfilled the ascetical demands of their indigenous tradition. They seem to have combined elements from both traditions to produce an easy-going lifestyle that inevitably lost its spiritual focus.

Consequently, compelled by need, almost all those in charge of the land wander away from the cloister as they please under the pretext of begging; there is no silence, no monastic discipline in the chapter-house, few are living in community, but they live in miserable huts outside the cloister in groups of threes and fours; they take up a collection and send to the village traders to purchase what they need instead of making use of the provisions of their properties. We are afraid to mention the contagion of the flesh, the association with robbers and murderers and others of the same ilk.[52]

The charges are repeated in a letter addressed to Pope Gregory IX by the Abbot of Cîteaux, in the name of the General Chapter.

> For in the monasteries of Ireland our restraint and rule is scarcely observed in anything apart from the habit, for there is no due service in choir, or silence in the cloister, discipline in the chapter, community meals in the refectory or monastic quiet in the dormitory according to the rules of the Order, not even as is kept by black monks; for they live as they like outside the walls in huts wretchedly built out of branches and they give their attention to all sorts of feasting and drinking; they reside together in twos and threes and fours, each of them having a horse along with his own boy-servant.[53]

Instead of simple loss of fervor, we may attribute some of these "abuses" to a clash of cultures between regimented continental monasticism and the lingering memories of the free-wheeling ways of the Celtic monks.[54] There are several simultaneous tugs of war occurring.

Enclosure— porosity of monastic boundaries
self-support— support by the faithful
silence —conversation
chapter decorum— freedom of expression
large building—"miserable huts"
formalized community—"twos and threes and fours"
separation—political involvement
careful economic management—a careless or carefree approach

Perhaps it was the sense of *anomie* thus generated that led to a more generalized "contagion of the flesh" — a situation not unknown on an individual level even in the best-ordered monastery. With the perceived erosion of several basic components of the Cistercian formula, Stephen concluded: "Internally all the spiritualities are dissolved, externally the temporalities are almost completely wasted, so that for the most part we can say in truth: there is nothing of the Order there apart from the wearing of the habit."[55]

Once the diagnosis was complete, a remedy had to be sought. Stephen was a well-educated man in the Anglo-European mold, but with little understanding of Irish culture and history. In retrospect, perhaps he seems to have set too much store by the education he himself had received and could not envisage any other manner of formation. "He had the instinctive fear of ignorance of one accustomed to an intellectual environment and he had the spiritual insight to see how much more damaging it was in an environment of silence and solitude.[56] In Stephen's assessment it was the lack of education that was the root cause of all the abuses, and potentially led to contentiousness, rebellion, violence and even heresy.[57] To his way of seeing things there were no schools in Ireland, so promising candidates should be sent abroad. Since language was part of the problem Stephen decreed that all should reach a level of competency in both French and Latin.

> So that there will be uniformity in the Order, it is strictly decreed that in future the Rule shall be expounded only in French so that the less well-ordered do not conceal themselves, and visitors when they come may understand and be understood by the monks. Whoever expounds it otherwise shall be subjected to the penalty allotted for breaking the silence. No one shall be received as a monk unless he knows how to confess his faults in French or Latin, regardless of whichever people he belongs to.[58]

A second and shorter redaction of his decisions applying to all the monasteries was drawn up in the following year, after his return to Stanley. Incompetence in French or Latin rises to the head of the list of concerns. The prospect of a European education is evoked and there is a hint that speaking Irish was deemed subversive.

> #1 No one shall be received as a monk, no matter whatever his nation, unless he knows how to confess his faults in French or Latin, so that when visitors and correctors of the Order come they may understand [the monks] and be understood by them.
>
> #2 The Rule shall only be expounded in French and Latin and the chapter of the monks conducted in French or Latin in future, so that in this way those who want to be received in future may attend school in some place where they may learn some gentle manners.
>
> #3 In punishment for the conspiracies having arisen throughout the Irish houses generally, it is strictly forbidden for anyone of that language to be appointed abbot, for a period of three years, so that their obedience to the Order may be fully tested and they may first learn to be students that in due time and place they may become more capable masters without danger to their souls and to the Order.[59]

He spells out his thinking further in a letter to the abbot of Clairvaux:

> How can anyone love cloister or Writ who knows nothing but Irish? (*Quomodo autem diligit claustrum, aut librum, qui nihil novit nisi Hibernicum?*) It is impossible to construct anything but a tower of Babel when the disciple does not understand the master, or vice versa, and cannot distinguish properly so that when he asks for bread, the other proffers a stone in place of bread, and for fish gives a serpent. For this reason we have enjoined on the Irish that, if they want to receive any of their people into the Order in future, they should send them to Paris or Oxford or other famous cities where they will learn letters and skill in

speech and ordered habits, and we pointed out to them very clearly that the Order does not intend to exclude any race but only the inadequate, useless and uncivilized.[60]

The same sentiment is repeated in a letter to the abbot and community of the Welsh-speaking monastery of Tracton.

> We do not intend this decree to exclude any people whether English, Scots, Welsh or Irish, but only those who are unsuitable for and completely unproductive to the Order. For how can anyone love the Order or observe the seriousness of the silence or the discipline of the cloister who does not know how to find any consolation at all in the Scriptures, or to meditate even a little on the law of God either by day or by night?[61]

In his own Anglo-Norman context, Stephen's prescription is sound. The problem was that his recommendations needed to be received in a profoundly different context. Irish Cistercianism is always presented as defective compared with the European norm. On the one hand, we hear no defense from the Irish. We have no means of knowing how objective are Stephen's reports of monastic misconduct. On the other hand, Stephen seems to have little knowledge or appreciation of local practice and it may be that some of his conclusions derive from fear, suspicion and incomprehension. Certainly there is no evidence of any attempt at "fusion of horizons"; the Irish are roundly condemned for their differences and called to conform to the European model.

The Irish had the advantage of having an identity and organization which was tenacious although it was very different, and this was under-pinned by a culture of considerable richness, supported by a religious distinctiveness of which the monasteries were an important part. All of this gave depth to the resistance which the Cistercian visitors were faced with in the

Irish monasteries. With the immigration following upon the Anglo-Norman conquest, there were two very different cultures and organizations continuing side by side in Ireland differentiated by racial composition finding its immediate expression in language, but very marked in social customs and mental concepts.[62]

Notwithstanding Stephen's efforts, "the spiritual and intellectual vigor of the monasteries appear to have declined steadily since the thirteenth century and the Cistercians were no longer capable of attracting the best minds of the age."[63] In the context of the theme of inculturation it is interesting to speculate whether this morbidity was primarily the result of moral failure or simply the necessary effect of ongoing cultural conflict. The Irish foundation was not a case of monastic **implantation**, to use the expression current at the time, but an attempt to **graft** the Cistercian reform onto an existing monastic stock. Different procedures were necessary. Because the pre-existing monastic culture of Ireland was not recognized, it was not understood, appreciated or respected. Instead of initiating a dialogue, the officials of the Cistercian Order conducted a campaign of suppression in the name of a chauvinistic uniformity which, of course, met with resistance. The opposing parties became polarized, particular observances were politicized. War began, peace evaporated and the spiritual focus of the monastery was lost. As St Benedict remarks of conflict between an abbot and his prior, "while they espouse contrary views, their souls are necessarily endangered by this dissension and those who are under them, currying favor with the parties, go to their ruin" (*RB* 65,8-9). In such a situation it was inevitable that a decline in fervor would follow, and that this lukewarmness would itself lead to further slackness and abuses.

There is a clear moral to this story. The pattern has been repeated often throughout the centuries and even a country as monastically youthful as Australia can provide several examples. There is a responsibility on the part of those making foundations to take seriously the culture of the country in which they settle, to become "lovers of the place." If they do not, the enthusiasm that accompanied the foundation will give way to alienation; and thence to frustration, anger and aggression. The final effect will be one of two extremes: either an exotic artificiality totally removed from its cultural ambiance or an equally inauthentic rejection of all that comes from elsewhere. In both cases there is no "fusion of horizons"—the purpose of making the foundation has been effectively voided. The founders may as well have stayed at home.

NOTES

[1] See M. Casey, "The Dynamic Unfolding of the Benedictine Charism," *ABR* 51.2 (June 2000), pp. 149-167.

[2] See M. Casey, "Marketing the Monastic Tradition within Monasteries" *TJ* 60 (2001), pp. 27-52 where I explored this facet of historical evolution with reference to the notion of "hybrid vigor" borrowed from animal husbandry.

[3] Colomban Pouilly, *Cultures traditionelles et foi chrétienne: Recherches sur l'inculturation* (Nouméa: 1992), p. 4. See also N. Standaert, "L'histoire d'un néologisme: Le terme "inculturation" dans les documents romains," *NRTh* 110 (1988), pp. 555-570.

[4] "The process of inculturation may be defined as the Church's efforts to make the message of Christ penetrate a given socio-cultural milieu, calling on the latter to grow according to its particular values, as long as these are compatible with the Gospel. The term 'inculturation' includes the notion of growth, of the

mutual enrichment of persons and groups, rendered possible by the encounter of the Gospel with a social milieu. 'Inculturation is the incarnation of the Gospel in native cultures, and also, the introduction of these cultures into the life of the Church'" (Paul VI *Slavorum Apostoli*, 8). International Theological Commission, "Faith and Inculturation," §11, in *Omnis Terra* 178 (May 1989), p. 265.

[5] The principle of monastic inculturation is affirmed clearly in the *Constitutions and Statutes of the Cistercian Order of the Strict Observance*.

Constitution 70, Adaptation to Local Culture: Wherever new monasteries are established, the founders are to become lovers of that place. Monastic life is not to be bound to any particular form of culture nor to any political, economic or social system but, as far as possible, what is rightly valued in the local culture should be welcomed as new means of expressing and enriching the Cistercian patrimony.

[6] "Ecclesia in Oceania, #16"; *Osservatore Romano* 5 December 2001, Special Insert, p. vi.

[7] OCSO *Statute on Foundations*, 3.

[8] It has to be noted that differences between the forming generation and those in the process of receiving monastic formation are not only national and cultural, they can be regional, generational, educational and deriving from social class. The impact of globalisation on the Internet generation sometimes makes generational diversities more significant than those based on country of origin. Gender differences can also figure in the equation in Orders such as the Strict Observance Cistercians which comprise both male and female communities.

[9] This image of living skin has been borrowed from some comments made concerning liturgical renewal. E. Schillebeeckx, "Zijn er crisis-elementen in katholiek-kerkelijk Nederland?" in *Katholiek Archief* 21 (1966), p. 347.

There is also the common unrest that is characteristic of persons abandoning old habits when this does not come from a personal, existential need that is experienced at depth, but which is imposed on them by the community in which they live. This is what happened in the sphere of the liturgy after the Council. To be sure, it is not the vocation of the Church to act as the conservator of ancient and outdated treasures but to try, first of all, to satisfy the Christian needs of the faithful. Meeting these needs has priority over saving from destruction the treasures of Gregorian culture. On the other hand, for older people who have lived the Catholic faith, these ancient treasures are not simply cultural treasures. They are part of the fabric of their Christian life: they are, as it were, the living skin of their religious experience, and not simply a garment that we can at any time take or leave, even sometimes regretfully. These are not simply religious forms of expression, but it is a case that their religious life has become what it is in and through these particular forms. Here there is no room for a dualism between what is inner and what is outer. A good number of such people inevitably feel as though they have been skinned alive, as though they have been stripped of their own flesh. (Translated.)

[10] See *RB* 2,11-12; 21,4; 64,2; 64,9. See also M. Casey, "Leadership in a Benedictine Context: An Interrogation of Tradition," *TJ* 22 (1982), pp. 5-103.

[11] See M. Casey, "Dynamic Element," p.151.

[12] See M. Casey, *A Guide to Living in the Truth: Saint Benedict's Teaching on Humility* (Liguori: Triumph Books, 2001), pp. 169-176.

[13] Garry Wills, *Saint Augustine* (London: Phoenix, 2000), p. xviii.

[14] *RA* 5.5-7. See Raymond Canning [trans.], *The Rule of Saint Augustine: With Introduction and Commentary*

(London: Darton, Longman & Todd, 1984), pp. 20-21, 34-35, 87-88.

[15] See Terrence Kardong, *Benedict's Rule: A Translation and Commentary* (Collegeville: Liturgical Press, 1996), pp. 308-309. On the approach in Byzantine monasteries see Herbert Hunger, "Zum Badewesen in Byzantinischen Klöstern," in *Klösterliche Sachkultur des Spätmittelalters* (Vienna: Verlag der Österreichischen Akademie der Wissenschaften, 1980), pp. 353-364.

[16] A full-time bath-attendant was employed at Westminster Abbey; between Prime and Compline he was able to accommodate only four customers. See Barbara Harvey, *Living and Dying in England, 1100-1540: The Monastic Experience* (Oxford: Clarendon Press, 1995), p.134.

[17] See Meredith Parsons Lillich in "Cleanliness with Godliness: A Discussion of Medieval Monastic Plumbing," in Benoît Chauvin [ed.] *Mélanges à la mémoire du Père Anselme Dimier* (Pupillin: Benoît Chauvin, 1982), T. 5, p. 123-149. The author thus summarizes the trend:

[Regarding the earliest hermits] their frequent aversion to bathing can probably be analyzed as a deliberate refutation of the lasciviousness of the late Roman baths.... The third century hermit St Anthony never bathed even his feet, except accidentally while wading a stream. He wore the same shirt all his life, as did his follower, St Hilarion, who stated realistically "that it was unreasonable to look for too great cleanliness in haircloth." In the 5th century St Jerome denounced bathing on the premise that it stimulated the senses. (pp. 123-125)

[18] *Benedict's Rule*, p. 309.

[19] Harvey, *Living and Dying*, p. 134.

[20] Lorna Price, *The Plan of St Gall in Brief* (Berkeley: University of California Press, 1982), pp. 32-33.

[21] This sometimes results in a "piety void" similar to what many experienced after the liturgical changes initiated by Vatican II. Newcomers may feel deprived of what have hitherto been their most potent sources of spiritual energy.

[22] Bernard of Clairvaux, *SC* 11.2; *SBO* 1.55.18-19.

[23] Paul VI, *Evangelii nuntiandi* 48.

[24] Gregory the Great, *Dialogues* II. 8. 10-11; translated by Hilary Costello and Eoin de Bhaldraithe in *The Life of Saint Benedict* (Petersham: St Bede's, 1993), p. 64

[25] Gregory's principles are set forth in a letter to Abbot Mellitus, the contents of which were to be passed on to Augustine of Canterbury. The idols are to be destroyed, but the temples retained after having aspersed them with holy water, given altars and relics. Pagan festivals are to be replaced with appropriate Christian celebrations. "It is impossible to eradicate all errors from obstinate minds at one stroke." See Bede, *Ecclesiastical History* I, 30.

[26] On the variations in the implementation of Benedict's directives on clothing see Pius Engelbert, *TJ* 61 (2001), pp. 21-44.

[27] The point is not so much to observe the Rule, but to **love** the observance of the Rule, not as an abstract ideal but as it is concretely lived in a particular monastery. Thus in the prologue to the Cistercian *Exordium Parvum*, the stated aim of the author is that his readers "may more tenaciously love both the place (= the monastery) and the observance of the Holy Rule there initiated somehow or other by ourselves, through the grace of God."

[28] In his fourth sermon for the Epiphany, Guerric of Igny gives as a sign of humility: "If you allow one who is less than yourself to have precedence over you." Sermon 14:7; *SChr* 166, p. 302.

[29] *Basili Regula* 6.5-11; *CSEL* 86, pp. 37-38. The corresponding section in the *Long Rules* adds, "To one, moreover, who has enjoyed any of the higher positions in society, and who aspires to imitate the humility of our Lord Jesus Christ, should be given tasks which may appear extremely humiliating to worldlings, to see whether he will prove himself to be a worker for God, wholehearted and unashamed." Translated by Sister M. Monica Wagner in *FC* 9, p. 261.

[30] The process of evolution into a more communitarian emphasis can be seen not only by comparison with the *Rule of the Master*, but also by noting the progressive modification of perceptual horizons as the later chapters are written.

[31] Herbert of Clairvaux, *De miraculis* 3:4; *PL* 185, 1316 ab.

[32] See M. Casey, *A Guide to Living in the Truth*, pp. 125-140. I have taken the title of this chapter from an article by Columba Stewart, "The Desert Fathers on Radical Self-Honesty," *Vox* 8.1 (1991), pp. 7-53.

[33] This was reinforced by losing one's name, hair, and secular clothes (especially one's trousers), as well as being divorced from one's family, background, career and interests and introduced into close contact with a already-existing group, most of whom were strangers. The whole experience was akin to rebirth. See Gerard Arbuckle, "Planning the Novitiate Process: Reflections of an Anthropologist," *Review for Religious*, July-August 1984, pp. 532-546. "Now is the time for the candidate to grasp more deeply the overall root paradigm for the novitiate—the death-resurrection paradigm." (p.541).

[34] Francis Fukuyama, "Life After God," [A Review of Deepak Lal, *Unintended Consequences: The impact of factor endowments, culture and politics, on long-run economic performance* (Boston: MIT, 1999)] in *Times Literary Supplement* 5020 (18 June 1999), p. 5.

[35] In this account, as will be evident from the footnotes, we are relying much on the published research of Professor Barry O'Dwyer formerly of Macquarie University, whose scholarly interest in the period and especially in the work of Stephen of Lexington has spanned several decades.

[36] See Jean Leclercq, "New Recruitment—New Psychology," in *Monks and Love in Twelfth-Century France* (Oxford: University Press, 1979), pp. 8-26. Joseph H. Lynch, "Monastic Recruitment in the Eleventh and Twelfth Centuries: Some Social and Economic Considerations," *ABR* 26.4 (1975), pp. 425-447. For exceptions see J. Lynch, "The Cistercians and Underage Novices," *Cîteaux* 24.3 (1973), pp. 283-297.

[37] *Ep* 357.3; *SBO* 8.302.17-18. Dated 1142.

[38] Thus Father Colmcille [O Conbhui], *The Story of Mellifont* (Dublin: Gill, 1958), p. 9.

[39] *Ep* 357.2; *SBO* 8.302.7-8.

[40] *Ep* 341.2; *SBO* 8.283.3-5. Dated 1140.

[41] Some qualifications regarding the Cistercian ideal of "unanimity" can be found in my "Unanimity First, Uniformity Second."

[42] *SMal* 1; *SBO* 6a.50.14.

[43] *VMal* 1; *SBO* 3,309. 19 (*de populo barbaro*), 20 (*de natali barbaro*), 21-22 (*inculta nobis barbaries*), 6; p. 315.15 (*exstipare barbaricos ritus*), 16; p. 326.20-21 (*barbaries ... barbaricae leges*), 19; p. 330.5 (*barbaries ... paganismus*), 31; p. 338.14 (*pulsa barbarie*), 41; p. 346.20 (*homo barbarus*), 46; p. 351.24 (*quod nimis barbarum sonet*), 55; p. 359.11 (*barbari*).

[44] *VMal* 16; *SBO* 3. 325.7-12.

[45] "The practice in Ireland had always been to mold and adapt external influences, on the conviction that the Irish cultural and monastic traditions were better suited to Ireland than those of the foreigners. The new

reform movement of Cîteaux was also expected to be molded and adapted in Ireland, and there was likelihood that it would not be a simple reproduction of French monastic life. The different attitude became evident even in the building of Mellifont, when most of the French monks in the pioneering group returned to Clairvaux, because it seemed that the Irish monks not only wanted a building more in conformity with the Irish monastic tradition, but they also wanted to introduce their own native customs." B. W. O'Dwyer, "The Crisis in the Cistercian Monasteries in Ireland in the Early Thirteenth Century (I)," *Analecta Cisterciensia* 31.2 (1975), p. 271.

[46] O Conbhui, *The Story of Mellifont*, p. 34. See the schemata adjacent to p. 42. The computation of the number of houses seems to vary from author to author. Not all monasteries survived until the suppression under Henry VIII (1536-1543); Geraldine Carville counts 34. *The Occupation of Celtic Sites in Ireland by the Canons Regular of St Augustine and the Cistercians* (Kalamazoo: Cistercian Publications, 1982), p. 14. Also to be noted is the fact that it is sometimes difficult to determine exact foundation dates due to conflicting evidence in the source material and different ways of establishing when the foundation took place.

[47] Since 1190, the Irish abbots were obliged to attend the General Chapter only once every four years, but were to be represented annually by a delegation (*Statuta* 1190,17; 1195,91). Chapter attendance, paying taxes to the Order and accepting the principle and practice of regular visitation remained contentious issues until the suppression.

[48] B. W. O'Dwyer, "The Crisis in the Cistercian Monasteries in Ireland in the Early Thirteenth Century (II)," *Analecta Cisterciensia* 32:1-2 (1976), p. 47

[49] A. Gwynn and R. N. Hadcock, *Medieval Religious Houses: Ireland* (London: Longman, 1970), pp. 116-117.

⁵⁰ Stephen was the youngest of four sons of a Nottinghamshire family. Having graduated Bachelor of Arts in Paris about 1215 he studied theology in Oxford. He entered the monastery of Quarr in 1221 and two years later became abbot of its daughter-house of Stanley. In 1229 he succeeded to the abbacy of Savigny and in 1243 became abbot of Clairvaux. At his initiative, and with papal encouragement, the General Chapter approved the establishment of the College of Saint Bernard in Paris in 1245 for the education of the monks of the Order. Despite the success of the venture he was regarded with hostility by other abbots and was eventually deposed by the General Chapter of 1255. He died shortly afterwards at Ourscamp.

⁵¹ On the violent reception Stephen encountered at Suir and Maigue see O'Dwyer, "The Crisis (II)," pp. 13-16.

⁵² *Letter 21*; Translated by Barry W O'Dwyer *Stephen of Lexington, Letters from Ireland 1228-1229* (Kalamazoo: Cistercian Publications, 1982), p. 44.

⁵³ *Letter 87*; p. 183.

⁵⁴ "This tendency to revert to or to continue the customs of the Irish monastic tradition had given rise to at least some of the irregularities to which there are many references in the statutes of the General Chapter." O'Dwyer, "The Crisis (II)," p. 56.

⁵⁵ *Letter 21*; pp. 44-45.

⁵⁶ B. W. O'Dwyer, "The Problem of Reform in the Irish Cistercian Monasteries and the Attempted Solution of Stephen of Lexington in 1228," *Journal of Ecclesiastical History* 15.2 (October 1964), p. 189.

⁵⁷ In the thirteenth century this was especially true of the lay-brothers, sometimes called *perversi* instead of *conversi*. Statements such as the following were commonplace in visitation reports: "We found the *conversi* of this house more contumacious and senseless

than elsewhere, insolent and notorious 'for constantly fighting and cursing.'" See Louis J. Lekai, *The Cistercians: Ideals and Reality* (Kent: Kent State University Press, 1977), pp. 342-343. In the Order of Grandmont there had been two major rebellions of the lay-brothers in 1185 and 1219.

[58] *Letter 80*, #40; p. 162. This is a circular letter containing all his injunctions, to the number of 97, for the Irish monasteries.

[59] *Letter 99*; p.210.

[60] *Letter 27*; p. 68.

[61] *Letter 42*; p. 91.

[62] O'Dwyer, "The Crisis (II)", p.42.

[63] Roger Stalley, *The Cistercian Monasteries of Ireland* (London: Yale University Press, 1987), p. 23.

Epilogue

THE MONK IN THE MODERN WORLD

This is the text of an address read at the symposium organized to commemorate the sesquimillenium of St Benedict's birth in 1980. It was intended to be a monastic Gaudium et Spes *and it is marked by the sort of optimism that was still alive in the Church in the wake of Vatican II. As such it reflects the period in which it was written. It strongly emphasizes the needs for monastic men and women to own the evangelical distinctiveness of their vocation, so that remaining faithful to their charism, they may serve as a foil to some of the less desirable features of modern industrialized society. The title of Part Two, "The Monk and the Future of Mankind" reads a little bombastically today, even apart from its exclusive language. There may have been a little irony in using it. The article was published in* Tjurunga *21 (1981).*

The most characteristic document proceeding from the labors of the Second Vatican Council was its pastoral constitution, *Gaudium et Spes*, on the Church in the Modern World. It is to our shame that, to a large extent, the substantial teaching embodied in this text has failed to win for itself a foothold in our *practical* understanding of the Church's mission. Its theoretical content has been applauded, but its fundamental preoccupations have scarcely begun to shape our conception of what is to be done to advance the Kingdom of God.

Perhaps it is also true that we who belong to the monastic tradition have not yet applied the teaching of *Gaudium et Spes* to our own mission within the Church. It is possible that we have been too concerned with uncovering and preserving our distinctive spiritual heritage and too little interested in translating this undoubted treasure into a spiritual force for the future.

In this paper, I should like to broach two topics, one general and the other specific. In the first part I shall address myself to a reconsideration of the question of the relation between the monk and 'the world.' In the second part I would like to propose a number of headings under which a creative interaction of Benedictines and society might be profitably considered.[1]

Part One: Independence from the World

In human relations a perfect bond does not exist between two parties when the relationship is a result of unilateral dependence of one upon another. A mature relationship is possible only where there is reciprocal freedom. An adult is not born except through emancipation from given relationships and the willingness to enter into relationships based on choice rather than on necessity.

Although such relationships are habitually built upon the common ground of similarity between the parties, their long-term fruitfulness depends on an apparent area of dissimilarity or complementarity, whereby one party conspicuously enjoys certain qualities which the other decidedly lacks. Choice is often made on the basis of perceiving in the other what is latent or potential in oneself. In this way, a mature relationship is a delineation of future growth. We select friends who have what we lack in order that our deficiencies may be remedied through them and, as their qualities rub off on us through association, eventually in ourselves.

The monk's fruitful interaction with society broadly follows the same principles. In order to attain to his identity, a monk has to recognize the extent of his dependence on the society which nurtured him, and by subjecting the given values and norms he has received to evaluation, he must assert his radical independence in thought and in action from the range of social expectations and customary practices.

This mature independence is the foundation of a monk's being able to incorporate into his own life all that is good in the thought and labors of human society. It is also the source from which stems the possibility of his being able to contribute something to the welfare and growth of mankind. There is question of a mature independence; it is not an adolescent or fanatic rejection of any bonds, nor is it the enthusiast's affirmation of total identity. It is a sober, reasonable, benevolent determination to work together unto good.

Let us now outline some elements which contribute to this creative outcome.

1. *Historical Identity*

The Benedictine monk is not defined by the role accorded him by the society in which he lives. His primary loyalty is not to any function he may fulfill, but to the tradition in which he stands. In his act of profession he pledges himself not to work at any particular task, but to live in accordance with St Benedict's *Rule*, under the direction of his abbot. It is this freely-determined fidelity to a specific past which gives the individual monk an identity and which unites communities in singleness of purpose.[2]

This allegiance to another age has the beneficent effect of offsetting the immediacy of claims made by the present. The beliefs, values and practices widely accepted in our own time can thus be evaluated by reference to a more remote age. Just as a traveler often returns from experience of other cultures with a heightened appreciation of what is specific to his own, so, an attempt to appropriate the values of another epoch can afford a more accurate standpoint for gauging current trends. A person devoid of historical sense often misreads his own situation.

A Benedictine in good standing with his own past is the heir of a particular spiritual tradition.[3] Within this sub-culture there are beliefs and values which help the individual to shape for himself a philosophy of life which is at once proper to himself and his situation and yet distinctively "Benedictine." It is a philosophy of life which is not learned only from books, but is communicated through sharing in a common life shaped by that tradition.[4]

The most significant aspect of the Benedictine tradition is precisely its antiquity. It is a way of life based on the Gospels which is formulated in substantial independence of movements in Western society since the sixteenth century. The great asset that Benedictine spirituality has is its relative freedom from the dehumanizing social ideologies which have prevailed over the last four hundred years. Almost no other strand of ecclesial life can give the lie to such recent errors so effectively as the tradition of life and thought called "Benedictine."

How many of the more recent spiritual traditions within the Church have come to maturity at a period in which Rationalism exercised considerable influence? Under the baneful impact of rationalist thought, we have seen the Western Church turn aside from mystery, poetry, wonder and ultimately from humanity itself. In their place were substituted systematic and analytic thought, a dangerous dualism which divided nature from grace and body from soul and concentration on interior states and phases of consciousness. Contact with and feeling for the symbolic world of the Scriptures and the Fathers was lost; liturgical awareness disappeared; mental and spiritual exercises came to assume an inhuman paramountcy at the expense of the whole man; the individual and his "experiences" were dissociated from daily life and communal interaction.

Something of the wholeness, the sanity and the balance of the Benedictine centuries has been lost during the last four hundred years. The world has become a vastly different place and within the Church not everything that has been good has been retained. And divisions within Christianity have increased.

Since that time many societies have been progressively dehumanized. Material production has achieved primacy over the welfare of workers and the demands of marketing what is produced largely determine how populations live. As societies become more complex, techniques of administration become less personal. Bureaucratic management is supplemented by improved methods of surveillance and sanction, and social control is all-embracing, though invisible and therefore without the resentment caused by overt violence.

Meanwhile propaganda machines promulgate the message that man has never been so free. The word "democracy" is attached to nations whose populations are powerless; "freedom" is redefined so that it does not exceed approved limits and "justice" is thought to be the effect of a system of positive law, even when legislators as a body are recognized to be without honor.

Perhaps it may be said that, on balance, contemporary Western society is no more exploitative and violent than other societies at other times in human history. What is frightening in the present situation is the complacency of large sections of the population in the face of such inhumanity. The fact of plural options has blinded many to the restrictions under which they live; different packaging often hides substantial similarity in the choices offered. There are approved areas of dissent which leave fundamental policy untouched. And if all else fails, there is the possibility of pleasurable escape into heedlessness—through drugs, alcohol, crowd frenzies, entertainment and other avenues of avoiding awareness.

It is not to be inferred that because the Benedictine has a long history, he is automatically free of the influences of society. He is not immune; he has been well dosed with the toxin long before he became a monk. What his commitment to the Benedictine tradition does offer him is the possibility of his becoming aware not only of the influences under which his views are formed, but also of the undesirability of some tendencies which he finds in himself. If he takes his commitment to Benedictinism seriously, he will soon find that he has to struggle against many aspects of modern life which he has internalized. His power to counter dehumanizing tendencies is not exercised on the level of declamation, but on the level of life by his individual and communal efforts in the opposite direction.

Because of his fidelity to values first formulated in the distant past a monk has the possibility of recognizing what is distorting in contemporary society and working for its improvement. This he does by submitting his own life to a process of purification through the pursuit of truth. At a communal level, this renunciation of what is false gives the community a character of authenticity and integrity which serves as a beacon to guide men of good will in their search for God and confirms them in their choice against the contrary attractions which would lead them to be satisfied with lesser goals.

The monastic community can, however, serve as a witness to the attractiveness of the evangelical ideal only to the extent that it concretely embodies this ideal in its way of life. Above all, our contemporaries demand honesty: we must ourselves pursue the goals we recommend to others.

2. Disengagement

If the monk is to take seriously his task of living for God alone, *soli Deo vacare*, he is obliged to leave aside many alternative occupations even though these might be useful, instructive or pleasurable. This necessary separation from normal society processes is never complete, but it can yet be substantial. The monk who deliberately renounces the many rewards offered by society as inducements to conformity, and who is not animated by ambition to ascend the social scale considerably weakens the hold of social pressures and enlarges his freedom to follow the Gospels.

Marginality is an important quality of monastic existence; the monk is in a position to contribute to human progress only to the extent that his life is patterned upon different presuppositions. His judgments are of value because they derive from a distinctive viewpoint. His witness to the truth is clear only to the extent that it is not obscured by compromise and irresolution.

In a recent article on "Monks and the Future of Worship," Nathan Mitchell addresses himself to this point with some acerbity.

> The monk's marginal but complementary relation to society is the ultimate source of his power to contribute something valuable to the world. Ultimately it is also his most difficult task. Because they must be responsive to social change, monks are always in danger of being domesticated, tamed into still another unimaginative puppet of the current social ideology. This seems to me to be the chief affliction of contemporary monasticism, especially in Europe and America. The problem is not that these monasteries are rabid centers of ultramontane reaction, nor that they are hotbeds of revolutionary subversion, but that they are so extravagantly bourgeois.[5]

It seems likely that much of what has passed for "renewal" in the Church in religious life during the past twenty years has not derived from an authentic response to fundamental sources of inspiration but from an overwhelming desire to be "normal"—to be quit of all those features of religious life which render their bearers in any way distinctive within society.

That there were present in many religious congregations false and exaggerated peculiarities is indisputable. Such contrived accretions express nothing of the personal character of those concerned and often formed a serious impedance to the task to be performed. The resultant scouring of religious life-style with a view to eliminating whatever sets the religious person apart from the secular is an over-reaction to the excesses of the immediate past. In many cases what has issued from such an enterprise has been a way of life devoid of any character and incapable of forming an identity and generating morale among those who adopt it.

The same is often true of the Church itself. In Australia, it is quite "respectable" to be a Catholic. Sportsmen, politicians and "media personalities" can now own to a Catholic background without prejudice to their ambition. Bishops are knighted. Catholics are pleased to be able to boast that their views generally conform to those held throughout society.[6] Catholic women have proportionally as many abortions as others. Many or perhaps most Catholics in this country have "liberated" views concerning the moral teaching of the Church in so far as it touches their own lives and activities. "Everybody's doing it" has become a justification of a particular line of action rather than the best reason for avoiding it.

There is real danger that monks will begin to allow their practical response to daily life to be pre-empted by an unthinking reversion to the standards of suburbia. Too much passivity before the mass media reinforces the undemanding banalities underlying conventional lifestyles and induces a state of permanent cynicism which blots out any statement of alternative values. Life becomes more predictable, less personal and further removed from the promptings of grace.

If it is true that one of the most urgent and important tasks facing Christian theology in the West is to counter the effects of Bourgeois ideology,[7] it follows that those whose call is to practice rather than to preach need to examine their lives that they are molded according to the teaching of Christ and not mindlessly determined by the priorities of practically non-Christian society.

Such an effort is liable to bring not peace but the sword. It will cause division among the adherents of the Church and the withdrawal of many privileges enjoyed by society's favor. There is no guarantee that individual and communal fidelity to Christ will bring popularity and applause. There is strong historical precedent for suspecting it will lead rather to rejection and even persecution. It is one of the paradoxes of Christian faith, however, that it is through death that life is brought to the world and it is by means of disengagement from the tyranny of social processes that the monk fulfills the condition for effective interaction with men.

3. Sensitivity to Good

The independence of thought and practice which is necessary for fidelity to the Gospels should not, however, lead to a new sectarianism. It is easy enough to grasp some partial truth and to use this as a means of celebrating one's own uniqueness and keeping all others at a distance. This can lead to no ultimate gain. On the one hand it causes the aspect of truth singled out for such attention to fall into disfavor with those who do not share one's precise perspective. On the other hand, it removes one from the forum of useful interchange and tends to preclude possibilities of further growth in truth. The possession of truth divides those who have it from those who do not; when the division becomes more significant than the truth itself then there is question not of liberation but of a new slavery. All social ideologies have something of truth as their kernel; all equally jeopardize the attractiveness of that truth by their preference for the part and their lack of interest in the whole.

One of the key concepts of *Gaudium et Spes* was the recognition that the Church, while maintaining its evangelical distinctiveness, must abandon its sectarian tendencies. There is question of renouncing any claim to a monopoly, the affirmation of the unity and universality of truth and the recognition that dedication to truth is best evidenced by a willingness to learn. By virtue of its own love for what is good the Church has the capacity to recognize the good in a variety of manifestations, no matter how disguised or deeply hidden.

The Church not only recognizes and affirms goodness outside its formal structures, it finds in this recognition a clear determinant of its own current mission. The "signs of the times" are not merely useful marketing indications, they are divine calls to future growth.[8] Without such sensitivity, stagnation and institutionalization are inevitable.

The same principles largely govern the monk's relationship with the world around him. His way of life is distinctive both in its practices and in the inner convictions and attitudes which support them. The fact that he is largely free from the wheeling and dealing which have become a constant adjunct to Church administration should equip him with at least a basic predisposition of sensitivity to the winds of change. This is not to suggest that he should feel compelled to add his measure of bluster to prevailing storms, but to infer that perhaps he might learn to trim his sails to catch the merest whisper of a breeze.

The only way the monk can keep up with the times is to stay ahead of them. If he is sensitive to the movements of change he is able to translate vague and diffuse aspirations into practice more easily than anybody else. He is largely free of the inertia imposed by involvement in complicated schemes of institutional existence. To a large extent he is not burdened by a system to be maintained. His disengagement permits a more rapid adjustment, his association with a long and creative tradition gives him the possibility of absorbing what is new without loss of identity, his fellowship with many brothers guarantees that at least a modicum of common sense and practical discernment will prevail.

In the second part, I should like to outline a number of areas in which such attention to the "signs of the times" can help us to recognize the priorities facing the Church and monastic life. Before concluding, however, I would ask you to call to mind a saying of Jesus which, it seems to me, contains a summary of what we have been talking about.

> You are the salt of the earth. If salt becomes tasteless, there is no means by which it can be seasoned. It is good for nothing, except to be thrown out and walked over by men (Mt 5:13).

Part Two: The Monk and the Future of Mankind

To project the monastic vocation against the backdrop of world history may seem to reflect an inflated appreciation of the significance of one person's response to the call of God. Yet throughout salvation history God has chosen to redirect the course of events through the interventions of chosen men and women. We regard them as heroes of faith because they said "yes" to God and actively co-operated in furthering his plans within their own limited spheres of contact.

To base our assessment of the values of a course of action on quantitative criteria is to risk depriving every *small* deed of any substantial meaning. It is to reserve greatness to those who spread themselves widely and to deny it to those who give themselves intensely but restrictively. It is to reprove those who try and create in their immediate ambiance a sphere of responsiveness to the divine call and to condone the inactivity of those who contend that evil is beyond any individual's scope to counteract.

The Benedictine solution to the problem of the salvation of mankind is rooted in the here and now. It does not envisage massive schemes of world-evangelization, but takes as its starting point the assent of the individual will to the promptings of grace and the creation of a band of like-minded persons to embody this assent in a communal life. It is a question of beginning a process without seeing clearly how far it will reach or where it will end.

It is, however, important to note that the object of what the Benedictine does is not the realization of personal schemes of holiness, achieved within the controlled environment of a monastic hothouse. The fundamental principle of animation within monasticism, as John Cassian clearly affirmed, is the pursuit of the Kingdom of God. No monk can separate himself from God's plan for the salvation of mankind and remain faithful to his call. To attempt to live an evangelical life is impossible without zeal for the coming of the Kingdom.

This is why it is inaccurate to contrast "monastic" holiness with "political" holiness.[9] There is no such thing as holiness which is not of benefit to others in an immediate sense. To be responsive to grace necessarily involves a degree of non-responsiveness to other influences, judging alternative claims to be less binding. To accept the call of God affirmatively is automatically a critique of other modes of behavior. It is to reject pressures to conform to social expectations and to establish a new code of priorities.

The very fact of trying to create a communal receptivity to grace is counter-cultural, though the degree to which this is evident will depend on the nature of the larger society. There are "political" consequences to every instance of independent assessment and action within a polity. Every concrete example of Christian wholeness is a threat and a challenge to an ideology which can produce only fragmentation: it is a self-evident protest which shouts louder than mere words.

> The protest is against both the dangers and the limitations of a materialist, positivist, extraverted, technological civilization. In opposition to the obvious dangers of this technological world with its power to manipulate, to control, to dominate, to enslave and to destroy human beings, there is the counteraction towards non-violence, receptivity, openness, empathy in our relationships with other people. In opposition to the intrinsic limitations of this technological world there is the search for a more complete human existence. We are becoming aware that some of our vital human faculties have been atrophied in the development of a one-sided civilization. In the process of the great achievements of our western civilization, a highly developed rational consciousness, men have lost the "sense of the whole". We have lost touch with the more intuitive, symbolic, contemplative consciousness, and we have isolated ourselves from the communion with the whole cosmos given in that consciousness. The technological civilization has led to an increasing domination over the material cosmos. But the domination is not to be identified with communion.[10]

That Benedictine life has had its influence on society throughout history is beyond dispute. There have been times when it seems that monks have sequestered themselves excessively, not as a means of giving prophetic witness but as a refusal of involvement, but these have been periods generally recognized as slack. In its finest moments, Benedictinism has been a force of direction and strength both for the Church and for society. This was achieved simply by dynamic fidelity to its own past.

Following are some of the ways by which a modern monk may contribute something to the world in which he lives and advance thereby the Kingdom of God.

1. Faith

Factors operative in Western society over the last few hundred years have caused a general loss of a sense of the sacred. The practical consequences of rationalism have robbed modern man of confidence in his own instinctive religious feeling. Religious institutions have been made to look ridiculous in his eyes, whether because of their own ineptitude or duplicity or because of bias in the presentations of the mass media. As a result there is massive alienation from the Church and a general feeling that religion is a matter for personal choice, like jogging or vegetarianism, and not a necessary component of universal human response to life.

Gaudium et Spes recognizes the growth of various forms of atheism in modern society.[11] In Australia this often takes shape as a passive agnosticism, refusal to credit any validity to ultimate principles due mainly to a lack of interest in the search for truth and complacency in a materially satisfying life. The overwhelming conviction that religion does not matter affects even those who profess and practice Christianity. There is a blunting in the missionary efforts of the Church due to a lack of confidence in the applicability of the Good News to those "outside."

In the growing void of positive faith there is a role for those whose faith is strong. The strength in question is not the undoubting simplicity of childlike acceptance, but the personal and communal witness of those who have lived with darkness and struggled with doubt and, by the grace of Christ, have attained to a commitment which is adult and undeviating. *Gaudium et Spes* says as much:

> The remedy which must be applied to atheism, however, is to be sought in a proper presentation of the Church's teaching as well as in the integral life of the Church and her members. For it is the function of the Church, led by the Holy Spirit who renews and purifies her unceasingly, to make God the Father and his incarnate Son present and in a sense visible. The result is achieved chiefly by the witness of a living and mature faith, namely, one trained to see difficulties clearly and to master them. Many martyrs have given luminous witness to this faith and continue to do so. This faith needs to prove its fruitfulness by penetrating the believer's entire life, including its worldly dimensions, and by activating him toward justice and love, especially regarding the needy.[12]

And in a recent book, J.B. Metz spells out the role of faith in history and society.

> Christian faith can and must be seen in this way as a subversive memory. The Church is, moreover, to some extent, the form of its public character. In this sense, the Church's teachings and confessions of faith should be understood as formulae in which this challenging memory is publicly spelt out. The criterion of its authentic Christianity is the liberating and redeeming danger with which it introduces the remembered freedom of Jesus into modern society and the forms of consciousness and praxis in that society.[13]

It is by practice of faith that the Church encounters the climate of unbelief. How many of the objections raised to belief by men of good disposition have to do with the Church's own infidelities? It is because it deviates from the plain teaching of Christ that the Church is most frequently criticized in a post-Christian world. It is not Jesus who is rejected by our contemporaries as much as the perceived duplicity of his followers.

A faith honestly professed and put into practice without shame is a service urgently required in the Church and ardently sought by those who are groping their way toward truth. From whom might this ministry of personal dedication be sought if not from monks?

2. *Continuity*

Rapid change in recent decades, together with a general awareness of different life-styles has caused many persons to become alienated from the groups of which they form a part. Settled patterns of belief and evaluation along with practices expressive of these have given way to pluriformity in viewing the world and in responding practically to its demands. As a result persons are assimilating the surrounding culture only imperfectly; they grow up without a convinced commitment to its way of seeing things and doing things. The capacity to endure the negative aspects of this culture is diminished; when the going becomes difficult loyalties are promptly transferred to something more immediately gratifying.

Geographical mobility is paralleled by a tendency to change in more personal areas. With each successive choice, personal commitment can often be more shallow. Far from putting down roots into the rich, deep, soil of collective consciousness, many of our contemporaries are in danger of becoming progressively enslaved to their own whims and easy prey for peddlers of something new. This has the effect of making identification with a particular institution on a long-term basis not only difficult but even incomprehensible.

In such an atmosphere the Church's preoccupation with its past is difficult to accept because it seems to preempt a creative response to the present. The past is seen as coercive and resisted; and the Church in its refusal to be completely swayed by current issues is seen as reactionary. There is a general lack of sympathy with what the Church is saying and the feeling that its message is too esoteric to have much bearing on practical life.

This reactionary image is particularly strengthened when there is excessive emphasis on more recent stages of tradition, and where attempts are made to make this recent past normative by collusion with conservative politicians. The distant past may be strange, but at least it is not marred by the mixed motivations of bureaucratic compromise.

The monk can be a proof of the vitalizing aspect of sound tradition. This is not to say that he is to become a custodian of antiquities, a curator of curious customs, reproducing the ethos of the past as a living tableau. It is not a question of perpetuating the past as much as of ensuring that the present is not without roots. Living in the past is as much a denial of continuity as refusing to admit the present has roots. It is a question of enriching the present by affirming its totality.

The faith of the Church is embodied and transmitted not by logical equations but through images. When Jesus spoke to the crowds he used parables and most of the Bible is written in poetic, symbolic, colorful language. To understand revelation it is necessary to enter into the symbolic world of which it is a part. Revelation is such a mystery that it transcends the banal categories of plain speech. It can never be clinically described; it can only be evoked through poetry. Many aberrations attend upon the failure to recognize this fact. Bizarre fundamentalist interpretations of the Scriptures are one example—denying continuity to revelation only results in rendering it implausible.

Those who maintain contact with the mythic world in which revelation found expression and celebrate it in ritual serve as the channel by which the Word of God is able to percolate through different strata of contemporary life. Without in any way reserving this role to monks, it remains true that monastic life offers great opportunity for the strengthening of cultural continuity within the Church. In this way the recapitulation of the wisdom of the past serves as a means of enhancing the present; not enslaving it to ancient norms but communicating to it ancient wisdom.

3. *Authenticity*

Monks are vowed to living an evangelical life; it is possible for them to embody their response to God's Word in a lifestyle. The whole purpose of setting up a distinctive way of life is to secure this possibility. Monks are not proclaiming anything else except what they live; their life is their proclamation. By what they are, monks attest to the faith of the Church.

This is of considerable significance in a period of history in which the prevailing attitude toward institutions is one of distrust and suspicion. Instances of dishonesty and duplicity within the Church confirm many individuals in their assumption that the official Church is more about power than about truth and love.

The monk is not only on the fringes of society; to some extent he is marginal to the ecclesiastical structure. John Cassian's admonition to monks to avoid women and bishops is aimed at preventing them from settling into some comfortable ecclesiastical slot or being tamed into domesticity.

Because he does not have to deal with administrative structures, the monk is exempt from the compromises dictated by pastoral prudence. "It is not the same for monks and bishops. Bishops have a duty toward both wise and foolish" says St Bernard.[14] The monk is also less likely to become consumed by a passion for bureaucratic correctitude. As St Bernard also says: "I shall not deal with the questions you ask me about canon law. Such matters have nothing to do with us, because we are monks."[15]

In the life of a monk there is potential for great transparency. Because of his disengagement it is possible that he might avoid some of the prejudice directed at more official Church persons. If his life is characterized by integrity, then it is possible that something of the purity of Gospel truth may be manifested to others.

4. *Simplicity*

To the extent that a monk gives priority to spiritual values, a degree of detachment from material goods and satisfactions result. To the extent that his life is ordered in accordance with his basic disposition, complexity recedes and undividedness follows. The monk who is content with little is happy most of the time; his life is exempt from the conflicting claims of multiple desire. He lives a simple life.

There is no doubt that many persons in our complex modern society long for just such a way of life, and not only those in the counterculture. There is more involved here than negative feelings aroused by an inability to handle the fruits of modern technology. Many of those most desiring to revert to a simple life are highly intelligent. It is not confusion which motivates them but the desire to rebuild fragmented existence on a simple human scale—to recover the natural harmonies of a life lived in union with other humans and at peace with the environment.

A life which is removed from the contrived covetousness of a consumer society and bases its use of things on necessity is not expensive. On the contrary one who follows such a regimen finds it possible to get by on modest means. As a result, there is a possibility of a simple economy which leaves ample scope for creative leisure on the one hand and which is happy to share the fruits of honest labor with the needy, on the other. The result is a life which responds to human values.

Having to deal directly with the practicalities of life without a lot of labor-saving machinery has the effect of giving the monk or anybody else involved in a simple lifestyle a firm sense of reality. Like the eagle of which St Augustine speaks, he may have his head in the skies, but his feet are firmly on the earth. The practical, concrete, down-to-earth realism of Benedictine spirituality is largely derived from the involvement of the monk in practical as well as spiritual matters. He prays AND he works: each activity enhances the other. To do away with simple household tasks and the need for physical work with a view to increasing its "spiritual" content is to risk destroying its wholeness and to expose it to increasing complexity.

In the simple life envisaged by St Benedict and realized at several stages of the Benedictine tradition we have a formula for living which not only accords with scriptural principles but is in fundamental harmony with the aspirations of many of the most thoughtful of our contemporaries. But this is not to say that because we are Benedictines then automatically our life is thus: **much** work remains to be done to achieve a simpler existence. There is need to "break visibly with the ways of the world, and to assert something more definitely" by our lifestyle.[16]

5. Discipline

The simplicity of monastic tradition is not regarded as an easy effect of "getting away from it all." It is something which is achieved progressively through a lifetime of learning and effort. Simplicity of life is only possible for those who are simple of heart and such inward unity never occurs by accident or through uncontrolled spontaneity and self-expression.

The essence of discipline is the willingness and capacity to learn. The root of the term is *discere*, to learn, and we still occasionally hear the word "disciplines" used to refer to branches of learning. There is more to discipline than self-control and willpower. Certainly constancy and the capacity to endure what is not presently pleasurable are necessary components of any successful learning process, but they are conditions rather than causes of growth. Mindless endurance profits nothing.

St Benedict refers to the monastery as a "school of the Lord's service"[17] and the image has reappeared often in subsequent tradition. A newcomer comes to monastic life in order to be infused with the *philosophia Christi*; it is the monastery's task to communicate something of its traditional wisdom to those who come seeking God. Perhaps it may be that monastic persons are today too diffident in this task of teaching; too unsure of the value of their own tradition; too overwhelmed by the complexity and sophistication of modern life: too convinced that modern youth are "unteachable."

Meanwhile sects and cults continue to attract legions of young people. Often there is question of a very austere regimen of diet, clothing, standard of living, sexual behavior and very little leeway is left for the infirmity of individuals. They are exposed to great masses of rote memorization and esoteric mythologies and the spirit of free inquiry is ruthlessly suppressed. Many come to them, including some from Catholic backgrounds, willing to submit to so much that is strange and harsh and narrow in order to learn something which they believe society and the Church cannot teach them.

Are we, as Benedictines, afraid to teach "old things and new" because we are uncertain about basic values, or is it because it might impose on *us* the burden of living in accordance with them? Is it faith or morality that is deficient? Certainly we have in our tradition ample guidance in practical mysticism and genuine Christian living, the question is, are we bold enough to assert its relevance to a world in search of just such teaching?

6. *Non-Instinctuality*

Learning to live a spiritual discipline involves progressive mastery of the instincts. It is not possible to achieve wholeness without coming to grips with the sub-personal forces which shape so much of our behavior, restraining us from so much good, inciting us to so much evil. It is not only our violent passions which lead us astray by making us covetous and aggressive; we are also distorted by our diffidence and timidity and fear. Our instincts not only lead us to do what is not expedient for us, they also induce in us excessive inaction and lead us into sins of monumental omission.

Traditional monastic spirituality placed great emphasis on *apatheia*, which does not mean "apathy," but is better rendered by "freedom." Unless a monk is free of the enslavement of his own biology and background, his behavior is not personal; it is the predictable result of a certain chemistry of events.

The assent to grace is dependent on our willingness to be drawn beyond the comfortable confines of a self-centered life. St Benedict expects his followers to live a moderate and abstemious life; the emotions are reined by reason; they do not reign independently.

In a permissive society Benedict's view seems very austere. Perhaps we need to examine the presuppositions of such a judgment. Is "letting it all hang out," "doing one's own thing" and "expressing oneself" really such a creative process unless the individual has first found himself? How often all that is externalized in such outpourings is the uncontrolled chaos of an unordered life, not the deep personal self which underlies behavior?

Violent emotional displays make good television; they do not contribute much to personal growth. Depression and fear and timidity can lead to a safe reputation and the lack of overt error, but they are not the stuff of creative living. Freedom to act as a person and creativity under grace demand the avoidance of both manic and depressive extremes. To resist emotional enslavement is a traditional Benedictine goal which has much to recommend it to the attention of our contemporaries.

7. Altruism

The most potent enemies of love are our own disordered instincts. To the extent that a monk is free of these, love becomes progressively easier, as Benedict notes at the end of his Prologue.[18] Although concern for the welfare of others is an acceptable and even popular tenet of contemporary "wisdom," it is often obvious that what is supposed to be done for the aid and comfort of others is in fact done for the doer's advantage. The interior virtues long espoused by monastic tradition such as humility and purity of intention are important for the emergence of genuine altruism. Without them, concern for others readily becomes a roundabout way of gratifying self, albeit in an unconscious manner.

A good monk is a great lover: not in the sense of restrictively loving only those who can benefit him, but according to the breadth of charity itself. If love is the most obvious feature of monastic living there will be no difficulty in attracting the finest and most perceptive of our contemporaries to follow the example.

8. Community

Since the sixteenth century, Western society has been sustained by individualist presuppositions. Individual experience has been accepted as paramount; the sense of belonging to a community has waned. The favored myth in capitalist countries is that of one who started with nothing and ended up with all he could desire. Communal existence is often regarded as an imposition on the one hand, or, on the other, as something which lacks reality, which is in the minds of community members rather than having a basis in being.

Defects in human solidarity have caused a counter-cultural wave of desire for genuine community to form. Many persons are independently coming to the conclusion that it is scarcely possible to live a rich human existence without being in a community which is capable of nurturing and supporting such a life.

This has led to the mushrooming of numerous small life-support groups which can offer the individual the assistance which the broader society cannot provide. Many of these groups have a clear insight into such neglected areas as harmony with nature, body-values, non-violence, and sometimes combine these with a non-specific religious orientation to life. Others less radical are simply affinity groups. All share the same concern for human growth and recognize that this is possible only within the context of community.

It is possible that the religious community can be viewed in this light, though in fact it is rarely a plausible assumption. When communities are so task-oriented that human values are secondary, when they are so institution-oriented that the community seems to exist *apart from* the individuals who make it up, then they do not appear able to satisfy the aspirations of the seeker of community. It is hard for a formal structure to have the casual, undemanding friendliness of looser associations, but this is not to excuse established communities from trying to incorporate something of spontaneity and joy into daily living.

I am not saying that religious communities should become aimless communes of free love, but that they should be challenged to see that they are communities in fact and not merely in name. The sort of behavior recommended by St Benedict in the 72nd chapter of the *Rule* is not the result of abandoning all goals and organization, but derives from the growth of genuine charity progressively externalizing itself in behavior.

We have in our tradition a practical guide to the formation of communities of love. This is especially evident in the sort of communal lifestyle achieved in the twelfth century and associated with such figures as St Aelred of Rievaulx. To implement the *Rule* as effectively in our situation as they did in theirs would be a powerful proclamation of the primacy of love in the Church and certainly an element in regaining the interest of many who have drifted away from what they believed to be a heartless and impersonal organization.

9. Creativity

Within the context of healthy community, individuals shed their repressions and latent talents begin to blossom. Culture flourishes only within the context of wholesome community: talented individuals stand on the shoulders of others who have brought their skills to fruition, who have provided them with support, sustenance and guidance whilst encouraging growth. Where a community encourages individuals to be themselves, in the best sense of that expression, creativity spreads.

Our society allows only limited scope for creative initiative; it tends to produce stereotypes, conditioned by the mass media, reliant on the same commodities and predictable in their reaction to new situations. This homogenization is one of the most significant means of social control. It goes unrecognized because scope for variation from the mean is inbuilt; by distracting persons with multiple choices our society conceals the severe limitations to freedom and creativity which it imposes.

The rebuilding of human society is ultimately dependent on the emergence of outstanding individuals who, by their personal vision and power of expression, can pioneer creative development. The Benedictine tradition can be proud that in the past it has engendered such individuals of talent. It will serve the world well if it continues to do so.

Within the Church this creativity has been traditionally associated with the liturgy. Much could be done to animate the people of God if Benedictines were able to contribute to the creation of a liturgy that is both faithful to the best traditions of ecclesial worship and authentically attuned to the noblest aspirations of men and women today.

10. Wholeness

The strength of the Benedictine tradition is found in the fact that throughout the centuries it has been honed down to a pattern of life devoid of extremism. It is a balanced life of different human activities lived under the influence of a paramount goal: seeking God. It is a life not built up by the application of theories, but by long experience of practical living; its basis is wisdom, not knowledge.

We live in a world which lacks wholeness, in which many pursue a style of life which is fundamentally unwholesome and inhuman, in which the instinct of destructiveness goes the whole way from seat-slashing in suburban trains to nuclear strike-forces poised for launching. If we do not create, it is because many are aware only of the urge to destroy the adornments and utensils of a world which has done them only harm. Those who have been hurt by the brutalizing aspects of our society become agents in the wounding of society itself.

To create and appreciate beauty is a necessary component of human life. Its first manifestation is not in producing beautiful objects, but in providing for a life that nurtures all that is noble in the human spirit and counters what is unworthy. A wholesome life is not only to the benefit of those who enjoy it; it becomes the means by which they can operate more fruitfully to serve others.

11. Peace

The Benedictine motto *Pax* is a challenge to all who profess the *Rule of St Benedict* not only to live in peace but to work energetically for the peace of all men, to become peacemakers in a world fraught by anxiety and fragmented by greed. Although this task will sometimes take the shape of attempting to inhibit the outbreak or continuance of conflict, generally it means accepting the obligations flowing from commitment to the coming of God's Kingdom.

No peace is possible without inner undividedness. The monk becomes a man of peace by enthroning within his heart the Prince of Peace and by making the Gospel of peace the determinant of his behavior. To the extent that Benedictines internalize their tradition of peace and embody it in their way of life, they have a contribution to make not only to contemporary society, but, indeed, to the future of mankind.

NOTES

[1] My use of the terms "monk" and "monastic" is not intended to exclude either women or apostolic religious. I use it in the broad sense and the common gender to include all followers of the *Rule of St Benedict*.

[2] The many attempts to propose a definition of monasticism in the 1960's foundered because they approached the matter too analytically, without paying sufficient attention to the historical determinants which give form and impetus to monastic tradition and which have a bearing on its identity in each new situation it enters.

[3] The phrase "in good standing" is important. The habit does not make the monk, nor does legal affiliation guarantee that he has creatively absorbed the wisdom of the past.

[4] Cf. M. Casey, "The Formative Influence of the Benedictine Community," *TJ* 14 (1977), pp. 7-26.

[5] *Worship* 50.1 (1967), p. 11

[6] Cf. Michael Hogan, "Wooing the Catholic Voter: Market Research Advice for Political Leaders," *Quadrant* 22.7 (July 1978), pp. 56-57.

[7] A whole issue of *Concilium* is devoted to the theme, "Christianity and the Bourgeoisie," (ed. J.B. Metz, #125) 1979.

[8] Cf. F. Houtart, "Les aspect sociologiques des 'signes du temps', " and M. D. Chenu, "Les signes des temps: réflexions théologiques," in Yves Congar, *L' église dans le monde de ce temps* (Unam Sanctam #65b), Cerf, Paris, 1967; pp. 171-204, 205-228.

[9] Cf. Claudio Leonardi, "From 'Monastic' Holiness to 'Political' Holiness," in *Concilium* #129 (1979), pp. 46-55.

www.ingramcontent.com/pod-product-compliance
Lightning Source LLC
Chambersburg PA
CBHW021050080526
44587CB00010B/193